The Most Difficult Revolution

BY THE SAME AUTHORS

*Women and Trade Unions in
Eleven Industrialized Countries*

THE MOST DIFFICULT REVOLUTION

Women and Trade Unions

A L I C E H. C O O K,
Val R. Lorwin, *and*
Arlene Kaplan Daniels

Cornell University Press

Ithaca and London

First published 1992 by Cornell University Press.

International Standard Book Number 0-8014-1916-6 (cloth)
International Standard Book Number 0-8014-8065-5 (paper)
Library of Congress Catalog Card Number 92-52747
Printed in the United States of America
Librarians: Library of Congress cataloging information
appears on the last page of the book.

♾ The paper in this book meets the minimum requirements
of the American National Standard for Information Sciences—
Permanence of Paper for Printed Library Materials, ANSI Z39.48-1984.

Contents

Preface   vii

Introduction and Setting   1

PART I
*Unions, Government, and International
Agencies: Law and Policy*

1   Government Policies on Work and Home Lives of Women   17
2   Women in Union Structures   42

PART II
Union Functions

3   Collective Bargaining   79
4   Union Education   107

PART III
Union Issues

5   Pay Equity   135
6   Vocational Training and Labor Market Policies   168
7   Part-time Work   191
8   Health and Safety in the Workplace   217

    Conclusion: Amelioration of the Work and Family Conflicts   255

    Abbreviations   269
    References   273
    Index   289

Preface

In 1975 the subject of this book was the center of a dinner-table conversation among colleagues in the School of Industrial and Labor Relations at Cornell University. The occasion was a visit that summer of an old friend and graduate of the School, Val Lorwin, distinguished professor of European History at the University of Oregon. He had returned recently from a trip to France, Belgium, England, and Scandinavia. Others at dinner had recently visited other European countries. My own special interests lay in Scandinavia and postwar Germany and Austria. All of us were concerned students of women's participation in the labor force. In addition, Val Lorwin and I had devoted much of our academic lives to comparative studies of trade union problems. I had just published the first edition of a comparative study of policies and programs affecting working mothers in nine countries, in the course of which I had given some, but not nearly enough, attention to women's roles in union structures and programs. As the dinner-table conversation continued, we realized we were planning a comparative study on this very theme.

We wanted to learn what was underway in European unions that might stimulate comparable progress and action in U.S. unions, similarly concerned as they were with the influx of women into the labor force. We decided to concentrate on four countries: Great Britain, Germany, Austria, and Sweden. The problems all these unions faced, we believed, were those of representing this growing body of potential new members and drafting programs to meet their most pressing needs. Among these needs, in addition to a place in the structures of the unions, we enumerated the achievement of equal pay for work of equal value, the remedy of conditions usually found in part-time work, access to skill training, and the inclusion of women's needs and interests in the growing programs on health and safety in the workplace.

We were fortunate that our plan gained the support of the then-new German Marshall Fund, established through a gift of the German government to assist U.S.-European studies and exchange on social policy, communications, and political and economic problems. Once the project was assured, we added Roberta Till-Retz to the investigating team of Cook and Lorwin. She was a recent doctoral student of Lorwin's and had written her thesis in Austria on women in labor history.

In the fall of 1976 we began our work in Europe by spending several days at the International Labour Office in Geneva, consulting its library and its staff experts on trade unions, collective bargaining, working women, and labor relations, focusing on special conditions and problems in the four countries we wanted to visit. We used this opportunity to talk with staff of several international labor secretariats, including particularly the International Metalworkers Federation and the International Federation of Commercial, Clerical, and Office Workers, about projects and people of interest for further study and consultation. With this background and our own knowledge of European unions gained in previous research, we began more intensive work in each of the four countries. Val took major responsibility for the work in Great Britain and I in Germany and Austria. We shared the Swedish experience. Roberta assisted both of us and did particularly intensive studies of the Trade Union of Private Sector White-collar Workers (GPA) in Austria and of the National Union of Public Employees (NUPE) in Britain.

We began our country studies with short visits to each to establish contacts; to test our hypotheses against local concerns both in the unions and in existing social policy affecting working women; to assess the state and location of research on our topic; and to assure ourselves of a welcome by the trade union federation and a number of its national unions. The selection of unions to be studied in each country was a result, in part, of our finding interested executives of these bodies; in part, of the application of a set of criteria we had outlined in our proposal for study. We wanted to become acquainted in each country with three or four unions, one of which would have a minority of women members, while others would have a majority or a very large minority of women. We wanted at least one of this latter type to be a white-collar union. We wanted at the same time to be able, in each country, to compare or contrast women in blue-collar factory work and in the service trades with white-collar workers, and to note differences or similarities between unions in the public and private sectors.

In the end we worked with the following union organizations: in Austria, the private industry white-collar workers (GPA), the metalworkers (IMBE), and the textile workers (GTBL); in Germany, the commercial, banking, and insurance workers (HBV), the metalworkers (IGM), and the independent white-collar workers (DAG); in Great Britain, the public blue-collar workers (NUPE), the local government workers (NALGO), and the white-collar section of the engineering union (TASS);

in Sweden, the metalworkers *(Metall)*, the private white-collar workers (SIF), the public blue-collar workers *(Kommunal)*, and the retail workers *(Handels)*.

We aimed to acquaint ourselves with the national governments' social policies affecting working women, the structure of each union organization in our study, its national coverage, the proportion of women to men within it, the union's policies on equality in the workplace, its methods of collective bargaining, its bargaining agendas, and its policies, if any, in respect to representation of its women members and their responses. In each country we became acquainted with and frequently consulted the woman who at the national federation level was concerned with women's (or, as in the Swedish case, with family) problems.

In addition, we endeavored to find in each country academics or professionals concerned with the interests and problems of working women. Twice we called together an ad hoc European advisory committee of some of these persons as well as trade union leaders, in Bad Homburg, Germany, for consultation on issues we considered salient. Among others at these meetings were Bob Fryer, then of Warwick University; Edith Krebs, chief of the Austrian Chamber of Labor's women's division; Gisela Losseff-Tillmans, labor historian and sociologist at the Fachhochschule at Duesseldorf; Karl Stadler of the Institute of Labor History at the University of Linz, Austria; Ilona Schoell-Schwinghammer of the Sociological Research Institute at the University of Goettingen; Helga Pross, professor of sociology at the University of Goettingen; Berit Rollen of the Swedish Labor Market Board; Birger Viklund of the Swedish metalworkers; and Margot Oedman of the TCO central bargaining committee.

Back in the United States, we formed a second advisory committee of women academics and trade unionists and consulted them on how best to utilize the material we had gathered. In this group—with whom we held two meetings, one while research was in progress and one at the end of our intensive European observations—were, among others, Barbara Wertheimer (Cornell University Institute of Women and Work), Dr. Jeanne Stellman (Women's Occupational Health Resource Center), Jackie Kienzle (American Federation of Labor–Congress of Industrial Organizations), and Evelyn Ferber (Women's Bureau, Department of Labor).

Our method was mainly the information-gathering interview. The major issues with which we were concerned are reflected in the titles of our chapters: the various national social and labor relations policies as parameters within which the work of the unions was set and played out;

the structure of the unions; the structure and method of collective bargaining and of women's participation in forming the union agenda and
conducting its negotiations; the unions' own training and education
programs; the issues, as we saw them at that time, of chief concern to
women—pay equity, part-time work, health and safety, and equal employment opportunity.

Thus the major studies and observations were conducted in the mid
and late seventies. Our hope was to produce two books. One, which
we would edit, contributing a chapter or two, would enlarge on our
own work to cover perhaps a dozen countries with contributions from
experts on working women's history and activity within the labor
movement. That book appeared in 1984 entitled *Women and Trade
Unions in Eleven Industrialized Countries.*

"Book II," as we referred to the other, was to be our report on our
own work in the four countries. Val Lorwin carried main editorial responsibility for Book II. Both Roberta Till-Retz and I spent several weeks
in the late 1970s on at least two occasions working with him in Eugene.
He called on an old friend, Arlene Kaplan Daniels, sociologist from
Northwestern University, for editorial assistance, and she became a val-
ued member of the writing team. On the second of my working visits
to Eugene, I was aware that Val was ill. The illness was cancer. Though
he continued to read and correspond and write, work slowed and then
came to a stop as he worsened and died. In a visit Arlene had with Val
shortly before his death, she assured him that she and I would carry on
the book that was the focus of his concern.

Already almost five years had passed since the major investigative
work had been done. On my continuing visits to Europe it was ever
apparent that further changes were in progress. To measure their impact and extent, I followed up on these new undertakings with interviews with union staff members, academics, and government specialists.
The most recent of these visits included attendance at the women's congress of the German metalworkers union in September 1988. Close and
continuous reading of union and labor relations publications from these
countries provided a focus for many of these interviews. At one point
Roberta, now director of Labor Studies at the University of Iowa, corresponded with her original informants for an update on Austrian developments.

Thus, working from Val's notes and drafts, from repeatedly updated
information and with the generous and indefatigable editorial help Arlene has continuously provided, I have written this book. May it serve
the purpose we all wanted it to serve.

My special acknowledgment of gratitude goes to Peter Agree of Cornell University Press, who has submitted at least two versions of the text to peer reviewers, each of whom has provided helpful comments.

ALICE H. COOK

Ithaca, New York

The Most Difficult Revolution

Introduction and Setting

Adjustment to the new revolution in women's rights and roles is the most difficult that
we have to face, and by "we" I mean both men and women.
—A. F. Grospiron, president of the Oil,
Chemical, and Atomic Workers Union

Grospiron's comprehension that the new revolution in women's rights
creates the most difficult problem unions have to face has been rare
among union officials and activists, at least until very recently. For all
the reporting of the movement for women's rights generally and the
growing numbers of women in the paid labor force, there has been only
limited discussion of what women were doing in trade unions and what
unions were doing about women workers and women's issues, either in
the United States or abroad.[1]

Equality of the sexes is a difficult idea for both workers and employers. Programs to bring about equality in the trade union world are very
new and very rare. Most such programs, whether within the unions or
more generally in the labor market, are so recent and so unevaluated
that one can read about them only in government and union bulletins.
One can know about them best by going to the scene of events: talking
to women and men at all levels in the unions, breathing the air of union
offices and meetings, classes and conferences. Further, one must also
talk with knowledgeable and concerned people in political and academic life and feminist organizations to understand the context within
which such programs arise.

Epigraph: Quoted in Katherine Stone, *Handbook for Oil, Chemical, and Atomic Workers
Women,* 1973, p.v.

1. In the United States, historians have been active in making visible the buried facts
of women's participation in organized labor. Among these, Barbara Wertheimer, *We Were
There: The Story of Working Women in America,* 1977; Ruth Milkman, ed., *Women,
Work, and Protest: A Century of U.S. Women's Labor History,* 1985; and Alice Kessler-
Harris, *Out to Work: A History of Wage-Earning Women in the United States,* 1982, are
outstanding. Discussions of current problems are fewer, but among the notable exceptions
are articles in a special issue of *Labor Studies Journal* 10 (Winter 1986) under the editor-
ship of Ruth Needleman, particularly the article by Ruth Needleman and Lucretia Dewey
Tanner, "Women and Unions: Current Issues." Also of interest are Karen S. Koziara et
al., eds., *Working Women: Past, Present, and Future,* 1987; and papers delivered at a
Pennsylvania State University Conference, "Women and Unions," organized by Frieda
Rozen of the University's Department of Labor Studies in March 1989.

1

Can people in the United States use information about what is happening in other countries? Trade unionists point to the 44 million women workers in this country, five out of every six of whom are not organized.

Male dominance is as deeply embedded in American unions as in other institutions: in union structures and processes, and in men's and women's attitudes and behavior on the job. Yet, new experiences can change perspectives. People learn, not only from their own experience, but from the experience of others like them. What people learn stirs interest in what is desirable and encourages demands for what begins to seem attainable. People can make their own uses of approaches tried elsewhere. Therefore, we have chosen to report on constructive practices in Europe that are relevant to American working women's needs.

✓ Our greatest interest had to be in the problems and the unions of the 80 percent or so of employed women who are not in professional, technical, administrative, or managerial positions. These are women in routine jobs, low-paid, mostly dead-end, and often stressful, unhealthy, and insecure. These women feel the greatest weight of the inequalities of gender, combined as they are with the inequalities of class, and in many cases also with those of race or minority ethnic status. These women are the most poorly organized and, even if organized, the least integrated into union life, although the most in need of the services that the unions are—or should be—able to give them.

We are interested of course in the problems, the handicaps, and the discrimination that professional women face. Yet, generally these women are more able than others to fend for themselves, through their unions or on their own. Consequently, we did not systematically study unions of teachers, upper-level civil servants, or other professions in any detail. Several of the unions we did study, however, organize women in a wide range of skills and responsibilities, and some include professional women and first-line supervisors along with the supervised. We report some of what we learned from them.

In each of the four European countries under examination here, we studied programs of the national trade union confederations and of three or four unions, blue-collar and white-collar, in both public and private sectors. In unions of metal and chemical workers, we observed the activities of women who were distinct minorities. Among white-collar workers and manual workers in the public sector, as well as in textile and clothing unions, we observed the activities of women who were a majority or a near majority. In addition, we studied white-collar employment in industry, in distribution, banking, and insurance, and in one British general union. We learned from women at the International

Metalworkers' Federation (IMF), the International Federation of Commercial, Clerical, and Technical Employees (FIET),[2] the European Trade Union Confederation (ETUC), as well as from people at the International Labour Organisation (ILO), the Organisation for Economic Cooperation and Development (OECD), and the European Economic Community (EEC) or Common Market.[3]

Because the labor unions in these four countries operate within systems of labor market and social policy which prescribe conditions of work and set normative standards for their maintenance, we begin by mapping this context. The second half of this chapter presents information on the political and economic settings and the labor movements of the four countries that are the context for our discussion of women's activities and trade union programs.

Government policies affecting the work and home lives of women are the subjects of Chapter 1. We discuss the issues surrounding protective legislation, government provision of maternity benefits and allowances, support for child care, including parental leaves following childbirth or adoption and when children and other immediate family members need at-home care. The special issues of equal opportunity in the labor market follow in the second half of Chapter 1. Here we examine specific legislation governing equal access to jobs and training, programs attacking job segregation, protection of women—and minorities—against being the first victims of unemployment. We are concerned with the special responsibilities unions may carry for the initiation and enforcement of gender equality.

We turn then in Chapter 2 to the structure of unions and the place women have in unions either by formal assignment or by informal consensus. We are concerned with whether provisions for women's sections provide an opportunity or a ghetto for women in trade union leadership and programs. We describe the women's divisions in German and Austrian unions that organize and activate women members and represent their interests in and outside the labor movement. We examine the programs adopted by about half the German unions for furthering women's leadership in union ranks. We follow the innovation in a large British union in providing reserved seats for women on executive bodies, as a provisional arrangement until women can compete for office on more nearly equal terms, and consider the debate about the value of

2. These are federations of national unions from many countries, organized in specific jurisdictions. Of the twenty so-called secretariats, many, but by no means all, are located in Geneva, Switzerland.

3. These are all intergovernmental agencies that include labor union representation. They all have offices concerned with working women's affairs.

are employed. The proportions are higher in Sweden, Finland, and Denmark, but most other Western societies are comparable. Yet in none of these societies—and in no society West or East—has women's participation in the labor force in itself resulted in a revolution in their rights and roles or in the privileges and roles of men. The revolution only becomes apparent when we sum up the improvements in union structures and policies.

People of good will have rushed to hail women's employment as women's equality. Yet the nature of women's jobs may be more telling than the number of women working, the quality of the jobs more important than their quantity. Employment will mean equality only when women have a preparation for work and a choice of occupations equal to men's, when they have equal opportunities for work and equal treatment at work, and when lifetime work arrangements permit both men and women to share fully in home life and parenting.

Women need to demand more than sameness with men's conditions. Millions of men, like women, have had feeble or unrealistic preparation for work life and little if any real choice in what work they take. Most jobs are without autonomy, creativity, or mobility; hours of employment prevent normal family life for many; employment itself is at the mercy of sudden employer decisions and unmastered economic trends.[4] Work for a great many men and women is marked by emotional stress, frequently by physical strain, and often by the frustration of having learned all one can from a job almost as soon as one has taken it. Yet, so deep is the present inequality between the genders at work that we could hail the beginning of a new era if women in fact had the same conditions and opportunities as men in the labor market.

Equality requires not only rights for women at work which are equal to those of men but also responsibilities for men in home and family life which are comparable to those of women. One of the great changes in our society this century, says a publisher's blurb, has been in the

---

4. Many social theorists have followed the work of Harry Braverman, who in his *Labor and Monopoly Capital: The Degradation of Work in the Twentieth Century*, 1974, discussed the history of management's efforts to increase workers' efficiency and productivity. From the beginning of this century to the present, through the work of such theorists as Frederick Taylor, management has encouraged the development of procedures to separate jobs into their component parts. This separation was designed to minimize the time workers spend learning the job and to deemphasize the necessity for any worker to have a variety of skills. In consequence, many workers today spend their time at quickly learned repetitive tasks with close monitoring and greater pressure to meet management-controlled production schedules. This degrading and deskilling of labor can be found not only in factory work, but also in clerical service and much bureaucratic work.

Metalworkers' Federation (IMF), the International Federation of Commercial, Clerical, and Technical Employees (FIET),[2] the European Trade Union Confederation (ETUC), as well as from people at the International Labour Organisation (ILO), the Organisation for Economic Cooperation and Development (OECD), and the European Economic Community (EEC) or Common Market.[3]

Because the labor unions in these four countries operate within systems of labor market and social policy which prescribe conditions of work and set normative standards for their maintenance, we begin by mapping this context. The second half of this chapter presents information on the political and economic settings and the labor movements of the four countries that are the context for our discussion of women's activities and trade union programs.

Government policies affecting the work and home lives of women are the subjects of Chapter 1. We discuss the issues surrounding protective legislation, government provision of maternity benefits and allowances, support for child care, including parental leaves following childbirth or adoption and when children and other immediate family members need at-home care. The special issues of equal opportunity in the labor market follow in the second half of Chapter 1. Here we examine specific legislation governing equal access to jobs and training, programs attacking job segregation, protection of women—and minorities—against being the first victims of unemployment. We are concerned with the special responsibilities unions may carry for the initiation and enforcement of gender equality.

We turn then in Chapter 2 to the structure of unions and the place women have in unions either by formal assignment or by informal consensus. We are concerned with whether provisions for women's sections provide an opportunity or a ghetto for women in trade union leadership and programs. We describe the women's divisions in German and Austrian unions that organize and activate women members and represent their interests in and outside the labor movement. We examine the programs adopted by about half the German unions for furthering women's leadership in union ranks. We follow the innovation in a large British union in providing reserved seats for women on executive bodies, as a provisional arrangement until women can compete for office on more nearly equal terms, and consider the debate about the value of

---

2. These are federations of national unions from many countries, organized in specific jurisdictions. Of the twenty so-called secretariats, many, but by no means all, are located in Geneva, Switzerland.

3. These are all intergovernmental agencies that include labor union representation. They all have offices concerned with working women's affairs.

these and other special structures that goes on among unionists, who may be alike in their commitment to equality but differ in their views of how to achieve it.

The next two chapters describe union functions that are basic to improvement of women workers' status and opportunities. Chapter 3 examines patterns of collective bargaining and political action, and women's roles in bargaining. This chapter also compares the roles of the unions' local bodies and their national and regional centers in bargaining on issues of greatest concern to women. Union education is the theme of Chapter 4. The search for ways to break down barriers to women's participation and women's leadership has evoked new ideas on the place, time, content, and method of labor education. In Sweden local union education representatives work to reach those who are most difficult to reach: ethnic minorities, shift workers, and women and men without adequate basic education. In Britain we report on an ambitious Trades Union Congress (TUC) program with the British Broadcasting Corporation's "narrow-casting" for the special audience of unionists. One European idea that has transcended national frontiers is the legal right to released time with pay for general or vocational education, for union training, and for the performance of union functions in the workplace.

In the following four chapters we discuss specific programs in which unions play an important role in improving women's working conditions and opportunities. The fifth chapter considers the demands often lumped together in two words, "equal pay," and the attempts to move from "equal pay for equal work" to "equal pay for work of equal value." We assess job evaluation as a way to approach the latter goal. Although often misused by management (sometimes in collusion with male unionists), job evaluation may be essential to give meaning and monetary content to the "work of equal value" demand. We report a path-breaking German study of the demands and strains on women in assembly-line operations, a study that suggests how various elements in their work may receive adequate weight in job evaluation. Then we examine the policy of "wage solidarity" as it was practiced for several decades in Sweden. It is not a job evaluation approach but the most sustained and successful effort of any labor movement to raise the wages of women and of all low-paid workers.

Labor market programs and vocational training are the subject of Chapter 6. Our discussion reviews union roles in the active labor market policies in which Sweden has pioneered. Strategies have included developing measures of vocational guidance, training, retraining, and placement of women entering or reentering the labor force, as well as guidance for the unemployed and those threatened by unemployment, or seeking to upgrade their skills. The chapter also touches upon programs in several countries to open nontraditional occupations to girls and mature women, and union programs for upgrading members in routine manual and white-collar employment.

Advances in the unionization and representation of part-time workers—almost all of whom everywhere are women—are the theme of Chapter 7. Distinguishing first among different types of part-time work, we consider unions that have organized many part-time employees, opened career ladders at work for them, and given them training for more effective union and civic participation. Our study of the best recent practices gives us a "Bill of Rights" for part-timers, both to protect those who need to work less than a full week, and to prevent their exploitation from threatening the standards of full-time workers.

Health and safety in the workshop are the subject of Chapter 8. Some of these standards are achieved by law, others through collective bargaining. In the 1970s all the countries that we studied mandated the training of safety stewards and joint safety committee members on employer-paid released time. These countries have recently been training large numbers (very large numbers by American standards) of men and women, elected or union-appointed, as health and safety stewards. These representatives have powers unknown to American safety stewards and safety committee members to protect the workers whom they represent. For example, in Sweden safety stewards may halt any process they consider an imminent danger to life or health, while the joint safety committees, with a union majority, control company health services. We also report some special efforts by unions and by women members in other countries in behalf of women's health on and off the job.

A concluding chapter considers issues of solidarity between women and men, reviews some of the last two decades' gains in equality, recognizes that they may be reversible in difficult times, and suggests some of the avenues for union action and demands that minimize fears of competition between men and women. This chapter also considers women's right to "equality in the face of unemployment," the necessary complement to women's right to employment. It surveys some elements that may survive retrenchment and reversal in an otherwise somber scene.

Employment Alone Is Not Equality

Where is the "revolution" in rights and roles of which Grospiron spoke? In the United States, more than five out of every ten adult women are employed. The proportions are higher in Sweden, Finland, and Denmark, but most other Western societies are comparable. Yet in none of these societies—and in no society West or East—has women's participation in the labor force in itself resulted in a revolution in their rights and roles or in the privileges and roles of men. The revolution only becomes apparent when we sum up the improvements in union structures and policies.

People of good will have rushed to hail women's employment as women's equality. Yet the nature of women's jobs may be more telling than the number of women working, the quality of the jobs more important than their quantity. Employment will mean equality only when women have a preparation for work and a choice of occupations equal to men's, when they have equal opportunities for work and equal treatment at work, and when lifetime work arrangements permit both men and women to share fully in home life and parenting.

Women need to demand more than sameness with men's conditions. Millions of men, like women, have had feeble or unrealistic preparation for work life and little if any real choice in what work they take. Most jobs are without autonomy, creativity, or mobility; hours of employment prevent normal family life for many; employment itself is at the mercy of sudden employer decisions and unmastered economic trends.[4] Work for a great many men and women is marked by emotional stress, frequently by physical strain, and often by the frustration of having learned all one can from a job almost as soon as one has taken it. Yet, so deep is the present inequality between the genders at work that we could hail the beginning of a new era if women in fact had the same conditions and opportunities as men in the labor market.

Equality requires not only rights for women at work which are equal to those of men but also responsibilities for men in home and family life which are comparable to those of women. One of the great changes in our society this century, says a publisher's blurb, has been in the

4. Many social theorists have followed the work of Harry Braverman, who in his *Labor and Monopoly Capital: The Degradation of Work in the Twentieth Century*, 1974, discussed the history of management's efforts to increase workers' efficiency and productivity. From the beginning of this century to the present, through the work of such theorists as Frederick Taylor, management has encouraged the development of procedures to separate jobs into their component parts. This separation was designed to minimize the time workers spend learning the job and to deemphasize the necessity for any worker to have a variety of skills. In consequence, many workers today spend their time at quickly learned repetitive tasks with close monitoring and greater pressure to meet management-controlled production schedules. This degrading and deskilling of labor can be found not only in factory work, but also in clerical service and much bureaucratic work.

exodus of women out of their homes and into paid employment. This is half fact and half nonsense. Women have gone into paid employment as never before but there has been no more an exodus of women out of their homes than there has been a rush of men to the kitchen stoves and baby cribs. Women have added paid jobs to their unpaid work at home and to their roles in childbearing and childrearing. They are, as Jeanne Stellman says, "on permanent, unpaid overtime."[5]

In the long effort to free women from the corset of Victorian stereotypes, let us be wary of new stereotypes, for example, that a woman is not a person unless she has a full-time, paid job, whatever the job and whatever her family responsibilities.[6] As Paula Wassen-van Schaveren of the Dutch Commission on Emancipation wrote a few years ago, "Emancipation policy should aim at giving women sufficient room to be themselves, instead of allowing them to be forced into roles that only partly fit them."[7]

Employment (or self-employment) is a right for both men and women. Either a man or a woman should be free to stay at home to care for family dependents as well as take on other family responsibilities, and parents should share the obligation to do so.

Equality in the Unions: Declarations and Realities

Most working-class women and men have little enough choice of roles. They must work if they are to raise families decently. Their need is for flexibility in work on a given job, for open career paths and ladders to other, better jobs, and for choice in their lifelong negotiation of time split between family and work.

Collective bargaining and legislation are two roads to improvement in the development of opportunity to work and to take leave from work during a lifetime. The concern of this book is chiefly with what unions have done within their own organizations and through their power in

5. Jeanne Stellman, *Women's Work, Women's Health*, 1977. For an appraisal of equality in the home ten years after Stellman, see Arlie Hochschild, *The Second Shift: Working Parents and the Revolution at Home*, 1989.

6. For some studies of the so-called nonworking women, see Arlene Kaplan Daniels, *Invisible Careers: Women Civic Leaders and the Volunteer World*, 1988; Arlene Leibowitz, "Women's Work in the Home," in *Sex Discrimination and the Division of Labor*, ed. Cynthia Lloyd, 1975; Marjorie DeVault, *Feeding the Family: the Social Organization of Caring as Gendered Work*, 1991; Meg Luxton, *More Than a Labor of Love*, 1980; Helene Z. Lopata, *Occupation Housewife*, 1971.

7. Paula Wassen-van Schaveren, *Planning the Emancipation of Women*, 1977, p. 9.

dealing with employers on these issues, and how they have worked through political parties and with other interest groups to achieve legislation and affect social policy.

Unions have claimed to be not only bargaining agencies for their members, but also an emancipation movement for all workers. Their weight in collective bargaining and in the politics of democratic societies includes the responsibility to represent women as well as men, and the interests of unorganized workers as well as the organized. Women and their organizations therefore should be able to look to the unions for support in the long struggle for equality.

In the labor market, unions are the sole representatives of wage and salaried workers. They participate in setting the fundamental conditions of wages, hours, and fringe benefits, and of the exercise of authority in the workplace. They can influence and in some cases even control how girls and women are trained for the world of work and how they are treated in the workplace. Those patterns of training and treatment affect not only women's working lives but also their lives in the home, just as their roles in the home affect their roles in the shop or office and in the union meeting.

Among those for whom the unions speak, the least well paid and the least autonomous in their work and in social life are the most entitled to concern. Women form a very large proportion of such workers, no matter in what ethnic group of Western society. How far the unions could reduce the inequality of conditions for women in offices and factories, hospitals and stores, one cannot say, since few unions have yet tried. While employers have the greater responsibility in the workplace, unions have the power in their own internal life to reduce discrimination that contradicts their official declarations on the equality of the genders. It is mostly men who must do this, since they control nearly all the unions. Social conditioning and social contexts tend to make women less demanding than they should be, in the union, the labor market, and the home, in Western Europe or in the United States.

In terms of social policy affecting women, male unionists have rarely been advocates of gender equality. They have typically waited for the chief impetus for advances in women's rights to come from others. They have waited until overtaken by general tides of opinion and events—wildcat strikes, legislation on equal pay or equal opportunity, the examples of governments as employers, the leadership of women in political parties. Even the progressive union leader quoted at the opening of this chapter called upon unions to "adjust" to the new rights and roles of women; he did not ask for women's leadership in achieving those rights. The exceptions are heartening—but their rarity confirms the general rule.

Some Words We Use

The general rule is that relations between men and women in unions are of the traditional order. These opinions as expressed in ordinary language and concepts reflect the hold the traditional order has in everyday life. Consequently we need to specify that we use terms somewhat differently from this customary usage, and to define some additional terms. Most of the words in this book are those of everyday speech; but everyday speech may be unclear or ambiguous, so here we explain a few words that we frequently use.

We still have to use the word "work" in the patriarchal sense, customary in both conversation and labor force statistics: work for pay. Thus it excludes all the important but invisible unpaid work of women in the home and for their communities. Of course most women have always worked. In the current usage, however, a woman "works" only when she adds a paid job to her activities in the home. This work usually means employment outside one's home.[8] The idea of work, since the industrial revolution, is so deeply associated with absence from the home that women who have done paid work in their homes, such as dressmaking, child care, or caring for boarders or lodgers, often have not called it "work," simply because it did not take them out of the house.

The term "equality" refers to gender equality, unless we specify racial or other forms of it. Equality of the genders, as of races, assumes the common human needs of all. That means much more than nondiscrimination. As with racial equality, it requires that society make special provisions to overcome present inequalities of education and training resulting from past inequalities of access. Unlike racial equality, however, gender equality recognizes a diversity of needs arising from the differences between the continuing social demands upon men and those upon women—primarily that in addition to childbearing, the social expectation is that women will do the child care as well as carrying other

8. There has been a growing movement toward home-based work. For specific studies, see among others Eileen Applebaum, "Restructuring Work: Part-time and At-home Employment," in *Computer Chips and Paper Clips*, ed. Heidi Hartmann, 1987; Kathleen Christensen, *A New Era of Home-based Work: Directions and Policies*, 1987; Carl Simon and Ann White, *Beating the System: The Underground Economy*, 1982.

family responsibilities. In the future, gender equality will mean that men must respond equally to these social demands so that women's responsibilities do not keep them in an inferior state.

"Inferior, who is free?" asked John Milton. The poet has reminded us that equality is not only a goal but also a means toward other goals. It is a means toward freedom from unjust constraints, freedom to participate in deciding one's fate, and freedom to take part in the public business. Participation, like equality, is both a goal and a means. Freedom and participation are conditions for self-respect and the respect of others; they go hand in hand to create and confirm equality of respect.

We use the term "family" to refer to all kinds of families: married and unmarried; two parents, single parents, and couples without children; old life-styles and new. In the same way we use "married" to designate women or men who share households in various patterns without reference to the nature of their contract.

The term "family policy" is used in many different senses. It refers to what government agencies and private organizations do, by action and inaction, to affect families as social units and individuals as members of families. The term covers explicit policies, such as those on child care and child support, social insurance benefits, health care, pregnancy benefits, and maternal or parental leaves. In some countries the term refers to all areas of social policy affecting women. It can also include implicit policies, or actions that indirectly affect family life, such as those directed at housing and the content of school curricula. Most immediately the term applies to family law, specifically law on marriage, divorce, and family planning.

Four European Countries

Great Britain, Sweden, Austria, and the German Federal Republic are all part of the same sociopolitical world as the United States. They are all political democracies, Britain and Sweden carrying on a continuous evolution in this regard, West Germany and Austria emerging in 1945 from the darkness of twelve years of Nazi rule. All have well-developed, democratic trade union movements that have organized considerably higher percentages of both men and women in the work force than have American unions. Two of the countries have small populations, the other two large populations. Germany and Austria are federal states; Britain and Sweden are unitary states, with Britain having some special institutions for particular requirements of Scotland, Wales, and Northern Ireland.

Two countries are Protestant: Great Britain, with a significant Catholic minority in the working class, and Sweden, the most secular of the four countries, although it still retains a state church. Austria is predominantly Catholic, while Germany is divided almost evenly between Protestants and Catholics. There are no longer Catholic and Protestant labor movements in Germany and Austria, as there were before Nazism. The United States constitutionally draws a sharp line between church and state. Nevertheless at many points in its history religious beliefs have played a crucial role in political life and in the formation of social policy. To see this role, one need only refer to the present deep differences between the opponents and proponents of abortion and of family planning, strongly affecting aspects of U.S. policy on foreign aid and domestic welfare.

Predominantly Catholic countries espouse traditional values and expectations for women in the family, placing these values and expectations ahead of equal opportunity for women in the workplace. Perhaps one should speak of the countries that we studied as more Catholic or Protestant in name than in fact, except of course for some deeply orthodox minorities, groups, and individuals. Yet, as opinion surveys show and history leads us to expect, traditional religious beliefs and attitudes have a pervasive influence on people's current behavior toward women's roles in society.

These countries all have "mixed" economies, with a complex and shifting balance between powerful private economic interests and widespread government intervention. In Sweden, private enterprise accounts for 90 percent of industrial employment. It is its emphasis on forms of government and trade union intervention in the private market economy that have made Sweden the nearest of the four countries to a genuine welfare state. The British unions consistently made an issue of nationalization of industry in the past. As recently as the early 1980s the plan of the Conservative government to privatize the mines led to a prolonged miners' strike that divided the labor movement itself. But while public ownership was greatly curtailed under Conservative governments in Britain, it continues to be widespread in Austria. None of the union movements, however, considers either that good industrial relations depend upon public ownership or even that public ownership assures good relations.

All four nations are heavily dependent—as the United States has come to be—upon export trade for their degree of prosperity and upon imports for much of their food and raw materials. Sweden and Germany are both economies of high productivity, higher these days than in the United States. Britain is the country least oriented toward productivity, and its wage level is far below that of the United States. Workers' incomes in Germany and Sweden average about the same as in the United States, although in different proportions of direct wages and fringe benefits, or "social wages."

The distribution of incomes among different social groups is more significant than any averages. The least unequal nations in distribution of income in Western Europe are Sweden, Norway, and the Netherlands. While Sweden is trying to achieve equality, Britain still has to abolish poverty. The proportion of poverty is highest in the United States among these Western countries. Among the poverty population, women-headed families in all these countries make up the largest sector of the poor.

The union movements in all four countries, as in the United States, are entirely independent of the state and of management though some work more closely than others with political parties and governments. As for political alliances of labor, each country where such a tie exists has a dominant federation of unions supporting a labor party. In Britain it is the TUC to which most but not all national unions are affiliated. However, individual national unions and not the TUC are the bodies that decide on support for the Labour party. Germany and Austria before World War II had multiple ideological trade union federations, each allied to a different political party. In founding the new unitary federations in 1949, each labor movement preferred that this body—the German Federation of Labor (DGB) in Germany, the Austrian Trade Union Federation (OeGB) in Austria—should maintain political neutrality in the name of trade union solidarity. Nevertheless, it is widely understood that most union members and leaders support the Social Democratic parties. In Germany a sizable Catholic minority of workers looks to the Christian Democratic party (CDU) of joint Catholic-Protestant inspiration as its political expression. In Austria a minority of unionists looks to the People's Party (OeVP) of Catholic inspiration.

Sweden has three federations. The Swedish Confederation of Labor (LO) is made up mainly of blue-collar unions with close ties to the Social Democratic party.[9] The Swedish Central Organization of Salaried Employees (TCO), the white-collar federation, is politically neutral, and the Swedish Association of Academic, Professional, and Managerial Officers (SACO/SR) is the union of professional and management personnel who are nominally nonpolitical, although many of their members belong to one of the center or conservative parties. The size and high

9. While LO is customarily called a confederation of manual workers' unions, its affiliates include a significant number of routine white-collar workers.

density of LO's organization ensured Social Democratic leadership of government from the 1930s for all but six years in the late seventies and early eighties and has strongly influenced Swedish socialist and labor market policies.[10]

The European Labour and Social Democratic parties are all reformist and gradualist in aims, temper, strategy, and tactics. The aims of the Swedish Social Democratic party have been the most ambitious and the most continuous. Each party has a left wing of some strength and union support, most important by far in Britain. The Communist parties are a negligible factor in the parliaments of all four countries. Communists and assorted left-wing groups have some strength in British unions but little in the other countries' unions. Whatever their relations to the parties, all the union movements regard themselves as the sole representatives of workers' on-the-job concerns and occupational interests.

Each country had some special interest for us as researchers. Americans have a natural curiosity about Britain, from which come some of the traditions of the founders of the modern American labor movement, including craft traditions that exclude women. When we started our work, Britain was the only one of the four countries to have either an equal pay or an equal opportunity law. (Both have been revised and amended in the intervening years.) Although British union leaders had much of the same ambivalence about equality legislation as their American counterparts, some unions have aggressively supported women's complaints under the equal pay law and have promoted equal opportunity in legislation, through collective bargaining, and in internal union programs.

In Germany and Austria the women's divisions of the confederations and national unions demonstrate that structures, in some cases originally designed to keep women "in their place," can be used by a more independent generation of women to advance their interests within the labor movement and in collective bargaining.[11] In Germany the DGB's women's division has also shown the advantages of operating as part of a general coalition of women.

Both Austria and Germany have a long tradition of protective legislation for working women and for maternity and child-care benefits. While the national government extended the protective laws in the postwar period, Austrian unions bargained for benefits beyond those that the law gave. Germany and Britain also maintain women's protective

---

10. In late 1991, the Social Democratic party lost heavily to a coalition of centrist-conservative parties.

11. For more details on the structure of these labor movements, see Chapter 2.

labor laws. In Britain some of those laws have been challenged by the Equal Opportunities Commission (EOC). Since the majority of the TUC supports those laws, however, the EOC recommendation for repeal or revision is unlikely to succeed in the near future.

All four nations have repealed their old patriarchal legislation in family matters, although attitudes have changed less than legislative texts. Sweden comes closest to achieving goals of equality, although women and men inside and outside the unions are quick to remind the observer that they still have a very long way to go to achieve the equality to which the nation is committed.

Sweden interested us for its advances toward equal pay by collective bargaining, by the active role of the unions in labor market policies promoting women's vocational training within a framework of near-full employment, by the wide reach and depth of the labor education for which the Scandinavian countries are famous, by the combination of collective bargaining, legislation, and educational activities in behalf of high standards of occupational health and safety, by its efforts to adjust men's as well as women's work life to a more egalitarian family life, and by the changes in school curricula to ensure that texts and teaching recognize the commitment to gender equality.

European nations have been on the defensive in recent years against unemployment and inflation. In most continental countries, people have not had to defend themselves against the sort of ideological attacks and antiunion activities that many employers and heterogeneous right-wing forces have mounted in the United States. In Britain, however, a Conservative government has legislated to clip the wings of trade union power. In Germany, also under a conservative government, legislation limiting strikes and other union activity is pending.

In our discussion an underlying assumption is that women in trade unions can do and have done much to improve their general quality of work life as well as their level of wages. An equally important assumption is that trade unions provide a valuable structure through which women's efforts—and those of their supporters—can be channeled. The European experience suggests a variety of approaches and strategies that women in the less advanced unions of the United States may consider. Whether in Europe or the United States, the trade union movement is now fundamentally committed to a philosophy of equality of opportunity which women can and should use to their advantage.

PART I

UNIONS, GOVERNMENT, AND INTERNATIONAL AGENCIES: LAW AND POLICY

Government Policies on
Work and Home Lives of Women

The economic organization of all industrial societies invites women into the labor force. . . . Even where strong ideologies of equality between the sexes prevail, ancient patterns persist: women are confined largely to nurturant, expressive, and subordinate roles; they increasingly combine childrearing and housekeeping with paid labor to make their "working hours" very long; . . . or they stay home, often restive or bored, feeling that they are on the sidelines.

—Harold L. Wilensky, "Women's Work:
Economic Growth, Ideology, Structure"

The difficulty in formulating exactly what we wanted at work was due in part to the lack of clear thinking on the issue of what we wanted at home. . . . What we never managed to achieve was to involve wide areas of workers into a general discussion on the relationship between the organization of working hours and private life.

—Paola Piva and Chiara Ingrao, "Women's Subjectivity,
Union Power and the Problem of Work"

Implicit in all our strivings of the last years has been an adaption to the world of work, rather than the adaption of that world to one that allows time for children, leisure, politics.

—Bea Campbell and Val Charlton

The influx of women into the labor market that has occurred in the past twenty years has produced a conflict of interests and loyalties among women that was unknown to earlier generations. Indeed, the very question of their right to equality in the labor market and civic life is still a matter of public debate, as the failure in the United States only a few years ago to adopt the Equal Rights Amendment to the Constitution amply demonstrates. For women themselves, the question of whether they can continue to meet the demands of homemaking and childrearing while they work is a besetting query to which most of them find no satisfactory answer. Voluntary associations, governments, and intergovernmental agencies have all to some degree recognized that women live in a world that has defined them as second-class citizens. Historically, in the family they have been legally subordinate to the male head of

Epigraphs: First from *Industrial Relations* 7:3 (1968); other from *Feminist Review*, no. 16 (April 1984), pp. 53, 64. The third is cited by Ruth Elliott in "How Far Have We Come? Women's Organisations in the Unions of the United Kingdom."

household; in the labor market, they have been assigned to marginal work where they variously have been perceived as a "reserve army," to be called up when men were insufficiently available. From biblical times they have been judged less productive than men and therefore deserving of less pay. Women are still widely held to be only temporarily in the labor market and therefore not worth the investment—either by themselves or their employers—in education and training. At best, only unmarried women or widows bereft of support have been seen to have a rightful place in the world of work. Women's proper place was in the home and not in the labor market.

Rather suddenly, in a subtle and complex revolution, all this has changed. Yet laws, policies, customs, and beliefs have by no means caught up with modern reality, although many forces, organizational and individual, are trying to bring these elements into line with the needs of what we call "working women," a phrase in which the unpaid but often arduous work in the home is overlooked and undervalued.

The developments that resulted from women's massive movement into the labor market are the focus of this chapter. We note the common assumptions about women and work that prevailed at the turn of the century and then explore how the values that informed them have undergone change, moving governments and unions unevenly forward to deal piecemeal with the realities of the late twentieth century.

Among these realities are the dilemmas women face when they enter the labor market as mothers of children and wives of male waged and salaried workers. Since the American and French revolutions, the modern world has been shaped by visions of equality, democracy,—even industrial democracy,—individual rights, and equal opportunity. A few women began 150 years ago to ask why they were not included among the citizens entitled to these rights, and to put forward demands for the right to franchise. This was the first step in the direction of the inevitable demand in this century for equal employment opportunity in the labor market and partnership in marriage. Let us see how far we have advanced toward this goal. Since our central theme is women in trade unions, we shall turn again and again to the role unions have played in setting goals and bringing about progress.

Origins of the Problem: The Domestic Code

Preindustrial life was organized around the home. While a division of labor existed between spouses and their children, they all labored for each others' sustenance with the home as center. This organization worked for agricultural and handcraft pursuits; perhaps only a little less so for persons who engaged solely in marketing and the provision of credit—the early form of banking. To the extent that the family farm continues to exist it is an observable relic of a preindustrial life-style. It is characterized by a division of household and production tasks, wagelessness, income through barter rather than by sale of surplus products, and a high degree of family self-sufficiency to which each family member contributes.

With the beginnings of industrial development, the first wage workers were those not central to the maintenance of the home—unmarried daughters and young children. These groups were recruited into the textile mills and other "light" manufacturing. Women stayed a few years in the mills until they married; they received low wages, commensurate with those of children with whom they shared not only the work but the rationale for being sent to work—they could be spared, and work was preferable to the mishaps that would surely befall the possessors of "idle hands"—those with no full-time assignments at home or outside it. Moreover, they could bring a cash income, however small, into homes otherwise largely dependent on agriculture or barter. They were temporarily in the labor force. They would in due course return to the work that women were made to do, production and reproduction in the home.

With the spread of industrial manufacture—aggravated in Britain by the land enclosures—men also moved early into wage work in iron and steelmaking, shipbuilding, mining, milling, and into the construction and printing trades. These men, unlike the women, left home for a lifetime of wage earning. In the cities that grew up around these enterprises, a new urban life-style developed. This way of living established the male as the breadwinner, the female as the mother of children and the homemaker. Although homemaking was her full-time occupation, it was unpaid; her husband worked entirely outside the home and brought home the sole source of money income for the family. The rationale for a decent income—or at least the demand for one—was that it was "a family wage." In response to his effort, the home became a refuge for the family head when he returned from his long day of arduous labor, often under brutal, back-breaking conditions. The fight for the family wage was undertaken so that he could spare his "weaker" wife and children, and keep the refuge intact.

The result was a new ideology of men's and women's roles and status, what Kessler-Harris calls "the domestic code." Under it, the male breadwinner was out in the world, earning the family income; the female was homemaker—cooking, cleaning, provisioning, bearing and rearing children, responsible for developing close personal relations, and carrying responsibility for culture and ethics. Whatever disaster might change this picture and force her also into the world of work, her paramount charge remained that of home and family. Although this code was in fact normative and descriptive only of the middle class, its assumptions were used by working men, and the early trade unionists, to justify their opposition to women entering the labor force and as a basis for their struggle for "the family wage."[1]

Still, the head of family could not always earn enough to provide for his family. Unemployment was a constant fear and seasonal work a recurring source of economic uncertainty. Children went to work early. Boys left home at ten or twelve to make their own way. Girls went out as children to do domestic work. Many husbands who died of industrial accidents and disease left their widows quite destitute. Under these circumstances, women had to seek work. They found jobs thought suitable for women at even lower pay than men received. They worked as laundresses, domestic workers, seamstresses—occupations presumably related to their domestic role. They ran boarding houses. They worked in textiles, clothing, and shoe factories. They took in "home work" by the bundle that they and their children fashioned in crowded tenements. In countries with late industrial development, such as Sweden, Norway, or Ireland, relatively few women, until recently, left home to work; but in countries such as England and Germany where textile industries were early established, and every middle-class home had servants, tens of thousands of working-class women worked for wages from the dawn of the Industrial Revolution—driven there by the need to survive.

The belief that women's place is in the home, with all the aura of domesticity and of innocence of wage work that clings to that concept, persists to this day. Such views are evident in the opinions of judges and arbitrators, of labor market policymakers, of educators, of churchmen, and inevitably even of many women themselves. Union men have shared the belief and only very recently have begun to see the actualities of the world through difference lenses.

Even now, in the late twentieth century, women still are expected to carry major, if not sole, responsibility for home duties, whether they work outside the home or not. At the same time, and despite this assumption, all modern countries have adopted laws and policies to achieve equality between the sexes in the world of work. Yet the very attempts to achieve this equality, as Campbell and Charlton point out, have forced

1. Alice Kessler-Harris, *Out to Work: A History of Wage-Earning Women in the United States*, 1982, and *Women Have Always Worked*, 1981.

women to make "adaptions" to the world of work, not "adaption" of that world to the home and to civic participation.[2]

An assumption underlying much of what has been done in the name of equality in the world of work is that men's organization of this world is right and proper, suitable to all workers of either sex. However, the reality is that the world of work has been shaped by men for men. Their assumption has been that work is the primary concern of the male worker while home, where the wife provides services of all kinds, is a refuge from the rigors of work.

Women who work outside the home cannot continue to operate in this way, unless conditions within the home are radically changed. This mode implies that they must adapt their work behavior to the male norm, without in any way motivating men to make a comparable adaptation to sharing home responsibilities. The consequences for women are those that Wilensky noted twenty-five years ago: either overload in carrying two sets of responsibilities or boredom at being confined to the home with little opportunity to be out in the world.[3] Yet as Piva and Ingrao observe, women, as well as policymakers, have not on the whole faced up to the consequences of a discussion of "the relationship between the organization of work and private life." Women typically have dealt with the problem by trying to carry "the double burden." Men, both husbands and policymakers, have tried to ignore the consequences for women of the fact that women's access to widened work opportunities has not at all mitigated their traditional major role in the home.[4]

In the face of these facts, conservatives of both sexes have tried to turn the clock back, to wish women back into their nineteenth-century homemaking stereotype, to privatize what they refer to as "every woman's choice," that is, to be either a homemaker-mother or a career woman. When pressed, they may acknowledge woman's right to equality in the labor market, but the private sphere, they insist, remains her individual problem and hers alone.

The progressives' agenda includes both spheres. They talk of "wages for wives," the "right of women to control their own bodies," the freedom to build families without marriage, "no-fault divorce," "compa-

2. Bea Campbell and Val Charlton, cited by Ruth Elliott in "How Far Have We Come? Women's Organisations in the Unions of the United Kingdom," *Feminist Review*, no. 16 (April 1984), p. 64.

3. Harold Wilensky, "Women's Work: Economic Growth, Ideology, Structure," *Industrial Relations*, 7:3 (1968), pp. 242–43.

4. Paola Piva and Chiara Ingrao, "Women's Subjectivity, Union Power, and the Problem of Work," *Feminist Review*, no. 16 (April 1984), p. 53.

rable worth," and "affirmative action." Yet, generally their views too are built on the assumption that women have and can exercise a wide range of choices about both their public and their private lives.

These two very separate spheres of public and private have produced two discrete areas of policy-making that only rarely have been interrelated. The shape and direction of these policy moves arise from, and are implicit in the ways women, whether in the home or in the workplace, became the subject of state policy.

The Origins of Policy-Making

Government policy-making about public and private life is of relatively recent origin. From medieval to very recent times, the Church laid down its binding moral principles on the family in canon law. Governments, both monarchical and democratic, then tended to take over the customs derived from these edicts and embody them in state legislation.

Early labor codes, to the extent they were recognized as such, were based on personal and moralistic doctrine as well. Churches, both Protestant and Catholic, had condoned the conditions of early capitalism. They saw long hours and unregulated conditions as preferable to slackness and no work at all. The early trade unions which sought to alleviate working conditions based their claims on new concepts of equal rights in the public sphere, as expressed by the American and French revolutionists and given especial reference to class and collective action in the Communist Manifesto. In this country, workers' protests and demands were summarily judged to be conspiracy against the republic; in monarchical Europe, they were treated as a form of lèse majesté.

For all their efforts and their occasional successes, the most these early unions did was to struggle for a better world of work for males. Like their rulers and betters, early unionists identified women primarily with family and home.

The domestic code was so widely accepted as defining women's separate and household role that women's work for wages could be either ignored as an unusual and temporary exception to the proper order, or actively opposed as dangerous competition in an area where men assumed they should retain hegemony. When active opposition to women's membership in unions became neither practical nor desirable, unionists created a form of second-class, "non-beneficial," low dues form of membership, a move which both sanctioned separate, low-wage scales for women and discouraged women's participation in these organizations by seriously limiting their rights and scope within the unions.

Protective Legislation

Out of these circumstances came union support in the late nineteenth century and well into the twentieth century for "protective legislation," laws prohibiting women from working overtime and at night, working underground or at heights, lifting heavy weights, or standing long hours. Although a few women workers protested that these rules barred women from much remunerative work in the prohibited areas, they were not heeded. Women's organizations supported these laws out of a concern for women's unprotected positions within the labor market, the heavy double burden of work outside and within the home, and the unions' policies that amounted to segregation and neglect of working women's needs. Whatever necessary purpose such laws served as they were enacted, they tended to sanctify women's secondary and short-term labor market status. Policymakers maintained that their primary responsibility was to mothers in the home. The courts made this concern eminently clear as they dealt with the issue of extending coverage of these laws to men. Women, they said, were to be protected, not as workers, but as potential mothers of the race.[5] Thus, labor market policy on women rests on their familial role. Acceptance of the "domestic code" was the grounding principle and governing force of national policy affecting women's work.

Early Family Policy

Family policy, of course, was equally invested in the "domestic code." As Folke Schmidt, a specialist in international law has observed, family policy has rested on the concept that

the adult man was a free person who would be able to take care of his own interests. A woman, even a grown woman, was . . . a dependent person. Whilst she was married (feme covert), she was protected by her

5. The Supreme Court in *Muller v. Oregon* made this point unmistakable: "That woman's physical structure and the performance of maternal functions place her at a disadvantage in the struggle for subsistence is obvious. . . . As healthy mothers are essential to vigorous offspring, the physical wellbeing of women becomes an object of public interest and care in order to preserve the strength and vigor of the race. . . . The [difference between the sexes] justifies a difference in legislation, and upholds that which is designed to compensate for some of the burdens which rest upon her" (200 U.S. 412 [1908]).

husband, who administered her property. . . . In France, the old rule of
the Code Civil that a wife was not permitted to exercise a profession (whether
as an employee or not) without the consent of her husband was in force
until very recently. . . . Its basis was a system of community property.[6]

In Europe, concern with family policy emerged after World War I as
natalism, an issue greatly aggravated by the massive loss of life in the
war. Not only were women to be protected as putative mothers; they
were to be encouraged to have as many children as possible. A rash of
programs developed to encourage women to bear more children and to
remain in the home. Family policy, Kamerman and Kahn note, first
took the form of financial inducements in income redistribution policies
favoring large families. Thus family policy addressed itself exclusively
to women's family role, defining that role as one of home responsibility
under the protection of the husband. Women, but not men, were identified with family and not with earning a living.[7]

Thus, two distinct kinds of protective legislation for women developed. On the one hand are laws restrictive of job opportunities in hiring, training, and promotion. On the other hand are those calling for
maternity protection during and after pregnancy and childbirth, child
allowances, and maternal and child health care. In these latter programs, the biological difference between men and women has been fundamentally compelling. Most European countries have insisted on
maintaining both kinds of protection. Only Sweden and the United States
in the last fifteen years have abandoned protections in the labor market
in the name of equality. Sweden has retained the protection of pregnancy and maternity and added to it rights of both parents to place care
of their infants above their responsibilities to the labor market. The
United States, which has never had a national policy on either maternity
or child care, has only recently, partially, and uncertainly moved to
protect the pregnant woman's right under certain state laws to return
to her job once her "disability" is over.

Child care programs were provided in Britain and the United States
during the wars in recognition of working women's double burden. In
contrast to earlier child care offered mainly by private welfare agencies
to children presumed to be neglected by mothers who had to work,
these wartime programs were offered by government to allow women
to work uninterruptedly in production. They ended abruptly with the

6. Folke Schmidt, "Discrimination because of Sex," in *Discrimination in Employment*,
ed. Folke Schmidt, 1978, pp. 126–27.

7. Sheila B. Kamerman and Alfred J. Kahn, eds., *Family Policy: Governments and
Families in Fourteen Countries*, 1978, p. 4.

armistice when, it was assumed, women were no longer needed in the workforce because men were coming home to take over jobs that women had held only for the duration.

Moreover, in Europe the postwar policies that focused on financial and patriotic inducements to families to have more children served a double purpose. They encouraged the now surplus women to withdraw from the labor market and remain at home. Yet, many women had lost their husbands and had no choice but to continue to work at whatever they could find—for the most part, "women's work" at low wages—if they were to support themselves and their families. Moreover, women had developed a taste for work and its concomitants of wages with a modicum of independence.[8]

Unions Become Policymakers

The demands of the modern wars for mass production greatly increased the numbers of both men and women in industry and services. The end of World War I may not have achieved peace in our time, but the overthrow of the German and Austrian empires and the democratization of the victorious monarchies hastened the rise of so-called industrial democracy. The achievement of this new development meant that workers under various schemes would participate in management or at least have some veto power over managerial excesses. By the end of World War I, except in the United States—which waited until 1936 to adopt the Wagner Act—unions or works councils or both were recognized in all the countries as legitimate representatives of working people; laws defining and limiting working hours and conditions were adopted; collective bargaining was recognized and labor-management agreements accepted as part of contract law. One democratizing outcome was the German unions' immediate post–World War II demand for the introduction of co-determination and its acceptance in the coal and steel industries.

The wars had required uninterrupted production, that is, industrial peace. To achieve that goal, governments initiated procedures of conciliation, arbitration, and wage and price control. Thus wartime experience provided models for peacetime labor codes in which labor organizations were legitimized and indeed even accepted as a social partner in the regulation of the labor market and its institutions.

8. Although the decade of the 1950s is stereotyped as a period in which women, in reaction to the hazards and hard work of the war years, devoted themselves to home and family, and the birthrate soared, the number of women in the labor force nevertheless returned to its wartime high by the mid-1950s.

Management and labor slowly developed a limited but substantial mutual trust. In this atmosphere they entered into agreements affecting areas wider than wages, hours, and working conditions. In Europe, national health and unemployment insurances replaced the efforts of workers' "friendly societies," the self-help mutual funds workers established as early as the first half of the nineteenth century to cover sickness and death. In the United States, collectively bargained schemes of health and retirement became widespread in the mid-twentieth century. Under national law, joint labor-management commissions, or in some cases unions alone, administered these programs. It became common practice that commissions set up to plan and implement all matters of labor policy included both labor and management representatives, regardless of the ideology of the ruling government.

Influence of the International Agencies

A major source of support and education for equality in the labor market has come from the international, intergovernmental agencies of which most industrial nations and many of the developing nations are members.

The International Labour Organisation, a branch of the United Nations, concerned with establishing norms of labor policy for both men and women, had adopted from its inception in 1919, as a guide to member nations, Conventions concerned with conditions of women's work as well as standards for maternity protection.[9] The governing body, the International Labour Organisation (ILO), is tripartite, made up of national delegations of trade union, employer, and government representatives. It meets at least annually to work through an extensive agenda of proposals from its many committees and staff members and is advised by many nongovernmental labor market bodies of which the various trade union confederations are a significant part.

So long as nations dealt with women's labor market issues by adopting protective legislation, the ILO Conventions affecting women were mainly concerned with legislation of this kind. Its standard-setting measures for maternity leave recommended that "all couples and individuals have access to the necessary information, education and means to

9. The United States, which has held intermittent membership in the ILO, has uniformly contended that it could not undertake to ratify these Conventions since labor standards were matters for the individual states and not for the federal government. The rationale is hardly relevant and has not been since the Roosevelt era of the 1930s, when the federal government adopted legislation regulating wages, hours, pensions, and collective bargaining, overriding the individual states in these matters.

exercise their basic right to decide freely and responsibly on the number and spacing of children." Postwar ILO decisions began to reflect the interdependence of work and family life. By the mid-1970s, the ILO had adopted Recommendation No. 123 on Workers with Family Responsibility, and by 1981 this was the title of Convention No. 156, now ratified by the four European countries we study here. This Convention and its accompanying Recommendation No. 165 note that

> the burden of household and family responsibilities, which in most cases falls mainly on women, can be an obstacle to achieving equality of opportunity and treatment in employment. Ssupporting measures should be encouraged, such as those designed to:
> a) make it easier for workers to combine home and work responsibilities;
> b) engender broader understanding of the principle of equality of opportunity and treatment for men and women and of the problems of workers with family responsibilities;
> c) promote such education as will encourage the sharing of family responsibilities between men and women.[10]

Other international governmental agencies including both the Organisation for Economic Cooperation and Development (OECD) and the European Economic Community (EEC) have, like the ILO, initiated studies and made recommendations that are meant to promote women's equality with men in the labor market. In all of these agencies a variety of international trade union bodies are advisers or members. Austria is the only one of the five countries in our study that does not belong to the OECD. Germany and Great Britain are members of the EEC, while all are members of the ILO.[11] Thus representatives of the national trade union federations are involved in all of the policy proposals that these international agencies have put forward.

Their recommendations, and (in the case of the EEC) mandates or directives, show support for such issues as equal pay for work of equal value, equal pension rights for men and women, shortened working hours, regulated part-time work, and improved workplace health and safety. In marginal and experimental ways they have begun to look at provision of support systems for working wives, mothers, and single parents and at least noted the need, if equality is to be fully achieved, of restructuring the division of labor in the household.

10. ILO, "Convention 156," *Official Bulletin* 63:2 Series A, 1985, pp. 89–92.
11. In 1990 Austria also applied for membership in the EEC. That organization received and postponed action on this and similar requests from Turkey, Sweden, and several of the former communist nations.

Thus, in the postwar years the governments of industrial countries generally have been confronted with proposals from many organizations, including trade unions and women's organizations, for correction of the anomalies and contradictions embedded in outmoded policies that treat the labor market as a male domain and the family as exclusively a woman's area. These countries have responded in distinct ways to these pressures to achieve, first, equality in the labor market and then equality in family policy.

Equality in the Labor Market

After World War II, economic life throughout the Western world boomed. Full employment was a serious possibility. Yet full employment in the 1950s was defined mainly in male terms. To meet the increased need for workers, European nations began by actively recruiting foreign male labor from Turkey, North Africa, the Caribbean, Greece, Southern Italy, Spain, and Portugal. Sweden was the one nation that from the beginning accepted family members of the foreign worker. Sweden was also the first nation to decide that the demands this program put upon the national infrastructure of schools, health services, housing, and transportation were too expensive. Before any other nation, it turned away from foreign recruitment and toward its internal potential labor market of married women; it began actively to encourage them to go to work. Unions and employers in 1965 established a joint office to represent women's needs and to monitor the introduction of a variety of equality measures. Its decisions to adopt an active labor market policy for women and to do it by granting them full equal rights placed Sweden years ahead of other countries.

Within ten years, all five of the countries of concern here had introduced some measure of gender equality in employment by law. The United States was nominally ahead of the other countries in doing so with its Title VII of the Civil Rights Act in 1964, although the rather sudden and unexpected inclusion of women among the "protected classes" of the law meant that implementation of this program was slow. While its enforcement was considerably weakened under the conservative Reagan administration, it is still an important part of American labor market policy. In addition, an executive order (no. 11246, as amended) adopted within a few years after the passage of the law greatly extended its coverage and used affirmative action, that is, positive programs for recruitment, employment, training, and promotion, as a significant enforcement tool. Partly as a result of this program, an important element of the gender equality debate in Europe is directed toward the proposed use of similar approaches, referred to there as "positive action" or even "positive discrimination." Aside from Britain and the United States, no country has committed itself statutorily to such a program.

Most of the countries we have studied are attacking the question by moving step by step to correct a long list of workplace inequities. These individual labor market matters have been addressed from different directions and to different degrees, depending upon the configuration of government, collective bargaining, and union interests.

Family Policy and Equality

"Family policy," as Kamerman and Kahn define it, is

> a field in which certain objectives regarding the family are established (e.g., large families, healthier children, less financial burden attached to raising children, more equality for women, well-cared-for children), and various policies and measures are developed to achieve these goals. As a "field," family policy has parameters which include population policy and family planning, cash and in-kind transfer payments, employment, housing, nutrition, health policies. Personal social services, child care, child development, and the whole field of social policy for women have all been defined . . . as part of the field.[12]

Programs of this kind are adopted because family is seen as an essential building block of societal organization. Yet the adoption of family policy is relatively recent. In no country, Kamerman and Kahn remind us, is family policy viewed as a single policy; rather it is a cluster of policies, measures, and benefits directed at the family.[13] One important factor in the resurgence of family policy in Europe, though not in the United States, has been the desire to stimulate population growth. Sometimes these policies have also been adopted to control women's participation in the labor force, sometimes to keep them out of an overcrowded labor market, and sometimes to encourage increased population without reference to labor market policy. Germany, for example, encouraged parents to have more than two children by paying a bonus to parents at the birth of their third child.[14] In the 1980s under the Christian-Liberal coalition, concerned with the trend to no-child marriages, the government moved to make such grants-in-aid payable for the first child with

12. Kamerman and Kahn, eds., 1978, p. 5.   13. Ibid., p. 8.
14. *New Society*, April 20, 1978.

increasing premiums for later births. However, despite whatever induce-
ment to increase population has been put in place, the birthrate in every
country falls in inverse relation to women's increasing labor force participation rate, although the relation of cause and effect is nowhere clear.

Although, as we have seen, women's role traditionally has been cast
in family life, the critical consideration for us is whether the woman
now is still assumed to be the chief contributor to family stability and
well-being, or whether this role is assumed to be shared by both spouses.
In the former case, social policy for women appears as measures introduced in the interests of máternal health, of the child's safekeeping and
its first steps in education. When, however, the family is viewed as a
partnership, these services and others are available also to the child's
father from the child's birth through preschool years, while the mother
is assumed to share in family economic support. Each of our four European countries regards women's role in the family and at work differently, and they frame spousal partnership in ways that either explicitly
or implicitly reveal their assumptions.

In Austria public opinion concedes a woman's right to work but in
effect constrains all but the single woman in the exercise of this right.
While gainful employment is acceptable for the married woman, it is
almost entirely rejected for the mother. Officially, however, women's
employment—although from early in this century always at a high level—
is taken for granted and when the statistics are noted, the health of the
national economy is even attributed in significant part to women's activity.

In terms of family policy, women have received paid maternity leave
since the days of the Empire. The mother—but not the father—of a
newborn may take up to three years' leave from work at nominal pay,
to care for her infant. The new marriage law has abolished the requirements that the wife take the husband's surname, follow him to his res-
idence, obey him, and keep his house. It views marriage as a partnership. Yet, according to one authority, traditional views about women
in both the labor market and the family are still deeply embedded in
national custom and behavior. A radical change in consciousness among
most managements and among workers in the skilled trades must take
place if the equality goal is to be realized.[15]

The postwar German government developed a policy that distinctly
approved of the family in traditional structures and restricted itself to
measures supportive of these structures. When the administration changed

15. Edith Krebs and Margarete Schwarz, "Austria," in Kamerman and Kahn, eds.,
1978, pp. 194–95.

in 1969 from Conservative to Social Democratic, the major change in the status of women was in the rewriting of marriage law, such that spousal-shared responsibility for children and ownership of property replaced the absolute authority of the male head of household. With the change back to a conservative government in the late 1970s, child allowances were extended, as noted above, to include payment for the first child in the interests of combating the trend to the no-child family. Under pressure to conform to the EEC equal pension policy, parliament adopted legislation that gives women credit under the social security program for years spent in raising children.[16] Both socialist and conservative governments have seen the child as dependent mainly on the mother. The father is not seriously expected to play any part of the nurturant role with his children, nor is any outside institution, including the child care center. Both Left and Right agree that mothers of children under three should be treated differently from mothers of children over that age. For mothers who must combine maternal and work roles, part-time work is the acceptable solution. Yet employment and training policy in recent depression years have made it extremely difficult for unemployed workers to claim eligibility for referral to part-time work. Germany has granted maternity leave and benefits since the early 1920s.[17]

Britain has never had an integrated family policy. What is protected are particular patterns of responsibility and a long established division of labor, all presented as natural or normal. Only women care for children, the sick, and the old. The unpaid work of women in the household is taken for granted. Marriage is assumed to be a relationship in which the husband is the breadwinner; social security does not recognize that couples share economic support of the family. Only the husband can sign the joint income tax return.[18]

In Sweden, the focus of family policy by the 1970s was to lighten the work burden of the two-income family to enable both parents to continue with gainful employment. The principles governing labor-market policy, tax policy, financial assistance to families, and social insurance have become adapted to a family with two breadwinners and to parents on an equal footing.[19]

16. The women's movement both in and outside the unions has strongly protested the fact that the women covered by this provision do not include the cohorts who were adults in the war years when women almost without exception had to carry full responsibility for the family. Extension of the law to include these classes is under active debate.

17. Friedhelm Neihardt, "The Federal Republic of Germany," in Kamerman and Kahn, eds., 1978, pp. 217–38.

18. Hilary Land and Roy Parker, "United Kingdom," in Kamerman and Kahn, eds., 1978, pp. 331–66.

19. Rita Liljestrom, "Sweden," in Kamerman and Kahn, eds., 1978, pp. 18–19.

The closest the United States has come to dealing with family policy occurred in the Carter-Mondale administration, but proposals then before law- and policymakers never reached consensus. The United States is the only modern, industrialized country without a maternity leave or child care policy. Although both the Census Bureau, in its abandonment of the head-of-household designation, and the tax law, in allowing exemptions for household dependents, have to some degree recognized changes in family life-styles and structure, the federal government has failed to deal with issues that most Europeans have long since accepted.[20]

Maternity leave and child-care provisions are minimal accommodations of European states to labor market demands on the two-earner family. Following the Swedish model, Germany and a growing number of other countries have introduced in limited form parental leave policies that allow either the father or mother paid time off from work for infant care. All of them have national health insurance programs that cover costs of pregnancy, maternity, and child health services as needed by all parents and children. Care of infirm and elderly relatives in any of the five countries in our study is still largely the responsibility of the woman of the family, but some are considering a broadened concept of family care responsibilities under the rubric of "Family Leave," exemplified in the draft bill before the U.S. Congress. This bill would allow workers to take a limited number of unpaid days leave per year to care for sick or infirm family members as well as very young children.

Toward a Definition of Equality and Its Achievement

How should gender equality be approached in Western societies where work and family are important to both men and women and yet where women, whether in the labor market or not, still carry most of the responsibility for children and family? Those who look at equality strictly as a legal concept see the central element in its achievement as the elimination of discrimination in the workplace; and the major efforts and successes have been undertaken in labor market terms. Those who see equality as a social issue have advocated changes in male and female roles within marriage and divorce, prompting family law to undergo

---

20. For a passionate attack on the lack of family policy in the United States and the deleterious effect it has on working women's status, see Sylvia Ann Hewlett, *A Lesser Life: the Myth of Women's Liberation in America*, 1985.

widespread reconceptualization. As a result much family law now describes both parents as equally responsible for maintenance of home and nurture of children, while property brought into marriage remains individually owned, and property acquired or earned during marriage or cohabitation is shared.

Although most countries have examined each sphere as separate and unrelated to the other, the Nordic countries have attempted to deal with the entire range of issues in a single social context. The result, preeminently in Sweden and Norway, has been the adoption of a labor market policy of equality focused on the family. To affect both work and home, the Scandinavians have pursued the roots of discrimination not just into the labor market, but into schools, the tax office, the social security administration, and—yes—the family.

This approach to policy on gender equity begins by identifying the joint and equal responsibility of parents for the upbringing of children. Thus, from childbirth on, fathers legally carry equal responsibility with mothers, not only for child support but also for childrearing. In consequence, fathers have equal opportunity with mothers to accept shorter hours of work when children are young. Both parents have equal access to assistance from the state in child care facilities, adequate and appropriate housing, full pediatric care, and school curricula and texts have been cleansed of class and gender distinctions. Each parent is taxed on his/her own income; each child receives a state cash grant of assistance paid quarterly to a designated parent. Every child and adult is fully covered by health insurance.

Equality cannot be just the absence of discrimination in the labor market, even when coupled with certain support systems that are provided for women who enter it. Equality flows from the treatment of women as discrete, independent members of society, who, when they have children, do so in an equal partnership with their spouses.

So long, however, as the majority of families in many countries are families with working parents, child care must be at the top of a list of support programs for working spouses and single family heads. In this respect, countries have varied a great deal in what and how much they have been willing to do, despite the large numbers of mothers of preschool children in the workforce. Sheila Kamerman, in a survey of child care in six industrialized countries, outlines five different goals underlying these programs: (1) supporting mothers at home; (2) supporting mothers in the labor force; (3) supporting parental choice in selecting how to allocate work and family roles; (4) supporting the opportunity for all adults to manage work and family roles; and (5) assuming that adults make personal and private arrangements in adapting to this life-style.[21]

Among the five countries to which our study directs its attention, Austria has adopted the first goal at least in respect to establishing paid child-care leave to which working mothers are entitled. In the mid-1960s, Sweden surveyed its policies on child care, and the resulting report proposed placing child health and care at the center of both social and labor market policy, with the understanding that both parents shared equally in responsibility and care for children. The government responded by instituting parental (and not just maternal) leave for the first year after birth or adoption, continuing its commitment to paid maternity leave for the mother before and after birth, establishing a free health-care program for mothers and children, and encouraging pre-school and after-school child care in a variety of institutional and family day-care arrangements. Kamerman uses Sweden as her prototype of the fourth goal.

Germany, Great Britain, and the United States are represented in the fifth goal, a laissez-faire approach to child care that leaves its financing and development to private welfare agencies as well as to cities, provinces, and states, with a heavy financial burden falling on parent-paid tuition.

Mary Ruggie has examined two countries, Great Britain and Sweden, to analyze how well each has developed an integrated policy of equality. She looks at the historical development of legislation and collective bargaining that each has taken, analyzes the motives underlying these steps and applies a measure of adequacy and equity to the results.[22]

Ruggie uses Rosabeth Moss Kanter's three models of policy analysis in approaching problems of women in the labor force. The first focuses on the individual, an approach that emphasizes women's personalities and capabilities. In this approach, differences between men's and women's behavior are attributed to their biological natures and to patterns of socialization, with both social and biological factors tending to keep women in inferior positions in the world of work. To the extent that the model allows for change, it places the burden entirely on women and their abilities to contend with the (male) requirements for success. It suggests the use of compensatory measures to help women overcome

21. Sheila B. Kamerman, "Child Care and Family Benefits: Policies of Six Industrialized Countries," *Monthly Labor Review* 103:11 (1980), pp. 23–24. For a brief statement of U.S. policy, see Kamerman, "Child Care Services: A National Picture," *Monthly Labor Review*, 106:12 (1983), pp. 35–39.

22. Mary Ruggie, *The State and Working Women: A Comparative Study of Britain and Sweden*, 1984.

their deficiencies—for example, assertiveness training and programs designed to prepare them to assume roles in management. While some of these measures identify not only personal but also employment problems, they may end by having pernicious implications in that they aim to make women behave like men, when in fact they are not free to do so (even if that was desirable).

The second, a role-related model, focuses on women's dual roles at home and at work. Day care is a remedy that grants a measure of relief, as is part-time work or flexible work schedules. The remedies here are support systems of various kinds to relieve the double burden and thus permit women to participate in the labor force. Still, participation in work alone, as the child-care issue exemplifies, amounts to the low-paid paying the lower-paid. It will not remedy women's secondary position in either home or workplace.

The third or "social structural" model focuses on the demand side of employment and aims at identifying factors contributing to the perpetuation of the "dual labor market," in which women perforce occupy a subordinate role: "The ramifications of this approach are . . . far-reaching, for they strike at a basic structural parameter: the hierarchy of sex-based inequality in society at large. Only this model rises above sex-based discrimination and allows full perception of the multiple dimensions of the problems women workers face." [23] Ruggie argues that only state intervention can affect structural problems, and thus intervention cannot be merely a single thrust but must operate in many dimensions of the market and society in considerable depth.[24] In detail she compares the degree of state intervention in the two countries' labor market policies. Yet while insisting that state action is essential, she does not fail to make this point:

> In both Britain and Sweden, legislation was built on foundations established by collective bargaining, [although] in Britain, this foundation was much weaker than in Sweden. . . . [As a consequence] in Britain [labor market policies] reveal that the role of the state is secondary to market forces. . . . In contrast, the Swedish labor market policies indicate that the state is to take a strong role in directing the best use of all labor market resources in conjunction with a well-developed industrial policy.[25]

23. Ibid., p. 93.
24. By "intervention" Ruggie means the extent of departure from the liberal principle that, left to its own devices, the market can take care of divergences between demand and supply and between wages and prices. For her discussion of state intervention in labor market function in Britain and Sweden, representing, respectively, "the welfare state" and "the corporatist welfare model," see ibid., pp. 12–17.
25. Ibid., pp. 180–81.

Ruggie argues that "for the achievement of greater equality for women, a concerted effort on the part of the state is required. Matters cannot be left to the goodwill of unions and employers, either individually or collectively."[26]

In sum, Ruggie believes only concerted and thorough-going policies directed at social structural change can result in equality for women in the labor market, and these policies must come from government.

The Process of Policy Formation

In some countries, the existence of equality in both labor and family policy is evident in the basic law of their constitutions, albeit in very general terms that promise equal treatment to all citizens, without specifying gender or ethnicity. In others of these countries, only individual matters are subject to equal treatment. In Japan, for example, until the late 1980s equal pay for equal work was specified but not equal access to employment. In still other countries, law consists merely of a statement of policy with no enabling legislation. In countries where the law lays out enforcement channels, it may not provide for enforcement administration or sanctions. In yet other countries, policy rests not on statutory requirements but on an array of traditional assumptions and practices embodied in a domestic code so widely accepted that they are repeatedly invoked even by the courts to form the basis of judicial decisions.

Germany and Austria have a relatively long history of defining specific labor rights and conditions in law and thus of applying them through established enforcement bureaucracies to all wage workers. Sweden has left much of the determination of both to collective negotiations.

Germany has built a carefully fashioned labor code that describes and prescribes in detail: labor relations; conditions of work; protection of job security; and a grievance system running through labor courts. It provides procedures for guarding and ensuring health and safety, and it prohibits or limits certain working conditions for women and young workers. Austria has faithfully followed the German example, though with adaptations to its needs. Sweden, in contrast, historically has left the bargaining parties to deal with most of these items and, although in the last ten years it has turned more to legislation than in the past, many statutes permit or encourage administration through labor-management negotiation. The United States came late to writing national

26. Ibid., p. 181.

labor law, having left these matters for much of its history to the individual states, with the result that both policy and administration vary widely. It has entered the field one step at a time, writing new statutes to amend old ones and achieving a patchwork of prescription and regulation.

In some countries in recent years, law, particularly that aimed at improving equality at work, has been promulgated with little previous history. This normative law sets new standards and deals with new issues rather than repairing old omissions or errors, and it has rarely gone through an evolutionary period. It has been the result of a relatively sudden moral awakening—of a subtle revolution. In the United States, these legal developments took place as a by-product of the Black Revolution, itself a product of a very few recent years of determined, organized, nonviolent, and radical action by the Black minority that stirred the American conscience to write its Civil Rights Act in 1964; women were included in it as an additional disadvantaged category of citizens.

Legislation on gender equality in other countries had very different origins. How did it happen that concern with the equality issue appeared almost simultaneously in so many different places? One answer is that in the twentieth century communication is instantaneous. Ideas spread rapidly around the world. In this context the processes of model-making by intergovernmental agencies such as the ILO have been consistently influential. The United Nations' Declaration on Equality for Women, its designation first of the International Women's Year (IWY) in 1975 and then of the International Women's Decade (IWD) 1975–1985, focused attention on these issues. The meetings held during the decade, of governments' delegates and simultaneously of the representatives of hundreds of nongovernmental organizations (NGOs) at Mexico City (1975), Copenhagen (1980), and Nairobi (1985), for all the conflicts played out at each, nevertheless established an international norm of equity concerned with both work and family. This norm spread through a network of women leaders in most of the world's countries. Practice in areas both of work and family has undergone more rapid change in the past twenty years than in the two hundred previous years since the Industrial Revolution. Family and labor market laws around the world reflect these changes.

Still, legislatures have not been the only arena of policy-making and policy change. Trade unions in some countries have preferred to deal with employment issues themselves, rather than allow the state to intrude on what they see as their proper sphere of determination. Swedish unions in 1977 in both public and private sectors signed agreements with employers, establishing a structure and a program to deal with matters of gender equality in shops and offices. In Germany in 1972, the trade unions declared a "Year of the Working Woman" and significantly attacked the problem of "the light wage" at the bottom of the wage scale in most German industries where the bulk of women workers were assigned. Yet, "despite some efforts and even some successes in combatting discrimination through collective bargaining, in most countries state intervention has become the final word," one expert observer concludes.[27] In Sweden in 1979, despite the unions' agreement with employers, a conservative government turned to legislation on workplace equality. To be sure in response to union pressure, law accepted administration of equity issues chiefly through the bargaining process, while instituting an ombudsperson to deal with complaints of nonunionists.[28]

Problems of Realization

The critical problem, no matter what the approach to equality, is to deal with the very wide gap between policy and practice. Nowhere do the dimensions of this gap become more evident than in the European Community (EC) where uniform requirements have been laid on all twelve member states in respect to three major issues: equal pay for work of equal value, equal employment opportunity, and pension rights. Almost every member nation at some time in the last ten years has been cited to the High Court of Justice for failure to comply fully with these EC directives. If nations are delinquent or even recalcitrant in complying with mandated behavior, individual or institutional evasion is much more likely.

The first test of the adequacy of such legislation—or collective agreement—is the kind of monitoring and enforcement that it specifies. Because the EC has a monitoring procedure, as well as a High Court of Justice where such issues may be brought for clarification, its decisions give some picture of what specific problems continue to exist and of suggested remedies. (The decisions have been compiled from time to time largely by the equality agencies and women's organizations). The highest authority (the EC Commission) has issued a "Women's Action Programme" stating not only goals but also the courses of action open to the member states to achieve them.

27. Thilo Ramm, "Introduction," in Schmidt, ed., 1978, p. 45.
28. Elisabet Sandberg, "Equality Is the Goal: A Swedish Report for International Women's Year," 1975. This report was written before the legislation was adopted, but it relates the history of Swedish concern with the issue.

The first program, which was to be achieved by 1985 (others have followed at approximately five-year intervals, repeating many of these points) included, among others, the following still unfulfilled recommendations:

[1] The introduction of law allowing "positive action," in addition to the passage of the law against discrimination. [2] Recognition that women's pressure to work and the numbers of women entering the labor market will not diminish, meaning that to seek as a matter of policy to confine women to the home as a response . . . would be to opt for an illusory solution. [3] A vast expansion of specific measures to encourage women into nontraditional occupations and to take account of women returning to the labor market. [4] Promotion of a more equal representation of women at different levels of responsibility. [5] Improvement of arrangements for legal redress by (a) shifting the burden of proof from complainant to defendant in charges of discrimination; and (b) provision for sanctions, such as back pay or fines, payable to the injured party or reinstatement at work, in cases where discrimination is proved. [6] Provision for the individualization of entitlement through reexamination of the "head of household" concept. [7] The introduction of parental leave and leave for family reasons, and the building of a network of public facilities and services. [8] Protection of women during pregnancy or motherhood by (a) abolishing discrimination against the recruitment of pregnant women; and (b) improving social security coverage for pregnant women, mothers, and the self-employed. [9] Desegregation of employment, first in the public sector and then in target areas through pilot projects. [10] Improvement in the quality of life by sharing occupational, family, and social responsibility by organizing public services and facilities, taking account of working hours, school timetables, and the needs of dual and single parents of young children.[29]

Much of this program has little to do with the adoption of new laws or even the creation of enforcement agencies. Much of the responsibility for implementing it rests on women's groups and the trade unions. After all, it is such groups that must assist individual women in bringing their cases to tribunals or even to the Community High Court of Justice. In Britain, for example, a collective of feminist legal workers produced a useful book, *Women's Rights and the EEC,* describing the European Community's organizations, powers, and actions in respect to British law and practice. It offers practical directions to British working women on exercising their rights within the EC.[30]

29. Commission of the European Community, *A New Community Action Programme on the Promotion of Equal Opportunity for Women, 1982–1985,* 1981.
30. Rights of Women in Europe, *Women's Rights and the EEC: A Guide for Women in the United Kingdom,* 1983. This book includes a table of cases before British courts in

In Germany the monthly publication of the all-German Council of Women keeps German women's organizations abreast of policy developments and debates, both on family and labor law, as does the trade union women's monthly publication.[31] In Sweden a series of publications from trade unions, the Equality Commission, the Equality Ombud, and the Bremer Association supplies material on diverse political views with information on Swedish policy development and practice.

In several European countries the law on workplace rights only allows for specific redress to the individual complainant, without obligation on the part of the offending union or employer to provide back pay. In Germany the only monetary sanction is for reimbursement to a successful grievant of actual out-of-pocket expenses in preparing her case; remedy is individual and does not correct a general problem. The judicial rules in the United States that allow a court to grant a single complainant class action status and thus to deal with a problem rather than an individual complaint is unparalleled in the other countries. Courts, to be sure, vary in their willingness to allow this strategy, and clients' lawyers must persuade the courts to agree to their petitions for it.

The fact that movement toward increasing women's earning power is slow is certainly a by-product of the worldwide no-growth or slow-growth economies characteristic of the 1970s and 1980s. Moreover, conservative governments in the United States, Germany, and Britain, with their tenacious hold on outworn concepts of women's family and labor market roles, have sought to slow or even reverse action that had earlier gained considerable momentum.

Yet, even a superficial comparison of attitudes, programs, and achievements over a long period reveals fundamental changes in the breadth of acceptance of principles of working women's equality. Such change is unquestionably easier to obtain in labor market than in family behavior, reports from many countries indicate. Behavior in the former area depends greatly on the degree to which the law makes labor market agencies responsible for the behavior of individuals and groups within their jurisdictions. Some systems of rewards and punishments can alter behavior in institutional situations, and the experience gained as a result can lead to changes in beliefs and commitment. This is not necessarily the case for the so-called areas of private life.

Indeed, it is precisely where family matters are concerned that the law

---

the early eighties, as well as cases brought by the British EOC to the Community High Court of Justice in the same period.

31. *Informationen fuer die Frau* is the monthly publication of "Der deutsche Frauenrat," Bonn–Bad Godesberg. *Frauen und Arbeit* is published bimonthly by the women's division of the German Trade Union Federation (Frauenabteilung des DGBs), Düsseldorf.

can set standards but may have great difficulty changing behavior and attitudes. Any family is comprised of a few individuals whose behavior is a consequence of personal socialization. In situations where individual interactions rather than the rules of groups, associations, or institutions are controlling, the law may correct discrete, egregious violations, particularly those that are criminal, but it is unable to address habitual thoughtless exploitation, as represented by the dual load of work assigned to working mothers. Change under these circumstances takes place only incrementally and slowly. Law can state norms and offer inducements, but it cannot swiftly change attitudes or wipe out the assumptions built into the lifelong socialization process. Hence policymakers have made conscious efforts in some countries to tie these new standards to the welfare of men as well as women, and to offer them in the name of child welfare. Such strategies to effect changes are of particular interest because they provide examples of changes both in goals and procedures that have taken place in traditional and in progressive societies. Examining limitations of the strategies and possibilities they command is an opportunity to assess their usefulness and adaptability for American working women.

CHAPTER TWO

Women in Union Structures

We can't talk about civil rights and human rights and then look the other way when women come to us demanding the opportunity to serve in key union positions.
—Douglas Fraser, president, United Automobile Workers

When men get together among themselves, that is called a cabinet or a synod, a board of directors or a trade union council. . . . But when women get together among themselves, there is always someone to fear that they are shutting themselves up in a "women's ghetto."
—Marijke Van Hemeldonck, Belgian
General Federation of Labor

Sex differences in organizational behavior have been recorded . . . since systematic research in organizations began, and the sex segregation of the occupational world is being increasingly recognized as a significant aspect of social structure. . . . When [these differences] have been commented on at all, they have been variously interpreted, but rarely related to sex segregation and differential sex power in organizations.
—Joan Acker and Donald R. Van Houten, "Differential Recruitment
and Control: The Sex Structuring of Organizations"

Women's organizations, particularly trade unions, are among the most effective channels for social and economic participation of men and women workers. Not only is collective action essential to protect individual and group interests, but self-managed, representative organisations alone permit the independent elaboration, expression and pursuit of ideas and programmes as basic ingredients of participatory democracy. Traditionally, trade unions have fulfilled this role for workers.
—International Labour Conference, 71st session, 1985

A recent study of unions in the United States by Richard Freeman and James Medoff asks the question, what do unions do? The authors point out that many economists view unions largely as labor market monopolies whose purpose is to raise members' wages at the expense of unorganized labor. These authors, however, see unions as having another, more beneficial role: "Unions can increase the development and retention of skills, provide information about what occurs on the shop floor, improve morale, and pressure management to be more efficient in its operations." Unionists go further, these authors point out: "Unions also provide workers both with protection against arbitrary management and

Epigraphs: First as cited by Mark Lett, *Detroit News*, May 18, 1977; second cited in *Europese Beweging* (April 1978), p. 1; third from *Administrative Science Quarterly* 19 (June 1974), p. 152; fourth from Report 7, *Equal Opportunities and Equal Treatment for Men and Women in Employment*, 1985.

with a voice at the workplace and in the political arena. . . . In the political sphere, unions are an important voice for some of our society's weakest and most vulnerable groups, as well as for their own members."[1]

It is this "voice" in a somewhat broader political sphere that we examine in this chapter. Freeman and Medoff treat the "voice" function of unions mainly as an expression of the unions' political activities, that is, in influencing the world outside the union itself in behalf of both unorganized and organized workers. Political voice, we believe, is heard in the internal politics of the union as well. Some of Freeman and Medoff's investigation, to be sure, is directed to this area. They inquire into members' satisfaction with the way the union works, not only to produce better wages and conditions for members in dealing with management, but to hear and respond to their voices regarding the management of the union and the formulation of its policies.[2]

In this chapter, we look especially at how the structure of the union defines its political life. In doing so, we particularly ask whether one special interest group within its membership—the women—can effectively voice their needs and take their place within this body politic. Does the union recognize the handicaps under which women have come into the world of work and then try to redress them? Does the union encourage its women to participate fully in the various levels of union activity? Does it open its education programs to women, its electoral system, its staff selection, its congresses, its publications? In these efforts, does it take into consideration the constraints on women's time and schedules? Does the structure of the union allow for the representation of women and their interests at decision-making levels of the union? Does it undertake affirmative action within its own ranks? To

---

1. Richard B. Freeman and James L. Medoff, *What Do Unions Do?*, 1984, pp. 3, 4–5.

2. Freeman and Medoff direct some of their investigation to the union's internal functioning. They inquire, for example, into members' satisfaction with the way the union works, not only its efforts to produce better wages and conditions for members in dealing with management, but also how the officers hear and respond to members' "voices" regarding the management of the union and the formulation of its policies. Despite attaching great importance to "voice" as a union function, the authors on the whole fail to examine unions analytically as political institutions in their own right. Among the union voices, they do not differentiate among Blacks and Hispanics, women and men, skilled and unskilled, production and white-collar workers. They provide no map of channels unions offer for hearing and responding to members' voices, or for assembling these voices into the collectivities of caucuses, special interest groups, or political parties within the union. They confine their inquiries and analysis essentially to unions' influence within the labor market, and to an evaluation of their benefit to the market, leaving their internal politics aside.

respond to these questions, we need to be clear about the nature of union structure and the location of political power within it, for it is within that structure that women as members learn to speak out, to organize, and to exercise their power. If the union does not respond positively within its structure to the questions we have outlined, these needs will not be heard in the union's voice projected to employers and to government. We turn then to unions in the four countries we visited for examples of their positive responses to women's growing presence in their ranks. Finally, we shall try to assess the usefulness of some of these European undertakings for our own needs in the United States.

Union Structure

In the democratic capitalist countries, labor unions have all adopted democratic structures in which members elect their leaders, vote on policy issues, meet in representative or plenary bodies, ratify agreements, conduct referenda, and otherwise behave like citizens of these organizations. In these many ways, members can use their voices. Yet the political life of autonomous organizations differs in significant ways from that of public bodies. Like most nonpublic organizations, unions do not normally provide for the expression of differing organized points of view, such as could be carried out by legitimized political parties or caucuses within the institutions.[3] In the few cases where caucuses are tolerated they usually take ad hoc forms. Since such structures are informal as well as temporary, they are generally unmentioned in bylaws or constitutions. Rather, unions stress the fundamental requirement of a militant organization, the need for "solidarity," for disciplined, united, unquestioning action when required. An American radical of an earlier generation created his own aphorism: "The union must be both army and town meeting."[4]

So long as equal emphasis is given to both aspects of union behavior, loyal trade unionists accept and live under these contradictory requirements with conviction. The situation changes when distinct groups within

3. In this respect, the Israeli unions are perhaps unique. The executive board of Histadrut, the national trade union confederation, is constructed of representatives of the various political parties within its membership, roughly in proportion to the constituencies they represent. In the United States, the typographical union during much of its history had an active multi-party life within its organization. (See Seymour Lipset, Martin Trow, and James Coleman, *Trade Union Democracy*, 1956.)

4. Credited to A. J. Muste, organizer of the Amalgamated Textile Union and longtime director of Brookwood Labor College.

the union—the unskilled, ethnic minorities, women, or young workers—feel their needs are overlooked or that they are discriminated against when they try to locate or build a channel through which they can voice demands and influence policy. Hence responses to questions about how unions are structured and function are essential to judging them as political institutions.

The Pyramid and the Location of Power

Because unions are usually national in scope, they are pyramidally organized, typically in three levels: local, regional, and national, with a bureaucratic and interconnecting structure in which power is more or less centralized at the top of the pyramid.

National industrial or craft unions in each country are affiliated to a national center or confederation. Its job is mainly to coordinate the work of its various affiliates. It is governed through national congresses meeting at regular periods, and by an executive body in command in the intervals. It maintains relations with other national confederations and with international trade union bodies such as the International Confederation of Free Trade Unions (ICFTU) and its regional groups, of which the European Trade Union Confederation (ETUC) affects most of the national confederations in this study. In a few countries the national confederation conducts peak bargaining on such matters as overall wage increases and general conditions or policies affecting the entire labor market. This was the pattern in Sweden for many years with all three of its confederations. Departmental staffs of professionals carry out special functions—research, journalism and public relations, law, lobbying, political analysis, adult education, and library collections, among others. Another series of departments concerns special constituencies within the union—youth, women, foreign or minority workers, white-collar workers, and skilled trades.

The confederation often establishes regional and local offices to which all the national unions functioning in that area are affiliated. In these centers, the unions can coordinate their relationships with provincial and local governments, as well as make meeting space available for the associated unions and conduct regional union education programs.

National unions organize in similar ways, assigning functions to their various levels of organization, whether by industry structure, employer organization, or governmental unit. Most functions are carried out through bodies representing the membership to which delegates are elected through shops or local unions.

The local unit is variously named. In Britain it is the branch; in Sweden, the club; in the United States, the local. In Austria and Germany the local body is made up not of all members but of representatives from all the organized shops, while individual shops and offices are governed through "works councils" that represent all employees there whether organized or unorganized.[5]

In any discussion of union democracy, "centralization" is a buzzword strongly suggesting concentration of power in the hands of top leadership as opposed to the town meeting democracy of the local membership bodies. An important test of centralization is to find the locus of bargaining power. This in turn is usually determined by the nature of the product market within which some or all of the national union's local bodies operate. The local labor and product markets of the service and construction trades suggest local bargaining. The national product markets of much of manufacturing speak for more centralized bargaining. In large countries like the United States we find wide variations in union structure, measured by the degree of centralization. In smaller countries, a much higher degree of centralization of power may well obtain. In highly centralized unions, the "voice" of special interests may be harder to put forward and may meet with less specific response than in local unions. Sweden may have the most centralized of the union structures in this study, though there are indications of important efforts at decentralization there, and Great Britain has the most decentralized.

Each level of union structure has its reason for being in the administration of the various functions the union performs. It is, however, the nature and scope of collective bargaining that most influences the concentration or distribution of power within unions.[6] Collective bargaining is, after all, the union's central function and reason for being. Its other functions—education, health and safety, political action, vocational training—allow for more local initiative and decision-making. Because these matters are in some degree less important than bargaining

5. In 1989, the DGB in Germany abolished its district offices in favor of local cartels of unions in a given locality. An article in the trade union journal examines activities which many of these local bodies have engaged in with other community organizations involving issues of women's rights, local ecology, the peace movement, the anti-atomic power movement, and local political campaigns. The authors find that these new projects and the networking they represent are an important grass roots innovation with significance for the future of the trade unions in Germany. See Oscar Negt, Christine Morgenroth, and Edzard Niemeyer, "Organisationsphantasie, Vernetzung, Projekte—neue Elemente der Einheitsgewerkschaft," *Gewerkschaftliche Monatshefte*, July 1990, pp. 446–55. For details on works councils, see Chapter 4.

6. See Chapter 3 for a closer examination of the structure and functioning of the union's collective bargaining. For its dealings with specific problems, such as pay equity, and part-time work, see Chapters 5 and 7.

in the building and exercise of union power, these departments are allowed more flexibility.

Power, Politics, and Ideology

An important element contributing to centralization is the unions' relation to political action. In this respect the unions of the United States and Europe differ rather widely, although they all give this activity a significant place on their agendas.

American unions throughout their history and with very few exceptions have refused to ally themselves to any political party, including those that professed to represent exclusively working class interests. They have, however, actively supported candidates in elections and lobbied for legislation. Because regional politics may vary from national party norms, and because local union bodies are understood to be autonomous in these matters, political action in this country has tended more to decentralization of union action than the reverse.[7]

European unions, on the other hand, have been historically closely associated with leftist parties. As deep-going ideological differences appeared from time to time within these parties, splinter groups have formed. To the extent that these were more radical or conservative, that is, more politically oriented, they were inevitably at war with the parent party. Unions under leadership from these splinter political parties formed new, often even more centralized, national union confederations. In several countries where the Catholic church was strong, it became alarmed at the inroads Marxists were making among its working-class members and formed Christian unions, ideologically at war with socialist ones. This history still explains to a large degree the multiunionism in Italy, France, Belgium, and the Netherlands.[8]

The unions in Germany and Austria before the Nazi takeover in 1933 followed such a multifederation pattern. When they reorganized postwar, they abjured political affiliations in the name of solidarity, while still finding that the Social Democrats were their closest and most dependable allies in the provincial and national parliaments. Indeed, the

---

7. Perhaps the last significant attempt on the part of U.S. unions to build a political link was during the 1924 presidential election in which Robert M. Lafollette was the candidate of the Progressive party. He was strongly supported by the railroad unions and by several individual national unions in the AFL, but not by the confederation itself. Since the American party system is not built on individual party membership and even less on association memberships, it is difficult to see how a close permanent labor alliance within either of the two official parties might develop and find a permanent place.

8. See Val R. Lorwin, "The Black and the Red: Christian and Socialist Labor Organization in Western Europe," 1975.

national union executives still reflect party affiliations, in the sense that Social Democrats occupy the majority of seats while Christians are assigned a limited number of union functions. For forty years the women's division of the DGB was headed by a Catholic, but after Irmgard Blaettl's retirement in 1989 she was succeeded by her long-time assistant, a Social Democrat.

The Scandinavian unions, located in Protestant countries with homogeneous populations and powerful social democratic parties, largely escaped this history. To the present, LO has maintained its close affiliation with the Social Democratic party (SDP), although the white-collar federation (TCO) developed as a nonpolitical association of trade unions. The third union confederation, SACO/SR, is made up of academics and professionals, and is likewise nonpolitical.

The SDP of Sweden—occasionally in coalition—governed Sweden uninterruptedly from the early 1930s until 1977; and after a six-year hiatus, in 1983 it again formed the government in power, only to be soundly defeated in 1991. This long hegemony could not have existed without union support, and the 1991 defeat suggests a weakening of union power. Many SDP parliamentarians are trade unionists in national, county, or local governments. Unionists are the majority members in party branches and study circles. Many of them are leaders in both party and union organizations. This close personnel identity between party and unions has assured a high degree of—though not total—unanimity between unions and party on matters of social and labor market policy. Unquestionably the egalitarian ideas of the party had great influence on the unions' support of gender equality in the labor market and the creation of equality committees within the unions.[9]

The British unions went still another route. The many different craft unions in their early years of organization sought to influence politics by lobbying liberal parties. In the early twentieth century many of them decided that this stratagem was not advancing their cause. In 1906 they launched the Labour party as an effective element in Parliament.[10] The two-thirds of British unions that are members of the Labour party, like their Swedish counterparts, supply it with national and local parliamentary candidates and play an important part in its inner-party life. In its parliamentary and branch structure, however, the party has not always seen eye-to-eye with the unions, and it has by no means had the success in national elections that its Swedish counterpart for several decades

9. See Alva Myrdal, *Towards Equality: A Report to the Swedish Social-Democratic Party,* 1971.

10. For this history, see G. D. H. Cole, *A Short History of the British Working-Class Movement, 1789–1947,* 1952.

achieved. Nevertheless, the party offers access to a participatory role that for many unionists is more congenial than activity in the unions themselves.

Although national idiosyncrasies provide women with differing opportunity for the exercise of political "voice," open channels for this type of activity exist everywhere. Moreover, since unions have tended to prefer finding solutions for women's issues in the political sphere through protective and maternity legislation, access to political activity is particularly important for women.

Women's Place in Union Life

Many women want to work in solidarity with the men and women whose work life they share. Some of them may well be stirred by the chance to serve other workers as shop stewards or local union officers, and to become full-time members of the union staff. Yet a woman's chances of active participation in union life, unlike a man's chances, depend for the most part on the many aspects of her family life in her home: how many children she has; what her own work schedules are; her husband's hours of work; his community commitments to party, union, neighborhood, athletic club, family; the traditional times for meals; the amount and quality of household equipment. She depends, too, on the arrangements she is able to make for child care for preschoolers and for after-school care of school children. These are all over and above matters of her own desires and capacities, and of her situation on the job. Her access to leadership depends furthermore on the structures and rules of the union and the ways the rules are applied by the men who are union officers. Finally, the barriers of past discrimination and current prejudices in education, training, and employment exist as well. "Inequality is cumulative," Dorothy Wedderburn has said.

In the several generations that have elapsed since unions first agreed to find a place for women in their ranks, one that would not disrupt their existing structures and leadership, male unionists have discovered a series of solutions to the "woman question." In the United States, an early addition to union structure was the Ladies Auxiliary. To be sure, this was often a device, men found, for aligning their wives with the movement that absorbed their own lives. It became, however, often the only place in the organization where a woman worker could feel at home and find a participatory role. In the original auxiliaries, women were given their traditional functions. In times of strike they set up soup kitchens and commissaries and cared for families whose men were in jail; or if they appeared on the picket line, they were wheeling baby carriages. They provided the social glue that made solidarity a reality, and they created the fabric of community as well—based on friendship and common undertakings. These auxiliary women did their traditional work and played out their traditional roles. They did not participate in the union itself.

For European women, an early shelter was either a women's union or, when that showed itself too vulnerable to exist, a women's section of the male union. Here women were sequestered. They developed their own social and intellectual life and a communal spirit, fed by their own journals and sometimes led by women of unusual power and international fame, of whom Klara Zetkin, Emma Goldman, and Eleanor Marx are examples. Women were nevertheless in a female enclave within a male world.[11]

✓ Within the unions in all the countries we studied, women historically have played some minor role and been given limited functions. In Germany and Austria, they have had their women's divisions since the 1890s, replicated at each level of confederation and national union life. In Britain, up to 1921 the Women's Trade Union League (WTUL) offered women a place within the labor movement. Thereafter, when the WTUL gave up its independent existence, the TUC agreed to give women a certain number of places on the executive board and to sponsor an annual meeting of unions "catering to women." This annual meeting has continued to draw up an action agenda for TUC on women's issues. The British national unions variously regard or disregard the role of women within their organizations. Perhaps the typical recognition of their concerns is to assign a woman staff member responsibility for creating an organizational place and program for women. In Sweden, in the 1960s a joint labor-management committee on women's issues was established and then in the early 1970s abandoned in favor of trade union equality committees of men and women both in the national unions and at workplaces. In the United States, a national Coalition of Labor Union Women (CLUW) emerged in the 1970s, with local chapters in many cities. It began to hold annual national meetings on women's is-

11. For full historical treatment of the role of women in the four European countries, see Gisela Losseff-Tillmans, *Frauenemanzipation und die Gewerkschaften, 1800–1975,* 1978; Norbert C. Soldon, *Women in British Trade Unions, 1874–1976,* 1978; Sheila Lewenhak, *Women and Trade Unions: An Outline History of Women in the British Trade Union Movement,* 1977; and Gunnar Qvist, *Statistik och Politik: Landesorganisationen och Kvinnorna pa Arbetsmarknaden,* 1974; for the United States, see Barbara Wertheimer, *We Were There: The Story of Working Women in America,* 1977.

sues, and its members then brought the resolutions from these meetings to their national unions for adoption.

A great debate has developed among feminists and their allies within the unions as to whether such special women's organizations can adequately meet the problems that the growing body of women have brought into union life. Positive moves toward equality are necessary, these women insist, including helping women overcome the disadvantages they bring with them and those imposed by their environment. These all-women classes, social events, and discussion groups are the most efficient way to help women surmount their lack of self-confidence and inexperience with union life, as well as the barriers—intentional and inadvertent—which they find at work and in the union meeting. Women's job segregation, it is pointed out, bars them from wide contacts throughout the workplace; their unskilled or semiskilled work accords with low status; male unionists see them as secondary earners, uncommitted to a lifetime of work and to union discipline. It follows that only men have the qualities for trade union leadership. If women's hands were to be on the tiller, the male members tend to feel, the labor movement would be unstable in a rough sea.

Indeed, women's roles in union life have differed radically from those of men. The results have been that women lost confidence in their ability to carry leading roles within the organizations. Women often insisted that men could better represent them than their women colleagues.

Because of women's intermittent working life and the consequent turnover in female union membership, men saw them as undependable and unorganizable. Consequently, the union put less and less staff and energy into recruiting them to union membership, and into training them for union leadership. In short, unless women behaved like men, conformed to a male model of unionism, elected men as leaders, little attention was paid to them. Ironically, when they did so conform, little attention needed to be paid to them.

How the unequal sharing of family responsibilities between men and women affects the latter's conformity to this male norm for union activities was shown in a survey reported by the Equal Rights Working Party for the National Association of Local Government Officers (NALGO) in the mid-1970s.[12] The report noted that this union, whose member-

12. NALGO, *Equal Rights Working Party Report*, 1975. For TUC's "Charter: Equality for Women with Trade Unions," see Judith Hunt and Shelley Adams, *Women, Work, and Trade Union Organisation*, 1980.

ship then was 542,000, included many articulate and competent women. In local unions ("branches" in British terminology) with women on the average comprising over 40 percent of their members, only 20 percent of the executive committees and 15 percent of local officers were women. Among local officeholders, more men were married than single or widowers. Among the women, more were widows than either single or married. Such a pattern suggests the differential career expectations for those with different types of family burdens. Only those women without family responsibilities, or expectations of them, could plan for the time that union activities require. Marriage helps a man. Many a union career has been built on the support of home comfort and stability created by a wife. Marriage, however, restrains a woman. Thus a widow (if she has no small children) has the best chance for office. Women have a much harder time than men in union careers because they have no wives!

The Working Party's recommendations in their report were based on the fact of women's inequality under the heavy burdens of family responsibility. The report urged the "acceptance by both sexes of joint responsibility for families"; this, of course, was with two-parent families in mind. The single parent, usually a woman, if she does not live with relatives, has no assistance. Recommendations included thirty proposals, some calling for changes in law and in the gathering of statistics, the latter so as to reflect more accurately women's opportunities for training and jobs. The report supported women's right to abortion. It included a number of specific proposals for improvement of union conduct. Among these were: that branches have the right (a right some had already won) to hold general meetings during working hours; that branches supply child care at meetings outside working hours; and that they hold more office and departmental meetings, in addition to the general branch meetings. The recommendations called also for a national committee on discrimination to monitor progress, and they suggested a review of trade union education policy. Point no. 30 urged the union to implement all these proposals for its own employees, as well as for its members.

The Union Meeting as Elementary Participation

The first barrier that women have to surmount is that of participating in union meetings. The NALGO report makes clear that women's mere attendance may not be achieved unless special arrangements for time and place are made. Apparently it is still necessary to point out to male union leaders that women continue to live under different constraints and even in another cultural atmosphere from men. The secretariat of the International Transport Workers' Federation (ITWF) has tried to do this in a "man-to-man" bulletin that reads in part:

(1) Ask those members, especially women, who do not come to meetings, why they do not, and try to act upon their replies.

(2) Ask members, especially women, when and where they think meetings should be held.

(3) Provide child-care facilities at meetings (and at other union activities).

(4) Get news and views of meetings and other activities to all members by official union channels, not just by male official to male shop steward to male-grapevine member.

(5) Encourage new members individually to come to meetings and to speak up.

(6) Train new and old members, especially women, in union procedures, terminology, public speaking, and chairing a meeting.

Similarly, the ICFTU (1978) reminds its affiliates: "Meetings must start and end on time because women have very little free time."[13]

In negotiations for union meetings on working time, public authorities have generally been more forthcoming than private employers, and white-collar unions have often led the way. In Britain, both NALGO and the National Union of Public Employees (NUPE) have successfully bargained for workplace meetings on working time.

They were able to do this in part because Britain's Employment Protection Act (1975) requires an employer to give members of all trade unions in an establishment reasonable time off—not necessarily with pay—for trade union activities. In 1978 the Advisory Conciliation and Arbitration Service (ACAS), an independent public body, promulgated a code of practice under the act.[14] The code points out that "to operate effectively and democratically, trade unions need the active participation of members in certain union activities, such as voting at the workplace in union elections or holding meetings during working hours, for example, where the urgency of the matter to be discussed requires a meeting."

As one approach to meeting needs that are not just those of women, the Swedish Metalworkers have urged their locals to experiment with meetings oriented to the family as a unit, at hours convenient for family participation. Such meetings might begin with activities for the whole

---

13. *ITF News*, "Women's Conference," 1988, p. 5. The original set of proposals was promulgated by the ICFTU in 1978.

14. ACAS, *Code of Practice on Time Off for Trade Union Duties and Activities*, 1978.

family—songs and skits. While members then conduct union business, nonmember spouses and children can carry on activities elsewhere and then rejoin the members for the conclusion of the meeting. On "equality questions" or family policy, the entire family can contribute to the discussion.

Surveys on participation problems show that "more information" is a chief demand women have. They, as well as many men, can find parliamentary procedure baffling. One Swedish women's group we observed was using its lunch hour to practice conducting meetings. In the Association of Scientific, Technical, and Managerial Staffs (ASTMS) in Britain we also found women meeting in informal office groups to develop competence and self-confidence of this kind. Educational programs often include a few hours of practice in chairing and participating in meetings. Union newcomers, and in this category women are apt to be the majority, are often baffled by the acronyms used in union life and by the jargon used in discussions of labor law or collective bargaining practices. Both information interaction and formal study sessions can help in informing new—and old—members about the terms most used in the conduct of union business.

A spontaneous workshop group developed at the public power authority in Gothenburg, Sweden. Two switchboard operators were working under crowded conditions, for relatively poor pay, and without any regular lunch breaks. Their attempts to air their grievances at the union meeting were put down by men on the grounds that they were not bringing them up in the right way. Moreover, the men said, women did not understand how collective bargaining worked and did not know what the union had already tried to do about the matter. In reaction, clerks and typists—all women— joined with the switchboard operators to form a study group that they limited to women, because as beginners they needed to avoid the risk of being dominated by men. The male local's executive board was suspicious at first that the women planned to break away from the union. The women assured them that only if no help were available from the union would they go outside. The union began to support the study group's efforts. In fact, the group succeeded in training about 50 of the 180 employees in the office. When we were there a year later, the women were ready for a short residential course in speaking skills at a nearby Folk High School and for training in group dynamics and union meeting procedures. The women's activity, moreover, threw a new light on existing salary arrangements just before a period of salary negotiations, with the result that the men agreed to push this issue.

Women as Union Officers

In Europe generally women are being chosen in larger numbers than before by their fellow workers as local union officers and especially as workplace representatives. The latter category includes shop stewards, health and safety stewards, union representatives, and works councillors.[15] Works Council functionaries typically perform their tasks during working hours, and under the law receive released time for training. One reason why more women have been elected in recent years is their influx into the unions, as more and more of them entered the labor market. Most of them are somewhat better educated than their sisters of earlier generations and have a greater commitment to work. Increases in the numbers and functions of workplace representatives improve the possibilities of women's election or appointment particularly when they carry out new functions, since such additional offices can be filled without competing with male incumbents. However, women's work continues to be highly segregated from men's; in consequence, women who achieve office are usually those elected from female-dominated departments.

The unit of election can determine whether a woman has any chance to be elected. Women, particularly those in low-prestige manual labor working under male supervisors, often may elect those very supervisors as their representatives, especially where first-line supervisors are organized in the same union. In NUPE this choice of shop stewards by women school cleaners working under male custodian supervisors presented a two-fold problem: women were not elected, and women with grievances had to take them to stewards who were their supervisors and sometimes even the source of the grievances. Leaders in NUPE began negotiating with the employers to recognize units of single occupational categories for election purposes. Such a correction addressed the root of both problems.

Unions are affiliated with many bodies within the labor movement.

15. Under German and Austrian law, these works councillors are elected every three years. While most of them are in fact union members and run on a union slate, some nonunion workers may also be elected. Since a major function of the council is to enforce the collective agreement, as well as the labor law, within the shop, it is important for the union that the council executive board members, who are for the most part released full-time from work to carry out these functions, and a majority of council members be union members. A substantial union education program consists in the training of works council members. A different group, union representatives in the shop (Vertrauensleute), have responsibility for collecting dues, organizing the unorganized, and disseminating union information.

Table 1. Membership growth, male and female in the DGB, 1950–1988 (selected years)

Year	Women	Index 1950 = 100	Men	Index 1950 = 100
1950	892,039	100	4,557,951	100
1955	1,047,805	117.5	5,057,067	110.9
1960	1,093,607	122.6	5,285,213	115.9
1965	1,030,185	115.5	5,544,306	121.6
1970	1,027,150	115.1	5,685,397	124.7
1975	1,313,021	147.2	6,051,891	132.8
1980	1,596,274	178.9	6,286,254	137.9
1985	1,705,131	191.1	6,014,227	131.9
1988	1,828,649	204.8	5,970,428	131.6

Source: Frauen und Arbeit, "40 Jahre Gewerkschaftliche Frauenarbeit," April 7, 1989, p. 27.

Delegates, elected from local unions to central bodies, state or provincial federations, and to national congresses and committee meetings, take on significant responsibilities. For the most part, members winning these representational posts customarily move slowly up a ladder leading from local to national delegation. Where a local is entitled to only one delegate, that one person is usually the top local officer and hence the top man. Where there are two or three delegates, a woman may have a far better chance.

Again, women with small children can seldom manage these extra meetings. Several British unions have introduced child care facilities at conventions. At least one union has become committed to maintaining these facilities even if at first they are underused. For years, delegates have understood that "you can't bring children with you." It may take years of positive action to get parents to believe that "you can bring children with you."

Guidelines governing the German national confederation's (DGB's) convention call for the election of women delegates in line with their proportion in the union whose members they represent. While the number and proportion of women attending these quadrennial meetings has increased slowly, the female membership of none of the affiliated national unions is adequately represented by this standard.

An example of the trend in Germany can be found in the considerable growth in female membership in the metalworkers' union, from 15.1 percent in 1950 to 21.9 percent in 1985. Over that period the number of women delegates grew from 14 to 80, or from 2 percent to 11.4 percent.

Similarly, the women's division of the Austrian metalworkers' union

Table 2. Development of the proportion of women delegates to the DGB national congresses, 1949–1986 (selected years)

Congress place and year	Total number of delegates	Female delegates Total	Female delegates %	Proportion of females in total membership
Munich, 1949	487	14	3	14
Berlin, 1952	356	25	7	17
Frankfurt, 1954	391	23	6	17
Hamburg, 1956	403	24	6	17
Stuttgart, 1959	418	26	6	17
Hannover, 1962	425	20	5	17
Berlin, 1966	439	20	5	16
Munich, 1969	430	19	4	15
Berlin, 1972	453	29	6	15
Hamburg, 1975	478	34	7	16
Hamburg, 1978	504	37	7	18
Berlin, 1982	525	60	11	20
Hamburg, 1986	525	80	15	22

Source: Frauen und Arbeit, "40 Jahre Gewerkschaftliche Frauenarbeit," April 7, 1989, p. 36.

has shown what can be done with only the vaguest guidelines to point the way. The union's statutes merely call upon the locals to "take into consideration" the numbers of women in their membership in electing convention delegates. The women's committees throughout Metall began to campaign for better-trained and better-informed candidates, Within a three-year period, and comprising only 16 percent of the union's membership, the women increased their share of convention delegates from a mere 2 percent to 8 percent of the total attendance.[16]

Although women have difficulty in being elected to union office, even in unions with a high percentage of female members, various kinds of affirmative action programs have been developed to increase their representation. The ICFTU, for example, urges its affiliates to act on the principle that "when there are elections or nominations at any level whatsoever, the list of candidates should reflect the membership structure of the organisation."[17] From 1972 onward the German women's division has with unvarying success carried through campaigns at the

16. *Frauen und Arbeit,* May 1982, p. 1. For further information on Austria, see ETUI, *Women in Trades Unions in Western Europe,* 1987, pp. 17–22; *Positive Action for Women in Western Europe,* 1989, pp. 50–51; and *Women's Representation in Trade Unions,* 1983, pp. 3–6.

17. ICFTU, *Integration of Women into Trade Union Organisations,* 1978.

time of every triennial works council election to increase the number of women elected as council members and chairs.[18]

Tested procedures by which women have achieved office include proper "positioning" or "blessing" of an intended successor by an incumbent soon to leave office, so as to assure smooth leadership transition. Although it is a strategy that has served to continue autocratic leadership within unions, it can serve more progressive ends, including the purpose of representing women members and minorities, when other ways seem closed. The fact that a woman is the president of the German public workers union, the second largest in the DGB, is a product of the resigning president's expressed preference. A mentoring relationship between an experienced officer and a likely, though little-known, candidate may provide her necessary training and guidance as well as placement on an otherwise unavailable inside track.

Affirmative action as an internal union policy is now accepted in several German unions, not least among them the powerful Metall. Its 1985 "Frauenfoerderplan" calls for the preferred appointment of women to positions in headquarters and regional offices in proportion to their membership in the union (now 21.5 percent). The plan made explicit that by 1990 there would be thirty-eight vacancies in regional offices. The announced goal was to fill the majority of them with women as well as to carry out similar actions in the case of other "leading political positions" as they became available.[19]

Many women have been hired by unions for staff positions, usually in the education department, and for administrative positions in research, publicity, and legal offices, all posts that carry little political power. Health and safety departments are a major new area that has begun to employ women. Yet the route to union elective office rarely runs through staff departments. Rather, election to national posts is a step-by-step upward climb through elected positions in local to regional and so to national office.

The ICFTU, in its recommendations on the integration of women, admonished its affiliates to assure them the chance to acquire qualifications for office: "Women members of trade union staffs should re-

---

18. See Tables 3 and 4 in Chapter 3.
19. IGM, *Frauenfoerderplan*, 1986, pp. 6–8. One of us attending the Metal Workers' Women's Congress in September 1988 witnessed an interesting demonstration of the women delegates after the union president attempted to defend his failure to follow the plan in the case of several district appointments to office. He pleaded that in these cases the shops employed only men, and that therefore a woman officer from outside would have been inappropriate. Following this statement, the auditorium was filled with boos and soap bubbles, this last a protest equivalent to "Blah, blah, blah!"

ceive training enabling them to stand as candidates for elected posts."
These training programs in Germany, for example, climax in advanced
courses at union residential schools, or in academies associated with
universities where one- or-two-year programs produce leaders trained
in labor law, economics, history, and public administration. Specialized
courses for various union functions in accounting, public speaking, bargaining, and industry economics are of shorter but substantial duration.
Many unionists will have completed a number of these courses, as their
movement through union office requires specific training.

For women, entry into such a career begins, as it does with men, with
attendance at shop and union meetings, activity on union committees,
travel to regional and national conventions, and enrollment in residential schools. All of these put demands of time on a woman whose days
and nights are already more than full. What will she do about her children, even school-age children? Will her husband accept her absence
from home in the evenings, on weekends, for a week or two at a time?
For most women the most favorable positive solution is to postpone
taking on this kind of responsibility until some of the pressures at home
have eased. One reason why women are more rarely in staff or elected
office than men is that many unions make it a condition that officers
accept assignments that call for a great deal of travel and evening work.
Such demands are mostly a heritage of the years of slender union trea-
suries and tiny staffs in the "heroic period." Nowadays such assignments are necessary only in crises. Even so, they may create family tensions that strong men dread; they deter women, and some men, from
seeking full-time union posts. The requirement of willingness to move
on demand (a demand rarely made in any case) could be dropped, as
one immediately feasible change. Yet the traditions of the formative
years of the labor movement disappear slowly. The problem of how to
adapt work life to family life, rather than the other way around, is no
less compelling for unions than for other employers.

Men have no trouble seeing women as suited to be women's officers.
Still, many a woman seeking a union career has felt a conflict between
performance as a union women's officer and that of a woman union
officer. The conflict concerns whether she should be a person representing women in particular and concentrating on women's issues, or functioning as a union officer who happens to be a woman. Where staffs
are small, women may find themselves holding both kinds of jobs,
women's affairs sharing time with other matters—education (teacher or
administrator), legal aide, or national organizer. In an earlier generation
quite a few men served as women's officers, and as late as 1977 in
Britain a man served as women's officer in the engineering (metal in-

dustries) section of the Amalgamated Union of Engineering Workers (AUEW) with one million male and 148,000 female members.

Women's officers do not handle grievances or participate in collective bargaining and consequently may well find they have little power. Yet, some of these officers, such as Pat Turner of the General and Muncipal Workers (G & M) in Britain, for years carried double responsibility— for women and as an industrial officer (national representative) for several industrial groups within the union. In addition she also represented the union on a large number of committees outside the union, such as minimum wage councils and industrial training boards. Inside the union she worked for equal pay and for equal opportunity in wage negotiations and in job evaluation exercises. Turner may well have been effective as a women's officer precisely because of her multiple roles. The issue is whether a woman can advance her own union career by doing a good job on women's problems alone. Many women, aspiring to union leadership, doubt that they can move into policy- and decision-making positions from leadership in the women's division alone. Thus, ironically, a woman officer's specialization in women's issues may create a new prejudice: "Women's officers," as one of them said in an interview, "are women who cannot make it by the regular route in union office." In the ideal situation, men and women would recognize that women's issues are trade union issues. Indeed, the ICFTU Charter of Rights of Working Women insists that women trade unionists "should be encouraged to assume responsibilities and to act as spokespersons of the trade union movement at all levels and not be confined simply to dealing with women workers' issues."[20]

When Grapevines Show Their Sex

We heard of many examples of men's solidarity and sharing of information with women coworkers and union representatives. We also heard of many cases where women shop stewards were cut off from grapevines that continued to carry essential information and influence from men to men. Newly elected women representatives, we learned, might fail to receive information transmitted from higher levels through official channels. As one woman remarked, "You can't get the word if it is posted only in the men's room."

The women's committees of the two largest unions in Austria, one a white-collar, the other a blue-collar union, have developed their own "information hot lines." These channels regularly carry information from

20. ICFTU, *Women's Charter of Working Rights*, 1978b.

the headquarters director of women's affairs to the women who are liaisons in the workplaces, on a broad range of union concerns—new labor law proposals, economic analysis and forecasts, recent findings on health and safety—as well as notices of task force and committee meetings, regional courses, and conferences. The white-collar union, in addition, regularly sends what is called "info letters" to women works councillors and their alternates. It also sends regular visitors to new councillors to offer help as they take on their new roles.

Reserved Seats on Union Executive Bodies

No union constitution these days forbids women to run for elective office. Yet, this fine impartiality is not enough. To be sure a few unions composed largely of women, such as the flight attendants in the United States and the telephonists in Australia, have put women in top offices. In Germany the second largest union, the Public Workers (OeTV), has a woman president. In Great Britain the lay president of the General Municipal and Boilermakers' Union is a woman and twenty-eight women are on its executive committee, making up 25 percent of that body. Few other mixed unions have done so much. In Britain the honorary office of the president of the TUC has several times fallen to a woman, and in all our countries the union leaders are at least aware that women expect soon to have at least proportional representation on executive councils, where they have not already achieved it. Nonetheless, nowhere is the representation of women in union leadership in any way proportional to their numbers in the membership. Indeed, in many unions, such as the Textile Workers of Germany or the two clothing workers unions in the United States, the ILGWU and the ACTWU, although women predominate heavily among their members, men make up the majority of chief officers.

In Britain a few unions, including the national confederation, the TUC, have reserved seats for women on their executive committees, largely as a result of historic incidents, notably mergers between men's and women's unions. The reserved seats for women on the general council of the TUC date from its absorption of the Women's Trade Union League in 1921. In 1981 reserved seats rose to five, but by 1989 women held fifteen of the fifty-four general council seats.

A blue-collar union in the public sector, NUPE, conducted what was in the 1970s a bold experiment. It had long been a centralized organization with little participation of the rank and file of either sex. By 1973 women—including many part-time workers—numbered about two-thirds of its 472,000 members, but there was no woman on the national or district (regional) executive councils or among the full-time officers. In that year a new national leadership, concerned about democracy and participation, commissioned a study of the union's structure and processes by a team of academics close to the labor movement.[21]

One of their recommendations was to create five new seats, reserved for women, to add to the twenty general seats on the national executive council and a comparable number in each regional body. Their holders would be chosen, like other members, by both men and women; there would be no special women's electorate. Women, at the same time, could continue to run for general seats on the executive body. The proposal was accepted for an indefinite period, and soon a sixth woman was elected in competition with a man for an established seat on the national council. By the late 1970s more women were being elected as shop stewards, more were taking training courses, and more were delegates to the 1978 national congress than ever before. Without its other efforts on behalf of women, NUPE's reserved seats would have had little meaning or vitality.

The British Sex Discrimination Act leaves the way open for such experiments. It specifies that it is not discriminatory for a union to have arrangements that ensure a minimum number of persons of one gender on bodies made up entirely or chiefly of elected members.[22]

Women Representing Unions in Public Bodies and Coalitions

Both by custom and by law, unions are entitled to representation on such public bodies as labor market boards, ad hoc commissions developing public policy, labor courts, and vocational and other educational commissions or institutions. The German Labor Market Board (BfA) calls for its tripartite members to name women to the board. Neither labor nor management has done so. However, both the Swedish and German staffs of their respective institutions have included women in high positions who came from or were acceptable to the unions.

All the labor confederations included in this study are represented by governmental appointment to their countries' ILO delegations. The same can be said for labor representatives on other intergovernmental bodies and national labor market agencies.

It is necessary that the representatives of unions to such national and

21. Bob Fryer, Andy Fairclough, and Tom Manson, *Organisation and Change in the National Union of Public Employees*, 1974, p. 38.

22. For a full discussion and the text of the British Act, see Rights of Women in Europe, *Women's Rights and the EEC: A Guide for Women in the United Kingdom*, 1983, pp. 27–32.

international bodies be able to speak for their confederations with a certitude possible only after considerable experience in high positions on their staffs or as their executives. With so few women at those levels, it may be genuinely difficult to find even a few who can be freed for such additional tasks. The absence of women in these bodies has meant a lack of sustained attention to women's issues, both in the national labor markets and in institutions establishing standards for national labor markets to follow. Unfortunately, it is still rare to find women included in national delegations, even in such international trade union bodies as the International Trade Secretariats (ITS), unless it is to their meetings of delegates from women's divisions.[23]

In their political and public relations work, unions often find it advantageous to enter into ad hoc coalitions with social and human rights agencies and with special interest groups having programs that affect the unions' members. Among these are civil liberties groups, women's organizations, associations of migrant or minority or ethnic people, welfare societies, adult education associations, and groups lobbying on various issues. Here, too, unions need to delegate women as their representatives to speak with special concern and authority from the feminist viewpoint.

Working Parties: Task Forces

The working party or task force is a temporary body established to inquire into a specific problem or problem cluster, to carry out a specific program and to make recommendations for future action. Because it is ad hoc, it may be permitted to draw in outside experts. In Britain NALGO went outside its own ranks for several members of its Equal Rights Working Party. The Working Party's twelve members included nine women, among them a representative of NALGO's own staff union and one woman from each of two social-action organizations, the National Council for Civil Liberties and the Child Poverty Action Group. The seventy-seven-page report the Working Party produced was sharply critical both of the public authorities for whom NALGO's members work and of union policies on women's work and women's capacities. It rejected proportional representation for women in union governance and reserved seats for women on national executives; but it did call for more opportunities for promotion and training of women among NALGO's own employees, for a comprehensive study of occupational pension

23. Heads of delegations from several countries have been women ministers or deputy ministers of labor.

conditions, and for the union to negotiate like benefits for men and women. It endorsed the right to abortions and for reasonable access to a state abortion system. It pled for a campaign for better trade union facilities in the workplace, including the right to hold meetings at the worksite on work time with child-care facilities. Moreover, it called for the establishment of a national monitoring committee to check on progress.[24] This combination of workplace and family issues indicates women's increasing perception of the interconnections of work and family and their growing conviction that employers—and unions—must recognize their responsibility for maintaining the connection.

National Conferences

Regular delegate conferences at local, regional, and national levels are essential parts of the operations of the women's divisions of confederations and national unions in Germany and Austria. In the TUC, with no women's division as such, an annual conference called the Conference of Representatives of Trade Unions Catering for Women Workers is the most important forum for discussion of women's issues for TUC action. The session we attended brought together 231 delegates from 52 unions. Although both men and women attended, a significant majority of the delegates was made up of women.

The conference itself, under the aegis of a women's advisory committee of the TUC's general council, sets its own agenda. The committee is composed of members elected in almost equal numbers by the general council and by the conference delegates. Conference proposals for action go to the general council for discussion and decision.

Women's Divisions

Women's divisions, or similar structures within unions, are a clear signal that women have a place. Such structures may, as they certainly did historically, place women's issues in a separate and powerless sphere; or, as in the case in most modern unions, a women's division may provide clearcut channels to executive and legislative bodies within the union. In the cases of Germany and Austria, women's divisions are an integral part of national confederations and of all levels of the national unions.

British unions prefer to establish ad hoc committees on women's issues as branches need them. The committees usually report to a special

24. NALGO, 1975.

official at national union headquarters; six major unions now operate in this way. The national women's official may also hold special conferences and organize special education facilities for women.

Sweden formerly had women's divisions, roughly similar to those in Germany, but in the early 1970s instead established family policy departments designed to include men as co-heads of families as well as union members concerned with problems previously seen as the sole concern of women. Despite this laudable objective, many spontaneous local organizations of women sprang up to provide a place where by themselves women could discuss and try to solve problems they met both at work and at home.

In the United States, women's divisions are not unknown—the Autoworkers (UAW) established one during World War II that has had a continuous and active life—but they are rare. More common is the assignment of a national woman staff member to deal with these problems, much on the British model. In the 1970s, women trade unionists formed their own interunion national organization, CLUW. Any organization certified to bargain collectively is eligible for affiliation with CLUW whether a part of the American Federation of Labor–Congress of Industrial Organizations (AFL-CIO) confederation or not. Thus the American Nurses' Association (ANA) and the National Education Association (NEA) can send delegates to its meetings, while women from independent unions such as the Teamsters for many years were included. Individual members of CLUW pay dues that finance both local and national bodies; CLUW has its own research department, distributes its own publications, and at one time drew up a plan with the Industrial Union Department of the confederation for jointly organizing women in several target cities.

The most integrated and developed of such women's groups are those in Germany and Austria. They have full-time staff at confederation and national union levels and in regional and local offices, wherever women make up substantial portions of union membership. The division head is an ex-officio member of the national union and confederation executives. Staff members help unions organize nonunion women and activate passive ones. They also carry on research on women's jobs and pay. They teach regularly at trade union schools and provide union education departments with curricula for special programs set up for women only.

The divisions are expected to function as special interest representatives for working women's demands within the unions. In Germany they are also important affiliates of the national umbrella council of all women's organizations, *Der deutsche Frauenrat*. The DGB women's division chief has repeatedly served as chair of this council. On matters of social policy, they speak with authority at the union congresses and to the executives on women's issues within the national community, as well as within the unions themselves.

The DGB women's division executive includes women representing DGB regional bodies as well as the head of each national union's division. Thus both geographical and industrial interests are included. They hold women's congresses a few months before the confederation or union congress. In the case of the DGB, these all-women meetings made up of delegates from the affiliated unions bring resolutions from their own women's division, and thus formulate a women's affairs policy program for the ensuing four years. The division in each national union operates in much the same way.

For the rank-and-file member these divisions become part of a women's movement with an articulated program and a terrain of understanding between labor and other women's organizations. In joint actions with individual organizations in the broader women's movement, they have surmounted some of the misunderstandings that might have prevented the labor movement and the women's movement from coalescing to serve all of women's common interests. Still, these women's divisions have no independent income or budget and, in Germany at least, they operate under certain limitations on their freedom of action laid down in the original charter and by-laws of the DGB from 1949. Recent attempts to define their status and function in more up-to-date forms have not yet been approved by the DGB executive committee.

A very early and still signal achievement of the DGB women's division, the Year of the Working Woman, illustrates how a national trade union movement can turn its attention to women's problems and focus on them in all of its programs.

The Year of the Working Woman was a designation for 1972, proposed by the division and accepted by the DGB executive committee and then by national affiliates. Union publications brought to the attention of millions of Germans, both women and men, the facts of gender inequality in economic, legal, union, and family life, and the needs for action. Rallies, conferences, exhibits, displays, talks, and discussions in schools, political party meetings, and church groups raised such issues as women's double burden of work at home and on the job, women's low pay, women's inferior legal position in matters of property and even of their rights to work without husbands' permission, the low percentage of women joining unions for the benefits they might there enjoy, and the low percentage of women in leadership positions within the unions and the political parties. A questionnaire was placed in popular women's magazines covering many of these issues and asking women to send in their responses. The questionnaire encouraged women to discuss these issues with their husbands and, with their permission, to include their reactions as well. More than 6,000 people responded. These replies were given wide publicity both in women's magazines and in union publications.

The women's division cooperated with the white-collar department of the DGB to launch an organizing campaign, financed by a DGB appropriation of DM 1,000,000 (about $500,000 at that time) to be supplemented by funds from the cooperating national unions.[25] Each affiliated union, moreover, undertook to abolish or correct the so-called "light-work" wage scales.[26]

Women's increased activity and influence were not limited to the national unions or the confederation during this year, but animated local and provincial women's division undertakings. Although most national unions preferred a position of neutrality on women's issues in the family, wanting to avoid alienating their Catholic members, independent activity at state and local levels came into play in a women's national campaign to legalize abortion and revise marriage and family law. Other less controversial action took place where social services had not kept pace with growing industrial employment of women. One regional DGB organization in Marburg (Hesse), headed incidentally by a woman, involved its women's committee and the press in a successful campaign to increase the number of child-care centers and kindergartens.

In the province of Hesse, a local DGB women's committee initiated a campaign, co-sponsored by other women's organizations, in behalf of improved factory inspection, better information to enable workers to

25. The DGB is made up of seventeen industrial unions organized by broad definitions of enterprise—metalworkers, public workers, chemical workers, mining and construction workers, commerce and banking workers—all of which include both blue- and white-collar workers. At the founding congress in 1949, white-collar workers sought a union of their own, but their proposal was voted down in favor of the consistent industrial structure. The proponents of the white-collar union then withdrew to from an independent union, the German White-Collar Workers Union (DAG), which still exists but which by no means drew all white-collar workers with it. The DGB established a white-collar department to serve the special interests of this group.

26. After 1955 when the Supreme Labor Court ruled that "women's wages" were illegal under the equal rights provisions of Germany's Basic Law (Grundgesetz), both unions and management agreed to add "light work" grades to wage scales. These appeared at the very bottom of the scale. They applied in reality to women's segregated, unskilled work in the factories and thus tended merely to replace the outlawed women's wages. These rates are fully discussed in Chapter 5.

detect and report factory violations of the safety code, and more adequate prosecution of violators, along with consistent monitoring on the part of provincial authorities.

The Austrian Way

The women's division of the Austrian metalworkers' union, in addition to creating a responsive network of local women activists (described in Chapter 1), trained shop-level union representatives and works councillors in the content and skills of bargaining. Its strategy was to prepare them on a whole range of issues in addition to special "women's problems," and as a result the number of women work councillors increased steadily. By 1982, women made up 19.3 percent of all metalworkers' councillors and chairpersons.[27]

More recently the division focused on overcoming job segregation by expanding opportunities for girls to train for skilled jobs in various metal trades. It began by attacking sex bias in job evaluation and job assignment. As a remedy the union, together with the Austrian Chamber of Labor, sponsored a study of the bias in elements of job evaluation in order to eliminate sex-biased content and introduce a method of considering different men's and women's jobs so as to establish "work of equal value" standards in its industrial sector. After receiving many complaints by women of unfair job assignment by hiring officers, the division persuaded union executives to place on their bargaining agendas the creation of workplace appeals bodies to review such complaints, whether from men or women.

The Union of Private Sector White-collar Workers (GPA) in Austria showed how a women's division already active in organizing, union education, collective bargaining, and lobbying could move male leadership into serious participation in the struggle for women's equality. In 1977, women made up 42 percent of the union's 310,000 members. The women's division took special initiatives in research, education, publication, and general publicity on equality issues. In its 1978 publication *Women and Men: Equal Partners in Society*,[28] it presented in popular and persuasive form the most important material from a massive government report titled *The Situation of Women*. Working parties of union members had analyzed this seven-volume report and applied these data to their own union and its members. On the basis of their findings, they persuaded the union's leaders to undertake a series of

27. *Frauen und Arbeit*, May 1988, p. 1.
28. GPA, *Women and Men: Equal Partners in Society*, 1978.

specific measures to give women more openings in union life and to take a strong public stand in favor of equality in the workplace.

The 1975 program of the International Federation of Commercial, Clerical, and Office Workers (FIET), a federation of national white-collar workers' unions, urged the revision of school books as essential to attacking the roots of labor market segregation. The GPA women's division took up this issue in Austria and produced *Our School Books: Reflection of Our Society*,[29] which similarly urged the revision of Austrian school texts. The division initiated a public inquiry, with the national union president presiding, to hear experts testify on the contents and consequences of sex-biased textbooks. The proceedings of the inquiry were widely disseminated among educators, parents associations and political leaders. The GPA then commissioned a research institute to prepare a model textbook to help children develop attitudes on equality.

The British Approach

In the Technical, Administrative and Supervisory Staff (TASS) section of AUEW, the women's division, although it represented only one-sixth of the total membership, turned its attention to recruitment and activation of women. These women were mostly in low-paid categories, without special training and with few chances of advancement in a union long dominated by well-paid, high-skilled men.

TASS developed a national pattern of women's organizations, headed by a female organizer and using subcommittees composed of representatives of the national union executive committee and of each of the twenty-six regional executives. These committees involved rank-and-file women in successful organizing of both men and women. In the ten years between 1967 and 1977, women's membership rose from 2,500 (3 percent of the total) to 27,000 (17 percent of a much larger total).

To develop active unionists out of new or passive members, TASS' women's committees experimented freely with purely social affairs, some involving men or whole families, and with mixed social-business affairs beginning with wine and cheese and turning to the next round of local bargaining. Women's committees also joined with nonunion groups in sponsoring community actions, such as establishing refuges for battered wives. They have become part of a movement to integrate women into both unions and the community. Women in TASS were also taking a larger part in the economic and political actions of the unions that were

29. GPA, *Our School Books: Reflection of Our Society*, 1979.

once only "men's activities." In both community and union, then, these committees have been breaking down sex segregation. The director of the program told us that where these committees have been most active, women have made most progress in attaining union office and electing delegates to union congresses.

Sweden: "No Specific Policies on Women"

In the name of equality, and in opposition to the idea of the separateness of women's concerns, the two major Swedish confederations eliminated their women's divisions, TCO in 1967 and LO in 1970. "We have no special policies on women," a TCO official said, "because we believe that women and men should have the same possibilities."

The new structures that all unions established to replace their earlier women's divisions were equality committees in TCO, and councils for family policy in LO. They involved both men and women and they assumed that equality for women would follow from the remolding of people's "traditional thinking on the roles of men and women in the home, the workplace, and society at large."[30]

At the grass roots, women—and some men—saw the problem somewhat differently from confederation policymakers. Immediate needs, they felt, were for the establishment of their own local groups, spontaneous or official, to attack the problems women faced in the shops and offices. When LO took its 1971 convention draft proposals on family policy to the membership for advance discussion and revision in study circles (a common practice in Swedish public life as well as in the unions), local working groups added proposals to lower barriers to women's participation. These proposals included decentralization of union training courses from residential schools to county towns; provision of childcare facilities at residential schools; holding union meetings during working hours; and election of more women to union offices at all levels. All of these proposals were adopted five years later at the 1976 congress.

The TCO White-collar Workers Union (SIF) led the confederation in the creation of equality committees. Almost all of the union's twenty-seven districts established them, usually with men as well as women members. We encountered an especially militant SIF committee in the Stockholm district. By intensive training of women, it had produced a corps of candidates for union office. Its program often began by recruiting women at the workplace to come to consciousness-raising sessions

30. LO, *The Trade Unions and Family Policy*, 1970, preface.

that opened with the question, "Have you encountered special problems because you are women?" It released a torrent of responses. The women then worked their way to collective solutions that took various forms: how to launch action for equality in the office; how to approach employers with demands for training; how to participate in union meetings; how to organize a meeting; how to speak in public.

At two later national conventions, women comprised half the Stockholm delegation, although they made up only one-third of the members. In 1977, for the first time, a woman was elected to chair the district convention. By 1978, SIF had reversed its stand on no special policies for women and had appointed a national women's officer. Even in progressive Sweden the time for special attention to women's affairs had not yet passed.[31]

The Debate on Special Structures

Thus far we have described three types of special structures to expand the voice women have in unions. First are measures that assist women's participation in union activities: meetings during working hours and instructions in the basics of trade unionism and the practices of union meetings. Second are structures that give special representation to women's interests and to the interests of the union in organizing and integrating women as members: women's divisions, women's officers, committees, and conferences. Third are measures and structures that help to promote individual women to positions of union responsibility. These include preference in education programs, reserved seats in executive bodies, and affirmative action plans to give women preferment in election and appointment to official and staff positions.

While the first of these measures has raised no opposition, the second and third types have engendered a continuing debate among unionists. On balance the debate is a contribution to the recognition of women's place in unions, by focusing attention on several vital issues for union democracy: the reasons for women's difficulties in participation, the relation between union structure and purpose, and the gap between the promise of equality and the realities of inequality. In the debate, however, both critics and advocates speak in the name of equality:

CRITIC: First, the women's divisions and conferences are too isolated from the men who hold power, both in unions and in society, to influ-

31. For a realistic picture of women in Sweden, see Hilda Scott, *Sweden's "Right to Be Human": Sex Role Equality—The Goal and the Reality,* 1982.

ence them very much. Whether on the "soft" issues affecting only or chiefly women or on the "hard" issues of collective bargaining and politics, women can petition, but have no power to command action.

ADVOCATE: Power is not a matter of all or nothing. True, women's divisions do not have formal power. They are generally advisory on broad union policies; but they have power to activate women to demand, and qualify for, greater participation in union life. "Once the 'outs' insist on participating with the 'ins', what is 'in' will not be the same."[32] Although women are still among the "outs" in the power structure, women's divisions give them some possibilities of participation even now. The supporters of special structures do not mean them to replace women's access to regular positions of leadership.

CRITIC: Second, the special structures give women the illusion of sharing power, when in reality, women holders of reserved seats or offices are only tokens. Take them out of these marginal roles and they will face the realities of power and win it on their own. As for women's conferences, there "women feel cozy talking to other women. But who is listening?"

ADVOCATE: Those who serve in the special structures make no secret of the narrow limits to their power. But "every forum is valuable. Do not take this away unless we have something to replace it." Moreover, "there is still a great need to debate issues facing women; every opportunity provides a platform."

CRITIC: Third, special structures and women's activities are divisive, pitting women against men, instead of uniting them in the class struggle or in the drive for "another pound in the pay packet and another hour off the work week." Instead of building solidarity, such structures consign women to a permanent ghetto. Separate women's activities lead only to more separate women's activities.

ADVOCATE: To be sure separation of any kind carries the danger of isolation, but recognition of this fact is some protection against it. These separate activities are temporary and are used to lead to full integration on terms of equality. After all, is there anything more divisive than inequality?

Despite the terms of the debate, women are not in a simple either/or position. No one suggests special structures for all needs, and no one suggests that they last longer than necessary to get women moving more rapidly toward equality. These structures, to be sure, are a sign of wom-

---

32. For a summary of this impact on British unions, see Hunt and Adams, 1980, p. 17.

en's weak representation in labor organizations; but they are not an acceptance of that weakness. Rather they are a sign of flexibility in adapting to women's needs.

Of course, the way these structures function varies in a number of ways from union to union. Union tradition and history make a considerable difference. The degree of job segregation within the industry, the degree of education of both women and men within the union, the resources union leaders have at their command in terms of education, of time for service to local unions, of staff and money that can be thrown into organization—all these play their parts. Much depends upon the depth of commitment of national leaders to equality. Even forces outside the union affect the success of its attempts to activate women members. Public understanding of working women's problem is a potential force against at least the most flagrant inequalities. Structures that a few decades ago, in another climate of opinion, may have helped "keep women in their place," now may promote equality, as when the DGB women's division began its ongoing campaign to elect women to seats in works council elections. One generation's "token women" may become another's "ginger group."

Opponents of special structures have the high ground of principle— "equality is indivisible: are you for it or against it?" Proponents are for practical arrangements that by definition do not yet embody equality but are only a means toward its attainment, over an indefinite period of transition.[33]

Back in the United States

Can any of the European experiences be adopted or adapted in the United States with advantage for women in the unions in this country? Institutions of all kinds, including unions, exist within their own social and historical settings; direct import of innovations from other countries will rarely find a neat fit. Nevertheless, many underlying questions are remarkably the same in all of the countries of concern in this study. To the extent that innovations tried abroad have arisen out of genuine universal needs of women, they suggest that adaptations could be useful in the American setting.

In recognizing this problem, one strategy is to provide special accommodations for women so that they can manage their roles in both fam-

---

33. For a profound discussion of "equality feminism" and its relation to "social feminism," see Naomi Black, *Social Feminism*, 1989.

ily and workplace. Some critics of this position see accommodation as special favor, ultimately weakening the assertion of equality between men and women in the workplace.

Another form of criticism from some feminists focuses on the issue of equality from a somewhat different angle. Why should equality require sameness? They stress the significance of a separate women's culture, generated by the requirements of women's work in the home for children and family. This culture creates specific competencies and sensitivities that women bring with them to enrich the workplace where appreciation for their ways of seeing and dealing with problems should have space, recognition, and rewards.

The universal need for women's voices in the union arises preeminently in issues involving the demands of work and family. The fact that the "domestic code" continues to pervade the thinking of many union members is the first hurdle to be overcome. Europe has gone further than the United States in recognizing that family issues must be addressed by both men and women. This achievement is evident mainly in the state's assumption of responsibility for child care, paid maternity leave, and the growing adoption of parental and family leave policies. Many such programs, particularly those affecting child and maternal welfare, are built into or upon a long-standing national health insurance program.

In this country, lacking a national health program, employees increasingly have had to look to the employer to provide such programs and, therefore, to unions to initiate them in bargaining. That some excellent programs are coming into existence by this route is evidenced by the 1989 agreement between American Telephone and Telegraph (AT&T) and the International Brotherhood of Electrical Workers (IBEW) and the Communication Workers of America (CWA) in the private sphere, and the agreements achieved by the Service Employees International Union (SEIU) and the American Federation of State, County, and Municipal Employees (AFSCME) in the public field, notably with the State of New York. Still, all such agreements leave 37 million Americans without health insurance coverage.

Whether the problems are tackled through bargaining, employer initiative, statutory mandate, or a combination of all of these, no country has yet resolved the question of how to bridge the separation between family and workplace without undue hardship on those responsible for the home—almost inevitably women. The answer for the United States seems to require a federally mandated floor of support for working family needs, like that established for wages and hours on the employment side. Unions can improve conditions above this floor through bargaining and will undoubtedly do so in respect to many kinds of family support systems, including child care and family leave.

The questions of power and empowerment of women also have arisen as women scholars have researched the ways women function in unions, the ways they have been excluded or included in specific areas of union work, and the ways women have dealt with these issues in new and creative strategies. Here women's culture often has played an important role, particularly in the accounts of women in French and Italian unions, as they devised new and different ways of taking charge in critical periods.[34]

In the United States, women's unhappy relationship with unions earlier this century sent them to the WTUL. Union men were ambivalent about this development. To be sure, women were in their place, a women's place; yet by aligning themselves with nonunion advocates, were they not really denying the official union movement? Was this an honest search for a home or was it subversion? When women brought forward out of their own organizations quite different issues from the standard union demands—for a cooperative lunchroom, minimum wages, night schools, free medical service by women physicians—and when they attracted public support for legislation and the idealistic goals of women's suffrage and peace, the male-dominated movement treated the issues as trivial and the women as unstable and politically unreliable. Revisionist historical studies of classic American strikes in the early twenties—such as those at the Colorado Fuel and Iron Company, by textile workers in Lowell, and by Jewish women garment workers in New York City— have found in all of them a special and particularly effective type of feminist militancy, derived in part from the very domesticity that was accepted at the time as the desirable role for women.[35]

A union movement that finds room for elements of women's culture of mutual aid, noncompetitiveness, appreciation of difference, and innovation in dealing with crises would have an attractive and more pleasing face for women than the present formal structure and outworn attitudes. Such a labor movement could even be more interesting and satisfactory for men as well.

---

34. See Margaret Maruani, "France," in *Women and Trade Unions in Eleven Industrialized Countries*, ed. Alice H. Cook, Val R. Lorwin, and Arlene Kaplan Daniels, 1984.

35. Colette A. Hyman, "Labor Organizing and Female Institution-Building: The Chicago Women's Trade Union League, 1904–24"; Ardis Cameron, "Bread and Roses Revisited: Women's Culture and Working-Class Activism in the Lawrence Strike of 1912"; Priscilla Long, "The Women of the Colorado Fuel and Iron Strike, 1913–14"; and Roger Waldinger, "Another Look at the International Ladies' Garment Workers Union: Women, Industry Structure, and Collective Action," all in *Women, Work, and Protest: A Century of U.S. Women's Labor History*, ed. Ruth Milkman, 1985.

Conclusion

The gendered division of labor in all of the countries in our study is unquestionably a root cause of much of women's weak position in society as well as in the unions. The effect of assigning women to so-called women's jobs is that women predominate in low-status, low-skilled work and at the lowest pay in the semi-professions. While positive changes have taken place in women's participation in some of the full professions, women's work in offices and factories remains highly segregated from men's. Indeed the introduction of new technology in both places has tended to replace middle management and semi-skilled operatives, thus cutting off on-the-job training and promotional opportunities for many women as well as men in the hands-on occupations.[36]

Where unions have made a separate space for women in which they can develop their skills, union and women have both profited. Organizations have grown, women's voices have been heard, and the pool of candidates for leadership has increased. In the United States, CLUW has come closer than most to providing women with this separate space. In CLUW, the approach has been that women lack power because they lack the skills for power. When these are provided, whether through union education programs, women's summer schools, or university labor education programs, women's special needs are met and they contribute to the labor movement.

Although separatism is widely accepted as a useful measure, it is nowhere viewed as the long term approach; rather it is a necessary, immediate aid, helping women to fit into the existing institution. When they have established leadership there, they can influence a true restructuring of the institution.

It is the issues surrounding the relationship between work and family and their effect upon women in the labor market that give rise to the most challenging question about women's contribution to union life. In restructuring unions to accept women as equals, is it not possible that women's culture may prove useful not only to women but to unions as well?

---

36. We assess the actions underway in vocational training as a partial remedy for these circumstances in Chapter 6. See Harlan and Steinberg for successful projects in vocational training of women.

PART II

UNION
FUNCTIONS

CHAPTER THREE

Collective Bargaining

We are learning to use the system, and well we should for it has certainly used us.
—Tish Sommers, Older Women's League Educational Fund

Almost every question arising in negotiation and collective bargaining has an equality aspect.
—Swedish Trade Union Confederation

As trade unionists, we shall realize our demands together with any government, or, if need be, against any government.
—Anton Benya, president of the Austrian Confederation of Trade Unions

Discrimination of women in union contracts does not arise because of animosity but out of unconscious attachment to patriarchal ways of thinking. This means a systematic ignorance of the content and mechanisms of discrimination. . . . Women's interests—insofar as they are recognized at all—are regarded as second-rate with the result that the contract, at least in part, reads as little more than a codification of patriarchy.
—Ingrid Kurz-Scherf, economist in the Wirtschafts- und Sozialwissenschafts Institut, DGB

Women who speak of "using the system," as Tish Sommers does, mean shaping and using social policy, usually enunciated in legislation and explicated in the administrative agencies and the courts. For trade union women, however, social policy is also a product of labor management negotiation of the terms of collective agreements. Unionism, like the law, long retained discrimination and inequality. Now women and men who seek to establish social justice for working women and ethnic minorities are finding increasing possibilities in using collective bargaining to supplement law. Labor and management can agree upon detailed terms for implementing equality within their jurisdictional sphere and can set standards above what is legally mandatory throughout the state or nation.

By collective bargaining we mean both its product in agreement between unions and employers and its procedures for enforcing the agreement. The functions of negotiation are the real reasons for unions' ex-

Epigraphs: First cited by Shelley Smolkin, "When a Homemaker Loses Her Job," *Working Woman,* July 1979, p. 18; second from LO, *This Is How We Work for Equality between Men and Women in Working Life and in Trade Unions,* 1980, p. 1; third from *Wochenpresse,* October 8, 1969, p. 4; fourth from *WSI Mitteilungen* 39:8 (1986), p. 537.

istence in capitalist nations—for it is through negotiation that joint administration of workplace policy replaces conflict and exploitation.

Where disputes and grievances arise over differing interpretations of the agreements or over violations of their terms, systems of mediation and arbitration exist to assure that labor-management conflict interferes as little as possible with production. In all four European countries these systems include a hierarchy of labor courts (called industrial tribunals in Britain). In the United States, systems of private arbitration perform this function and are usually included in the collective agreement, as a final and binding step in settling grievances under the contract—thus determining "rights" in American labor relations. State and national governments offer conciliation services to aid in breaking impasses over the terms of contracts arising in negotiations. The resulting agreements are referred to as establishing "interests." [1]

The main function of unions during the terms of a contract is to represent their members in enforcing the workers' rights as they are laid out in these agreements with management. National laws recognize the importance of this function as a means both of keeping industrial peace and of protecting the individual workers from exploitation through the otherwise superior power of management. Laws may specify the powers and behavior of both unions and management in carrying out their negotiations and enforcing their bargains, and particularly in resolving any intractable disputes. Union bargaining structures, in turn, are shaped by such legal prescriptions.

At the same time union structures themselves influence the content and style of bargaining; this is evident in the differences between the way industrial and craft unions organize and represent their members. These differences vary from union to union and country to country. Whatever they are, it is the unions' collective bargaining structures and the persons who participate in negotiations that emerge as the source and seat of internal union power. [2]

Since collective bargaining is the very center of union power and functioning in the Western world, its significance for women in the labor market is primary, including for women who are not union members. Union achievements inevitably establish norms in wages and working

---

1. When contract negotiations are at an impasse, occasionally arbitration is used by agreement of both parties in the private sector to make a binding determination on clauses of the contract itself, which is known as "interest arbitration." In government labor relations where strikes are forbidden, "interest arbitration" is sometimes used to achieve a contract.

2. Alice H. Cook, "Dual Government in Unions," *Industrial and Labor Relations Review,* April 1962, pp. 323–49.

conditions for everyone in union and nonunion plants throughout a product market. In some countries, labor ministries may actually extend union agreements to cover all of these workers. Germany and Austria practice this so-called extension of agreements. It is the provincial labor ministers that may extend a regional collective agreement to cover firms in the industry or geographic area that were not members of the association negotiating the agreement. Such extensions are more important in Germany, where less than half of all employees are in unions, than in Austria. Extensions particularly affect favorably the conditions for the many women workers in small establishments that often do not join employer associations.

In other countries, the conditions laid down in union contracts may become the standards accepted by government for its own contractors, as with the Davis-Bacon Act in the United States. In many instances, employers who do not wish to deal with unions nevertheless accept, or may even improve on, union conditions. In this way they aim to avoid worker dissatisfaction and attempts at organization by their employees based on what the organizing unions could portray as inferior conditions.

The growing number of women in the labor force has resulted in more women joining unions, so that the proportion of working women who are represented by unions has greatly increased. It is these women union members, many of them new to work as well as to unions, to whom unions have had to learn to direct their collective bargaining interests and energies.

Union Structures and Bargaining Structures

Since union structures and their bargaining patterns differ from country to country, we outline here the way in which each country conducts its bargaining functions, indicating important changes and transitions.

British union structures are the products of a long, unbroken history in the first industrial nation. While they differ decidedly from those on the continent and in the United States, they have strongly influenced patterns in the U.S. unions. The British national confederation, the Trades Union Congress, has 110 affiliates—three very large, general unions and the remainder a variety of local craft unions, mixed unions, and large industrial unions, each categorized by law into the profit sector, the private nonprofit sector, or the public sector.

The general unions tend to dominate the scene, chiefly by their size. They organize all grades of manual workers in a multitude of indus-

tries: the biggest, the Transport and General Workers (T&G), is over
two million members strong and has substantial numbers of women
members. Industrial unions and many craft unions operate in fields of
production where male employees predominate. Their women may belong to semi-autonomous white-collar sections. National white-collar
unions in both public and private employment tend to have a near majority of women. In contrast to the historically male-dominated unions,
many of these organizations have actively supported equality measures.
Most employers deal with several unions, some of them with overlapping jurisdictions. The result is multiunion bargaining in most industries
and even in most large plants.

The law permits what the British call the "closed shop," or what
Americans would call a "union shop," that is, compulsory union membership after entry on the job, but not before it. While managements
having formal or informal closed shop agreements have frequently expressed satisfaction with this type of union security, the Conservative
government's legislation in recent years has made the establishment of
such agreements more difficult, and thus it has become easier for individual employees who are dissatisfied to opt out of membership.

Bargaining in Britain, with a few important exceptions, tends to be
conducted at the enterprise or plant level. The elected shop stewards
often achieve great power within the local and may even function quite
independently of the national union in respect to the contracts they negotiate and administer or in calling strikes.[3] As a result, Britain presents
an irregular—indeed often a chaotic—model in which local unions frequently bargain with individual plants or firms. Even where national
unions have endeavored to establish their hegemony, locals may continue to operate in the old way, relying for justification of their independence on what they refer to as "custom and practice." Under this
concept, bargaining over rights as well as interests may take place inter-
mittently during contract periods and local strikes may even be called.
One American observer with whom we talked noted that "workplace
managements make concessions to different union stewards on different
issues at different times. The results are 'disorderly pay structures' and
'competitive section wage adjustments,' as the Donovan Commission
pointed out in 1976." Attempts by British governments, including both
Labour and Conservative governments, to regulate wage agreements have
only rarely been successful.

3. For more details on the British system, see Hugh A. Clegg, *The System of Industrial
Relations in Great Britain*, 1972.

Before the Hitler period, Germany and Austria also had competing unions dealing with management. Their competition was not jurisdictional but ideological. They were affiliated to federations that carried political labels: socialist, Catholic, liberal, and in embryonic form, communist. These all disappeared in the maelstrom of Nazism. After the war, both the German and the Austrian unionists who survived this catastrophe completely rationalized their trade union structures, erecting them without political or religious attachments. What emerged were purely industrial federations: in Germany, sixteen national unions—now seventeen—affiliated to the German Federation of Labor; in Austria, fifteen affiliated to the Austrian Trade Union Federation. In most cases, this reorganization meant that the national unions included both manual and white-collar employees, not always an easy integration of interests. The OeGB largely avoided one of these conflicts by making a major exception to the principle of industrial unionism and establishing one of its nationals as a union for all private-sector, white-collar employees, the GPA. In Germany the DGB at its founding congress in 1949 held firm against such an exception, whereupon a large number of white-collar employees left the federation to form the Independent White-collar Union (DAG), which still exists outside the DGB. Thus, to the degree that women make up an important part of the white-collar sector, the women in Austria can draw upon the strength of the national confederation if need be, whereas those in Germany in the DAG might feel themselves too weak to achieve their goals.

German bargaining is conducted by district offices of the national unions in the various branches of each major industry within the area. The national union makes its professional staff members available to these bargaining committees usually composed mainly of union chairpersons of the works councils in the leading plants.[4]

Austrian bargaining is highly centralized and for many years existed within the social partnership of management, labor, and the state in a process called "concerted action" *(konzitierte Aktion),* a process which served to link wages and employment to national economic indicators. Bargaining on other than economic issues is conducted for the most part nationally by the individual unions.[5] An Austrian government agency,

4. For more details on Germany, see Joachim Bergmann and Walther Mueller-Jentsch, "The Federal Republic of Germany: Cooperative Unionism and Dual Bargaining System Challenged," in *Worker Militancy and Its Consequences, 1965–75: New Directions in Western Industrial Relations,* ed. Solomon Barkin, 1975.

5. For more details on Austria, see Helga Duda and Franz Toedtling, "Austrian Trade Unions in the Economic Crisis," in *Unions in Crisis and Beyond: Perspectives from Six*

the Chamber of Labor (Kammer der Arbeiter und Angestellten), is closely and complementarily related to the trade unions and carries on many activities that support their work, including training works councillors for their jobs in the works councils, carrying out vocational training programs, conducting research, and disseminating a great deal of information on labor law to employers as well as to employees.

Sweden, which like Britain has had a continuous union history, is now in the process of rationalizing its union structures, mainly by merger and pruning, without having gone through the Central European trauma of death and transfiguration. Its trade union movement is composed of three labor confederations. There are twenty-five unions in the Swedish Confederation of Labor, organizing mostly, but not exclusively, manual workers. Sweden also has a highly developed white-collar unionism in a confederation of its own. The Central Organization of Salaried Employees is comprised of five unions that together have almost half as many members as LO. A third confederation, much smaller but influential, is the Swedish Association of Academic, Professional and Management Officers, which represents university-trained employees, senior civil servants, and other professionals.

For many years and until recently, the Swedes worked under a system of peak bargaining, by which the confederations, sometimes in concert through organization of ad hoc union cartels, bargained with the top employers of the Swedish Employers' Federation (SAF). Details of the bargain would be administered through union "clubs" located at plant level. This system has given way to decentralized bargaining, in part because of the trauma of the general strike in 1981, but in part because members of the national confederations have grown more and more dissatisfied with the constraints the peak bargaining system put upon them. In the shock following the assassination of the prime minister, the peak organizations returned to their old mode of individual union bargaining. Swedish collective bargaining is in structural transition.[6]

The labor organizations of all the continental countries, relatively centralized as they are for bargaining, command large financial resources and are well staffed. Top union negotiators generally meet as professional equals with the representatives of employer associations and

Countries, eds. Richard Edwards, Paolo Geronna, and Franz Toedtling, 1986, pp. 227–68.

6. For a description of the "peak bargaining system" in Sweden, see Casten van Otter, "Sweden: Labor Reformism Reshapes the System," in Barkin, ed., 1975, pp. 194–233; and Lennart Svensson, "Class Struggle in a Welfare State in Crisis: From Radicalism to Neoliberalism in Sweden," in Edwards, Geronna, and Toedtling; eds., 1986, pp. 269–308.

public employers. The unions' bargaining is supported by well-staffed research, policy, education, and information departments that advise the bargaining officials. British unions, with much lower dues income, have smaller staffs in relation to membership, fewer professionals involved in negotiations and more limited—if now increasing—research, education, and information systems. Employers are strongly organized nationally for bargaining purposes in the continental countries; less so in Britain, where plant and local bargaining are more common.[7] Indeed, the Confederation of British Industry (CBI), the employers' organization, has only indirect influence through its members on the pattern or content of bargaining, but it is influential within government circles on matters of labor relations policy.

By contrast, in the United States, the National Labor Relations Board (NLRB) administers the National Labor Relations Act (1936, as amended). It determines bargaining units and grants unions representing the majority of workers within a unit exclusive bargaining rights to represent all employees within that unit. It also determines what is termed "mandatory subjects of bargaining." Thus, an employer deals with only one union for a given unit of workers. The large number of national unions—still, after many mergers, nearly one hundred—together with any independent national organizations outside the AFL–CIO, such as the NEA and ANA with their hundreds of local unions, present extremely varied sets of hybrids. Many of these have long historical roots crossed with modern growths, and the specific combinations influence bargaining patterns.[8]

Are women better served under unions that are centralized in their bargaining or decentralized? Officers at the top of many unions, particularly those with large female memberships, tend to be more inclined than local leaders are to keep women's interests in mind. Yet, officers of decentralized unions, however supportive their sentiments about women's needs may be, are quite reluctant to interfere with local fellow-workers' decisions, even when overtly discriminatory. Few women have yet arrived in the national executive boards of unions, or even as chief executives in regional offices, although their numbers are increasing among local stewards and works council members. We observed situations in all the countries where from time to time local women took action into their own hands, often winning the support of male departments in the plants and finding sympathizers in neighboring firms

7. Jill Rubery, "Trade Unions in the Eighties: The Case of the United Kingdom," in Edwards, Geronna, and Toedtling, eds., 1986, pp. 61–113.

8. For a careful comparative study of collective bargaining, see John P. Windmuller, ed., *Collective Bargaining in Industrialized Market Economies: A Reappraisal*, 1987.

or other branches of the same company. Even in highly centralized organizations, such as in Swedish unions where the official position clearly supports sex equality but where no women are on the executive committees, the degree of sex segregation within the workplaces and the unions is one of the highest in the world. Moreover, Swedish women in our interviews complained of sex bias in their local plants and offices, and strongly felt the need for the reestablishment of women's groups within the unions in order to make their complaints more audible and more influential.

Nevertheless, one of the few cases where national bargaining has been of unqualified benefit to women is Sweden's solidary wage policy. The policy was advanced by LO to narrow the gap between low- and high-paid union members. It was conceived of not as a women's issue but as an effort to narrow the pay gap between low- and high-paid workers regardless of gender. Because women were almost always low-paid the policy worked to their benefit. The gender interest in the policy was never addressed, thus making it difficult to generalize about the relative benefits of a centralized versus a decentralized organization.

Works Councils and Labor Courts

Two institutions unknown in the United States, which nevertheless play significant roles in all four European countries, are works councils and industrial tribunals or labor courts. The first is a means of providing representation for unorganized as well as organized workers. The second, the labor courts, is a means of handling grievances of all workers, through a public institution rather than through the system of private arbitration which in the United States varies from union to union and is embodied in the collective agreements.

Works Councils

Following World War I and under the Weimar Republic in Germany, revolutionary demands for workers' participation in management resulted in a law providing for the establishment in every workplace of a works council. A compromise that unions accepted at the time was to have the councils represent all workers in every firm, whether union members or not. Under the Nazis, these became part of fascist corporatism with their union element abolished; but after World War II, the old law was reinstituted and then amended in 1972. In both Germany and Austria today, works councils handle some plant-level bargaining.[9] The two countries' systems are almost the same, but the German system is more elaborate.

Under national law, works council members are elected triennially by the votes of all employees in a plant. Local unions put up slates for these elections. While candidates for the works council need not be union members, most councillors are union activists. All councillors have paid leave for training, which is offered both by employers and unions, but in fact most training takes place in the union schools and nonunion councillors not infrequently join the union. Observers of the system note that works councillors, much like British shop stewards,

> set the limits of union policy and determine how it is to be executed within the factories. The institutional interests of the factory councillors, moreover, tend to be curiously out of phase with those of the national union leaders. When the economy is booming and the labor market is tight, as it is in many sections of the German economy, the union's bargaining power is enhanced and factory councillors may establish themselves as barons, relatively independent of the unions' central control.[10]

The works council's power to negotiate is limited to making improvements above the basic wage scales of the regional agreements, negotiating methods of wage payment, job and bonus rates, and other performance-related pay standards. It schedules hours and vacations, and establishes criteria for layoffs or dismissals in case of lack of work. Together with the company, it administers welfare services—canteens, vacation homes, and housing—that the company may provide.

Thus, the functions of the council and its individual members can be of crucial importance to women in the plant. As the depressions of the 1970s and 1980s deepened, causing companies to lay off or even dismiss workers, the works councils under the law had veto power over the lists of those scheduled for unemployment. The women's committees of the unions complained that many of them were agreeing with the companies to lay off married women first, regardless of seniority, skill, or experience, and to protect men's rather than women's job security.

The councils are also crucial for women because they are the primary

9. Sweden also has a system of works councils. They exist not by law but by collective agreement between the national labor and employer confederations. The unions have seen to it that the councils are not independent bodies but are a subordinate part of union structures without collective bargaining power, used mainly for consultation.

10. Charles Sabel, "Rationalization and Unemployment in Germany: Their Impact on a Fragile Truce," IRRA 32d annual meeting, *Proceedings*, 1979, p. 318.

agency for taking up employee grievances. For example, a great deal may depend on the attitude of male councillors in approaching women's problems. When a works councillor cannot or will not resolve a grievance, the affected employee may take his/her complaint to a labor court, if possible with the help of the council. Women in both Germany and Austria have had cause to complain of indifference or half-heartedness on the part of works councils in pursuing such cases into labor courts, while many women have found it very difficult to find their way there alone without experienced assistance.

Although women are elected to works councils in ever increasing numbers (see Table 3) they usually come from the departments in the firm where women predominate. As such they are typically seen as less representative and less important than men from the skilled trades who tend to be better known.

A certain proportion of works council officers are released from work for full-time council duties. These are invariably the council officials who because of their positions, particularly in the large firms, do the local bargaining and whom the union selects to be members of the regional bargaining committees. This practice tends to exclude women from the bargaining function itself and to limit their activities to their own departments and plant-internal affairs. For these affairs, women councillors typically are selected by their council colleagues to deal with social services and social functions, and only rarely represent the council in dealing with the employer.[11]

The Labor Courts

In the European system these statutory bodies take over much of what in America falls under the bargained grievance procedure. They are organized on a tripartite basis, usually with a professional judge who presides with two lay assistants, one representing unions and one management. In some countries, the judges appoint these lay members; in others, laymen are named by their respective labor and employer organizations. In some countries, the labor courts are empowered first to conciliate disputes and only if conciliation fails, do they resort to adjudication.[12]

Labor court procedure is less formal and hence less intimidating to a

11. In addition to the works councillors, unions have their own representatives, Vertrauensleute, in each plant or office. These are responsible for union interests—maintenance of membership, circulation of information, collection of dues, and other nonbargaining activities—plus exercising varying degrees of support and stimulus of works council actions.

12. Benjamin Aaron, "The NLRB, Labor Courts, and Industrial Tribunals: A Selective Comparison," *Industrial and Labor Relations Review* 39:1 (1985), pp. 35–45.

Table 3. Works council elections: Elected female works councillors reported by four unions, 1959–1987 (all election years)

	1959	1961	1963	1965	1968	1972	1975	1978	1981	1984	1987
Chemistry, paper, ceramics	1,440	1,458	1,484	1,479	1,416	2,094	2,418	2,602	2,973	3,021	2,652
Commerce, banking, insurance	1,539	1,827	2,169	1,990	1,839	3,829	6,373	8,237	10,668	10,976	12,295
Metal	3,188	2,631	3,900	4,221	3,918	5,765	6,872	6,984	7,562	7,316	8,812
Textiles	4,949	5,238	5,271	5,019	5,535	7,199	7,441	7,722	7,738	7,031	6,585
All DGB unions	15,281	15,469	16,707	16,175	16,246	23,409	30,006	33,319	38,356	38,043	39,032
Total councillors (both sexes)					142,412	173,670	191,015	194,455	199,125	190,232	176,104
% women councillors					11.4	13.5	15.7	17.1	19.3	20	22.2

Source: *Frauen und Arbeit*, "40 Jahre Gewerkschaftliche Frauenarbeit," April 7, 1989, p. 24.

worker than the process, for instance, of a U.S. district court. However, it is certainly more formal than the U.S. practice of carrying a grievance through a contractual procedure within the firm. Its advantage over the U.S. system is that a worker whose steward has decided not to involve the union in the grievance may him/herself take the complaint to the court or tribunal. Workers before the court may plead their own cases, or they may be represented by a union or their own lawyer. Decisions are made without lengthy delays.

The British courts, called industrial tribunals (ITs) are more informal than the first tier of labor courts on the continent, but their main features are generally similar. An IT is presided over by a legally qualified person (often more qualified in legal than in industrial relations matters), not usually a judge. He—it is almost always a man—is flanked by one or two persons, each chosen from panels proposed by the TUC and the CBI. Appeals from ITs' decisions (only on points of law) go to an Employment Appeals Tribunal (EAT), presided over by a High Court judge, assisted by one or two lay persons each from the labor and employer panels. Here, unlike the IT, decisions set legal precedents. In rare cases, appeals are permitted from EAT decisions to the court of appeal of the regular judicial system and finally to the House of Lords.[13]

As was pointed out earlier, the degree of union support given an appellant can be decisive. In Britain, as well as on the continent, local steward's or councillor's decisions to support a woman's complaint of discrimination can rest as much on fellow workers' attitudes as on national union policy. In the famous British case of *Snoxell and Davies v. General Motors*, the chief steward in the plant where the women worked refused to help the women, although their own shop steward was convinced of the merits of their case. His support assisted them in appealing a lower tribunal decision to the higher EAT where they won. The union was T&G, whose chief officer at that time, Jack Jones, was an outspoken supporter of gender equality. Because grievance handling was decentralized to the local union in this organization, Jones made no

13. In cases in Britain where interpretations of the anti–sex discrimination or equal pay statutes have been at issue, the EOC has repeatedly referred cases to the Community High Court of Justice in Luxembourg for interpretation under EC directives. One such case was that of Mrs. Garland, a retired employee of British Rail Engineering. Before her retirement, her husband and children had received free railway passes for travel; after her retirement passes for her family were denied, although her male colleagues continued to receive such passes for family members. Her case went up to the House of Lords. There the issue of whether her case fell under the equal pay law was raised and referred to the European High Court, which ruled in her behalf. Jennifer Corcoran, "U.K. Sex Discrimination and the European Court," *Equal Opportunities International* 1:1 (1981), pp. 18–22.

effort to interfere with the negative decision of the chief steward. His behavior was explained in another, similar arbitration hearing when a T&G officer, who was asked about the possibility that Jones would discipline a local officer, responded, "It is foolish [for him] to discipline shop stewards. If [officers] did, we would soon have no union at all."[14]

In Germany, union support often depends on workshop decisions. A group of women cable spinners sought for eighteen years to have the company recognize their grievance for a change in labor grade. Over the years, the work underwent a great deal of development. Instead of working on four kinds of cable, they now spun eighty-two different kinds, for each of which they had special training. Each day these women had to lift 4,000 pounds of weight. Moreover, the company had greatly increased the work norm over the period. With the support of their union, Metall, they appealed the case to the district labor court in Wetzlar and were awarded a two-grade improvement in their rating.[15]

In a similar case, women in a honey concern sought upgrading. The matter went to the Supreme Labor Court before the women won, but win they did with the help of their union's representation. In this case it was the Food and Restaurant Workers Union (NGG) that supported them.[16]

Thus, the Europeans resort in stubborn cases to special courts for the settlement of individual or collective grievances. Most women have so far fared about as well—or ill—under the labor court system as they have in the United States under private arbitration or court action. Judges—and in America, arbitrators—have been slow to understand the special position of women, and particularly of married women and women heads of family, who come to the work force already burdened in a way that men usually are not, where they are assigned to the ghetto of so-called women's work.

The Content of Bargaining

The unions in Germany, Austria, Britain, and Sweden are essentially pragmatic bargaining organizations. Although ideologies influence them

---

14. This case illustrates again the overriding independence of the local union stewards in Great Britain and the policy, possibly born of weakness, of national officers' unwillingness to impose policy on local officers. Despite the unions' higher degree of centralization on the Continent, a similar outcome is predictable where union works councillors also may not necessarily respond to national union directives.

15. "Nach 18 Jahren Lohnstreit, Hoehergruppierung," *Frauen und Arbeit* August/September 1980, p. 20.

16. *Frauen und Arbeit*, December 1980, p. 13, and July 1986, p. 7.

and they have close political ties to the labor parties, they are primarily neither ideological nor political in outlook and concerns. Their prime targets (as with American unions) are wages, working conditions, and union security.

In Sweden, for reasons we have already discussed, the direction and strategy of the unions is somewhat unclear while the whole collective bargaining process moves into a new mode. Since the solidary wage has largely been achieved, with women in blue-collar work earning on the average 90 percent and in the white-collar fields about 80 percent as much as men, equality issues must center now on the role and conditions of part-time workers, mainly women, who make up more than 25 percent of the female labor force, and on shortening the workday.

In Germany and Austria, a major goal is increasing the degree of co-determination—union participation with management in a broad range of decision-making. In Germany, the Socialists' failure through most of the 1980s to win even local elections, and the rising support for the Greens, during that period, to some degree shifted political attention away from working demands and toward ecology, nuclear power, and disarmament issues. Moreover, high unemployment during that period weakened union power, as did the scandals connected with the management and attempted sale of the unions' housing corporation, Die neue Heimat. Under these circumstances, the unions' chief issue (put forward as a countermeasure to unemployment) was the achievement of the thirty-five-hour week. While men and women were united behind the general demand, they remained sharply divided on how best to implement the program. Most union leaders advocated a shorter work week—four-and-a-half days, for example—while women advocated a shorter work-day, necessary if both parents are to have more time with children and to share household tasks.

Other issues put forward by the women's division of the DGB include elimination of discrimination in job training and wages, as well as provisions for retraining to make women eligible to compete for the new technical demands in office and workshop; reduction of excessive strain and demands on the job; and consideration for the fact that women are doubly burdened with full responsibility at home while they work for wages outside the home.[17] The women also constantly remind the employers that they have a responsibility to open more job categories to women—not an easy demand to achieve as long as the unemployment

17. "Arbeitsmaterial fuer die gewerkschaftliche Frauenarbeit zur Durchsetzung der gleichen Rechte und Chancen der Frauen," *Frauen und Arbeit*, July 1980, pp. 2–10.

rate over-all exceeds 10 percent, with women at an even higher rate than men.

Despite periodic loss of political power, European unions generally have more power than American ones. One reason, of course, is the higher rate of organization among both men and women in Europe. Another is that European employers have not yet engaged in on-going antiunion campaigns, instead accepting the bargaining system and the unions as social partners. Moreover, since many of the issues over which American unions still negotiate at the bargaining table have been regulated by law—covering such provisions as health insurance, pensions, paid vacations, and severance pay—the unions have more power and time than American ones to devote to wages and some of the newer, non-pecuniary issues, such as the phasing in of new technology, the work environment, the shorter work week, and industrial democracy.[18]

European governments, like the U.S. government, set many of the essential conditions for labor-management relations, although generally in less detail and with fewer restrictions than does U.S. law. In times of inflation and recession, they seek to influence the size of the wage settlement in major negotiations, as the American government has done from time to time, though never with outstanding success. Generally, however, European governments do not interfere directly in the determination of wages by management and organized labor. The possible exception is Austria, and there consideration for the national economy in setting wage levels is a function of union and management agreement and not of government imposition. In the United States, the government has determined some wage issues that in Europe are left to the bargaining parties, notably the national minimum wage and the rates of overtime pay.[19]

18. One labor expert has called attention to a useful by-product of management's campaign against unions in the United States. He says that "by pushing labor's back to the wall, they have given some unions new incentive to strengthen alliances with environmentalists, civil rights activists, women's groups and other liberal organizations . . . to launch a broad attack on a wide range of corporate practices after the company refused to negotiate a new labor contract, and it became clear that more narrow, traditional tactics such as strikes would not win an agreement." Among the new issues he listed are environmental concerns at a huge surface mine, a struggle against an oil company engaged in toxic dumping, and a boycott against a major oil company doing business in South Africa. He concludes by saying that "companies should expect more campaigns of this type." Matt Witt, "Labor Tries a New Tactic," *Washington Post National Weekly*, May 28, 1987, p. 32.

19. The Center for Research on European Women reported in late 1991 that the European labor ministers were preparing a directive on minimum wages for submission to the Council of Ministers. *CREW Report*, October 1991, p. 11.

The weight of government action in Europe has been in labor's favor on many issues, more so than in America. These include not only national health insurance and paid vacations, but pregnancy and maternity leaves, and parental leave to care for newborn infants and sick children. They also cover compensation for dismissals without just cause and aggressive training programs for persons dismissed because of plant closures. In the United States, in contrast, legislative emphasis has been on the scope of bargaining and the content of such concepts as "bargaining in good faith" for both labor and management. The law has further created the doctrine of "the duty of fair representation" by unions. These concepts (potentially of great importance to women and minorities in that they can compel the union to deal with members' grievances without equivocation) in turn flow from the assignment of exclusive bargaining rights to the majority union.

As a result of this legislative emphasis, American collective agreements are longer and more complicated than European ones. They are longer, in part, because they detail a step-grievance procedure leading to binding arbitration, whereas in Europe the grievance process at an early stage turns to labor courts. They are also longer because many matters that in Europe are regulated by government—length of paid vacations, pensions, long severance notice and severance pay, health insurance, and paid maternity leaves—are left to collective bargaining in the United States.

Bargaining on Women's Issues

Although unions are self-described agents of change, historically they have not rushed into the struggle for women's equality. Indeed, history suggests that unions prefer the easier route of dealing with the issue by expressing a supportive attitude in a resolution of principle nonbinding on action. This paradox raises the question of how women's equality issues can reach union bargaining agendas and become issues that the union will retain in the bargaining process and even strike to gain.

In her devastating critique, Kurz-Scherf has analyzed the sex discrimination in union agreements in Germany over recent negotiating years. First, she notes that every German noun has a gender ending and that contracts are almost invariably written in the masculine. Only low-level jobs are written in both genders, though mainly in the feminine. More specifically, she points out that women's wages continue to be associated with the "light wage groups," that is, with the wages for "light work" at the bottom of the scale. The typical characteristics of women's work—the problems of nervous and psychic stress, monotony, repetition in use of a few small muscles, and lack of big muscle activity—are systematically overlooked and become by default legitimate reasons for paying low wages. Thus, the work to which women typically are assigned is seen as having little value. Even where formal educational requirements for different technical work are much the same, work done by men is higher paid than that employing women, with the result that even qualifications carry a sex label. Kurz-Scherf goes on to show how the seniority principle as it is used in Germany further discriminates against women. Because it assumes continuous employment as the norm, a condition few women have been able to achieve during the childbearing years, women are handicapped. Further, since years of employment in a single firm are often taken as equivalent to enriched experience and even advancing skill, these qualities are rewarded with wage improvement. Without the seniority that males achieve, women are often deprived of opportunities for on-the-job training that could lead to advancement. Seniority frequently determines access to other better work conditions and eligibility for certain privileges. Among these can be leaves from shift work or eligibility to early retirement, separation pay, and the amount of sick pay. Thus, rewards presumably based on loyalty to the firm are in fact measured by uninterrupted employment as expressed in seniority.[20]

The failure of union contracts to represent women, Kurz-Scherf points out, is the consequence of the union's inability to check the employer's "massive economic interest" for cheap and interchangeable women's labor. When the union asks, for example, for increases in pay for the low-wage grades, it does not usually deal with the issue for what it is— a general social and economic problem—but rather as the demand of a specific interest group to which it attaches minor relevance, as compared to other issues deemed of concern to a majority of members. The consequence is that negotiators can always find a broad-based issue to which this specific demand must defer. She believes this will "change only when the union recognizes that sex discrimination is not merely the concern of a special interest group but is a structural problem of the entire social order."[21]

Union agendas, like political ones, reflect three kinds of pressures. The first comes from impersonal, long-run forces such as the introduction of new technology, increasing governmental intervention in the

20. Ingrid Kurz-Scherf, "Von der Emanzipation des Brunnenmaedchens in Heilbaedern: Frauendiskriminierung, Frauenfoerderung durch Tarifvertrag und Tarifpolitik," *WSI Mitteilungen* 39:8 (1986), pp. 537–48.

21. Ibid.

conditions of employment, and changes in the patterns of family life. The second comes from cataclysmic events that reshape society: wars, depressions, the rising of a new social movement such as civil rights, ecology protection, and the revival of the women's movement throughout the world. The third comes from identifiable individuals who influence union decision-makers. This third, as it affects union programs, generally comes from within the labor movement itself.

A strong force since the late 1960s has been the formal union caucuses and committees that have identified women's problems and expressed them in programmatic demands. They exist in the ETUC, in most of the trade secretariats, in the national confederations of TUC, OeGB, and DGB, and in LO and TCO, and they are echoed in the national unions within these countries.

One example of how action in the international bodies finds its way into the work of a national confederation is illustrated by a report on the twentieth FIET World Congress that appeared in *Frauen und Arbeit*. FIET actions included resolutions on equal opportunity and comparable pay for women, shorter working hours, control of the new technology, job security and job creation, and a strong trade union organization. The article noted that these were all addressed not just to national unions but to local organizations and to the enterprises with which they negotiate.[22]

Typically, organized women's groups within the unions have been able to make themselves felt. No better example in the 1980s exists than the women's division of the German metalworkers. As usually occurs in the German unions, these women held their convention a few months before the national union congress. They adopted resolutions on legislation, internal union policy, women's trade union education, abortion, foreign workers, and right-wing extremism. Twenty-eight resolutions dealt with collective bargaining issues of concern to women, in addition to which various local organizations and national departments introduced resolutions affecting women. The executive of the women's division established priorities among those to be passed on to the national union congress. As a result of this initiative, among the resolutions adopted by the national congress and serving as instructions to bargaining committees were ones on the effect of new informational and communications technology on women's work, and on the continuing problem of women's wages held low through the hidden biases in job descriptions and grade evaluations.

22. "FIET Weltkongress," *Frauen und Arbeit*, January 1984, p. 16.

Austrian white-collar workers in GPA began with an earlier step. The women launched a study of all the union's collective agreements to underscore the differences in their treatment of men and women. We were told that these differences, as they were accumulated in the report, "leaped to the eyes" of the male officials to whom the women brought the study results. Of course, these inequalities were not previously unknown. What was new was that they had been shown to be part of a systematic pattern that the women felt thwarted gender equality within the union. It was the difference, in effect, between dealing with a series of individual complaints and facing the evidence of systemic inequality.

A similar approach served union legislative goals in Britain. There a TUC study of women's and men's grievances over forced quits (what in the United States are called "constructive dismissals") caused the national union congress to insist upon a provision in the 1974 Trade Union and Labour Relations Act making such employer action unlawful, establishing a procedure for redress in labor courts, and entitling victims to compensation.

Despite the decisions and recommendations throughout the broad network of national and international trade union affiliations, union leaders react positively to an internally orchestrated demand from their rank-and-file members. An example of how powerful these internal actions can be is the history of a women's strike at a single Ford plant in Britain. Although it took years to settle the women's complaint, it had ripple effects that did not merely bring attention to this grievance but eventuated in determining TUC policy on equal pay for women with men.

The episode began in mid-1968, when 187 long-frustrated women sewing auto seat covers at the Ford plant at Dagenham went on strike for an upgrading of their jobs from semiskilled to skilled status and for equal pay with men at those grades. Although they struck on their own, their union at once made the strike official. Their strike brought Dagenham to a halt and inspired a sympathy strike at another Ford plant.

The company protested that the strike was in violation of a contract. A male union leader conceded this but replied that equal pay was an issue of principle that took precedence over contract obligations. Although the strike won the women only part of the raise that they claimed, the bargaining on pay structures at Ford went on and on, actually taking some nineteen years to settle—perhaps a record in union foot-dragging. Indeed the strike reached far beyond the Ford company. It put the equal pay issue on the active agenda not only of the union to which the women belonged but also of the TUC, which had paid no attention to it since passing its first equal pay resolution (in quite another spirit) eighty years earlier.

One consequence of this locally initiated chain of events occurred at the 1968 TUC convention. Although a number of unions represented there overtly opposed equal pay, a majority of delegates endorsed strike action if necessary to achieve equal pay. In the next year, Britain's biggest union, the T&G, made equal pay the subject of one of the two resolutions it had the right to put to the annual TUC congress. T&G's Frank Cousins, at that time the nation's most powerful union leader, in his last TUC speech denounced unions that still had "women's wage rates" and demanded "equal pay for work of equal value on behalf of all people employed." Other efforts—women's equal pay strikes and demonstrations, and the creation by the unions of a new Labour Party National Campaign Committee for Women's Equal Rights—finally moved the issue beyond the unions; the Labour government after long hesitation put through the Equal Pay Act in 1970. By 1975, as the United Nations Women's Decade was inaugurated, the TUC held a monster march and meeting in Trafalgar Square in support of a broad range of women's issues, including equal pay.[23]

Women on Bargaining Committees

"Do the unions represent the interests of men better than those of women?" asked a 1975 public opinion survey in Belgium, where the public correctly perceived the unions' bargaining as a major element in shaping labor market policy. Sixty-four percent of those replying said that the unions represented the interests of men better (of the wage and salaried workers among those queried, 51 percent agreed with this majority); seven percent said that unions better represented the interests of women. The remaining 29 percent of the respondents had no opinions to offer.

The responses would probably have been similar in almost any other country, even in Scandinavia. Other questions would no doubt have brought out the fact that the unions, despite their male biases, have of course benefitted their women members in many ways, but chiefly by raising the earnings of union members, including women, above those of unorganized workers. Still, union leaders generally have been indif-

23. For a brief, dramatic summary of these events, see Sheila Lewenhak, *Women and Trade Unions: An Outline History of Women in the British Trade Union Movement,* 1977, pp. 285–91.

ferent to the special concerns of women, including their own members. For example, leaders' concern with child care as a subject of collective bargaining, has often carried the patriarchal imprint of their belief that mothers should take full responsibility for infant and child care. The sense of parental and not just maternal obligation to children is only beginning to awaken among men. It shows itself most clearly in the widening positive acceptance of parental leave policies.

Would matters change, would women's issues appear more often and be advocated more consistently, if women were on bargaining committees? Or, as most men and many women believe, do men work more effectively with their male counterparts on management teams than do women? What is the experience with women at the bargaining table?

Although women are appearing with greater frequency in union executive positions, there are so few women with collective bargaining experience that generalizations are difficult to make. With almost half of its members women, Sweden's TCO in the mid-1970s had only one woman serving on the collective bargaining commissions of its five affiliates. The self-generated educational and political activity of women throughout the union has resulted not only in policy statements on increasing the number of women officers but also in women both among the actual bargainers and among those on the enlarged bargaining committees that advise bargainers and initially ratify agreements.[24]

In Britain, where much of the bargaining is still local or with single firms, women presumably have more of an opportunity to mainstream their issues, particularly because the shop stewards have come to act almost autonomously in many locations, disregarding national and local officers where that seems the necessary tactic to achieve their local goals. So far, however, women in Britain participate in local bargaining no more frequently than women elsewhere in Europe at the same or higher levels.

In all the countries where bargaining takes place on a regional or national scale, many contract details still remain to be worked out between local union officers (or in Germany and Austria, the works councils) and the local firm. The German Basic Workplace Labor Relations

24. For reports on women's status in European trade unions, see ETUI, *Women and Trade Unions in Western Europe*, 1987, and *Positive Action for Women in Western Europe*, 1989. Unfortunately women's participation in collective bargaining is not used in these reports as a measure of status. Among the events that establish a trend of more women on the executive policy boards of unions in all countries were the election in 1984 in Great Britain of a woman president of the Society of Graphical and Allied Trades, and, somewhat earlier, the election of a woman president of the second largest union, the public workers (OeTV), in Germany.

Law (BVG), adopted in 1952 and amended in 1972, states the aim of electing women to the councils in proportion to their numbers within the work force, but it provides no implementing measures and no penalties for nonimplementation. In contrast, the unions' women's divisions put great emphasis on increasing the number of women's works councillors and chairs. In the first twenty-five years by 1981, women had neared their proportion of DGB members—somewhat over 20 percent—in holding 19 percent of the works council seats. By 1987, women had increased their numbers among council chairs to 23.2 percent of these offices. It is these chairs, particularly in the key firms of the industries, upon whom the unions call to participate in regional bargaining and as members of the bargaining advisory commissions. (See Table 4.) Since under the BVG councillors are entitled to released, paid time off for training during their three years in office, an increasingly competent group of women is emerging, not only in the councils, but also in the bargaining commissions as well. (See Chapter 4 on Trade Union Education.)

The British experience is also hopeful in this respect, particularly in the white-collar unions and sections, where the main trade union growth has taken place in the last decade. When it was still the white-collar section of AUEW, TASS bargained for the most part on a single plant or establishment level, through office committees. The national office sent out the word in the mid-1970s, "Office committees must ensure that women are present at negotiations, both to learn and to affect the outcome."

The General and Municipal Workers Union (GMWU), one of the three big British general unions and comprised mainly of blue-collar workers, engages in a considerable amount of job evaluation as an integral part of its wages program. Its manual, *Bargaining for Equality*, instructs its local to have women elected or appointed to serve on job evaluation teams.[25]

In the United States women have appeared as national presidents of five unions, two in the entertainment field where bargaining is mainly in the hands not of presidents but of executive secretaries and is carried on in a unique way with associations of agents and their artist clients. The Airline Flight Attendants (AFA) and the Retail, Wholesale, and Department Store Union (RWDSU) are two unions headed by women and using standard patterns of bargaining.[26] Other unions, mainly in the

25. GMWU, *Bargaining for Equality*, n.d.

26. For the history of women's bargaining in one of the major airlines, see Georgia Painter Nielsen, *From Skygirl to Flight Attendant*, 1982.

Table 4. Works council elections: Chairwomen elected by unions, 1978, 1981, 1984, 1987

	1978			1981			1984			1987		
	Plants	Chair-women	% women	Plants	Chair-women	% women	Plants	Chair-women	% women	Plants	Chair-women	% women
Chemistry, paper, ceramics	2,489	217	8.7	2,573	276	10.7	2,596	320	12.3	2,564	304	13.1
Commerce, banking, insurance	5,054	1,117	22.1	6,107	1,565	25.6	5,918	1,701	28.7	6,181	2,040	33.
Metal	10,528	361	3.4	10,158	442	4.3	9,877	469	4.8	10,181	605	5.9
Textiles	2,762	1,384	50.1	2,699	1,458	54.0	2,445	1,349	55.2	2,280	1,260	55.3
Total DGB	35,294	3,803	10.7	36,307	4,731	13.0	35,332	5,036	14.3	34,844	5,179	14.9

Source: Frauen und Arbeit, "40 Jahre Gewerkschaftliche Frauenarbeit," April 7, 1989, p. 25.

public sector, have begun to add women to their executive boards. To the extent that these women board members are responsible for women's affairs, they do not normally carry bargaining responsibility. (See Chapter 3.) An exception is the present head of the women's division of the United Automobile Workers (UAW) who, when she took that office, stipulated that she should retain her staff responsibility for bargaining in an industrial region as well. Because successful participation in bargaining is a major route to top union leadership, perhaps what is most needed to assist women in their advancement to such positions of power are affirmative action plans constructed on the principles used by German unions committed to positive action in behalf of women.

Grass Roots and Women's Place

Are women's issues finding a central place on union bargaining agendas? Is it important to have women doing the bargaining? Under what circumstances do they participate in bargaining? What progress has been made? Do European experiences offer American practices any usable models?

Issues

Evidence from official union pronouncements is available to show that at least union decision-makers are aware that women's issues deserve attention. This awareness is evident in provisions for child care and parental leave, and movements toward equal pay. Yet providing child care for working mothers is a response grounded in the still widely accepted view that children are the mother's chief, even sole, responsibility. When employers set up child-care programs, it is because they need women employees to do "women's work," or, in periods of business boom, they find women are desirable employees, in part because they are cheaper than men in scarce supply. On the whole, European employers and the unions see this problem, as they do many women's issues, as matters for government to deal with, rather than as subjects of collective bargaining. In the United States, the reverse is the case.

In this country, where the government has been particularly delinquent in dealing with child care and other matters affecting mother-and-child services, unions are under more pressure than in Europe to take up these issues in bargaining. The employers who have most often responded are the hospitals. Nurses must be on duty around the clock and in recent years have been a scarce commodity. Under these circumstances, employer-sponsored child care has been seen as a solution to finding and employing nurses in sufficient numbers.[27]

Union leaders who have espoused such programs have often had to face a divided membership. In the first group are those women who are past the child-bearing years and most men. In the second group are young parents and single women heads of families. Those in the first group prefer to have fringe benefits tailored to their needs rather than to those of young women whom they perceive as intermittent members of the labor force. Only about 600 American firms out of some 40,000 major employers have agreed to offer child care even as an alternative benefit, and some 400 of these are hospitals.

Equal pay (discussed in Chapter 5 in much greater detail) is also an issue that many individuals and unions see as properly within government purview, that is, as a problem for enforcement under the Equal Pay Act or Title VII of the Equal Employment Opportunity Act (EEOA). Moreover, the issue in its comparable worth form has been put forward almost exclusively in the sphere of government employment, particularly at local and state levels.[28] Under the pressure of women's organizations inside and outside the labor movement, major unions in the public sector have made it their paramount issue. Not only do they consistently bargain for its realization—though often under conditions that cut corners and take half a loaf—but also they have pursued cases in the courts, lobbied legislatures, conducted studies, employed expert consultants, and carried on educational campaigns among their own members on behalf of the pay equity goal. Part of the motivation has been the desire to recruit the many women in public employment to union membership and thus to increase their collective bargaining power generally. Under the present conservative swing in American politics, neither legislation nor judicial decisions can be counted on to support the goal of pay equity. Collective bargaining remains the most successful approach to its achievement, and many women members of these unions have worked for years to achieve the goal.

Women Bargainers

Do women bargainers make a difference? It is hard to say because there have been so few. Moreover, the economic system itself is in tran-

---

27. BNA, Special Report, *Work and Family*, 1986b. See particularly Chapter 4, "Case Studies," pp. 25–67.

28. For a full report on union initiatives in this area, see Alice H. Cook, *Comparable Worth: Experience in States and Localities*, 1985, and *Comparable Worth Supplement*, 1986.

sition, and the unions have had to work under conservative governments intent on limiting union powers.

Another factor is women's own assessment of how they can best enhance their positions within the unions. For example, where women are doing the bargaining in mixed unions, they are often reluctant or even averse to putting women's issues first. They feel compelled by their exposed position to do "as good a job as any man," and do it within the confines that a man would lay down for himself—the best that can be done for the majority of members, even at the price of abandoning women's issues. In a women's union, in contrast, taking the experience of the AFA or the ANA as models, women's issues become the paramount ones: in the case of the AFA, major concerns include eliminating discrimination against women who marry; issues related to pregnancy, age, and weight restrictions; opposition to the exploitation and commercialization of feminine behavior to placate customers;[29] and equal pay. In the case of ANA, the issues concern flexible schedules, part-time work, and child care.

Progress

It is clear that many unions now accept that more women should be in policy-making positions in the unions. The programs of these unions call for a variety of measures for finding and placing these women: reserved seats, training programs, persuading women to run for office, and affirmative action programs. Despite the nearly uniform support of top union leaders for increasing the numbers of women in official ranks, these views are all too often carried out with reluctance and even hostility at the local levels where women have to begin to gain leadership experience. Many male rank-and-filers are fearful that a new order of equality can endanger their own hard-won gains and status. They see what women achieve as something taken away from them—gender equality as a zero-sum game. If these views are as widespread as they seem to be, then the very place where women have made the most progress—in the local union organizations—may become a battlefield with the outcome of the struggle uncertain and in any case long-drawn-out.

Have women done better under centralized than local bargaining? In Sweden in certain respects, they have. In Austria, they clearly have not. In neither country are women on the executive boards and the central

29. See Arlie Hochschild, *The Managed Heart: Commercialization of Human Feeling*, 1983.

bargaining commissions. Women have gained in Sweden because Swedish public policy has been built on the welfare of the child. From this central concept have developed social policies that the unions accept. These policies focus on equal parental sharing of responsibility for children through parental leave and shorter working days. The policies accept part-time workers as legitimate participants in the labor force. The unions also accept social policy that requires treating each worker, regardless of sex, as an individual under tax, pension, and family law. Policies require that equality in the shop be analyzed and monitored by shop committees. Perhaps most important of all was a union/management commitment to a solidary wage policy to narrow the gap between low- and high-paid workers, regardless of gender (but since women are the majority of the low-paid, this is a significant benefit to women, with the result that they receive in earnings 80–90 percent as much as men).

Thus, it is not centralization that has benefited women, but a social policy that has placed child welfare at the center of national welfare and makes parents equally responsible for the nurturance of their children. This social policy is an equality policy widely but not invariably manifested both on the shop floor and in the home.

Measured by the situation twenty years ago, women have made progress throughout the Western world. The "woman question" is on the agenda not just of unions but of nations. For the most part, it is seen as a set of badly needed support systems for working mothers, who make up the vast majority of women in the work force: child care, maternity and parental leave, equal pay, equal employment opportunity, access to all kinds of jobs and to the training needed for each of them. A doctrine of equality has been accepted and largely legislated by governmental policymakers and given at least lip service by the institutions of the labor market—employers' and workers' organizations. Horizons have widened and brightened enormously. It is the slowness of the achievement of these goals that rankles. Barriers still exist; implementation is dilatory and inadequate; attitudes have changed only at the edges. Despite legislation and resolutions, women still have a long way to go.

Unions have not led the forward movement of the last two decades. Rather, they have adapted to the women's movement and the governmental and intergovernmental policies laid down by legislatures. Where these have slowed down or reversed goals through economic depression and conservative reaction, the unions with a few exceptions have slowed, too. The comparable worth movement in the United States and the affirmative action initiatives in Europe are the two greatest exceptions.

Model

European unions' experiences with internal affirmative action are unmatched in the United States, although our EEOA still serves as a model to them for improving employment equality. Many European women have come to the United States to study Title VII's influence and implementation here. (They tend to substitute the phrase "positive action" or "promotion of women" for "affirmative action.") Paradoxically, our EEOA serves as a model to Europeans although in many respects in this country it does not operate as "positively" for women as does the British Anti-Discrimination Act for women in Britain.

In addition, the task of the European unions is to some degree alleviated by the historic achievement of social legislation on national health, child welfare, maternity protection, and child care. The unions, placed within that statutory framework, have a shorter, more focused bargaining agenda. While the AFL–CIO has endorsed child care legislation, pay equity, and a parental leave bill, its weakened position in terms of membership and political power under national conservative leadership has left it less influential in attaining these ends than might have been the case in a less anti-union climate. In the United States, the major immediate hope for the attainment of women's goals must rest with the unions that represent large numbers of women workers. Yet, millions of unorganized women will only marginally profit from gains these unions may be able to make for their members. The effectiveness of collective bargaining to meet the needs of working women in the United States is limited by the weakness of the trade union movement in numbers, coverage, and influence.

CHAPTER FOUR

Union Education

Workers' education is the talent scout for the labor movement, as well as its working arm.

—Barbara M. Wertheimer

There is a need for a major review of the trade union education program to make the union aware that discrimination against women is a trade union issue requiring a trade union response.

—NALGO

Workers' education is the fundamental tool used by the ILO, in close cooperation with and support of . . . trade unions, to foster women workers' active participation in trade union life. It involves the twin objectives of creating among women workers awareness of their conditions and of their need to join trade unions, and of providing them with the necessary training to be able better to protect their interests, and to participate effectively in trade union activities and the conduct of their business.

—International Labour Conference, 71st session, 1985

The labor movements of Western countries took part in the struggle for universal free education for the young. In their own educational work, they have helped to expand the social, political, and cultural horizons of generations of workers. They have trained many men, and recently an increasing percentage of women, in the responsibilities of union rights and union duties.

In the life of the union, informal education and training accompany the formal. The informal arises from participation in union activities, ranging from meetings to collective bargaining and strike action. "To be active in the trade union movement means that one is constantly learning something new," reports the IGM recruitment brochure. The formal activities are those of the unions' own education departments, sometimes in cooperation with other institutions of learning or communications. The traditional structures of union education were established chiefly by men for men, rarely with the special needs of women and families in mind.[1]

Epigraphs: First from *Focus on Women Unionists,* 1975, p. 2; second from *Equal Rights Working Party Reports,* 1975, p. 32; third from Report 7, *Equal Opportunities and Equal Treatment for Men and Women in Employment,* 1985, pp. 90–91.
1. Many of the innovations in workers' education in the United States in the early days of the movement, just after World War I, as well as other innovations in the past decade,

European and American Labor Education Contrasted

The framework of European union education and that of the United States share similar ideals and experience similar difficulties in broadening access to training for women. There are, nonetheless, several characteristics of European union educational work that differ from those of the United States.

(1) European unions have utilized labor education, not only to train their officers and activists but also to encourage practice of "labor culture" through music, drama, and art. They have offered programs planned to broaden the understanding of economic and social developments, politics, and international issues among union members. Publications include discussions of theoretical questions and new studies from the trade union research centers. The scope of interest tends to be broader than in comparable American journals.

(2) Educational programs in Europe in the unions' schools are more structured than in most of ours. Courses generally follow a recognized order, beginning with the basic, through intermediate, to the most advanced or the most specialized knowledge.

(3) Unions in Europe stress residential programs far more than American unions do. Confederations and many of the strong national unions maintain their own residential schools. Most residential programs in the United States are sponsored by universities offering labor studies, in both credit and noncredit week-long courses.

(4) Under law or collective agreement, union activists in Europe are more apt to be entitled to educational leaves, usually without pay. Unions may cover these expenses.

(5) Governments in Europe give more direct aid to workers' education. One form of aid is financial assistance to union schools, workers' education associations, or youth schools offering certain recognized programs. Another form is the obligation by law that employers grant paid leaves for the training of such union-designated or elected workplace representatives as safety stewards, works councillors, and shop stewards. Most of these, including some who are not union members, nevertheless may receive training in union schools. Neither government aid nor employer-paid released time alter the unions' control of their own educational programs.

(6) Historical differences in class structures between Europe and the

---

have come from focusing labor education on women's needs. Many more are now in the planning stage. See Barbara M. Wertheimer, ed., *Labor Education for Women Workers: An International Comparison*, 1981; and Joyce Kornbluh and Mary Fredrickson, *Sisterhood and Solidarity: Workers' Education for Women, 1914–1984*, 1984.

United States are reflected in the role of universities. In Europe, during the years of union formation and growth, class barriers convinced unions to assume responsibility for training their own leaders and active members. Universities were open only to the graduates of elite secondary schools, while workers customarily left school at the end of a required seven, eight, or nine years of elementary schooling to enter apprenticeships or go to work as unskilled laborers. At the turn of the century, Ruskin College was established at Oxford University as a center for trade unionists and Labour party leaders. In 1921 the German unions established the Academy of Labor at Frankfurt University (later followed by two other such university-level training centers at other universities). In the United States workers' education, at least since World War II, has been included largely as one of many extension programs offered by the state and some private universities, in both credit and noncredit programs.

Structures of Union Training Programs

Most union training, in each of the four European countries we studied, is aimed at newly elected or incumbent shop stewards and activists. Basic training stresses the history and practice of trade unionism, important aspects of collective bargaining, industrial relations law, social security law, and protective labor legislation. This training is offered at three or even four levels, beginning with short courses in the locality or workplace, then more advanced regional weekend or several day-long courses, and finally still more advanced or specialized courses of one to six weeks in residential schools maintained by national unions or confederations. Ruskin College and the German academies offer one- and two-year programs.

Even at the first level, much of the content of union officers' training comes from syllabi prepared by national union or confederation education departments. These may also certify and contribute to the payment of local teachers. Regional and national schools are usually entirely in the hands of the national union. Centralized education is characteristic of Germany, Sweden, and Austria—all countries with more centralized bargaining and higher percentages of organized workers than is the case in the United States or the United Kingdom.[2] National unions

2. This refers to union density; the proportion of organized workers in the total work force has declined in Germany and England though by no means as sharply as in the United States. With the exception of England, where, as in the United States, a conservative government has joined employers in fighting unions, labor organizations in Germany,

and confederations staff their residential colleges well and equip them handsomely.

The British unions' educational structures are rather fragmented, as compared with the three continental labor movements, but less fragmented than British collective bargaining. National unions and the TUC function on very modest dues, which have lagged far behind price increases. Hence they have fewer full-time staff and fewer officers (in proportion to membership) for educational work, internal administration, and collective bargaining. Consequently, they are able to train smaller proportions of their work-place representatives and their officers than do their European counterparts.

Unions in Britain rely heavily upon the facilities and staffs of the polytechnic institutes (somewhat comparable to U.S. community colleges), upon the Workers' Educational Association operating as extramural branches of many universities, and upon some of the adult education residential schools.

The TUC, however, is gradually strengthening its educational structure to meet the challenge of the numerous new tasks in bargaining, safety and health, and private pension fund administration. It envisions a systematic course structure for union representatives in which training would move from fifteen-hour introductory coursework at local facilities, to the most advanced or specialized residential courses of up to six weeks. These forms of training constitute an objective for negotiation of agreements, allowing released time for union representatives to attend these programs at employers' expense.

A framework is already in place (Table 5) in the TUC, the national unions, and regional and local union bodies. Though the model when adopted in 1978 had to remain a "middle term plan" pending the generation of expected agreements with (mostly local-level) employers, it presents a summary picture of the British movement's general structure of officer training.

Unions in both Sweden and Britain for generations have stressed their independence from state action (except for a few special issues that called for legislation). The unions financed their education programs out of their dues income, with the aid of some volunteers and of the respective workers' education associations. In the past twenty years, unions in Sweden, Germany, Austria, and Britain have turned to legislation when it could expand the scope of collective bargaining and guarantee protection of their members and organizations in the workplace. Their ex-

---

Austria, and Sweden, as more widely throughout Europe, are accepted and trusted elements in national society.

Table 5. Trades Union Congress (Great Britain): System of courses for union representatives

	Stage 1	Stage 2	Stage 3	Stage 4
	Induction	Basic introductory	Further training	Advanced training
For whom?	Newly-elected shop stewards, staff representatives, safety representatives.		Representatives with special responsibilities: senior stewards, pension fund trustees, safety stewards, members of company boards. Updating for all representatives as new needs arise.	Key representatives, mostly as in stage 3.
How long?	15 hours at least.	10 days at least.	10-day courses.	Longer courses, up to 6 weeks.
Where?	In plant, union district office, union college, or educational institution.			Normally at residential schools.
What subjects?	Union officer roles; collective bargaining, agreements, and grievance procedures.	More systematic study of stage 1 topics; employment and job security laws and rights; new developments in industrial relations.	Union or TUC modular courses on rights at work (new legislation), health and safety, work study and job evaluation, company pensions.	Wider trade union, industrial, economic, social, and political studies.
Who teaches?	Conducted by union officers or senior shop stewards.	Union courses or TUC courses, latter offered by local college, WEA, or university extension department.	Union or TUC modular courses, tailored for some unions	
When?	As soon as possible after representative's election.	Within a year of taking office. As soon as possible for officials already in office who have not yet had such training.	At least 3 courses within 3 years. As soon as possible for those meeting new needs.	As required.

Source: Based on TUC, *Paid Release for Union Training: A TUC Guide* (c. 1978), pp. 14–17. Used with the permission of the Trades Union Congress.

panded training programs have relied to some degree on both government and employer contributions while the selection of students and teachers and the control of curriculum remains in union hands.

The unions' budgets still cover much of the cost of their resident facilities, the expenses of administration, the preparation of teaching materials, and the teachers' salaries. The unions compensate workplace representatives for loss of earnings where employers or governments do not do so, and they cover the costs of training their own full-time staff.

Government financial aid has not weakened the unions' willingness to use their own dues income for education; on the contrary. In the nation where government has given least, in Britain, the unions' outlay (in proportion to membership) has been least adequate. Where the government has given most, in Sweden, the unions' outlay has been largest.

The British labor movement, in building its case for more government support, has begun to use an argument that the Swedish movement has already used with success (though in dealing with a more friendly government than British unions have had to face): governments everywhere spend far more for management education in universities and polytechnic schools than they do for workers' education and union officers' training.

Barriers to Women's Participation

Barriers to educational opportunity for women continuously come from fellow workers, used to thinking of women as not belonging in male-dominated trades, resentful of their presence, and fearful of the low-wage competition they may offer. Barriers also come from employers who are reluctant to place women outside the jobs commonly designated as "women's work" and who resist women's issues in union disputes and negotiations. Barriers also are built by women themselves. Many women still assume that union affairs and leadership are best left to men, who have managed these functions since the unions were founded. As relatively new members of the labor force, they are keenly aware of their lack of experience and that they occupy low-status jobs in the plant or office. Much of this attitude is the result of the prejudice and indifference of male gatekeepers in providing opportunity for women at union schools. Many married women, moreover, still cannot escape the everyday obligations of family, work, and child care as they enter the paid labor force. Moreover, some are wives of possessive husbands unwilling to see their women go off to an evening class or residential school program that men attend.

In all of these countries women, nevertheless, have been joining unions at higher rates than men. Some have joined out of conviction. Others have become members as a result of peer pressure; such members—male or female—are a special challenge to union education. Some women come from ethnic minorities without union traditions and at the edge of poverty, resentful and uncomfortable in the presence of the native majority; resentful, too, of having to pay dues with no representation in the union's power structure.

In short, many women who are in unions are conscious of having less experience, power, and seniority than men. At the same time they are unsure how to attain and develop the qualities that might enable them to attain equity. At home, they have less free, uninterrupted time than men have to read the union publications that might inform them on social and economic issues. At best these women are passive members. When they come to union meetings, they hesitate to speak, especially on controversial issues or on matters they see as outside their experience. Education secretaries rarely see such members as likely candidates for leadership training; they are looking to train activists for leadership.

Even when urged to apply for educational programs, many women hesitate simply because the pressures from home and workplace outweigh any benefits they can foresee as results of the sacrifice in time and effort that an education program implies. They need not only information but also active support. In addition, some of these women report that their applications, once made, have been rejected or lost in a maze of bureaucracy and prejudice.

For the very reasons, then, that women have a greater need than men for training, they are less likely to get it. More than men they have to search if they are to discover union education. Fortunately, in a number of unions that we observed, union education is trying to discover them.

Some Remedies for Neglect

Affirmative Action in Recruitment

Some unions have long had a tradition of choosing a few women for their training courses under the "ten-percent rule." With rising proportions of women members, such a percentage has become clearly discriminatory: not a concession, but a restriction.

A number of unions are taking affirmative action. In Britain the Sex Discrimination Act permits unions and employers to discriminate in training programs in favor of the underrepresented sex. Nevertheless, it remains a problem for women to be nominated at the local or regional level. The union with the largest female membership in Britain has reversed the rules it had been using to select candidates for residential schools, namely to accept students only if their names were proposed by local and regional offices. Instead, it now gives preference to those of either gender who have had no training, or at least no recent training. A national union office with such a commitment to equality can in this way open training opportunities to the very persons who under normal selection procedures might be overlooked. In such unions, education agencies operate as the preparation centers for potential union leaders.

Broadening channels of information is another way of recruiting more women into education programs. Our interviews with women unionists in each country found many of them eager to participate in programs but unaware of existing possibilities. We also found several examples of successful union efforts to direct information to women.

In England, for instance, we observed a manual workers' union regional weekend school in which women were vastly overrepresented. In the past the central office had notified only the chief stewards of plants about upcoming education programs. This time the regional education officer had sent special notices to women and gone personally from plant to plant promoting the course. Women responded despite the problems of child and husband care. Some used their vacation time to attend.

One education secretary, at the suggestion of a woman member, sent his description of correspondence courses directly to women tied to home and family. Within a few weeks hundreds of applications flowed in from them.

The women's divisions of the two largest unions in Austria developed a telephone network—their own hot line—for communication with women in the shops. As the union offers new courses, phone calls go out to women works councillors and union representatives from Graz to Linz, Klagenfurt to Wiener Neustadt. These local leaders then begin to prepare women candidates for the courses that best meet their needs, often long before news filters down through the official hierarchy.

Child Care at Union Functions

Child care is often the key not only to women's working but also to women's studying. Particularly at residential schools, but to a considerable degree at local schools, the existence of child care may determine women's attendance or absence. The life-cycle squeeze works against women's union training and careers just as it works against their chances for on-the-job training and promotion in factory or office. Union schools can be filled with men in their late twenties and early thirties, whose wives (at home) are in their childbearing and childrearing years. Most women in union schools are childless or mothers of children nearly or already in their teens.[3] They waited ten to twelve years longer than their male coworkers for recognition and training. Experimental provision of child-care facilities at LO residential schools as early as the 1960s produced a marked drop in the average age of women attending, compared to those at schools without such facilities.[4]

Unions and their male members who have been supportive of day-care during their own and their wives' working hours have been slow to see the need for it in union life.[5] Several German and Swedish unions provide cash baby-sitting grants to participants with children under school age. The German white-collar union, DAG, arranged for parents participating in union courses to place their children in a nearby kindergarten. The Swedish retail and wholesale employees' union, Handels, has a majority of women members and introduced child care at one of its schools in 1977. One of the LO schools offers a summer course for families.

Similarly, several German unions have experimented with "family seminars," to which wife, husband, and sometimes children are invited. Some of these seminars try to educate all members of the family on the aims of unions and the family implications of women's work.

3. A Swedish study of 1,073 participants in programs at four union schools showed that 50 percent of the women attending had no children, while only 35 percent of the men were childless. Of the women with children, 50 percent had children over eleven years of age, but 56 percent of the men had children under six years of age. While most men were fathers of young children, the women either were single or had put off attending until their children were able to some degree to take care of themselves.

4. In 1977 the Brunsvik school surveyed eighteen months of parents' experience in bringing children to the school. Many had done so at first with deep misgivings. Afterward, all were enthusiastic, with a single exception. The children's presence, they said, had pulled parents with children together with childless adults into closer relationships. The childless helped parents during recreation breaks and evenings; drinking declined. Parents said that if they came again they would gladly bring their children. The DGB has offered such courses, sponsored by the women's division, since 1977.

5. The German unions' women's division journal, *Frauen und Arbeit*, reported in 1985: "Since 1984 the demand of parents and especially of single mothers and fathers was responded to. Now at each Federation School one course each year is set up and offered with provisions for child care. This offering is extended in 1985 to a total of 14 courses (additional to the two courses for women only)." A list of the courses where child care is available follows (August 1985, p. ii).

Decentralization

All such opportunities are of no use to women who cannot leave husband, children, or an infirm relative to attend a residential school. Recognizing such barriers, unions in Austria and Sweden have been decentralizing advanced courses from residential to local or nearby regional schools so that participants may attend without having to leave home. This mix of local and residential schools is less costly and more flexible than the older separation of function which, while useful, did not facilitate women's participation. Even short courses in a local setting may be hard for some women to attend after work hours. It is always part-time workers and young mothers who are at the greatest disadvantage.

The Austrian textile union reorganized course content in a way that allows it to bring education programs closer to its members. It decentralized teaching by restructuring the material presented in long and intensive residential programs into shorter modules so that they could be offered in weekend or other short local programs.

The combination of new demands and limited residential facilities may call for even further decentralization. The LO saw the need in 1977 to train about 50,000 new shop stewards and other workplace and company-wide representatives every year. Only about 10 percent of this number could possibly find places at existing residential centers. Local courses were imperative for this reason alone, but local courses would also attract women more readily. Decentralization soon became such a central point in LO planning that the residential colleges came to be used mainly for training teachers and group leaders for such new programs as health and safety, while the programs themselves were conducted locally.

While local groups profit from the resulting autonomy, problems have arisen both in Sweden and Britain when local groups want to choose the subjects of their courses. Swedish metalworkers found that some of their local study circles were indulging in a kind of dilettantism or faddism in these choices. As a result, "many of the union members who went on to the residential courses lacked the previous knowledge and study routine."[6] British TASS leaders faced this problem as well. The positive side of local initiative is illustrated in the experience of a textile local union in Bielefeld, Germany. The union's women's group orga-

6. Birger Viklund, "Education for Industrial Democracy," *Current Sweden*, no. 152 (March 1977), p. 4.

nized a support network to enable women to get to midweek and weekend courses. Retired women members provided transportation and child care for mothers of young children. One of our team, riding in such a car pool, heard the driver give young women her vivid recollections of her own and her mother's part in women's struggles for union recognition in the factory where the young women were now employed. The car pool and the child-care network, in which old and young women joined, maintained this union's vitality in an economically ailing plant.

Central services may do much to remedy diffusion of effort in choice of subjects. To assure that students in residential courses arrived with a common background for advanced work, the Swedish metalworkers' educational department provided local courses with complete packages of the basic study-circle materials, while encouraging local leaders to modify it in the light of local conditions.

Teaching Methods

Among the changes and experiments in Europe of special interest to women, in addition to the decentralization of programs just discussed, are the democratization of classroom style, the modernization of correspondence courses, and the use of television.

While many union educational programs are as formal as the academic lecture, others rely heavily on small groups in study circles. Indeed in Sweden, the study circle is the means by which all manner of organizations, from the church to the political parties, reach their grass roots. Unions may have as many as 10,000 study circles functioning at any one time.[7] The Swedish unions stress democratic methods of teaching. Their basic position was laid down by the 1976 LO congress:

> Studies based on learning through cooperation give social training and stimulate democratic activity. The teacher becomes a resource person for small working groups and four-fifths of LO courses take place in these small groups. . . . Adult students bring special resources to their studies. . . . [They] come with concrete experience of the need for change. Therefore, they do not study only what has been achieved, but also what it is possible to achieve.[8]

7. For a discussion of Swedish methods of reaching the rank-and-file, see Norman Eiger, "Labor Education and Democracy in the Workplace," *Working Life in Sweden*, no. 22 (April 1981), pp. 7–8.

8. LO, *Education—Preparing for Work and Democracy: Report to the 1976 Congress of the Swedish Trade Union Confederation, Summary*, 1976a, pp. 12–13.

Central Europe was long one of the world's historic shapers of re-
pressive authority patterns. Yet, in a residential school of the German
metalworkers we observed teaching sessions that departed radically from
these old patterns. Students remained in large, introductory sessions for
only a day or two; then they began to work in groups of four, five, or
six. The teacher's knowledge was an important resource but only one
among many. Students drew on their work experience and supple-
mented it with library research and with fieldwork in the community.

The Workers' Educational Association (WEA), founded in Britain in
1903, began by encouraging students to select their own tutors and
construct their own course plans. Discussions centered on student experience and moved from the known to the less known and from specific experience to social generalization. Its founder wrote that "[p]erhaps
the principle which gave most life and vigor to the classes was that each
student was held to be a teacher, and each teacher held to be a student.
A tutorial class consisted of thirty-one teachers and thirty-one students." [9]

Correspondence courses in union education have been used more in
Europe than in America. While these programs are no longer a large
element in the union's education menu, several unions have reviewed
the contents of their courses with women's needs in mind. One such
innovation combined the Swedish practice of setting up study circles
with provision of discussion materials in correspondence course instruction. A British union with a majority of women members, most of them
with minimal formal education, has established such pilot programs.
Small groups of students discuss the study guides and questions and
then write individual answers. Persons interviewed at such a program
expressed confidence in this approach, believing that they learned more
than they could have done in isolation.

Another approach to worker education is narrow-casting. In the three
years between 1975 and 1978, the TUC sponsored the "Multi-Media
Study Project with BBC." It consisted of thirty half-hour television programs developed in close argumentative and yet effective collaboration
among representatives of TUC, WEA, and the broadcasting company.
Participating unionists could receive course credits in one of three ways:
by completing the correspondence course materials, which included study
books for each year's series; by attending TUC-sponsored day-released-

9. Albert Mansbridge, *An Adventure in Working-Class Education,* 1920. The WEA is
not a trade union institution but an independent organization. Its students are no longer
all workers. It offers the elements of a liberal adult education rather than training for
union functions. Its long experience in workers' education has provided models in teaching methods for the union programs that have followed.

time classes of the WEA; or by forming their own study circles to watch the programs and work over the discussion questions. Video-cassette recorders permitted discussion groups to meet at their own convenience, unconstrained by the normal broadcasting times, which were Sunday mornings at 9:45 and Wednesday evenings at 7:05.

First-year programs were devoted to the topic of trade union issues at the workplace. Gender equality in the workplace and the union rated the longest chapter in the study guide. Second-year programs were devoted to the topic of trade unions and the economy. Although this series required more reading and study of abstract materials, its study guide was lively.

The first two years' experience persuaded the sponsors to drop plans projected for the third year under the title "Trade Unions and Society." Instead, they returned to practical workplace issues under the heading "Democracy at Work." The issues selected for study included history of collective bargaining, safety and health organization, work satisfaction and dissatisfaction, company pension plans, and democracy within the union itself. A section called "Sisters and Brothers" took up women's problems with promotion, nursery facilities, and bargaining for improvements in statutory maternity leaves.[10] Recognizing that many of their audience would not normally think of television as a tool for serious learning, the authors of the study guide provided a number of practical tips on systematic study at home.

Experience with this program produced its lessons. One was the importance of strengthening face-to-face discussion groups. The third year's publicity urged union members to establish self-help groups in their union branches and workplaces. Over half the participants in the first two years of programming said that the series had led to discussions with other members and union representatives, with full-time officials and with management. "In many cases, particularly with less experienced trade unionists, this reflected a growth in confidence, which was often fragile and which depended for its development on the support of other active trade unionists."[11]

American concern with teaching methods in workers' education owes a great deal to the women's summer schools of the 1920s and 1930s, and to the programs of the Affiliated Schools for Workers, their umbrella and successor organization. Teaching methods have remained an

10. Tony Matthews, *Trade Union Studies: A Partnership in Adult Education between the BBC, the TUC, and the WEA,* 1978. This booklet is unusual in the informative candor with which it discusses difficulties organizers encountered, as well as lessons they learned in innovation and achievement.

11. Ibid., p. 26.

ongoing concern of the present University and College Labor Education
Association (UCLEA) and particularly of its committee on programs for
union women.[12]

In the United States, concern with teaching methods in labor education has been more active among the men and women directing university programs in labor education than among education directors in the
unions. The close relationship between these two branches of labor education has allowed, however, for considerable interorganizational discussion, jointly sponsored by the education department of the AFL–
CIO and the UCLEA. Over many years, a continuing flow of American
labor educators has visited both Sweden and England for observation
and study in the adult education centers and union schools of those
countries, with resulting enrichment of programs.[13]

Educational Leaves: A New Right for Labor

Educational leave and training on paid released time or during working hours offer a complex and far-reaching pattern of employee rights
that have grown up in many European countries, including all four of
those we studied.

Two types of leave are involved, both of importance to women. One
is initiated by individuals for their own instruction and satisfaction. This
type rarely includes any right to replacement of lost earnings. The second is more widespread and usually qualifies for reimbursement. This
type involves the right to leave for training in industrial relations or
health-and-safety training. The right is typically attached to an office
that individuals hold: shop steward, works councillor, member of joint
safety committees, or representative of special categories of employ-

12. On methods, see particularly the first two sections of Barbara M. Wertheimer, ed.,
1981. On the Affiliated Schools, see Doris Cohen Brody, "American Labor Education
Service, 1927–1962: An Organization in Workers' Education," Ph.D. diss., Cornell University, 1975. For studies of the individual summer schools for women workers, the WPA
programs, and current union programs for women, see Kornbluh and Fredrickson, 1984.
For contrasts and continuities in methods, see the transcript of a 1981 discussion among
four teachers in the early women's schools as their experiences relate to current issues
and problems in union women's education (ibid., "Memories of a Movement," pp. 325–
42). For ongoing programs for women, see the regular reports of the Committee on Programs for Union Women in UCLEA's *Labor Studies Journal*.
13. Among these are Eiger, 1981 (Sweden); Al Nash, *Ruskin College: A Challenge to
Adult Education*, 1981; Alice H. Cook and Roberta Till-Retz, "Labor Education and
Women Workers: An International Comparison," in Wertheimer, ed., 1981; Robin Miller
Jacoby, "The British and American Women's Trade Union Leagues, 1890–1925," Ph.D.
diss., Harvard University, 1977.

ees—women, youth, or migrant workers. Entitlement to paid educational leave arises from the functions these officers have been elected or selected to perform, or from educational or employment disadvantage. Their training is their duty as well as their right. Paid educational leave is a benefit that derives primarily from the right of fellow employees in shop or office to be represented by men and women with specific knowledge and skills that enable them to perform their functions. Such leave is the product of continuing union demands won through collective bargaining or legislation.

Governments and management in Europe, with exceptions chiefly in smaller enterprises, have widely accepted the need of paid leave for training. In their view, union negotiations and labor participation in shop government will proceed more correctly and expeditiously if worker representatives understand labor law, health and safety requirements, and collective bargaining practice.

Germany and Austria led the way with laws requiring the training of works councillors. (See Chapter 3, "Collective Bargaining.") While not all councillors are union members, the vast majority are union activists. German national legislation grants them three weeks of educational leave during their three-year terms, with four weeks for newly elected councillors. Although management-sponsored schools offer such training as well as the trade union institutions, most councillors attend union schools.

Austrian councillors are entitled by law to two weeks' paid leave during a three-year term, but with easily arranged extensions. There, most training is in the schools of the union-oriented Chambers of Labor, a unique Austrian institution.[14]

A British law requires employers to grant paid released time to officers of all recognized unions for training in industrial relations functions. The training course must be approved either by the TUC or the union in question.

In Sweden, released-time training is available for employee representatives at higher echelons as well as for those in the workplace. These include representatives on company boards of directors and on company pension fund boards. Health and safety now pose the most chal-

---

14. The Chamber of Labor was established to parallel the Chamber of Commerce. In Austria neither is a private institution. Under law, the Chambers of Labor are employer-financed by a very small payroll tax on every employee. With this income they run schools for labor education and vocational training, provide homes for apprentices, and maintain libraries and research staffs on labor law and working conditions. The Chambers of labor exist in each province and at the national capital, Vienna, and operate in the wide dissemination of labor market information, not unlike the U.S. Department of Labor, Women's Bureau.

lenge to unions for training. In Sweden and Britain, employers are required by law to give paid leave for the training of health and safety representatives named by the unions. In Germany and Austria, employers must do so for works councillors whose duties include health and safety. In Sweden, as many as 85,000 safety representatives may be trained per year. The unions are the chief training agent; materials are prepared, however, by joint union-employer committees.

The first and chief claimant upon union resources for education almost everywhere is the training of officers and workplace representatives not entitled to paid leaves. In Britain the TUC sees little possibility of reaching substantial numbers of these rank-and-file workers.[15] Inquiries show that the workers who take courses in their spare time are chiefly those with better education and higher occupational status, not those in routine manual, clerical, and service jobs, where women are concentrated. Moreover, the educational handicaps confronting lower-class workers and women are cumulative throughout life, so that today's older women and men have greater needs for formal education than their young coworkers.

With these considerations of workers' increasing need for education gaining recognition, the ILO in 1974 adopted Convention no. 140 on paid educational leave. As the Convention and its accompanying recommendation state:

> Paid educational leave shall be available to all workers without any discrimination. (Art. 8,1)

> The term "paid educational leave" means leave granted to workers for educational purposes for a specified period during working hours, with adequate financial entitlements. (Art. 1)

> With a view to facilitating the continuing extension and adaptation of the knowledge and occupational skills of workers and as an investment in the interest of workers, employers, and the community as a whole, each member shall formulate and apply a policy designed to promote, by methods appropriate to national conditions and practice and by stages as necessary, the granting of paid educational leave for the purpose of—

15. "A real increase in opportunities for working adults will take place only with an increase in the right to paid educational leave. Without such leaves, workers can only carry on some of the lifelong education in their spare time, that is especially vital to those who leave school at the minimum school-leaving age. Without general rights to paid leaves, most post-school education and training . . . will always be cornered by those who know what is good for them and how to get it. The first step must be a greater public understanding of the gross imbalance in opportunities between the educational 'haves' and 'havenots' " (TUC, *Trades Union Congress Report,* 1978, pp. 184, 189).

a) training at any level;
b) general, social, or civic education;
c) trade union education.[16]

In Germany, ratification of the Convention produced no results at the federal level, but five of the eleven provinces *(Laender)* adopted laws for short paid leaves for general education, political, or trade union studies.[17]

The importance of union action in helping workers to use educational leave provisions is illustrated by the operation of the collective agreements in one branch of the women's underwear industry in Germany. Employer payments of one percent of payrolls since 1964 have financed a union center for education, leisure, and convalescence. Union members in this industry are generally workers of low skills, most of them women—the very groups that generally make least use of provisions for further education. Introductory classes "reintroduce participants to learning processes and to a group exploration of political and economic subjects," and provide an unusual long-term program of study alternating with employment, all distinguished by a "low pressure approach."[18]

The nation that has done most to make study leave possible is Sweden. The definition of what constitutes a study program is very broad. Legislation gives employees in private and public employment the right to study leaves for as long as their educational programs demand. While the law does not specify paid leaves, considerable public financial aid is available, especially for participants in priority programs. These include programs for immigrants, people suffering from lack of early schooling, handicapped workers, those on shift work at unsocial hours, and those working under conditions of great mental and physical stress. Leaves may be taken in installments, with the proviso that they not unduly interrupt operations. Employees have the right to return to the same job or one equivalent to it. If they interrupt their studies, they may return sooner than their original notification to the employer.

16. ILO, *Report IV (2)*, "Paid Educational Leave: Proposed Texts," 59th Session, International Labour Conference, 1974b.

17. Of the countries with which we are concerned, Germany, Sweden, and the United Kingdom ratified Convention 140 in November 1976, September 1975, and April 1975, respectively. The United States, in its comment following the 1973 discussion of the Convention, responded to the ILO that "[it did] not favor the adoption of a Convention, considering that too little is known about the economic and social implications of paid educational leave to warrant the adoption of a binding instrument" (ibid., p. 8).

18. Konrad von Moltke and Norbert Schneevoigt, *Educational Leaves for Employees*, 1977, pp. 101–2.

Trade Union Outreach: The Swedish Model

Since the Swedish unions probably are more successful than any others in reaching a high percentage of their membership with their educational programs, it is useful to have a more complete picture of their organization and financing. Both manual workers' and white-collar unions have developed positions for "trade union study organizers" designated as "education representatives," who come from the groups whose members they try to reach. They may take paid leave for their own training, which is financed through both LO and TCO federations using government aid. Their function is to acquaint fellow workers with study leave possibilities. People in priority categories may receive financial aid to participate in courses of their choice.

The Swedish union action—"pragmatic and missionary at the same time"—was directed first to immigrants, who make up about 10 percent of LO members.[19] Their efforts were directed not only to workers in the shops but to their wives at home. After the breakdown in negotiations for a collective bargaining agreement on the subject, the unions obtained a 1973 law giving immigrants the right to 240 employer-paid working hours of instruction in the Swedish language and information on Swedish society and unions. Representatives called upon the women of immigrant families to discuss with them general study courses to help them understand Swedish society and learn Swedish.

Many union members may also attend study circles of such allied organizations as the Workers' Educational Association (ABF), the Social Democratic party, the social-democratic consumer cooperative movement, while the People's High Schools throughout the country are often available for short residential sessions in nearby localities.[20] In the early 1980s, LO reported that some 17 percent of their members participated in some form of trade union education, of whom 12 percent were in courses both residential and external at the People's High Schools. About 1 percent attend centrally organized residential courses of a week or longer at one of LO's six residential colleges. The white-collar unions of TCO likewise have active, widely available educational programs.

19. Ibid., p. 121.
20. These residential schools, first organized for young people from farm families in the late nineteenth century, operated chiefly in the long Swedish winters to augment their often minimal education. Some adapted also to the needs and interests of urban young people, and many now function year-round. They may be sponsored by any of the Swedish interest groups and associations from religious to secular and from right to left politically. Many are available to local trade union groups for short sessions. The term "high school" is a literal translation from the Swedish. They are in fact adult education centers for persons of all ages seeking residential instruction in a wide variety of subjects.

Financing comes from many sources: the unions' own funds, national and local government grants, and employer contributions as provided for in collective agreements. A source of funds unique to Sweden is the adult education levy paid by employers to the national government, equal to about 0.25 percent of payrolls, funds that are, as LO observes, "money that the unions have refrained from taking out in pay claims at pay negotiations." According to LO, finance for trade union education and training should derive from production. The Swedish trade union movement regards it as evident that trade union education should be seen as part of the cost of production.[21]

In the early 1980s LO's goal was to provide twenty-hour introductory courses in trade unionism on paid leave for all workers as they start their wage-earning lives. One union, Kommunal, the organization of blue-collar workers in public employment with an 80 percent majority of women members, had already in 1975 introduced such a requirement, though without paid leave. Over 30,000 new members took courses that year in the basics of trade unionism, despite the fact that many were part-time workers.

One of the most intensive forms of grass-roots consultation and education is the "remand" method of LO and TCO as well as other Swedish labor and political organizations. (The method is sometimes called in English by its Swedish name, the "remiss.") Remand involves reaching thousands of members in small study groups and sometimes, later, in regional conferences with informative materials and specific questions related to a single, major issue on which the organization is developing its position. Thus, in the LO remand on the pending national occupational health and safety bill in 1973, over 85,000 members expressed their views and brought about a major change in the draft law enacted the following year. An LO remand may center on preparation for a convention debate or on the public debate of a major issue significant for the labor movement.

Kommunal uses the remand to prepare for its bargaining. It holds conferences of members on the pending issues, before, during, and after these nationwide negotiations. These meetings provide a forum for members' discussion of issues uppermost on the list of demands, as well as for ratification of any package of issues submitted for discussion.

To be sure, critics from right and left see such activities as mere brainwashing by the union. While we were in no position to form or offer a general evaluation, we were impressed with the way criticism from within the metalworkers' union was handled. Gøran Palm worked

21. LO, *Trade Union Education in Sweden,* 1979, pp. 29, 32.

for a year as an hourly-paid operative in various assembly sections of the big L. M. Ericsson plant in Stockholm. His books criticized both employers and his union for what he saw as an inhuman organization of work.[22] The union responded in a series of articles in its national journal, after which many locals asked Palm to lead discussions of his views. Both LO and TCO local bodies presented reports to their conventions in which they took up Palm's observations on the content and meaning of work and the need for the union to insist on its more democratic and humane organization.

Women's Courses

Many unions offer separate courses for women at the introductory level. The reason often given for doing so is that women new to the union movement and its ways of functioning are reluctant to meet with men, who, they anticipate, will outnumber and outclass them in terms of the union experience they will bring to a discussion. Many of the arguments for special women's structures within the union are repeated in the education context. (See "Women in Union Structures," Chapter 2.)

Although the Swedish unions decided in the early 1970s to abandon in the name of equality their women's divisions and special classes for women, we nevertheless found women meeting together in nearly all of the unions and shops we visited. Some meetings were initiated by women shop leaders, others by women members, and both were tolerated but not strongly supported by skeptical local male leaders.

In most countries, women's courses are part of the regular design of the education program. The women's courses seem to serve four functions: induction of the inexperienced; members' exposure to female role models; their mobilization as pressure groups for equality; and reassurance for possessive husbands. The courses help women overcome shyness in working in organizations steeped in male custom. At their induction stage, women seem to find an all-female atmosphere more supportive and less competitive than that found in mixed classes.

In the metalworkers club at the ball-bearing plant in Gothenburg, women numbered seven hundred, or one-fifth of the total membership. We were told that earlier only one woman was enrolled in the union's

22. Gøran Palm's two Swedish books appeared in 1972 and 1974. The English translation of one of them, *Flight from Work*, appeared in 1977.

study circles, despite attempts of the local education officer to recruit others. When, however, he offered two courses for women only, each enrolled some fifty members.

It is the A-level courses which usually are organized for women alone. Some unions have started courses for new women officers with several sessions in which the women meet alone, and then join men for the remainder of the course in mixed sessions. Most of the women are reported to make the transition without difficulty.

Many women's courses are taught by women staff members or officers. Consequently, women may meet more female officials of their union in this way than they would in mixed courses. These women teachers may be role models as well, inspiring some of the participants to think of union careers for themselves.

Women's courses may focus and inform members on issues within the union, on collective bargaining demands, and on equality issues in the larger society. In Britain, the white-collar unit of AEUW, TASS, used women's courses to mobilize support for union-wide acceptance of the concept of equal pay for work of equal value. After courses on equal pay, women in all regions succeeded in swinging the large male majority of TASS to give their demand high priority in local bargaining throughout the country.

In Austria and Germany, women's courses have helped inform and mobilize unionists in campaigns for more vocational training opportunities, expanded maternity benefits, equality in pension rights, and marriage law reform. On such issues, union women have been among the best informed and most influential lobbyists in the provincial and national legislatures.

Women's courses may also be an effective way of overcoming the objections of possessive husbands to their wives' attendance at mixed residential or even mixed local evening schools. At one course we attended in Britain, the women were so enthusiastic that the education officer asked why they had not attended other courses. Almost with one voice came the doleful answer, "Our husbands!"

In the United States, where the women's movement has had more power and prominence than in many European countries, there has been little controversy and broad acceptance among trade union women about special programs for women. Sponsored, or at least encouraged, in many locations by the Coalition of Labor Union Women and taken up by many university labor education centers, a broad variety of programs for women has been developed. Such programs were spurred by a study that Anne Nelson and Barbara Wertheimer did in the 1970s of women

in New York City local unions.[23] The findings showed clearly that women
were insufficiently represented among union officials even in locals where
they made up the majority of members. It showed further that little
attention was paid to their issues or their needs in education programs.
The result was the establishment of an education program for women
trade unionists at Cornell University's Extension Center in Industrial
and Labor Relations in New York City. A labor advisory committee
worked with the authors/educators in shaping its content; the Ford
Foundation made a substantial grant to establish the Institute for Education and Research on Working Women as an ongoing part of the
Center's program. The institute continues to flourish.

Similarly, at much the same time, Pennsylvania State University, the
University of Michigan, and the University of Connecticut, among others, set up comparable programs that, through UCLEA and its committee on programs for union women, have held a series of regional summer schools annually for trade union women throughout the country.
A 1980's Cornell University program trained minority women for union
leadership. Courses in this program, organized both as evening classes
and as summer residential schools, have included women who now occupy top positions in many large local, regional, and even national labor unions.

Women's courses raise two related but different issues: (1) whether
mixed or separate courses provide the best educational atmosphere for
women; and (2) whether their interests and needs call for study on the
same topics as those laid down in the standard male-oriented curriculum.

When the Austrian textile union developed a special A-level course
for women based on issues of particular concern to them—protective
legislation, maternity leave, pensions—graduates were found inade-
quately prepared to enter the B-level course with the students who had
completed standard A-level coursework. The union's solution was to
abandon the special women's A-level program forthwith. So fixed was
the union's acceptance of its A-, B-, and C-level progression that no
consideration was given to including women's issues in the standard
curriculum for discussion by men as well as women.

This episode is only one of many that raise the question: Are wom-
en's courses self-imposed ghettoes, or are they bridgeheads to equality?
The answer must be dependent on whether women's issues are perceived as of concern only to women or whether they are seen as impor-

<hr>

23. Anne Nelson and Barbara Wertheimer, *Trade Union Women: A Study of Their
Participation in New York City Locals*, 1975.

tant for the education of both men and women as union leaders. The issue of determining the context in which new women members—and other categories of new members as well—will learn most rapidly and gain the most self-confidence at the A-level becomes a matter for case-by-case judgment.

Still, for many, experience suggests that all-women courses are preferable. The Austrian metalworkers' secretary for women's affairs whom we interviewed was clearly in favor of continuing to offer special courses for women: "Separate courses indeed carry the threat of isolation, and we are conscious of that danger. But we have found that these courses are the best way to strengthen the confidence of union women, to bring them into contact with each other, to reduce feelings of competition and create bonds of solidarity and mutual support among them, while giving them the specialized information they need for their union jobs."

Education of Men on Equality

As new legislation, research, and information on equality issues find their way into standard courses in collective bargaining, job evaluation, and labor law, it seems likely that women's status in the labor movement and in unions will rise. Still this may be the teaching illusion, "the hope that a change in the system of education will be sufficient to transform the social structure."[24] Such educational initiatives can succeed only if there is continuing support for equality policies in the labor market and the workplace, in social legislation and in public education, along with progress in admitting women to leadership in unions and in political life.

The experience of the German metalworkers' union in introducing two model courses into their curriculum illustrates an innovative attempt to attack the problem of dealing with women's issues despite its difficulties. In the Ruhr we attended a union course and heard a group with a majority of men discuss women's work and its challenges to traditional patterns of family and work life. A useful teaching device, meant to enlist the strong in defense of the weak, was to ask the shop stewards present to write up some of the cases women had brought to them and to report what they did with these complaints. Sharp and enlightening critique—not all from the women—followed.

The women's division of the German chemical workers' union pre-

24. Centre for Educational Research and Innovation, *Development in Educational Leaves of Absence*, 1976, p. 91.

pared self-contained units of instruction on three themes: fair job classification for women, women's wages, and healthy working conditions
for women. These modules included a teacher's guide to the relevant
trade union terminology along with data on collective agreements and
legislation that can be used to introduce material of this kind into standard courses.

Another approach we discovered was to bring men in small numbers
into courses designed for women only. From their women colleagues
these men could hear, often for the first time, how women feel about
working in a male-dominated environment. Some men seem to come
away with two new impressions: the extent of male prejudice in the
union, and the extent of women's capacity to participate as equals when
space is made for their contributions. Such experiments teach more by
demonstration than by lectures.

Targeting men for programs on equality may help both men and
women escape from the inequality trap. Some male Swedish administrative officials have been taking courses in which they first meet by themselves to examine sexism in their treatment of female employees and
specifically their own secretaries. Meanwhile, the women meet on their
own. When the two groups join, they deal in general terms with the
divisions of tasks in their offices and the possibility of upgrading the
women's work. During working hours participants move from equality
principles to equality practices. Men take over routine duties such as
typing. Women take an active part in committee meetings and do not
act as coffee waitress or secretary.

In order to uncover sources of inequality, identify practices of discrimination, and then act on this information, the women's division of
the Austrian Trade Union of Private White-collar Workers began with
a study of their union's structures and processes. The union published
the unpleasant findings with an introduction by the president who called
a press conference to launch the publication. Not excusing any of the
discrimination it revealed, he committed the leadership of Austria's largest
union to the struggle for equality. Later, other national leaders of the
union called on women members to continue their many forms of pressure for change. The women's division responded through formal educational channels, through informal channels, and through the mass
media. As a consequence, a high number of GPA women have become
active unionists, keenly enthusiastic and loyal to a union that, though it
may still be imperfect, is positively responsive to their call for help.

One way that national leaders can show their support for dealing
with equality issues is in financial support for experimental approaches.
For instance, the British white-collar union, APEX, normally covered

two-thirds of each region's costs for educational work. For courses on equal pay and equal opportunity, the national office paid all costs. Most attendants at these courses were men (although women comprised about 55 percent of the membership).

Seeing Things as They Are

"The demands and needs of women will gradually alter the structures and discussions within the labor movement, as demands of other groups in the past have done." This was the hope, expressed as prediction, of one national women's organizer.[25] Her own union, as well as others, has a new vitality as a result of welcoming women into active membership and developing educational work on equality issues. This vitality enriches the women members, the life of the union as a whole, and the national community. The close tie that exists in Germany between the Federation of Women's Organizations and the DGB women's division has illustrated how fruitful such coalitions can be for both community and union.

With forces such as these slowly gathering momentum, many women have begun to ask, not merely for a place in the unions as they are, but for changes in the unions which will allow them growing influence over issues closely related to family well-being.[26] These issues grow in importance as women continue to enter the labor force while work remains bound in rigid patterns that allow little time for family life.

25. Judith Hunt, *Organizing Women Workers*, 1975, p. 12.
26. See Karen Shallcross Koziara, "Women and Work: The Evolving Policy," in *Working Women: Past, Present, and Future*, ed. Koziara, Michael Moscow, and Lucile Dewey Tanner, 1987; Alice H. Cook, Val R. Lorwin, and Arlene Kaplan Daniels, eds., *Women and Trade Unions in Eleven Industrialized Countries*, 1984; Suzan Lewis and Gary L. Cooper, *Career Couples: Contemporary Lifestyles and How to Manage Them*, 1989; and BNA, *Work and Family: A Changing Dynamic*, 1986b.

PART III

UNION
ISSUES

CHAPTER FIVE

Pay Equity

And thy estimation shall be of the male from twenty years old even unto sixty years old, even thy estimation shall be fifty shekels of silver, after the shekel of the sanctuary. And if it be a female, then thy estimation shall be thirty shekels.

—Leviticus 27:3–4

Elimination of sex bias in wage scales requires more than simply union strength. It operates in the broader context of societal assumptions about the value of female and male labor and laborers.

—Jean Quataert, "Women in the Free German Trade Unions"

If men wanted equal pay for women, they would get it. We have given a tremendous amount of lip service over the years to the problem of the lower paid.

—Frank Cousins, general secretary, Transport and General Workers Union

Whoever in the DGB wishes to see an anti-discrimination law must first convince six million men.

—Helga Toelle, DGB women's division

Historically, pay equity begins with a demand from organized workers for equal pay for equal work. It was a demand raised in all the industrializing countries at some point in the nineteenth century. The early socialist parties and their affiliated unions raised it in the name of equity; but the strong emotions that moved the demand were roused not so much out of concern for women's wages, as out of fear that men's hard-won standard rate might be diluted or reduced if women did men's work. Indeed, some labor leaders made it quite clear that they believed raising women's wages to those of men would mean that women would no longer be employed and that men would thus be completely freed of women's competition.

Epigraphs: Second from *The World of Women's Trade Unionism: Comparative Social Essays,* ed. Norbert C. Soldon, 1985; third from British Trades Union Congress, *Report,* 1967, p. 534; fourth from "Do We Need an Anti-Discrimination Law?" Friedrich Naumann Foundation conference, Bonn, August 1980, p. 161.

How Did the Low Value on Women's Work Originate?

As many countries entered the industrial age, women and children made up the bulk of the labor force. Men were supervisors, mechanics, and operators of heavy machinery inside and outside the factories. They built railroads and ships. Women were lower paid than men, only in part because their work was less skilled and carried less responsibility. This pattern of unequal wages was primarily based on the belief that men were the breadwinners and women were men's dependents. Women's earnings might help the family but they were not meant to be its main source of income. It was inconceivable that women could do the same work, at the same level of speed and accuracy. In the earliest days of factory employment single women's wages were often paid directly to their fathers. Women were to make only a short commitment to their employers and to the labor force before marrying and becoming fully occupied with homemaking. Under these assumptions, women warranted neither an employer's investment in training nor their own investment in an education or apprenticeship (assuming they could have been accepted by a master worker). Compared to the back-breaking toil in which men were often engaged, women's work was "light." Small muscle activity was seen as less demanding and less important than men's work and therefore deserving of lower remuneration. These assumptions, characteristic of all evaluation of women's early industrial employment, have continued to define women's status and women's low wages in modern employment.

In the early women's professions, still another factor encouraged low pay. Teaching, nursing, social work, and librarianship all had their origins in the volunteer activity of middle-class women, supported by their husbands, working out of motives of Christian charity, offering service to the less privileged, and "doing good works." Remuneration was not part of such a package, or if it appeared then only as a gratuity. Many of those involved felt that the service could not be equated with money; neither the giver nor the receiver could or should attempt to state such an equation. Moreover, all of these services, even teaching, were dispensable. School did not "keep" during planting and harvesting seasons. It often did not keep during bitterly cold weeks in northern winters. Teachers practiced their "profession" for a few premarital years and received much of their pay as "found" board and room, moving month by month among the parents of their pupils. When crops were bad, a teacher might receive no money at all, but at best a payment in kind or in "scrip." In their origins these teaching and helping professions enjoyed a wage relationship only in a remote sense. The volunteer's services were a gift, not a right that the recipient could claim or even expect.

A third factor in women's low wages was their heavy involvement in the service trades, as domestics, laundresses, food workers, maids in hostelries, or seamstresses—where all tasks were closely related to their household duties. As in housewifery, they were paid partly, sometimes mainly, in kind—in meals, bed, and board—and with minimal or no wages.

A comparison with male rates was not possible since women's work was never performed by men. Moreover, single women were thought not to need much, so long as they received enough to keep them off the streets. Many services, and particularly sewing, women could perform in their own or other women's homes. As sewing became a factory operation, women might still carry bundles of work to their homes from a contractor. Paid miserable piece rates, reduced still further by the fact that in effect they supplied their employer with space, light, and tools as well as with labor power, they worked long or short hours (mostly in the season, very long hours indeed) and often impressed their children into auxiliary tasks in order to finish still more bundles. In all these service trades, wages were low because the comparison was to unpaid housework, to "women's work," a category inviting exploitation. Neither women nor men knew or thought of gender equality. Without role models, and with an ideology that subordinated them to men, they could not envision such a possibility. Exploitation of women, even more than of men, was the accepted rule of the day.[1]

Who Wanted Equal Pay and Why

Nevertheless, the demand for equal pay was raised from three different sources. First, in the socialist movement it was part of a genuine striving to realize equality generally.[2] Second, many pragmatic union

---

1. Sidney Webb in *Problems of Modern Industry* 1902, summing up his chapter titled "Women's Wages," wrote, "Women workers appear almost invariably to earn less than men, except in a few instances of exceptional ability, and in a few occupations where sexual attraction enters in. . . . The general inferiority of women's work seems to influence their wages in industries in which no such inferiority exists. In the 'genteel vocations' women habitually receive less than men; and in the case of clerks and teachers for work of quality and quantity often equal to the men's" (pp. 74–75).

2. Marxist and even pre-Marxist movements thoroughly accepted the view that capitalism was responsible for the fact that women had to work. Hence in nineteenth-century Germany, a demand of the Lassalleans was to ban factory work for women altogether and to limit them to work which could be done at home. The Trade Union Congress at

men, focusing on immediate gains in wages and working conditions, viewed with consternation and alarm the increasing number of women in all kinds of employment, and all working at low wages. Particularly alarming was the threat to men's standards when from time to time women moved into the male trades. Equal pay might protect women, but it would surely protect men too in the sense that employers would refuse to employ women if they were as expensive as men. Third, the middle-class women's rights movement arose out of shock at revelations of the conditions of working-class women, who seemed caught between "white slavery" and "wage slavery" in their need to work.

Most unions over the years have conformed to the common view of women. They have uncritically accepted the premise that women's true domain was the home; that in the world of paid employment their skills, productivity, dependability, and need were all inferior to men's, and naturally, therefore, women's wages should be lower than men's. The result was to establish women's wage scales parallel to and below those of men with no possibility of crossover for women.

In many countries these differentials were deeply embedded in custom. In Germany in 1957 the courts had to remind unions and employers that since the nation's Basic Law required equality between men and women, special women's wage scales had to be considered illegal. Yet unions and employers, undaunted, found ways around a literal reading of the law. They defined women's work as "light," and using this differentiation between the work assignments of men and women created a pay grade with the title "light work," which they placed at the bottom of the wage scale. The rationalizations that government commissions have found or invented over the years to justify continuing to pay women wages that are less than men's are richly elaborated and clearly documented in country after country, time after time.

Investigations and Studies

In 1893 in Britain, for example, a royal commission including several

---

Erfurt in 1872 adopted a position "against all women's work in factories and workshops." Karl Kautsky, the Austrian socialist leader, in 1899 pointed to the increase in the employment of women and children as proof of the Marxian theory of increasing misery. Modern Marxists in such developing communist countries as Romania and Cuba carry more than a trace of this view in their ambivalent approach to the problems of working mothers. On the one hand, women who have been exploited at work under capitalism deserve, they say, to be allowed to be the mothers of families under socialism. At the same time, equality goals and the basic law insist that women share with men the right and duty to work.

lady assistant commissioners issued a study called *The Employment of Women* covering, among other matters, women's wages and "the competition between the labour of men and women." With few exceptions, they found that women almost never earned more than half of what men did. Carpet manufacturing, they noted, paid women fifteen shillings a week to men's thirty-five. Moreover, when women were first introduced into one such factory, men struck against their admission and for a time kept them out. Though the employer did in the end hire women, he instituted a sharp division of labor based on gender. Women were moved into less skilled, lower paying jobs, often physically separated from men. Even in the few cases in the royal commission study where men and women did the same work, women's wages were significantly lower—half or less—than men's.[3]

By the early 1900s, studies such as M. B. Hammond's in 1905, "Women's Wages in Manual Work in the United States," had been done in several industrialized countries. Hammond was trying to discover why and under what circumstances women were paid less than men. She concluded that "it may also happen that wages of women are lower than is their productivity." She attributed the causes for this inequity to "their lower standard of living, their practical dependence on other means of support and their lack of combination, [all of which] prevent them from obtaining their true economic wage."[4] Thus eighty-five years ago, Hammond found women earning less than they deserved because (1) they were not organized; (2) they were supplementary earners and hence did not need what breadwinners needed; (3) they were tractable; (4) they lacked training; (5) they would work only until they married; and (6) they were assigned to light jobs with other women, where they were all low-paid. Under any objective modern measure they were exploited.

The World Wars and Women's Work

In both wars, the simultaneous mobilization of men and the pressing need for munitions and supplies created new job opportunities and an influx of women into the labor force and into jobs previously reserved to men.

---

3. Reports by Eliza Orne, Clara E. Collet, May E. Abraham, and Margaret H. Irwin (lady assistant commissioners) in Great Britain Royal Commission on Labour, *The Employment of Women: A Report to Parliament on the Conditions of Work in Various Industries in England, Wales, Scotland, and Ireland*, 1893.

4. M. B. Hammond, "Women's Wages in Manual Work," in *Trade Unionism and Labor Problems*, ed. John R. Commons, 1905, pp. 421–22.

World War I. In the United States the National War Labor Board (NWLB) set forth two principles of wage payment that became the subject of a presidential proclamation on April 8, 1918: "Women doing men's work shall receive the same wages as do men," and the acceptance of a "living wage" for all workers, "including common laborers." This "living wage" was defined as a "minimum wage to 'insure the subsistence of the worker and his [sic] family in health and reasonable comfort.' "[5]

The principle of equal pay for equal work was then adopted by the War Labor Policies Board in 1918: "If it shall become necessary to employ women on work ordinarily done by men, they must be allowed equal pay for equal work and must not be allowed tasks disproportionate to their strength."[6]

In Britain the Ministry of Munitions early in the war issued an instruction to all employers to give women equal pay for doing men's work, but women employed in "women's work," that is, work previously done by women and girls or "boys, lads, and youths" was not covered by the statutory order.[7] In fact, in 1915 women's rates were expressly set to equal those given to boys and youths. A postwar investigation by a War Cabinet committee, of which Beatrice Webb was a member, reported that most women's work in munitions came about not by women taking over men's work, but by their assuming boys' work and the boys moving up to the work of skilled men. All of the adjustments fell short of equalizing men's and women's wages for the same work, although women made some gains.

The War Cabinet committee also predicted the postwar likelihood for equal pay for women. They considered three categories of work: occupations in which only women or only men were employed; those in which both were employed but with definite demarcation into "men's work" and "women's work;" and occupations in which both men and women were employed on the same or closely similar work. The first required no further study—women would definitely be paid less than

5. U.S. Department of Labor, Women's Bureau, *Equal Pay for Women in War Industries,* Bulletin 196, 1942b, p. 18.
6. U.S. Department of Labor, Women's Bureau, *Your Questions as to Women in War Industries,* Bulletin 194, 1942a, p. 5.
7. According to a Women's Bureau study in 1942, summarizing World War II practice in the United States, women working during the war similarly fell into two categories: those who had worked at women's trades, such as textiles and clothing, before the war and then moved into shipbuilding and munitions, and those who first worked during the war and moved into previously male-held civilian jobs such as positions on urban trolleys. See U.S. Department of Labor, Women's Bureau, 1942b. In the United States, however, both were considered war work and deserving of equal pay.

men, for there were no men with whom to compare them. Did equal pay in the other two circumstances mean "rate for the job," "equal time rates," or "equal pay for equal value?" Most troubling was the problem of equal time rates for men and women on the same work. The committee concluded that they were "unable at this juncture of the national life to recommend a change bringing such doubtful advantages to men fraught with such serious injury to women [unemployment] as we believe would result from the adoption of the formula of 'equal time rates.' "

Webb wrote a minority report. She found no difficulty in eliminating sex differentials on time work rates, providing they were built above a minimum and yielded a decent living standard. In her opinion "we have no ground for making sex a reason for differentiation in the conditions of employment. . . . There is no justice in and no economic basis for the conception of a man's rate and a woman's rate." The committee was unmoved by her views. It recommended against continuing even the limited wartime equal pay policy into peacetime.[8]

During the First World War Germany, Sweden, and Austria paid little attention to the equal pay issue. In fact, "in the pre- and post-war wage agreements negotiated by union leaders, women's rates were institutionalized as a separate category."[9] Nonetheless, it was already an issue of importance, as seen in the International Labour Organisation charter, adopted at the organisation's founding in 1919 and calling for equal pay for equal work.

World War II. Questions of equality in wages and opportunity were somewhat more urgently addressed in most countries—perhaps with the exception of Sweden—during and immediately following World War II.[10] In Germany and Austria (after 1938) the Hitlerian concept of women's familial role dovetailed with the widespread doctrine in the depression of the 1930s that would take women out of the labor market and, if and when they were employed, pay them less than men. Yet by 1939, with war imminent, women were already needed in industry. In a very real sense, "home"—where women naturally belonged—was in

8. War Cabinet Committee (The Atkin Committee), *Women in Industry*, 1919; for the minority report, see pp. 254–333, particularly pp. 278–84.

9. Jean Quataert, "Women in the German Free Trade Unions," in *The World of Women's Trade Unionism: Comparative Historical Essays*, ed. Norbert C. Soldon, 1985, p. 108.

10. Professor Qvist, author of a history of employed women in Sweden, stated that he knew of no study on women's employment there during the wars, although noncombatant Sweden mobilized a high proportion of its men, and women were substituted for them in many kinds of wartime employment.

effect redefined to include "whatever could be encompassed by the spirit of motherhood," and thus the Nazis could state that "our home is Germany, wherever she may need us." [11]

The German government of the Third Reich was not quite impervious, however, to world opinion. In responding to an ILO periodic request for reports from member countries on compliance with the equal pay principle, the German Minister of Labor dealt with the question in January 1939 by saying, "It has not yet been possible to apply the—in itself—fair principle of equal wages for equal work, owing to the effects which an increase in women's wages would undoubtedly have upon the price level." He had regard also for "undesirable psychological repercussions among certain groups of less well-paid workers (male workers in other industries and women employed at light work in the metalworking industry)." [12] In 1940, the German Minister of Labor again looked at women's wages and now, after the war had begun, in a press conference noted:

> In cases in which collective rules fixed the rates of wages for women or explicitly provided that their wages should be the same as those for men [a comment indicating that collective agreements still existed and were honored] there was no cause for doubt. Where no such provision had been made, account had to be taken of the fact that in the past, remuneration of women had as a rule been lower than that of men. Except in special cases, that principle had to be maintained. [13]

Great Britain has been the country, above all other participants in the Second World War, that most rigorously called up its women for war

11. For a detailed study of this development in Nazi ideology see Annemarie Tröger, "The Creation of a Female Assembly-Line Proletariat," in *When Biology Became Destiny: Women in Weimar and Nazi Germany*, ed. Renate Bridenthal, Atina Grossmann, and Marion Kaplan, 1984, pp. 237–70. As she sums it up, "Ideology and the image of 'women's role' was [sic] modernized too. It now encompassed both motherhood and some notion of vocation" (p. 265). Roger Chickering, in a review of Dörte Winkler's *Frauen in Dritten Reich*, similarly states, "Despite an ideological commitment to driving women out of the labor force and into the home, Nazi officials were reluctant to undertake the massive intervention in the economy that such social restructuring would have required" (*Business History Review* 54:136 [Spring 1980]).

12. *International Labour Review*, December 1941, "The Employment of Women under the National-Socialist Regime," p. 648. This script is reminiscent of the reluctance of one of the British royal commissions on equal pay. Although members of the commission concluded in general that equal pay was just, they could not recommend it because it could only apply to that small group of women actually working alongside men at "men's work." Such a limited application would be unfair, the commission judged, since it would represent an injustice to the vast majority of women not working with men and hence ineligible for equal pay. War Cabinet Committee, 1919, p. 186.

13. *International Labour Review*, December 1941, p. 649.

service in the factories. "The thorny problem of equal pay for women on war jobs new to them" was worked out under pressures generated by a variety of motives and demands. Unions stipulated that the movement of women into men's jobs should continue only for the duration of the emergency and that the introduction of women to men's jobs should not be used to break down wage rates. The result was that in at least sixty-five occupations, arrangements with unions provided that women on men's work would have a suitable probationary period and, after that, should receive "specified proportions of men's rates." Where impasses arose in negotiations over women's wages, cases could be, and some were, referred to the Industrial Court. An American visitor to England in wartime noted that "in all these cases, the courts upheld the principle that a woman doing the full work of a man should receive the man's remuneration for the job." [14]

In the United States the NWLB became the arbiter of all wage changes, including equal pay. In the first major case to come before the board (*General Motors*, 1942), it summed up the decision on equal pay as follows: "The Board has directed the parties to include in their new agreement a provision that wage rates for women shall be the same as for men where they do work of *comparable* quantity and quality in *comparable* occupations" (emphasis added).[15] Thus the first major decision of the board accepted in principle equal pay for comparable work, although it also permitted differentials based on special costs to the employer where women were involved, such as requirements for extra supervision.

Helen Baker, in her 1941 survey of the practices of sixty-two American companies in employing women, found that as far as wages were concerned, "the proportion of companies that reported a policy of 'equal pay for equal work' suggests that this has not been a widely accepted standard in American industry." [16]

In September 1943, the *Bendix* case before the NWLB raised the question of sex bias in job evaluation, probably for the first time. The board's chair insisted in his findings on "a reevaluation of job classification on the basis of job content and not of sex." [17]

---

14. Janet M. Hooks, *British Policies and Methods in Employing Women in Wartime*, U.S. Department of Labor, Women's Bureau, Bulletin 200, 1944, pp. 29–33.

15. In the *General Motors Cases*, September 1942, the NWLB stated further that "the national War Labor Board has accepted the general principle that wages should be paid to female employees on the principle of equal pay for equal work. It believes there should be no discrimination between employees whose production is substantially the same on comparable jobs" (U.S. Department of Labor, Women's Bureau, 1942b, p. 16).

16. Helen Baker, *Women in War Industries*, 1942, p. 44.

17. BNA, *In re Bendix Aviation Corporation, Bendix Products Divisions, and the United*

In 1945, in the *General Electric and Westinghouse Electric* cases, the union complained that women's rates fell below minimum job and common labor rates; but here the board found insufficient evidence that men and women were doing equal or closely similar work. Consequently, women's rates could be set lower than men's because the differential was justified on the grounds of women's incapacity to handle "heavy" work. Mary Anderson, chief of the Women's Bureau in the Department of Labor, in summarizing the board actions in matters of equal pay during the war, noted that "the Board refused to abrogate collective bargaining agreements for the purpose of equalizing rates for men and women. . . . It enunciated the policy of equal pay for equal work only where the terms of a new contract were disputed."[18]

Although the two labor federations, CIO and AFL, both endorsed equal pay, local union policy in negotiations of such agreements varied widely. The board chose to honor collectively bargained agreements, regardless of the degree of gender equity involved. Principles adopted at the top of the union hierarchy, as Baker noted, did not guarantee that local leaders would adhere to them.[19]

Dorothy Douglas, a Smith College economist, sought at the end of the war to strike a "balance sheet of labor" on American women's experience in working during the war. "For women," she concluded, "the end of the war saw . . . the return of greater sex discrimination."[20] In 1948 Syracuse University's Marguerite Fisher reviewed the wartime experience with equal pay and concluded that "the WLB took a stand in favor of the principle and applied it in more than fifty cases. In most industry, however, women's wages remained 25–50 percent below the wages of men, even when comparable work was done by both sexes."[21]

Automobile Workers, Case 2941-D, September 20, 1943, in *War Labor Reports: Wage and Salary Stabilization,* vol. 11, 1944. The War Labor Board (WLB) had two functions, only one of which was setting wages. The other was dispute settlement. When the first appeared to aggravate the second, the board's usage was to remand troublesome issues back to the parties for further bargaining. In *Bendix,* when this tactic did not produce the desired industrial peace, an arbitrator was assigned to make a wage determination. Agreement was hard to achieve, because the company insisted on paying women ten cents less per hour than men. The union, in the end, consented to the company position. For cases, see U.S. Department of Labor, Women's Bureau, 1942b, including "extracts from Decision of the War Labor Board in the General Motors Cases."

18. Mary Anderson, "Women's Status in World War II," in *Yearbook of American Labor: War Labor Policies,* vol. 1, ed. Colston Warne, 1945.

19. Baker, 1942.

20. Dorothy Douglas, "The Balance Sheet of Labor," in *Labor in Postwar America: Yearbook of American Labor,* ed. Colston Warne et al., 1949, p. 645.

21. Marguerite Fisher, "Equal Pay for Equal Work Legislation," *Industrial and Labor Relations Review* 2:1 (1948), pp. 50–57.

Fisher looked to the possibility that with the demise of the NWLB at the end of hostilities, states would adopt equal pay legislation, but by 1947 only nine states had passed such laws.

Thus, despite wartime initiatives and despite much debate and many resolutions, equal pay remained more a happenstance than a fixed policy. Industry's limited instituting of equal pay programs was regarded simply as a war measure that would satisfy both women and men, but it was not seen as in any way setting postwar social policy. Yet the equal pay issue did not die. Slowly emphasis shifted to what has been called "pay equity," an attempt to compare the value of men's and women's work even when their jobs were not equal or closely similar. Such a comparison could be carried out through the application of standards of comparable worth to the given employer, measurements usually achievable through job evaluation. Most job evaluation schemes themselves, however, had first to be cleansed of their own gender bias, constructed as they were to measure the value of men's work.[22]

Pay Equity: Equal Pay in a New Form

By 1951 the ILO had adopted a new standard on equal pay. Its Convention 100 of that year calls for "equal remuneration for men and women workers for work of equal value."[23] "Equal value" was defined as "rates of remuneration established without discrimination based on sex." Article three of Convention 100 outlines four approaches to the

22. For elaborations of this view, see Donald J. Treiman, *Job Evaluation, an Analysis Review: Interim Report to the EEOC*, 1979; Donald J. Treiman, Heidi I. Hartmann, and Patricia Roos, "Assessing Pay Discrimination Using National Data," in *Comparable Worth and Wage Determination: Technical Possibilities and Political Realities*, ed. Helen Remick, 1984; Helen Remick, *Strategies for Creating Sound, Bias-free Job Evaluation and the EEOC: The Emerging Issues*, 1979; Donald J. Treiman and Heidi I. Hartmann, *Women, Work, and Wages: Equal Pay for Jobs of Equal Value*, 1981; and Joan Acker, *Doing Comparable Worth: Gender, Class, and Pay Equity*, 1989.

23. The possible contradiction between the doctrine of the "family wage" and that of "equal pay for work of equal value" was a subject of major discussion at the 1950 session as the ILO considered Convention 100. The family wage was paid in several countries to "the breadwinner" (always male), in the form of a state allowance for each dependent member of the family, added to base pay. The concept underlay many adverse court decisions on women's equal rates and was advanced by employers to justify differentials between men's and women's pay. The conference noted presciently that "this system penalises women who have to support a family, whether of children or of other dependents." It cited a study of the U.S. Women's Bureau, showing that in 1946, 18 percent of the then-working women were heads of families. ILO, "Equal Remuneration for Men and Women Workers for Work of Equal Value," 1950, pp. 110–11.

implementation of this kind of equal pay. Implementation may be achieved through (1) national laws or regulations; (2) legally established or recognized machinery for wage determination; (3) collective agreements between employers and workers; and (4) a combination of any or all of these. Since its adoption, Convention 100 has been ratified (although not always implemented) by over 120 countries, including all four European countries studied here. The United States has consistently insisted that it cannot ratify ILO conventions because of its federal structure.[24]

The European Economic Community

There are presently twelve members of the Community; two countries in our study, Germany and Great Britain, belong to the EEC, and both Austria and Sweden are applying for membership. In 1975 the EEC began to play a decisive role in much of the progress that has been made in Europe on pay equity. Article 119 of the 1961 Treaty of Rome (the EEC's founding charter) requires member states to accept a policy of equal pay for equal work, despite the "equal value" position taken ten years earlier by the ILO. For a decade or more after the EEC's founding, little was done about enforcing the equal pay mandate, perhaps because the equal pay clause in the EEC treaty had been written not to gain pay equity for women but to avoid what might have been unfair competition among employers within the various Community states. By the time of the 1975 celebration of the U.S. International Women's Year, however, the Community commissioners (who have mandatory authority) had issued several directives on equal treatment, including the adoption of the ILO norm of equal pay for work of equal value. They now require reports at regular intervals from member states on details of implementation of these recommendations and directives.[25]

Enforcement consists of the Commission's proceeding to go to the Community High Court of Justice (CHCJ) against member nations whose laws fall short of complete compliance with the EEC directive on equal pay. In addition to the High Court's rendering judgments on such pleadings, equality agencies and courts in each country can address inquiries to it for interpretations of Community directives. It is largely

24. This point had some merit in 1919 but none at all by 1950, when the federal government had long since ceased to leave the field of social and labor legislation solely to the states.

25. For a summary of such reports, see "Equal Value: A Union Update," *Equal Opportunity Review*, no. 22 (November/December 1988), pp. 34–37.

through the resulting determinations that more precise definitions of wage equity are being derived.

In the first equal pay case brought before the High Court, the Defrenne case brought by Belgium, the court made clear that Article 119 is not only a mechanism to prevent distortion of competition but also a means to improve working and living conditions, particularly for women. Great Britain's Equal Opportunities Commission has been the most frequent user of the CHCJ and, in endeavoring to comply with its dicta, has presented the British government with a series of recommended amendments to the equal pay section of its antidiscrimination laws. On the whole, these proposals have been adopted.

Application of the law in each member state proceeds through its own agencies for labor law enforcement. In Germany it is through the system of labor courts, while in Britain complaints move through the tribunals with the House of Lords as the superior instance.

The United States

The United States is one of three countries in our study which is not a member of the EEC. The pay equity issue took on renewed life in the United States after the war, although mainly through state rather than federal action. In the late forties the Women's Bureau of the Department of Labor sent to all states a model equal pay act that read much like Convention 100. By the mid-1960s, about fifteen states had defined equal pay as some version of equal pay for work of equal value,[26] though no state undertook to enforce that legislation in terms other than equal pay for equal work.

By 1963, the U.S. Congress adopted the Equal Pay Act (EPA), having debated both possible definitions and settled on equal pay for equal work. More states, in the interest of conformity with national legislation, took up the equal pay question and by the mid-1970s all but nine had equal pay laws modeled on EPA or (in a few cases) on the earlier version of comparable worth. For its first fifteen years, the federal statute was enforced by the Department of Labor as part of the Fair Labor Standards Act of 1938 that defined minimum rates of pay and set maximum hours of work to be performed without overtime penalty. In the late 1970s, administration of EPA was moved to the Equal Employment Opportunity Commission (EEOC) that had been created to administer Title VII of the Civil Rights Act of 1964 as amended in 1972.

26. Alice H. Cook, *Comparable Worth: The Problem and States' Approaches to Wage Equity*, 1983, p. 2.

A year after the adoption of EPA, Congress passed the Civil Rights Act, of which Title VII on Equal Employment Opportunity forbids discrimination in all phases of employment, including compensation. Thus, in effect, two laws deal with pay equity, the one calling for equal pay for equal work, the other referring without further specification to equality of payment. The question of whether Title VII goes beyond the EPA and offers an opening for the application of comparable value to differing men's and women's jobs remains moot.

By 1979, when the director of EEOC addressed the first national conference on comparable worth it was clear that she was prepared to opt for a broader interpretation of Title VII than simply equal pay for equal work. She established a national commission of experts who were to recommend guidelines to incorporate this approach. With the change in administration in 1980, however, came her displacement. Subsequently, the new Reagan administration filled a majority of seats both on EEOC and on the U.S. Civil Rights Commission (USCRC) with persons hostile to the comparable worth concept. The issue nevertheless had taken hold in many unions and local governments.

Austria

Austria adopted an equal opportunity act in July 1979 that forbids any discrimination on the basis of sex but is not specific about setting wage rates. Wage discrimination is defined as any inequitable differential that is instituted without a "material justification." Administration of the act is in the hands of the eleven-person Equal Treatment Commission, headed by the Minister of Social Affairs, and consisting of two members each from the Chamber of Labor, the Association of Austrian Industry, and the Austrian Trade Union Federation and one each from the Ministry of Social Affairs and the Office of the Chancellor of the Republic. The commission is empowered to take up all questions relating to equal pay. At the request of any of the interest groups represented on the commission, it may examine problems related to discrimination in general or determine in any particular case whether there has been a violation of the equal pay law. Its decisions may be published in the *Government Register*.

The chair of the OeGB's women's division, at a women's conference in September 1979, noted that this law could at best be regarded as a first step. Since it contained neither clear definitions nor remedies it could not deal with the interwoven and widespread causes of wage discrimination against women. She listed women's low occupational status, poor promotional opportunities, almost total absence from the ranks of management, and traditional belief in women's presumably native qualities of deftness and patience as factors that together result in a pay gap of almost one-third between men's and women's work. She called attention to a study of discrimination against women in Austrian collective agreements that showed insubstantial improvement in meeting these problems through collective bargaining. At this meeting, affiliated unions offered more than 150 resolutions for OeGB congress approval of pay equity. This broad support, however, found little echo in national union action.[27]

As might be expected, the union taking the most aggressive action was the GPA. It initiated a variety of studies examining the inferior status of women as depicted in the media, in education, in union life, and in the workplace, and it instituted internal procedures aimed to activate its women members to continuously voice the issues of special concern to them within both the national confederation and its member unions.

Sweden

Sweden is not a member of the EEC though it also has applied for membership. It did not abolish special women's wage scales until 1960. However, the unions in LO already had begun to develop a solidary wage policy that was ongoing. The notion of wage equity underlying this approach was not meant to correct pay differentials between men and women but to narrow the gap between low- and high-paid workers. A government study conducted in 1965 made clear that at that time most low-paid workers were women. Since then, women have been a major beneficiary of the long-term policy carried out through peak collective bargaining between LO and SAF. In successive stages, beginning in 1952, the bargaining partners agreed to raise the wage rates of low-paid workers at a greater rate than those of high-paid workers. The result has been the closest approach to pay equity achieved in the Western world. By the end of the 1970s, women in blue-collar occupations were earning 85 percent of men's wages. By the 1980s, this proportion had reached almost 90 percent before the centralized bargaining system broke down. Under the individual union bargaining which has succeeded it, the policy appears to have been abandoned.

The Swedish Central Organization of Salaried Employees (TCO) fol-

27. These fears were all confirmed in an article that appeared in 1982, summing up in detail the unequal positions of wage and salaried women workers in Austria. See Josef Christl and Michael Wagner, "Die Stellung der Frau in der oesterreichischen Lohn- und Gehaltspyramide," *Wirtschaft und Gesellschaft* 8:1 (1982), pp. 77–96.

lowed a different tactic both politically and in its approach to equity. It too signed a central agreement with SAF for the private sector and with government personnel agencies for the public sector. The white-collar workers' federation has achieved a reduction in the pay gap among its workers as well, though still below LO levels.[28]

The anti-discrimination law of 1981 took into consideration that labor market organizations were responsible for its enforcement through wage agreements and through the establishment of equity committees in individual plants and offices. The Office of Equity Ombud, headed by a woman judge, was established to deal with complaints brought by unorganized workers and other matters arising outside the labor market. In addition, the powerful Swedish Labor Market Board (AMS), comprised of representatives of unions and employers, in 1977 issued far-reaching guidelines on equity, including pay equity, in the labor market.

Germany

Germany, one of the two EEC countries in our study, emerged from the war with the Basic Law (1952) granting equal rights to women and men. In 1957 the Supreme Labor Court declared that under the Basic Law special women's wage scales were unconstitutional. Unions throughout the country had to take action to bring their wage bargaining into conformity with this decision. Their typical solution was to create a new category in the wage scales, usually named "light work," and place it at the bottom of the scale. Most women's work fell into this category. The attack on this subterfuge took some time to mount, but by the late 1960s it was a major subject of discussion throughout the women's divisions of the unions.

The DGB women's division, under new, more aggressive leadership than it had had in its earlier years, persuaded the confederation to designate 1972 as the "Year of Working Women." Each affiliated national union pledged to place the problems of women's place in the wage scales on its next bargaining agenda for improvement in evaluation of the light work jobs.

More important, the DGB called upon the Minister of Labor in the then Social Democratic government to undertake a study that would show "whether it would be scientifically justifiable to characterize a job

28. Two papers by Siv Gustafsson fill in details on Sweden's treatment of equality problems, including equal pay: "Male-Female Lifetime Earnings Differentials and Labor Force History," 1979a, and "Trende in der Entwicklung zur Gleichberechtigung," March 18, 1986.

as 'heavy' if it involved high muscular exertion, but to classify it as 'light' if it merely led to nervous stress and strain with slight physical exertion."[29] This study, undertaken by two well-known specialists, one in industrial engineering, the other in industrial medicine, was completed in 1975. The experts concluded that such a distinction was not scientifically supportable, and the Minister of Labor submitted the report to the unions and employers for their approval and implementation. The DGB and its largest affiliate, the metalworkers, after a considerable period, accepted the report, but the employers—who took several months longer for their appraisal—rejected it. A change in government in 1976 effectively ended official support of the report's recommendations. The unions had to begin again, with hostile employers and a now indifferent state.

Statutory action, whether on specific equality measures or on equal pay, has been slow to reach legislative enactment in Germany. In 1980, after many delays and laborious studies, Parliament adopted an act respecting equality of treatment at the workplace, including equal pay for work of equal value (Article 612 [3] of the German Civil Code). Administration of Article 612 [3] is through the labor courts.

The courts usually have chosen, however, to treat wage discrimination cases either as equal-pay-for-equal-work issues, or, where no males work in a disputed classification, to treat the cases as narrowly and locally as possible. Thus, the Supreme Labor Court has found for a few individuals and one or two groups of women. It has in these cases ordered equitable wage payment but without back pay, and with reimbursement limited to minimal costs covering such items as postage, copying, and travel to the court hearings. Germany has received at least two CHCJ citations for its both inadequate and inactive commitment to wage equity.

Great Britain

The second EEC country in our study, Great Britain, approached the wage equity issue through legislation. By the mid-1960s, all political parties had committed themselves to the principle of equal pay; but

29. Walter Rohmert and Josef Rutenfranz, *Arbeitswissenschaftliche Beurteilung der Belastung und Beanspruchung an unterschiedlichen industriellen Arbeitsplaetzen,* 1975. Discussions of this report and its impact are included in Alice H. Cook, "Collective Bargaining as a Strategy for Achieving Equal Opportunity and Equal Pay: Sweden and West Germany," and Christof Helberger, "Work Analysis as a Means to Achieve Equal Pay for Working Women," both in *Equal Employment Policy for Women: Strategies for Implementation in the United States, Canada, and Western Europe,* ed. Ronnie S. Ratner, 1980.

when the Labour party came into office in 1964 after several years out of power, it was constrained from presenting the necessary legislation on the grounds that the cost to employers and to the society would be economically unbearable in the ongoing depression. By 1968, however, tripartite discussions began among the CBI, the TUC, and the government. As a result, a bill on equal pay was adopted in 1970 that allowed British employers five years to comply fully. The plan was designed to be implemented in stages during that period.

The law contained two definitions of equal pay: the first was for work done by men and women of "like or broadly similar kind," and the second, for "work rated as equivalent" under a job evaluation scheme. Both definitions applied only to men and women in the same employment in both the public and private sectors. The EOC monitored enforcement of the Equal Pay Act. It also conducted research in the field and made recommendations for changes that might make new legislation necessary.

Individuals, unions, or the EOC may bring cases to industrial tribunals and, on appeal by employer or complainant, to an employment appeals tribunal and thence to the House of Lords. Complaints about discriminatory collective agreements are made, not to an IT but to the central arbitration commission (CAC) by a party to the agreement or by the Secretary of State for Employment. In certain cases the CAC is empowered to assign experts to assess equal value. As a result, the CAC may even change the collective agreement or advise on what changes need to be made to comply with the EPA. Specifically, the CAC may make such amendments to a collective agreement as are required "to extend to both men and women any provisions applying specifically to men only or to women only, and to eliminate any resulting duplication, so that only the more favorable provisions remain."[30] On the matter of a pay structure, only the employer or the Secretary of State can make the appeal, although as one commentator notes, "There is nothing to stop an employee or union nudging the Secretary of State into action." The CAC is concerned more with how and under what conditions the contract is working than with what it says. For example, a clustering of men or women in specific pay grades can suggest to the CAC that despite unisex terminology, "it can hardly be by accident or fortune that women are distributed disadvantageously throughout the pay structure."[31] This provision of the law is unique among the countries studied

30. IDS, *Employment Law Handbook: Sex Discrimination and Equal Pay*, 1984, pp. 137–38.

31. "Negotiating for Equality," *Equal Opportunity Review*, no. 22 (November/December 1988b), p. 31.

in permitting government intervention in collective bargaining and pro-viding for corrective action where agreements have not resulted in sex equity in wages. Thus, individual women, a group, or a department of women can appeal to a government agency over the heads of union officials who have negotiated inequitable wage scales.

By 1980, as a result both of CHCJ rulings and of several years' ex-perience with the law, the EOC, as it was empowered to do, recom-mended a number of amendments, including adding the phrase "work of equal value" to the definition of equal pay.[32] To some extent the original law had allowed for comparisons of women's and men's wages that were not "closely similar work," but only where the employer had conducted a job evaluation. (In the law the EOC was not authorized to inquire whether the job evaluation itself contained sex bias.) The EOC also proposed an amendment—that was not adopted—that would have allowed a woman in a firm where no job evaluation scheme was in operation to be "otherwise rated" in order to achieve a comparison with a similar man. The EOC further recommended that a woman be allowed to compare her work with that of a hypothetical male where no actual male counterpart existed, but this recommendation too was not adopted because CHCJ interpretations of wages as including pen-sions, fringe benefits, bonuses, and other employer-granted schemes were adopted in the 1983 amendments, thus considerably expanding the def-inition of wages. The rejection of this recommendation was a significant loss. A woman earning low wages with deficient or no benefits, but without a male comparator, had no way of gaining an outside review.

For many women in Britain, however, the Equal Pay Act had an in-disputably favorable effect, at least for a few years. Women's hourly wages rose from about 63 percent of men's in 1970 to almost 76 per-cent of men's wages in 1977. Real and relative gains then ceased to

---

32. The first time the conservative government presented its bill amending the Equal Pay Act of 1970, it did so with considerable reluctance, only to withdraw it from discus-sion because of the scale of legal objections and the number of speakers scheduled to appear in opposition to the bill. Before the bill finally passed in 1983, the TUC had met with the Minister of Labour to outline the unions' many criticisms and objections to the government bill. The union representatives were told that the draft was simply to fill the gaps in U.K. legislation disclosed by the European Court's judgments and was not in-tended to make wider changes in the act. Not surprisingly, the TUC unions remained most critical of the law as it went into effect in January 1984. Labour objections included the fact that employers could still use "market forces" as a defense of unequal pay; the phrase "material factor" in the amendment replaced the original "material difference" as a basis for an employer's defense of his wage scale; the role and expertise of the proposed "expert" were ill-defined; and the burden of cost in taking a case to a tribunal fell mainly on the plaintiff. Altogether, the TUC questioned whether these procedures complied with EC requirements. *TUC Women Workers' Bulletin*, no. 4 (March 1984).

Table 6. Ratios of female to male hourly earnings for manual workers in manufacturing (selected countries and years)

Year	Germany	Sweden	U.K.
1955	.628	.692	.585
1965	.688	.720	.568
1975	.721	.852	.665
1980	.727	.899	.688
1982	.730	.903	.688
1984	.727	.900	.688
1986	.729	.904	.679

Source: OECD, *Employment Outlook* (Paris: 1988), p. 58.

grow and by 1982 had retreated to about 74 percent. The EOC, in releasing its annual report in 1983, had to say, "Progress toward equal pay appears to have halted over the past five years."[33]

The British have endeavored to deal with the issue of comparable worth by encouraging job evaluation and by directing complainants to find a male comparator. The EOC has acted not only to investigate complaints but also to advocate statutory changes.

For all the countries, with the exception of Sweden, the measures undertaken to implement pay equity policies have had only a slight effect in raising women's wages.[34] (Table 6 provides a broad comparison of women's and men's wages country by country.) Swedish unions, having adopted an approach that seeks to narrow the gap between low- and high-paid workers, have improved the income of their women members more dramatically than unions have done in any other country.

The German and Austrian approaches allow only correction of individual complaints.[35] No guidelines exist on how comparisons may be undertaken. Offending employers are not subject to monetary sanc-

33. EOC, *Annual Report*, 1983, p. 4.

34. Among studies covering the sex equality provisions adopted by the Community commissioners, two are particularly thorough: Ruth Nielsen, *Equality Legislation in a Comparative Perspective: Toward State Feminism*, 1983; and Eva C. Landau, *The Rights of Working Women in the European Community*, 1985.

35. The head of the Labor Inspection Service in Austria, charged with enforcement of all aspects of the act, notes that a staff of three hundred labor inspectors is too few to deal with the 200,000 enterprises in the country and warns against too high expectations from this quarter in enforcing the Equal Treatment Law. Moreover, the inspector states that the commission can only compare wages of men and women within a given branch of employment. It cannot, for instance, compare wages in textiles and energy. In any case, the article concludes: "Austria lies far below international standards and with admission to the EEC will be required to undertake an immediate upgrading" (p. 4).

tions, and employees must take their complaints through a long judicial process to gain a wage upgrade.[36]

The EEOC in the United States in 1980 was prepared to deal aggressively with comparable worth as a measure to pay equity. Under new political leadership, however, the commission has refused to deal with comparable worth cases, falling back on the more limited equal-pay-for-equal-work approach. While many states have addressed the issue successfully for public employees, no federal legislation requires state or local government action.

The Unions and Pay Equity

Trade unions play an important role within this complex of issues and approaches, depending on two factors. One factor is how much the state relies upon unions to fulfill the purposes of the law through collective bargaining on wages. The other factor is the consistency and commitment of unions in combining their power with that of the state enforcement agencies to aid in implementation.

British unions' behavior varies widely, running a gamut from innovative and aggressive attention to indifference, rationalization, and overt hostility to the law and its goals. The unions often regard the Equal Pay Act and its enforcement procedures as a last resort, to be used only when collective bargaining fails. A study conducted in 1988 by the journal *Equal Opportunity Review* of the cases unions have handled before tribunals shows that thirteen unions have backed applicants in fifty cases since the 1984 amendments. The three most frequently involved were the Association of Professional, Executive, Clerical, and Computer Staffs (APEX), the General and Municipal Workers Union (GMWU), and the Transport and General Workers Union (TGWU). They took or supported cases against over thirty employers.[37] In addition, the Manufacturing, Science, and Finance Union (MSF) is backing equal value claims by over 1,300 speech therapists and the National Union of Miners (NUM) is supporting over 1,000 canteen workers.[38] Unions also can initiate a complaint action, in contrast to simply supporting a member plaintiff. An Office of Management Education study surveyed examples of the positive measures that national unions have taken to enforce pay eq-

---

36. Information that would facilitate monitoring and enforcement is seldom available and as far as we know has not been collected systematically.

37. "Equal Value: A Union Update," *Equal Opportunity Review*, no. 22 (November/December 1988), p. 14.

38. Ibid., pp. 13–15.

uity.[39] Among these TASS, at the time the white-collar section of the AUEW,[40] campaigned actively with its members on behalf of aggressive action on equal pay. Tass's equal rights pamphlet laid out a range of approaches which the union had supported and would sponsor, among them a revision in minimum rate structure for TASS members and a new departure in policy that encouraged women in "women's jobs" to assess them for what they believed "hypothetical men" would earn if they were doing them. "We evaluated the jobs' work content and then put them in salary brackets where, in our judgment, *they would have belonged had they been done by men"* (emphasis added).[41] The union anticipated that this self-styled "rough and ready justice" would have two benefits: self-examination that could have a useful effect in reshaping men's as well as women's attitudes; and a practical and immediate effect on the wages of TASS women members. Jean Coussins, in a study for the National Council on Civil Liberties (NCCL), found that "the record of industrial action and negotiation for equal pay far surpasses the achievements of industrial tribunals over the past year."[42] Other observers, however, report somewhat different pictures of union activity. They find, for example, that the union at shop level may behave much less satisfactorily than at headquarters. The authors of the Office of Management Education (OME) study noted:

> About a quarter of the companies we visited told us that they had experienced union pressure for equal pay, but in about ten, it was contended by managements that its introduction had been blocked by the attitudes of the male union members. In some cases, the men had resisted pay changes that would have narrowed the differentials between themselves and female employees and had successfully demanded the same percentage increases.[43]

Other examples of noncooperation from unions included instances of incompetence or negligence on the part of a union official, of a union official who acted as an employer witness in opposition to women's claims, and of cases where unions' manipulations of pay scales to women's disadvantage had compelled women to complain to the tribunal against the union. (In one such case the tribunal gave the decision to the women.)

39. OME, *Equal Pay: First Report on the Implementation of the Equal Pay Act of 1970,* 1972.

40. TASS has since formed Manufacturing, Science, and Finance Workers Union (MSF) in a merger with the white-collar union, ASTMS.

41. TASS, *Equal Rights,* n.d., p. 4.

42. Jean Coussins, *The Equality Report,* 1976, pp. 73–77.   43. OME, 1972.

Underlying these instances of male resistance to pay equity appears to be union men's fear that extra money for women means less for them. At least one union has tried to combat this fear. A statement from an equality paper issued by the GMWU reads:

> The GMWU's policy is to obtain the best terms and working conditions for *all* workers. This *includes* equal rights for women. . . . It is important to note that longstanding notions and prejudices towards women workers persist amongst our own membership. . . . The achievement of equality for women members is not in conflict with our efforts to ensure improved wages and working conditions for our male members. Nor can equality of pay and treatment be separated from the wider trade union objectives.[44]

Valerie Ellis similarly found complacency on the part of unions who have achieved formal compliance with the Equal Pay Act but whose indirect discrimination is all too evident. One union, for example, admitted having done nothing to encourage members to implement the act, since "we have removed from the wages structure and the rule book any reference to men and women, as the same applies to all our members."[45] Rhetoric has never served as a guarantee of equity.

Yet, determined women in many cases have engaged in local action that has brought support from their male colleagues and generated positive action within the national union in behalf of their demands for equal pay. The strike of women sewing machinists at the Dagenham Ford plant, recounted in Chapter 3, resulted in a nation-wide impact. In another case the TUC supported a resolution on "making progress toward equal pay by encouraging national unions and local branches to take 'industrial action' if need be," despite the general council's contrary recommendation.

Many British unions and the TUC in the 1970s established special working parties and committees on the issue. The TUC, for example, established an equal rights committee, while thirteen centers had separate women's departments with staffs of between two and thirty-five persons. The largest national unions set up special women's conferences and issued publications on equality. The National Association of Local Government Officers established the "Equal Rights Working Party" that included representatives not only of its women members but also of its own employees' association. Its report rejected job evaluation as a means of improvements for the lower paid in favor of "flat rate pay increases

44. GMWU, *Bargaining for Equality*, n.d.
45. Valerie Ellis, *The Role of Trade Unions in the Promotion of Equal Opportunities*, 1982.

and the institution of a national committee on discrimination to monitor progress."[46] In 1977 the TUC held a special conference on equal
pay that brought together various unions to discuss their experiences
with implementation. It also drew up a model collective bargaining clause
on equal rights, including compensation, for use by its member unions.
Such models legitimate and encourage local initiative.

British unions during the 1970s exerted considerable and frequent
pressure on their constituent branches to implement union commitments to pay equity. In large part this activity was a result of the increase in women's membership and the recognition that women workers held major potential for union growth.

The German Federation was not enthusiastic about the legislation the
conservative government proposed when it took up EEC directives on
equality. In 1983, when Parliament received and debated the biennial
report on enforcement of the law on pay equity, both the DGB and the
national organization of employers testified that the law had been ineffective. A major reason the unions gave was that it had no enforcement
penalties; it specified no reinstatement rights and offered no back pay
and no money award in lieu of any of these. The law, they said, is a
"should-law" and not a "must-law."[47]

The DGB had just published a set of demands to their own activists
for the elimination of wage discrimination. In describing the situation,
the federation admitted that "women with like qualifications are regularly paid less than men; women working under the same requirements
of responsibility, stress, ability, and productivity are not properly evaluated and therefore not placed appropriately on the wage scale; when
agreements have been worked out with the employer allowing for payments above and outside the contract scale, women are rarely included." The DGB at its 1982 congress called on union leaders in the
workshops, in collective bargaining, and in the educational institutions
to include women in their activity and to check constantly on the wage
scales, on union demands for improvements, and on enforcement of
equality standards. Thus, official policy of the German national federation offered a model for all its affiliates and their regional and local
units.[48]

46. NALGO, *Equal Rights Working Party Report*, 1975, pp. 34–35.

47. Deutscher Bundestag, *Unterrichtung durch die Bundesregierung ueber Erfahrungen
mit der Gleichbehandlung von Maennern und Frauen am Arbeitsplatz betreffenden Teil
des arbeitsrechtlichen EG-Anpassungsgesetzes*, 1983.

48. "Forderungen des DGB zur Durchsetzung der gleichen Rechte und Chancen der
Frauen-Lohndiskriminierung: Lohngleichheit fuer Maenner und Frauen," *Frauen und Arbeit*, no. 10 (October 1982), pp. 7–8.

In addition to these initiatives, the DGB congress approved a critique of the law submitted by the women's division. It recommended making the law mandatory, while allowing the unions and not only individual plaintiffs to have the right to take employers to court. The women also wanted to strengthen the powers of the works councillors in both public and private sectors in respect to participation in job and wage assignments within the firms.[49]

Because the German law on equal pay and treatment was made a part of the BVG in 1952, its enforcement falls to the labor court system. Despite the discouragingly long process, women and their unions have taken their complaints on equal pay through this system with occasional success. For instance, the case of the women at the Heinze Photo-Lab was a clearcut victory. Twenty-nine women, backed by the printing and paper workers union, carried their plea for equal rates for night work from the district court to the court of appeals and then to the federal labor court. A few days before the decision was to be made, the union rallied several thousand members, including many men, to a demonstration in behalf of the women. In its decision, the court expressly stated that it was in no way influenced by events outside the courtroom. Although the court further insisted that its verdict in favor of the women was not meant to set a precedent for other equal pay cases, commentators in the press widely believed that the decision must inevitably have a favorable effect on a range of other equal pay cases making their way through the system.

In this case, the work of men and women differed, but pay was determined by whether workers were ranked as semiskilled or skilled. The men were all paid as skilled; the women who required a year of training on the job were treated as semiskilled and earned DM 1.50 less per hour than the men. Yet the women's jobs were described as involving great stress, close observation, and quick response to frequent mishaps on the assembly line. The district court judge and her two assistants arrived unannounced at the factory to see for themselves in several hours of inspection how the work was organized and conducted. Before the judge arrived at her decision, however, she was moved to another district and the case had to begin again with a new district judge. The first judge, nevertheless, had set a precedent for careful investigation of circumstances with which a judge is not familiar. The union women believed her approach should be used by other judges in arriving at decisions related to women's work.[50]

49. DGB, *Kongress Protokoll* 1983.
50. *Frauen und Arbeit,* June 1983, pp. 11–13.

One handbook on equity law, written by two professors of law and issued in 1985, recommends that women with complaints of discrimination turn to their works councils and unions for relief. The authors outline the powers these bodies have under current labor law, if they choose to use them. At the same time, they recognize that women have severe difficulties in the unions, since "the unions are reflections of society itself."[51] These male-dominated organizations, the authors admit, in many cases seem little concerned with the needs of their female colleagues, despite the circumstances under which women work and the nominal existence of their legal rights. Yet the works councils can be decisive in the effort to achieve equality of men and women in the workplace.

The two European countries not in the EEC are in a decided contrast to one another in public policy and programs on women. Austria is by far the most conservative of those we studied and Sweden the most progressive. They contrast in their programs on equal pay, as well as in other approaches to labor market equity. These differences are rooted in differing attitudes toward working women. Traditional values control Austria's approach to women in the work force, but egalitarian values characterize Swedish labor market policy. A basic assumption in Austrian policy is that women will have an intermittent work-life pattern. As a consequence, the central elements of policy have been maternity protective measures, including three years of paid maternity leave. Only in 1990 was this broadened to include limited paternity leave as well. Sweden, in making a decision in the sixties to recruit married women to meet its increasing work-force needs, committed the state and the collective bargaining partners to gender equality with women's full participation in the labor force. At the same time the Swedes retained full maternity protection.

At the beginning of the nineties, however, with the equal treatment law a decade old, Austrian concern with the wage gap became more active. Austria has addressed the problems of equal pay very late indeed, and is only now with a reorganization of the Equal Treatment Commission and the appointment of a new chairperson beginning to look at the equal value aspect of pay equity.

Over the years there have been at least two studies of the unions' attitude toward the equal pay issue. In 1978 an examination of three hundred collective agreements showed that 20 percent allowed differ-

---

51. Heide M. Pfarr and Klaus Bertelsmann, *Gleichbehandlungsgesetz: zum Verbot der unmittelbaren und der mittelbaren Diskriminierung von Frauen im Erwerbsleben*, 1985, p. 150.

ential payment of the same work.[52] A 1982 study undertaken three years after the passage of the equal treatment law found that while many discriminatory features of these contracts had been removed, completely equal treatment of men and women was far from being achieved. This study showed that 5 percent of the collective agreements still paid women less than men for very similar work; and another 5 percent under certain circumstances permitted differences in payment of bonuses and allowances. Among contracts allowing payment of widely different rates were those in woodworking, glass, clothing, food and restaurants, and paper manufacture.[53]

The new chair of the Equal Treatment Commission, Ingrid Nicolay-Leitner, appointed in January 1990, could state that "although the collective agreements have finally abolished separate women's pay scales, the difference in income between men and women workers has not become less, because these agreements now contain, instead of the women's scales a 'light wage' category . . . with the result that the incomes differentials have not been changed." At the same time she called for a new study of women's wages. She further announced changes that would improve administration of the law through the appointment of provincial ombuds persons for handling women's work questions, and the shifting of the burden of proof of discrimination from the complainant woman to the defendant employer.[54]

While unions must carry much of the responsibility for allowing these pay differentials to continue even after the law presumably made them illegal, employers have contributed to the underpayment of women by compensating many male workers well above union scales, thus contributing to substantial wage drift. The differences in some industries where women under union contract supposedly earn at equal rates with men—in glass and woodworking, for example—amount to as much as 10–18 percent, attributable primarily to bonuses, overtime, and allowances that favor men. These differentials, which were found to obtain in every age cohort, even with like education, result in a lifelong disadvantage for women, since retirement pay is typically scaled to lifetime earnings. Yet because such differences have existed for more than one hundred years, many researchers into income gaps by gender believe

52. Oesterrichische Studiengruppe Automation und Industrielle Arbeit, *Differenzierende Bestimmungen fuer Manner- und Frauen-arbeit in den oesterreichischen Kollektivvertraegen,* 1978.

53. Christl and Wagner, 1982, p. 95.

54. *Frauen,* "Kollektivvertraege Ueberpruefen: Die Gleichbehandlungskommission bekommt eine Vorsitzende," December 1989, p. 4; also, "Frauenarbeit neu Bewerten," February 1990, p. 3.

that nothing less than affirmative action programs, such as exist in the United States and Britain, can begin to remedy the tradition-bound situation. Within the unions, the chief advocates for pay equity are women, including those in the women's divisions of the OeGB and its affiliates, in the women's division of the Chamber of Labor, and particularly in the Trade Union of Private Sector White-collar Workers in GPA.

The basic problem in Austria, however, lies with the equal treatment law itself. Women's work is so segregated that very few jobs fall within the law's defined scope of equal pay for equal work. The union women continue to press their organizations, and to some extent the Parliament directly, to amend the legislation to cover equal pay for work of equal value. This attempt seems doomed, however, for it receives only half-hearted interest and little support from the male-dominated unions. Ingrid Nicolay-Leitner, chair of the Equal Treatment Commission, indicated at the beginning of her term in 1990, however, that "the amendments to the Equal Treatment Law which the Social Affairs Minister has sent out for comment will come soon to Parliament where they can be adopted without further change."[55]

In Sweden both unions and employers are committed to equality goals attained through negotiation. This commitment was fully embodied within the law on equal opportunity adopted in 1978. Despite some recent severe and prolonged disagreements that have ended in abandonment of the system of centralized bargaining, both parties have agreed on a number of radical measures affecting labor market equality generally and pay specifically. The commitment to equality, however, did not originate with the particular goal of benefiting women. It has a forty-year history that began with another issue altogether.

When the LO unions turned their attention to a new pay policy in 1961, they described it first as a "rational wages policy" based on the introduction of a job evaluation system that would be worked out with the affiliated unions and their members. The goal shifted fairly quickly to the acceptance of "reducing wage differentials" in what came to be known as the solidary wage policy. The unions conceived this policy both in terms of stabilization of the Swedish economy and as a distribution objective. If the policy was to be achieved, it required centralized control and coordination of bargaining. Thus until very recently, wage bargaining was a function of the central federation. The design of the first central wage agreement, negotiated in 1952, became a model for subsequent ones. A flat minimum increment secured a better than average percentage improvement for low-wage workers and this advan-

55. Ibid.

tage was combined with a general increase set at a higher level for women than for men, with similar exceptions for other low-wage areas as well. In 1960 there was a "women's agreement" that phased out special wage rates for women over a five-year period. It was at this point that Sweden became a signatory to ILO Convention 100. Successive advances of women's relative wage positions followed all through the 1960s, a trend supported by the increased demand for women workers.

By 1964 the wage settlement included a "wage kitty" to be used particularly for the adjustment of low earnings positions. At this point, unions were given power to negotiate separate increments for low wages where wage development had been unfavorable. By 1969 the wage kitty was calculated on each worker's earnings position as compared to a fixed low-wage line. Thus, "the efforts of the LO focused entirely on narrowing the range of wages, first among unions, thereafter among groups and finally among individuals." In contrast to Britain and the United States, the original intent in Sweden to use some kind of job evaluation was never realized. Sweden's approach has remained unique to the Scandinavian countries.[56]

Such a policy could never have been carried out without a high level of union discipline, particularly on the part of the skilled workers who broadly shared a commitment to the goals of social democracy. Union and Social Democratic party education, of which the skilled workers had been the chief recipients, also contributed to the program's acceptability in the very quarters where it might have faced determined opposition. The 1960s and 1970s were also a boom period when regular increases could be readily achieved. In addition Sweden, as a small and relatively homogenenous country, provided a setting that was conducive to centralized wage bargaining. A high percentage of Swedish workers belonged to trade unions and were thus covered by the agreements. Moreover, wage policy-making in Sweden has for decades been integral to and integrated with national economic policy.

The white-collar federation, TCO, with almost a million members and a growing majority of women, although lacking LO's long history and its affiliation with the Social Democratic party, nevertheless had a higher representation of women in its local branches and women with higher levels of education. TCO women were in a somewhat better position to articulate demands. On the pay question, TCO went a different route from LO, relying on the job evaluation LO had never adopted. Its job evaluation emphasizes the human and social conditions of work. A TCO affiliate, SIF (composed of white-collar workers in private in-

56. Rudolf Meidner and Berndt Oehman, *Fifteen Years of Wage Policy*, 1972, p. 19.

dustry), espouses still another approach, an "individual salary system," individual in the sense that earnings depend upon the individual's performance and the technical requirements of the jobs—a kind of merit system, established to satisfy career aspirations. All of these approaches have failed to rectify wage discrimination completely. In 1975, Scott reports, TCO decided to "castigate both private and public employers for their discriminatory employment policies. 'The lip service' to equality that was so characteristic of the sixties is no longer enough. The seventies must be a decade of action."[57] While Sweden has progressed further and faster than other countries toward pay equity for women workers, its full achievement of this goal has been slowed by job segregation, which in Sweden is even more decided than in other countries. Wistrand notes that "such occupational segregation is a serious obstacle to the realization of full equality in the labor market, both in terms of pay and of job opportunities."[58]

In a perceptive comparison of British and Swedish policy on women's wage equality, Mary Ruggie has weighed the relative merits of legislation and collective bargaining as routes to equality goals. While she believes that each alone is insufficient and both are necessary, she notes that in Sweden "legislation draws on the process of collective bargaining to construct a . . . unified effort for achieving a common purpose."[59]

How does the pay equity issue in the United States compare with these experiences? In the United States the Equal Pay Act (EPA) requires equal payment for equal work. The Equal Employment Opportunity Act prohibits sex discrimination in matters of compensation, among other employment conditions. The question for years after the adoption of Title VII was whether its provisions on equal pay allowed a broader base for approaching pay equity issues than did the EPA. *Gunther v. County of Washington* (1981) seemed to end that debate in favor of the broader interpretation and appeared to open the way for legalizing comparable worth measures of equity. The U.S. Supreme Court, however, has never again dealt directly with this issue.

A broad coalition of women's groups, the status of women commissions, and unions have backed the comparable worth issue as the remedy for sex-based wage discrimination. With the advent of the Reagan administration, a hostile administrator and a majority of commissioners

57. Hilda Scott, *Sweden's "Right to Be Human": Sex Role Equality—the Goal and the Reality*, 1982, pp. 52–53.
58. Birgitta Wistrand, *Swedish Women on the Move*, 1982, p. 55.
59. Mary Ruggie, *The State and Working Women: A Comparative Study of Britain and Sweden*, 1984, p. 181.

on the EEOC have taken the position that the issue is at best moot. They have refused to investigate cases brought to them under Title VII. As a consequence the advocates of comparable worth or pay equity have no alternative but to go directly to the federal courts in the hope that some of these cases will reach the Supreme Court for a clear definition of Title VII in this matter.

In at least one case, the *Illinois Nurses Association v. the State of Illinois,* the EEOC went so far as to enlist the Department of Justice in submitting an amicus brief in support of the defendant state and against the nurses' claim for equity. The EEOC's position in this case was supported by the U.S. Commission on Civil Rights, the agency having oversight of all federal civil rights enforcement.[60] Nevertheless, in every Congressional session in the 1980s, supporters of pay equity introduced bills calling for a study of pay practices in the federal government, with a view to establishing a system of comparable worth there. None of them reached the floor of Congress for a vote.

With the federal door closed, the issue has been redirected to the states. As early as the 1970s, several states had initiated studies preliminary to instituting systems of pay equity in public employment within their jurisdictions. They have been followed by programs in a thousand or more cities, counties, school districts, and other local public agencies.[61]

Growing experience with the introduction of comparable worth in the public sector indicates that the cost of bringing female-dominated wage groups up to the level of comparable male-dominated occupations, as determined by a system of job evaluation or a comparability study of some other kind, is not prohibitive. In Minnesota and Washington, where the first two statewide programs were implemented, the cost was less than four percent of payroll, and even this modest amount has been absorbed over several years. The mayor of Colorado Springs, Colorado, who introduced such a program in the early 1980s, an-

60. U.S. Commission on Civil Rights, *Comparable Worth: An Analysis and Recommendations—A Report,* 1985. Secretary of Labor Ann McLaughlin in 1988 stated the official position of the Reagan administration on this subject: "What's . . . disturbing are proposals from some advocates to make comparable worth legally binding nationwide through a system of strict law enforcement, lawsuits, and all other appropriate action. These proposals imply a level of government intervention that, I believe, is ultimately mistaken. . . . These comparable worth proposals would, I think, take us in the wrong direction" (*Social and Labor Bulletin,* February 1988, p. 145.)

61. See Alice H. Cook, *Comparable Worth: A Case Book of Experience in States and Localities,* 1985; *Comparable Worth Supplement,* 1987; and "Implementation of Comparable Worth in the United States," 1990. See also Sarah Evans and Barbara Nelson, *Wage Justice: Comparable Worth and the Paradox of Technical Reform,* 1989; and Acker, 1989.

nounced a few years later that everybody there was happy with it because absenteeism had been reduced and productivity and job satisfaction increased.

In the actual initiation and implementation of most of these programs, unions have played a major and positive role. Many have begun by negotiating for studies of job segregation. Not surprisingly, such studies have invariably shown that female-dominated jobs are low-paid in comparison with comparable jobs occupied predominantly by men. Further negotiations have produced agreements on how this situation can best be remedied. These have provided for a variety of joint labor-management agreements covering such matters as monitoring and implementation, determination of how and where the normative pay line is to be drawn, and the period of time over which the pay increases are to be phased in.

Private sector labor and management have not followed the example set by public sector unions and officials. Exceptions are unions in telecommunications, newspaper publishing, hotel administration, and clerical services that have been active in putting forward demands and plans, and in using their own job evaluation studies to establish the probable degree of discrepancy between men's and women's pay, the breadth and depth of job segregation by gender, and the invariable linkage of this division of work with low pay for women.

Private sector management is particularly unwilling to accept union proposals on pay equity because, as *Business Week* pointed out in 1985, managers fear revealing wage scales to competitors.[62] This suggests that legislation may be the more effective approach. At one point in drafting legislation on the subject the state of Hawaii included both the private and the public sector in a bill, but by the time the legislation was in its final stage the private sector had been omitted. However, if pay equity is to become a standard of equality for women—and indeed for minorities generally—legislation is probably the only effective approach.

In the meantime, the movement in the public sector is now so pervasive that federal judicial and administrative opposition have had little effect on its spread and continuation. As for judicial opportunities for remedy, they have again and again proved disappointing. Courts hearing complaints based on comparable worth theory have rarely responded positively. Nevertheless, plaintiffs who have not been successful through collective bargaining continue to turn to the courts in the

62. *Business Week,* "Don't Duck Comparable Worth," January 28, 1985, pp. 140–41. This article reports, however, that private enterprise is in fact introducing comparable worth rather widely and on its own initiative as a preventive measure to ward off possible law suits.

hope of finding judicial confirmation of their position. Despite this generally negative attitude of federal courts, some legal procedures continue to encourage plaintiffs to take the litigative route.

American law, for example, permits plaintiffs to petition for class action status. When they are successful—and it is up to the presiding judge to decide this issue before he/she hears such a case—the plaintiff's individual case can stand for all like employees, even in cases where these number into the thousands. A single complaint may affect a whole class of employees in similar circumstances for the entire period of demonstrated discrimination. Back pay judgments form a significant penalty and may be dated to two years before the initiation of the court case. Furthermore, under the law the EEOC can ask the Department of Justice to prosecute landmark cases, thus framing a case as *U.S. v. the defendant employer*. In such cases, the personal plaintiffs bear no financial outlays and the case carries the Solicitor-General's imprimatur.

All of these factors in American legal procedure, until recently, made this country the cynosure of European equal rights advocates. However disappointing the American judiciary's current decisions on pay equity may be, the pressure of the unions and the women's groups on legislatures and in bargaining goes forward. Moreover, these efforts continue to result in occasional successes.[63]

63. For periodic updates on implementation in the United States, see National Committee on Pay Equity, *Newsletter*, Washington, D.C.

CHAPTER SIX

Vocational Training and Labor Market Policies

There is in all barbarian communities a profound sense of the disparity between man's and woman's work.

—Thorstein Veblen

In a technological age, if ever there is an argument that ought to be thrown away by us, it is the one that there is such a thing as women's work.

—Frank Cousins, general secretary, Transport and General Workers Union

The right to vocational guidance and training is a fundamental right like the right to education. It is due to every individual; it should be free of charge, but it must not be an authoritarian measure. Vocational guidance and training constitute an indivisible whole, which should be designed to allow individuals to become aware of their personal capabilities and vocational abilities, and to answer the needs of the economy in terms of labor.

—Commission of the European Communities

A system of education and training, and especially of vocational training, emerges and grows within the historical process and is the result . . . of political decisions made on the basis of certain norms, values, and ideologies.

—Joachim Muench

The attainment of labor market equality for women is heavily dependent on unimpeded access to vocational training. To describe the labor market in countries in our study is to note first, as Veblen did in 1899, its deep occupational segregation into men's and women's jobs. This segregation is rooted in family and school socialization; its growth is visible in the majority of men's and women's choices in secondary and professional schools; and its fruits are evident in employers' job assignments. Assessing the effectiveness of programs designed for women's training is therefore, first, a process of analyzing how much they open employment opportunities for women to a wider range of occupations than is presently available.

A second measure of effectiveness, however, is the one that Muench

Epigraphs: The first is from *The Theory of the Leisure Class,* 1899; the second is from the British Trades Union Congress, *TUC Report,* 1969, p. 506; the third is from *Vocational Guidance and Training for Women Workers,* 1976, p. 38; the fourth is from *Vocational Training in the Federal Republic of Germany,* 1986, p. 11.

emphasizes, namely the degree to which training programs for women can be and are fitted into the national system of vocational training. For women, this means not only preparation for nontraditional jobs, but also training adapted to their relatively late entry into the labor force, or their reentry after some years devoted to raising a family. Yet other measures include the availability of remedies for inadequate school preparation for technical jobs, and the encouragement of clearly stated career patterns with information and counseling on further training requirements for each step of the promotional ladder.

Moreover, there are relative differences in training available for men and women, boys and girls, both across and within occupations. These differences may relate to the length of training courses, the relative openness of admission for each gender, the kind of pre- and post-training counseling available, the relationship of general public education to vocational education, and the roles of parents, schools, employers, and unions in the various systems and programs.

In theory, most countries and most unions subscribe to the individual's right to vocational education with freedom of individual choice of vocation, aided by state support, and with programs structured to meet the needs of the national economy but without authoritarian determination of choice or capacities. Yet in no country has the sum total of its best practice measured up to the professed national goals of equality.

General Education: A Background

"Vocational guidance and training constitute an indivisible whole," the EEC commissioners said as they approached the problems in the European community in 1976. At the same time, national programs, policies, and approaches vary with each country's structure of its educational system and the place given vocational training within it.

In general, in European educational systems, the elite and middle grades of workers are separated at an early age from those predestined as manual workers. The systems immediately postwar established eight years of compulsory education, but by 1980 most countries had raised this to nine. Children completing these years terminated their schooling at fourteen or fifteen. Then their parents sought an apprenticeship contract with an employer who would produce a skilled worker for a lifetime career. Boys and girls often had little choice; indeed they were seen as too young to choose. Thus, the apprentice contract was typically between employer and male parent. Children destined for academic education moved at ten years of age into a lycée, gymnasium, or preparatory school and pursued a general classical program until they were eighteen or nineteen in preparation for the university, and so into academic, management, or government careers. A terminal modern language and science program was available for children who would move at sixteen or seventeen into technical schools or preparation for the semi-professions.

At the time these systems were constructed, ten-year-old boys and girls entering secondary education were segregated into schools. Inevitably these schools prepared them for life in very gender-labeled ways. The introduction of coeducation in the public school systems came relatively late and was first widespread after World War II. To the extent that vocational training was built into the school curriculum it differed sharply for boys and for girls. This segregation corresponded to the generally accepted definition of gender roles and was seen as responsive to women's and men's needs and capabilities.

Although radical changes have taken place in women's roles and status, these systems still largely obtain. To be sure, efforts have been made to update curriculum within the system and to some degree to open vocational courses equally to boys and girls; but the gender stamp on occupations—and on preparation for them—is still marked and widely accepted. A 1986 Organization for Economic Cooperation and Development study showed that "[first,] enrollments of girls in vocationally-oriented education and training still lag behind their participation in general programmes; and second, and possibly more serious, is that subject choices are still markedly divided by gender and that the typically female tracks, in both the general and vocational sectors, tend to be precisely those that now suffer declining value in the labor market." The study also notes the influence of class on women: "Much of the progress . . . has been concentrated among those from privileged social strata. A student who is both female and of working class origin . . . faces a double educational handicap."[1]

Equally important with the gender handicaps of elementary and secondary education is the hampering effect of early decision-making on boys' and girls' careers. Children of ten or eleven cannot be expected to make wise or independent choices. Yet parents who contract for apprenticeships are apt to look to past rather than to future indicators for their guidance in choices for their children. Unsound career choices have,

1. OECD, *Girls and Women in Education: A Crossnational Study of Sex Inequalities in Upbringing and in Schools and Colleges*, 1986, pp. 13, 27. For comparable effects in the United States, see Aaron V. Cicourel and John T. Kitsuse, *The Educational Decision Makers*, 1963; for Great Britain, see Paul E. Willis, *Learning to Labor: How Working-class Kids Get Working-class Jobs*, 1981.

to some degree, been mitigated by school systems providing bridges between tracks in secondary schools as well as opportunities for adults to return in later years both to general and to vocational training. Moreover, general education provides the base and to some extent sets the limits of vocational training. Wilensky and Lawrence noted that education has "an enduring effect on the capacity to learn new jobs quickly. 'Vocational Education' is an illusion unless it builds on basic literacy, discipline and flexibility of mind."[2] This emphasis on learning new jobs and new procedures for existing jobs is a major characteristic of the change in vocational needs in a rapidly mechanizing and high-tech world of work.

Stages and Types of Vocational Counseling and Training

In-School Counseling

In many European countries vocational counseling programs for school children are in the hands of the labor ministries rather than the school system. This arrangement has the presumable advantage of placing them more realistically in the world of work than the schools might be able to do. It has the disadvantage of placing counseling outside the curriculum, and of bringing outside representatives from the Ministry of Labor into the classroom, with little provision for follow-up within the school.

Yet, whether located within the schools or outside of them, both in Europe and the United States, vocational counseling as well as training tend to lag behind the needs of the economy and the promise of equal opportunity for girls and boys. Councillors need constant refresher training, not only on occupational trends but also on the economic and social forces promoting changes, on the abiding effects of gender, and on ways to present these issues to the pupils of both sexes. A 1985 report covering the member states of the EC found that "only in a few EC Member States are girls offered intensive orientation possibilities in the form of active school career guidance covering areas beyond the traditional range of subjects and occupations."[3]

"The isolation of schools from working life must be broken," the

2. Harold L. Wilensky and Anne T. Lawrence, "Job Assignment in Modern Societies," in *Societal Growth*, ed. Amos H. Hawley, 1979, pp. 221–26.

3. M. V. Alemann, "Vocational Training for Women in Europe," cited in Monika Oels and Suzanne Seeland, eds., *Equality of Training Opportunity and Vocational Training Five Years On . . . Vocational Training Measures for Women in the European Community.* 1985, p. 14.

Swedish LO has urged, even though that isolation is less in Sweden than in most countries.[4] The LO advocates more contact with the world of work for both boys and girls and suggests that these contacts include work in community services, as well as in private enterprises, in offices and health care facilities, as well as in factories. Swedish children in the final months of compulsory school spend time observing people at work for a week at a time at a variety of installations in which they have indicated interest.

The unions have sent women unionists who have made careers in nontraditional work to speak in the schools about their training and work. In the LO's view, teachers as well should get rid of their stereotypes about work and workers by gaining experience of other workplaces than the school.

Apprenticeship

In the United States, most young or new workers learn on the job or in specialized private and public vocational schools before finding work; the European systems rely much more heavily on apprenticeships. With its remote origins in the medieval guilds, apprenticeship has been the gateway to opportunity in manual work and many of the service trades. In Germany over half of those leaving school at fifteen are in the apprentice system.[5] Of those without apprenticeships, "two-thirds of all young people who fail to find a training place are girls, irrespective of the level of schooling reached."[6]

Apprenticeship, wherever it exists, has been doubly biased against women. Most apprenticeships open to girls lead to occupations with little prospect of personal fulfillment or advancement. Most enrollments are in cosmetology or hair-dressing, and much of this training is never put to use. Of the proportion of girls enrolled in this field, only a fraction are able to gain permanent employment. The system further operates against women reentrants to the labor market who in mature years are beyond the usually acceptable ages for apprenticeship or even for first employment.

4. LO, *Education—Preparing for Work and Democracy: Report to the 1976 Congress of the Swedish Trade Union Federation, Summary,* 1976a, p. 6. An update of this policy, *LO's Role in the Framing and Implementation of School and Educational Policy Reforms in Sweden,* appeared in 1985.

5. Joachim Muench, *Vocational Training in the Federal Republic of Germany,* 1986.

6. Oels and Seeland, eds. 1985, p. 15.

Learning on the Job in Britain

Most countries now require an integration of practical training with a day or more a week in vocational school for general and theoretical training. In Britain, a somewhat different system of learning-on-the-job is combined with classroom work at the technical schools.

There may be a formal period of instruction, or the newly hired worker may be put in the hands of a colleague to learn the job in informal and unsystematic ways. The British call this pattern "sitting next to Nelly." It tends to be narrowly specific to job and company. One British personnel officer commented about the hazards of such training for women:

> It is not unusual to find that while a new male colleague is quickly included in meal breaks, given helpful information on the personalities, likes and dislikes of superiors, and generally assisted in adapting to the new employment, the woman entrant in a male-dominated or mixed department is often left pretty much to her own devices. Not for her the helpful shortcuts and supportive atmosphere; instead she is often left to learn for herself by trial and error.[7]

To counter such receptions of female workers in male-dominated or mixed jobs, the Swedish Labor Market Board, in an operation we observed, trained a group of twenty-five women for work in a paper plant. As part of their prework training the women discussed their reactions to a possibly unfriendly reception from men who had never worked before with women. Their decision was to remain cool for the first two weeks in the hope that such a reaction would effectively counter unfriendliness or hostility. An important factor in the situation was that the women were distributed among shifts and departments in couples. The strategies worked. In their preliminary training the women were prepared to carry their full share of the load. Both employer and union had agreed to support them should any harassment occur. Training involved more than technical content and relied significantly on developing a support system made up of women colleagues, the union, and the personnel officers.

Retraining and In-Service Training

In-service training is employer-initiated and designed for the employer's benefit in his accumulation and disposition of human resources.

7. Suzanne Richbell, "De Facto Discrimination and How to Kick the Habit," *Personnel Management*, November 1976, p. 31.

Retraining may also be employer-initiated, but employees themselves may see the technological handwriting on the wall and seek retraining through their own initiative and at their own expense. While retraining is a problem for the individual, it should also be a concern of those responsible for training policies, since its lack may be a matter of public concern.

People today must change occupations more frequently than they did in days of less rapidly changing technology, business organization, and markets. The concern for flexibility arises from these considerations as well as from other points on the training agenda. Oels and Seeland found that where women have a choice between taking retraining at an educational institution or in a firm, "they tend to take the school option."[8]

Broadly speaking, however, the choice of where to retrain is not often open. Women predominate in the service trades, which for the most part do little or only short-term training, and where jobs have a short career ladder. Most women, moreover, are in small or medium-sized establishments that can rarely set up on-the-job training programs. Further, in the part-time work that is mainly done by women, chances for on-the-job and in-service training are almost nil. The one choice for such women is whether or not to retrain on one's own initiative outside the firm.

For a study of in-service training for women in Germany, Hegelheimer selected four firms in different branches of work: a department store, a bank, a computer firm, and a public agency. In all but the public agency, the firm sought out young, unmarried, and childless women for training opportunities; but the women in the public agency pool included a number of married women over thirty-five years of age with family responsibilities. Each firm explained its failure to promote and train more women on grounds of "women's family role and residual, traditional prejudices regarding the assignment of women to managerial positions." In the public sector, marital status and number of children were of no relevance. Rather, "target groups are determined by the post concerned, career regulations, and the conditions governing admission to a competitive selection procedure."[9] In Hegelheimer's view, the public sector using these criteria generally does better than the private in maintaining standards for promotion of working women.

8. Oels and Seeland, eds. 1985, p. 14.
9. Barbara Hegelheimer, *Equal Opportunity and Vocational Training: In-firm Training and Career Prospects for Women in the Federal Republic of Germany*, 1982, pp. 11, 41.

Refresher Courses and Reentrants

The most used form of refresher training consists of short technical courses to update professional workers such as nurses and laboratory technicians. These are often conducted by manufacturers of new equipment. In contrast, rapid changes in office technology—from typewriter to word processor, for example—have often left the user to find her own way.[10]

In the case of workers who want to reenter the workplace, few opportunities exist for updating earlier training that is no longer current. Even in occupations with labor shortages, such as nursing, institutions tend to leave this "catching up" to the worker herself. Those who find a way to update their training become reentrants; those who cannot, remain unemployed or find work at an unskilled level.

Many would-be reentrants, however, had minimal original training, or what they received even a few years ago bears little or no relation to current employment requirements. Some labor market agencies have undertaken to prepare women psychologically and socially for reentry into the world of work. After years spent in the company of small children, many lack confidence in their capacities to deal with adults who are not neighbors or family members. Oels and Seeland tell us that these women "are too often persuaded to accept short-term or outdated training courses, leading to low-skill jobs." Many women reentrants need specialized counseling, training, or retraining—or at the very least, refresher courses—as well as help in placement and follow-up counseling after initial placement.[11]

The many women who are "displaced homemakers," older women who have never worked for wages and have been caretakers of elderly parents and homemakers for husbands and children, now widowed or divorced and without independent skills or means, present problems not

10. A study done by 9 to 5, National Association of Working Women (*Hidden Victims: Clerical Workers, Automation, and the Changing Economy*, 1985), in a discussion of training, noted, "When new equipment is introduced, workers are required to learn how to operate it. This process is often done with a minimal amount of help or supervision, or entirely on one's own. Sixty-eight percent of respondents claimed that they learned on the job and 35 percent said they had a demonstration by the manufacturer. A majority (57 percent) reported they had trained themselves, using the manual that came with the machine. Furthermore, clerical workers are usually only given the opportunity to learn machine-specific skills. They are unlikely to receive the broader training necessary to advance to better and higher paying jobs" (p. 25).

11. Oels and Seeland, 1985, p. 16. For an overview of policy and programs in several countries, see Alice Yohalem, *Women Returning to Work*, 1980.

met by programs for younger job applicants. The Displaced Homemakers in the United States has fashioned pretraining courses for its members that enable mature women to make a new start at work. Such courses deal with writing resumes, participating in job interviews, and presenting household experience in business and professional contexts. They also help women to understand the conditions that can make them eligible for employment benefits such as pensions and health insurance, to know what to expect in standard working conditions, and to appreciate how training may contribute to better opportunities.

Continuing Education

"It is impossible to prepare an individual for a working life of forty years during ten years of youth, a few years of adolescence, and the first years of adult life," say von Moltke and Schneevoigt in their argument for policies of educational leave.[12] While many of the adult education facilities in all our countries are aimed at general education or even at hobby proficiency, many have a strong vocational component. On the whole, it is those who already have better education and training who most often take up these opportunities. Although women make up the majority of participants in general adult education, many fewer women than men sign up for adult vocational courses.

Outreach and extension personnel in some adult education institutions include support staff who can help women see the reasons for making long-range plans and who are available for consultation and advice as the plans progress. In Britain the technical colleges, in Germany the "bridge schools," and in the United States, the community colleges are all available to part-time as well as full-time students, allowing women who are still caring for children, or who have started to work, to begin systematic studies. Sweden has opened all secondary schools to adults who wish to return and has designated some of these schools only for adults. This loosening of old rigidities is a significant change in the training system and fundamentally important to women.

Within the EC countries, a powerful thrust for improved vocational training has come from the European Center for the Development of Vocational Training (CEDEFOP), located in Berlin and largely financed by the EC Social Fund. Women's training has been an important target for this agency. It selects and supports pilot projects in member states as submitted by labor market agencies and private local organizations

---

12. Konrad von Moltke and Norbert Schneevoigt, *Educational Leaves for Employees,* 1977, p. 30.

to meet locality needs. With its foundation in 1977, CEDEFOP stated, that it funded projects that "in the longer term were to make a contribution towards ensuring a more equal distribution of labour within the family, at the workplace, and in society." At a conference in Manchester in 1983, CEDEFOP focused on innovative training measures for women and the problems of implementing them generally under four objectives: (1) the possibilities girls and women have of choosing an occupation; (2) improving their chances in the labour market; (3) return to work after the family phase; and (4) qualification for new occupations and functions. Any country that will adopt and carry out these objectives must be willing to introduce special measures for women: "These extend to information and motivation, to financial incentives, to compensatory education to fill in gaps in knowledge, and to sociopedagogic supervision during the programme, the job-seeking phase, and the early period of work."[13] Such requirements are designed to meet women's special needs.

The Special Needs of Women

Women have moved in massive numbers into the labor market just as Western economies have moved from predominantly manufacturing to service-oriented workplaces. Though this transition has increased the demand for women, it has not affected their status in the labor force because job segregation still confines them to a few occupations that are comparatively poorly paid, presumably require low levels of skill, and have short promotional ladders and limited training opportunities. Two centuries of industrialization have made such working conditions for women culturally acceptable and produced social policy based on "the domestic code." As a result working women are segregated from the dominant male society that has created the conditions in which women work, conditions that assume women's primary interests and abilities are those of homemaking.

Nonetheless, radical changes have taken place, creating the conflicts that women face in trying to meet the demands of both home and work—the changes themselves are the circumstances that shape women's special needs. Neither CEDEFOP nor other labor market agencies are unaware of the facts of job segregation and of women's low status both in the world of work and in the family. Indeed, their programs are a response to the worldwide demands for equal treatment, equal employ-

13. CEDEFOP, *Innovative Training and Employment for Women*, 1983, p. 20.

ment opportunity, and equal pay. The fact that this equality is measured by the norms for men, and that women's circumstances seldom
allow them to live as men do, is much more rarely taken into account.

It is therefore difficult for men—whether policymakers or fellow
workers—to understand the nature of women's special needs, to appre-
hend that the playing field in employment is not in fact level. The male
referees do not question that men should define the standards and rules
of equality as they have always been defined for men. By these standards, they see most women as unqualified to play the employment game
the way men have always played it. Women's disadvantage turns into a
matter that men tend to see not as a social but as an individual problem, a matter to be solved by their personal choice and natural preference. In short, there is no place for women on the team.

Hegelheimer analyzes the complexity of issues relating to redressing
inequality in the study she did for CEDEFOP of German programs for
training women to enter nontraditional work. Such women, whether
new workers or reentry women, were without either skills or jobs. She
found that the severest problems arose not from the training itself, but
from traditional assumptions and attitudes of trainers, participants, and
employers about the social roles of the two genders. Most difficult was
the problem of motivating the young women to enter training. This
reluctance extends often to their parents and peers, creating for the
trainees a negative social environment. Where they surmount these difficulties their motivation during training is apt to be high; but at the
point of employment, doubts and fears appear again. Will men in the
trade accept them? Will work in the real world be like work in the
training program? Such considerations determine women's decisions about
further training, requests for promotion, and their estimates of their
chances for continued employment.

Trainers and teachers whom Hegelheimer interviewed recommended
that schools provide more and better vocational counseling, that they
disseminate information about the programs more widely, that they rely
less on bureaucratic requirements to measure learning, and that they
develop flexibility in selecting and instructing students.

Programs for unemployed women seeking relocation in the labor
market, she found, presented an even less optimistic picture. Dropping
out was a regular occurrence, as women who had been out of school
for many years struggled with new pressures in addition to pressing
family demands. To take these matters into consideration, sponsors were
convinced, meant putting heavier emphasis on support staff to help
women manage these pressures. It also meant building into teaching

modules more material aimed at improving motivation and addressing serious deficits in general education.

Reentry women have special needs resulting from outdating of the skills some of them once had, the disuse of skills for a long period, new technical or procedural job qualifications introduced while they were out of the labor market, and the need for updated information on conditions, rights, and procedures in the world of work. Program sponsors can help women understand how skills developed in household management can be applied to the work they now wish to undertake.[14]

Experience Abroad

Austria

Austria's program and performance are characterized by: (1) acceptance of a gender-segregated labor force in which women historically occupied a relatively large place (for over one hundred years the participation rate has remained at about 40 percent);[15] (2) the longest maternity leaves in Western Europe, wherein women's total years at work nonetheless vary not at all from men's; (3) a training system that until the 1970s depended almost entirely on gender-segregated apprenticeship. Then, alarm over youth unemployment resulted in the opening of additional publicly sponsored training facilities in the form of full-time vocational schools in most provinces;[16] (4) a public policy based on tripartite understandings that have been successfully implemented, to control inflation, expand welfare measures, and maintain a steady growth of gross national product.[17]

Little special attention has been paid to women's needs except in periods of labor scarcity. The Employment Promotion Act of 1969 allowed agencies concerned with vocational training and employment to consider the special needs of women.[18] Yet, there is little evidence to

14. Hegelheimer, *Berufsqualifikation und Berufschancen von Frauen in der Bundesrepublik Deutschland*, 1977, pp. 26–30.

15. Traudl Brandstaller, *Frauen in Oesterreich: Bilanz und Ausblick*, 1982(?), pp. 51–55.

16. George Aichholzer, Peter Kowalski, Lutz Burkhardt, and Gerd Schienstock, *Vocational Training in Austria*, 1986.

17. Theodor Tomandl and Karl Fuerboeck, *Social Partnership: The Austrian System of Industrial Relations and Social Insurance*, 1987.

18. Detailed provisions of the Employment Promotion Act include: "occupational guidance for the choice of a career or a career change, assistance to people looking for jobs and apprenticeships, information to employers about suitable workers, and help to

suggest that these provisions have ever been used to modify the high degree of job segregation. Aichholzer et al. have noted that the weight of women's training continues to fall on the retail trades, office jobs, and hairdressing: "The degree of segregation is far greater among female trainees than the males. Over 87 percent of all girl apprentices are training in the ten skilled occupations most frequently chosen by their sex. Among boys, the figure is 54 percent."[19] Careers, and with them chances for success in choice of careers, are largely determined by sex and number of years of education, characteristics that are determined before work entry. The rest of the difference derives from seniority at work.

The system results, according to Gaudart, a senior civil servant in the Social Affairs Ministry, in men moving more rapidly into establishing a career and being promoted within it, because they stay at a probationary stage for shorter periods. Women, she says, are much more apt to spend their entire working lives at the same grade of work than are men. After a break in their careers, women come back typically to the same grade of work, while their male colleagues meanwhile have advanced to higher grades.

In order to overcome some of these barriers and to improve women's chances as well as their vocational training, the Employment Service instituted an information service for children ten to fourteen years of age and conducted mainly in the schools. Gaudart noted, however, that the number of hours the guidance counselors can come into the schools is limited by the insufficient number of counselors. The result is that "limits are set to what we can do. It must be clear that the time available is not enough to do away with the prejudices and misconceptions of women's capacities and attitudes."[20]

The greatest positive effort thus far in Austria to counter a deeply embedded traditional view about women's roles was undertaken by the GPA, the union with the largest number of women members, in its study of working women's status in 1977. (See Chapter 2.) At the time of the study, the head of the Employment Service, Oberrat Burgmuller, recognized the continuing difficulties of Austrian working women and placed much of the blame on the employers and their prejudices. At the same time he admitted that one of the aims of the Service is to endeavor to

---

people in adapting to specific jobs and apprenticeships." The Ministry of Social Affairs has established over the years a number of kinds of financial grants to assist employment and training schemes.

19. Aichholzer et al., 1986, p. 40.

20. Dorothea Gaudart, "Gleiche Berufsschancen fuer Frau und Mann," *Enquête der Gewerkschaft der Privatangestellten,* 1977, pp. 33–41.

meet employers' wishes in respect to gender as well as other qualifications. "In the last analysis, we have to expect, and, if we can, overcome, objections that may arise when we send a woman to interview for the job instead of the man they wished for and expected."[21]

When an employment officer thus defines his functions in terms of acceding to employer gender preferences, he is stating his powerlessness to impose or greatly influence equal employment opportunity. Austria's law on equal opportunity was not enacted until 1979, but since it provides no affirmative action requirement and has only vague enforcement provisions, it is almost totally ineffective.

Nevertheless, the Austrian placement office has from time to time offered pretraining programs for women who have never been in the labor market and who come late to it. These programs have been made available mainly when male labor was scarce and the office felt obliged as a last resort to turn to older women seeking work.

While Austrian vocational training is described as a dual system, made up of both in-firm apprenticeships and programs in vocational schools, the major emphasis is still placed on the former and with small employers. Under these circumstances, according to Aichholzer et al., "It is possible that qualifications are acquired (and required) that are no longer of much use in the employment system."[22] They fear, moreover, that this condition may have been aggravated by the addition of school-based training, which they see as a questionable preparation for the realities of employment.

Union influence over the system is equally problematic. The OeGB as early as 1975 drafted a reform of the 1969 Employment Promotion Law. Their amendments became operative in 1978 and allowed for "modest co-determination" in basic vocational training matters. However, neither the unions (with the exception of GPA) nor the new vocational schools in their out-of-firm training have given much attention to changing the gender-segregated characteristics of the labor market. Girls comprise the vast majority of pupils in the commercial schools and boys in the technical/craft schools. Nor have pilot projects been undertaken that might demonstrate ways of surmounting the barriers to a wider range of occupations for women or to their placement in new occupations not yet male-dominated.

---

21. Oberrat Alfred Burgmuller, in ibid., p. 11. Recent information contained in several 1990 issues of *Frauen*, the publication of the Office of the Chancellor's Adviser on Women's Questions, outlines amendments to the equality law aimed at correcting these weaknesses.

22. Aichholzer et al., 1986, p. 46.

Germany

Germany, which operates a similar though less rigid system of schooling, on the job training, pre-reentry programs, and refresher courses
has, by contrast, a record of considerable innovation. Germany's vocational training has been built on its apprenticeship system, originally in
the hands of the employers, then linked to public vocational schools,
and after World War II extended to include full-time vocational schools,
advanced and technical schools, technical institutes, and universities.[23]
    Girls have consistently had fewer vocational training opportunities
than boys and have made less use of formal skill training.[24] Somewhat
less than one-third of all women work, and women make up 37.3 percent of the wage-earning working population.[25] As in Austria, women
are concentrated in a narrow range of jobs and men and women are
customarily trained for quite different skills. Women tend to choose
shorter training programs and occupations with lower levels of skill
than those men select. Women's occupations for which training is available have distinctly lower levels of upward mobility than do men's.[26]
    In her study of fifty years of the development of standards of equality,
Willms noted a decided change in the German economy in the 1970s,
reflecting a change to a welfare state in which public sector work expanded and women moved from agricultural work and the production
of consumer goods into the service sector. The result, she notes, is a
new set of occupations for women but a continuing polarization of historically gender-defined occupations.[27]
    In 1969 the federal government adopted its Employment Promotion
Act, defining training responsibilities respectively of federal and provincial governments, of private employers, and of such nonprofit institutions as trade unions and employers' associations. Administration of
the federal program lies with the Federal Labor Market Board (Bundes-
anstalt fuer Arbeit) composed in equal parts of trade union, employer,
and government representatives. Attached to it is the National Institute
for Vocational Training (BIBB), which produces regular labor market
studies and program evaluations.

    23. For a full description of the system, see Muench, 1986.
    24. ETUC/ETUI, *Women in Trade Unions in Western Europe*, 1987, p. 78.
    25. Hegelheimer, 1977, p. 30.
    26. Angelika Willms, "Auf dem Weg zur beruflich Gleichstellung der Maennern und
Frauen? Entwicklungsspezifischen Segregation des Arbeitsmarktes und ihre Determinanten, 1925–1980," 1983, p. 72.
    27. Ibid., pp. 13–14.

For several years CEDEFOP played a particularly important part in sponsoring innovative training programs for German women. These were sponsored by a variety of labor market and non–labor market institutions. The unions and the women's organizations allied in the national women's council were important interest groups persuading provincial and federal agencies to take advantage of CEDEFOP aid.

Many of these programs have suffered reduced enrollments in recent years from tightened requirements set by the BfA in the mid-1980s for admission to them, conditions that have been particularly onerous for women. These conditions include lowered amounts of financial support for trainees, requirements that their previous employment must have been insured, specifications on the duration of unemployment, and the trainee's commitment to enter trades covered by unemployment insurance in any future employment. The women who are adversely affected include those who have worked part-time or who have interrupted work at intervals. Despite these difficulties, a 1983 evaluation of vocational training reported distinct increases in the number and percentage of women in these programs.[28] The numbers, however substantial, still represent a very low proportion of female unemployed and an even smaller proportion of the labor force.

The 1983 CEDEFOP conference in Manchester, while on the whole praising the efforts in Germany to meet women's special needs, noted their inadequate provision of child care. It further noted that while pilot projects had been innovative and in themselves successful, they had not stood the test of influencing major changes in the basic training system.

Unions' participation in training programs, beyond their representation on the policy-making BfA, is best seen in the German Federation of Labor's Bildungswerk, its vocational advancement institution. It did indeed offer a few programs particularly for women in the late 1970s, in technical jobs in the metal, woodworking, and construction trades. But rising unemployment that persisted well into the 1980s discouraged a continuation of these efforts. In 1988, when we followed up in Germany with interviews at DGB headquarters, there was no evidence of plans to undertake further programs of this kind.

The unaffiliated white-collar union, DAG, had an active training program directed to white-collar workers in several occupations. In a series of four-month programs with thirty participants each, it trained ninety women within a year. Hegelheimer noted that the chief reasons for any

---

28. Renate Weitzel, *Berufliche Bildung nach dem Arbeitsfoerderungsgesetz von Frauen in Vergleich zu Maennern*, May 1983.

failure to complete these courses lay not with the training itself but were due to illness, financial difficulties, age, and family problems related to children.

Since its founding, the DGB has had an active department devoted to its young members, mainly those still in apprenticeship. Special attention has gone to recruiting young women to this youth division of the unions, where a number of women have achieved positions of leadership and thus laid a base for later activity in the union. Under the law, young workers are entitled to have a representative on works councils. Thus there are two avenues for them to bring their problems and grievances to the attention of their senior colleagues—the plant council and the union itself. These queries or complaints, however, focus on local working conditions rather than on the apprenticeship system itself. The program is administered by the employers' organizations.

In several provinces and preeminently North-Rhine-Westfalia, not so much the unions as an aggressive women's division in the government has continued to offer programs designed to meet young and older women's special needs, with staffs that include social workers and special educators to lend support to women through their transition from training to work. These warrant study both within and beyond Europe for the way they have been sensitive to women's needs and responded to them, both with staff and with flexible teaching methods.

Training for nontraditional jobs has frequently been perceived (as it was for a time by the unions) as training for jobs in the construction trades or heavy industry. Hegelheimer concluded that the CEDEFOP supported programs had demonstrated that many nontraditional occupations existed outside these fields and were well suited to women. Moreover, she pointed out, many social and training problems could be overcome through devoting time and effort to giving information not only to young women but to their parents and husbands as well; that trainers and their assistants needed special preparation for working with women; and that evaluators in the research institutes needed to be conscious not only of teaching and training methods but also of the social and psychological needs of the participants.[29]

Great Britain

British working women confront equality issues different from those faced by their continental colleagues because for many years they ex-

---

29. Hegelheimer, *Equal Opportunity and Vocational Training: In-firm Training and Career Prospects for Women in the Federal Republic of Germany*, 1982.

perienced a lower rate of unemployment than British men, unlike gen-
derbased rates of unemployment elsewhere. Thus efforts to provide
training for this group have been taken by the Ministry of Labour as
less pressing than attending to the training needs of the high percentage
of unemployed youth.

Employers have long managed vocational training on their own, for
the most part on an as-needed basis. The TUC has criticized the narrow
and undemocratic basis of vocational preparation on the grounds that
it left most boys—and the vast majority of girls—who could not go on
to university with little valid preparation for working life. For some
time, the TUC pressed for a central labor market board in Britain on
the Swedish model.

In 1973 the government amended the training act to provide for the
establishment of an independent Manpower Services Commission (MSC)
overseeing two agencies: the Employment Services Agency with responsibility for planning, development, and use of public employment services; and the Training Services Agency with responsibility for the national training efforts and the industrial training boards (ITBs).[30]

The MSC not only involved unions in formulating training policies
and activities but also enhanced the amount and the quality of training
for girls and women in traditional occupations. It also broadened opportunities for training and retraining of mature women, and it made a
start at opening opportunities for women in the crafts from which they
had been excluded. Spurred by women union representatives and other
staff members, several ITBs made innovative efforts to attract girls into
modernized forms of apprenticeship. For example, the Engineering ITB,
on the initiative of a woman union representative, established a scholarship in electronics.

As has so often been the case with nontraditional jobs, the problem
is finding enough young women recruits. The Engineering ITB in Birmingham aimed its advertisements not just at girls but at their parents,
stressing the value of the two years' scholarship and the Engineering
Board's commitment to place each trainee elsewhere if an employing
firm failed.

The program covered four years, the first two of which combined off-
the-job schooling at a technical college with training in company workshops with all costs covered. The last two years the girls were employed

---

30. The ITBs represent various industries and occupations. They consist of equal numbers of union and employer representatives and a smaller number of educators. Their
function is to ensure adequate supplies of trained men and women at all levels of activity,
to improve the quality and efficiency of training, and to spread the cost of training more
evenly among firms.

by participating firms and given in-service training together with paid leave to finish courses at a technical college.

Employers are permitted by the Sex Discrimination Act to give preference in training programs to women reentrants. It allows for affirmative action for "persons who are in special need of training by reason of the period for which they have been discharging domestic or family responsibilities to the exclusion of regular or full-time employment." Two government-financed programs—TOPS (Training Opportunities Scheme) and WOW (Wider Opportunities for Women)—were both designed for reentry women.

In the mid-1970s, the TUC had urged the government to develop a universal scheme of vocational preparation for the mass of school graduates not going into craft apprenticeship or to university.[31] The germ of such a plan was established by the MSC in 1978 with the Youth Opportunities Program (YOP). The MSC paid girls and boys a flat-rate, tax-free allowance of about $43 per week in the first year, for an average of six months of industrial experience, while employers provided jobs and training. About half of the 160,000 participants were girls. Several unions responded vigorously to the YOP, among them APEX, which encouraged its local officers to help design programs and monitor employer participation.[32]

The Conservative government of following years began in 1980 to abandon both TOPS and WOW, and to place responsibility for training once more on private rather than government initiative. A number of ITBs were closed down as early as 1981 and a very restrictive policy in respect to training for adults, including the women's programs, went into effect.[33]

Not only have these earlier training initiatives been slowed under Conservative government, but also new labor market policy has reverted to an unwillingness even to accept women as permanent entrants

31. For the full text, see TUC, Department of Employment, *Youth Unemployment and Vocational Training: The Material and Social Standing of Young People during Transition from School to Work in the United Kingdom—United Kingdom Contribution to a Comparative Study in the Member States of the European Communities*, 1980, pp. 59–69.

32. APEX, Research Department, *Topics: Unemployment*, 1978. APEX reminded its local officers that work experience schemes must be approved by the unions in the enterprise, and that adequate counseling, training, and supervision must be available for the participants.

33. CEDEFOP observers summed up the situation as follows: "The British continuing training policy must be judged at present by criteria of economic efficiency and political expediency, to which criteria relating to social justice have taken second place" (Reiner Broedel, Erna Schmitz, and Erwin Fauss, *A Comparative Study of Denmark, the Netherlands, Ireland, the United Kingdom, and the Federal Republic of Germany*, 1982, p. 241).

into the labor market. The attitude is not far from the traditional view of women as a reserve army to be enlisted in a national emergency and dismissed when it ends.

Sweden

In Sweden in 1985, more than 78 percent of all women between sixteen and sixty-five were in the labor force, working under a labor market policy that aimed at full employment.[34] Long-standing programs of placement, counseling, and training have consistently gained in importance since the mid-1960s, because they are focused on avoiding unemployment. The crucial area in the 1980s was with the age cohorts 16–19 and 20–24.

This program was administered through twenty-four county labor market boards and the Employment Service's 290 offices. Its mandate covered job creation as well as training and placement. In the mid-1980s its budget totaled 4 billion krona, of which two billion krona went to training grants for trainees and employers. Because the majority of board members are union representatives, labor and management have become jointly responsible for "ensuring the development and smooth implementation of the necessary labor market policy programs."[35]

Much of the work of AMS goes toward preventing unemployment. Employers are required to give several months notice of layoffs both to employees and to the Employment Service so that the affected people are notified of opportunities for counseling and retraining well in advance of layoff. Most training is conducted in AMS centers, but in-plant training programs also exist. Relief work is used as a means of giving unemployed workers work experience. Localities are encouraged to increase public job openings if necessary to provide employment opportunities.

Subsidies are available to private employers who hire unemployed workers, who set up new establishments in areas where unemployment is severe, and who conduct in-firm training. These are accompanied by additional incentives to balance the labor force participation of men and women. Special effort goes into counseling young men into what have been predominantly women's jobs in nursing, health services, child care, and care of the elderly, while women are trained for nontraditional jobs.[36]

34. B. Jangenas, *The Swedish Approach to Labour Market Policy*, 1985.
35. AMS, "Labour Market Training," 1985, p. 17.
36. For descriptions and evaluations of such projects, see Berit Rollen (now deputy director of AMS), "Equality on the Labor Market between Men and Women: A Task for

In Sweden, with a high degree of union density, most employees are in unions, and unions strongly influence social policy. Society is broadly committed to concepts of equality in every area—education, labor market, economy, politics, and social welfare—and employers, until very recently have joined in this commitment. The approach to vocational training is guided by the goal of full employment for both women and men, and hence has its roots in the public education system as it serves all ages and elements of the population. The Labor Market Board endorses the concept of lifelong continuing education in the form of retraining and new training to respond to changing forces in the economy. It assumes that women will constitute their proportionate share of the labor market. It looks on workers as parents of children, who may for some period prefer part-time employment. These workers are as eligible to promotion and training as full-time employees and training is as available to them. Only a few countries, and those chiefly in Scandinavia, share these principles. In these countries, vocational education is organized to serve the commitment to full employment rather than the varying needs of the business cycle and of an economy aimed to maximize private profit.

The United States

In considerable contrast to the Swedish model is the approach in the United States. Over the past fifteen to twenty years, U.S. citizens have experienced a variety of vocational programs, established through federal legislation, each intended to meet a specific need of an economy that has been on a roller coaster. It is not surprising that these bits and pieces of response fail to comprise a labor market policy. The fact that many of the programs specifically directed to women have been abandoned without adequate replacement diminishes the possibility of measuring any positive consequences of those programs, where they existed.

In a recent book, *Job Training for Women*, Sharon Harlan and Ronnie Steinberg have brought together a comprehensive review of vocational training programs for girls and women in this country.[37] Individual essays in the book evaluate as well as describe most of the

the Labor Market Board," in *Equal Employment Policy for Women: Strategies for Implementation in the United States, Canada, and Western Europe*, ed. Ronnie S. Ratner, 1980, pp. 180ff.; also Hilda Scott, *Sweden's "Right to Be Human": Sex Role Equality—:The Goal and the Reality*, 1982, Chapter 2.

37. Sharon R. Harlan and Ronnie J. Steinberg, eds., *Job Training for Women: The Promise and Limits of Public Policy*, 1989.

undertakings of recent years. In summary, the book makes five points about the current status of American practice:

> The government has taken responsibility for programs for the economically disadvantaged in a way and to an amount unknown in the 60s. While funding has been reduced after 1980, the legitimacy of the government's role is no longer debated.

> Services and opportunities are in greater demand by women.

> Deep occupational segregation keeps alive the question of how much training investments are worth to women and whether changes in both education and training would reduce gender inequalities.

> All facets of the training system have had to grapple with the implementation of equal employment opportunity law.

> Technological changes have always been an accepted reason for government involvement in training. They are occurring rapidly. Training women to adapt to them is a high priority.[38]

The critique emphasizes that most women are still being trained for a small number of traditional female jobs. Since training operates outside labor market law or policy, employers tend to undervalue graduates of private vocational schools, with the result that few women are hired. The government programs have not addressed the issue of how participants are to gain access to the internal labor market of large firms that ordinarily hire at entry level and do their own training.

Skill training alone is not enough for women. Most of them, as European programs amply demonstrate, need support for child care and transportation, and from counselors and social workers, if the end goal is to be training that promotes self-sufficiency and empowerment. "Empowerment is teaching women about the limitations of personal options and the necessity of community action in the stark realities of local and regional economies that provide an inadequate supply of jobs that pay a living wage."[39]

Whether in the U.S. or Europe, women's work experience bears common marks: gender-bias in school curricula, in educational and vocational counseling; in women's continuing need to carry family responsibilities along with paid work; in the persisting discriminatory barriers

38. Ibid., pp. 3–4.   39. Ibid., p. 8.

to their acceptance in any work that is not already low-paid, and low-skilled. The fact that these characteristics are not common to the needs of men and boys may say more strongly than anything else that women have special needs.

The European programs that merit further study are those that address parents as well as school-leavers, that combine remedial with theoretical and practical training, that include comprehensive services extending to child care, consultation with husbands and family, the creation of a nurturing environment, and follow-up during job search and on the job.

The role of unions in these programs will be played out largely at the policy level by their representatives on agencies and boards responsible for finance and oversight of training programs. To the extent that they have jurisdiction over skilled crafts, their obligations under the law to support affirmative action should include as a minimum opening gates of access to women and providing within the workshops an atmosphere of welcome to those who are hired.

Part-time Work

It is not sufficient to grant to women the rights of men. One must also extend to men the responsibilities of women. Emancipation should benefit everybody. So, if the right of women to a full-time job should be defended, the right of men to a part-time job should also be upheld.

—National Advisory Commission on Emancipation, the Netherlands

The continued commitment of industry to a uniform work week and year is a concession to the convenience of management.

—John K. Galbraith

Once the working week is reduced to 25 hours, it will be normal for everyone to have a job and for the family income to consist of the joint income of two parents. It will also become normal for men as well as women to devote an equal part of their free time to bringing up the children and looking after the home.

—Isabelle Savoy Clot, "What Equality for Women: The Swiss Experience"

Regular part-time salaried employees should without restriction have the same rights and obligations as those in full-time salaried employment. Their interests must be covered by legislation and collective agreements. Their wages, salaries, and other remuneration should be proportionate to those of full-time salaried employees.

—International Federation of Commercial, Clerical, and Technical Employees

Most women working part time have a second-class status in comparison with those working full time, much as most women working full time have a second-class status in comparison with men working full time. The choice among part-time occupations is more limited, the pay is lower, the fringe benefits are fewer, there is less opportunity for training or promotion, the jobs are less secure, and union organization is weaker. Moreover, part-time jobs are not interchangeable with full-time jobs and they become tagged, as a British study has noted, as "generally unskilled and low-grade in nature."[1]

Epigraphs: The first is from the Netherlands National Advisory Committee *Report,* 1977; the second is from *Economics and the Social Purpose,* 1973, p. 237; the third is from *Labour and Society,* January/March 1984, p. 102; the fourth is from *Program for Women Salaried Employees,* Geneva, 1975.

1. G. Clark, *Working Patterns: Part-time Work, Job-Sharing, and Self-Employment,* 1982.

The lack of security which is further characteristic of part-time work makes the European Commission refer to part-timers as "a largely marginal labor force,"[2] which would be the first to be made redundant in an economic downturn. Indeed, only in a very few countries is part-time work described in any direct and uniform way for purposes of defining the legal rights and entitlements of part-time workers or of dealing with part time as a legitimate way of working.

Since it is largely women who make up the part-time labor force, and since women part-timers are largely assigned to menial and unskilled jobs, they are even more segregated into female-dominated occupations than are women working full time. As a consequence their earnings and outlooks are even more limited than is the case for full-time women workers.

Full-time workers who look upon part-time work as another world might recall that their own forty-hour weeks would have been only part-time at the turn of the century. Before the First World War, a standard white-collar week was six days of ten hours each, and the production workers' week was even longer. The thirty-hour weeks that some women part-timers have now is what some unions have set as their collective bargaining goal for a standard work week. The distinctions are blurred further by the fact that employees who work part time at one phase of their lives have worked (or will work) full time at other phases.

What Is Part-time Work?

The definition of part-time work agreed upon in the International Labour Organisation is "voluntary work performed on a regular basis where employer and worker agree to shorter hours than a normal week." "Regular part time" distinguishes it from casual or temporary labor (both of which are generally even more subject to exploitation). "Voluntary" is meant to imply that the part-time worker chooses this mode of work over full-time or no work. In fact it implies very little about the choices that women in a patriarchal society have about the number of hours they can work outside the home and fulfill family obligations as well. "Voluntary" means that, given all their personal circumstances, part-time work is the only choice many women have.

"Voluntary" distinguishes part time from the reduced work week that is called "short time" or "work-sharing," in which normally full-time

2. Olive Robinson, "Part-time Employment in the European Community," *International Labour Review* 118:3 (1979), p. 310.

employees, through no choice of their own, have their regular work week curtailed by slack business or plant repairs or shortages of power, fuel, or supplies. (There may be some choice in work-sharing, if a union and an employer agree to spread the diminished amount of work among all employees rather than having some laid off while others remain full time.)[3]

In the United States, by 1985 statisticians had moved to a five-point characterization of part-time work: (1) those voluntarily at work part time; (2) those normally working full time but working part time for such reasons as holiday, illness, or vacation; (3) those working part time for economic reasons; (4) those normally working full time but not at work during the reference week; (5) those looking for part-time work. These categories were populated as follows: 14.7 million working part time voluntarily; 3.8 million working part time for economic reasons; and 1.5 million looking for part-time work; together with 1.7 million normally full-time workers now working part-time.

Both numbers and proportions of part-timers increased steadily during the period that Nardone studied. (See Chart 1.) Indeed, part-time in the period 1968–85 grew faster than full-time employment. Much of the increase, however, was in involuntary part-time, suggesting that the depressions in the 1970s and early 1980s were responsible for workers having to shift from full-time to part-time employment. Nardone attributes the consistent growth in voluntary part-time work to the rapidly growing service industries. For example, in wholesale and retail trade, 33 percent of the employees by 1985 were on part time, while 11.6 percent of workers in banking and finance but only 8.4 percent of those in manufacturing worked part time.[4] Nardone concludes that the rate of part-time employment varies significantly by age, with workers in the youngest cohorts having the highest incidence. Breakdown by gender shows that women make up a consistently high majority—white women part-timers were 27.6 percent of the white work force and black women part-timers comprised 20.1 percent of the black employed.[5]

Comparative figures for the other countries in our study underscore these trends both as to the proportion of part-time workers in the total

---

3. The problem of identifying "voluntary part-timers" statistically is difficult since, according to de Neubourg, only the United States distinguishes between full-time workers temporarily working part-time and regular voluntary part-time workers. The Swedes distinguish further between long part-time of twenty hours or more per week and short part-time of up to nineteen hours. See, Chris de Neubourg, "Part-time Work: An International Quantitative Comparison," *International Labour Review* 124:5 (1985), p. 560.

4. Thomas J. Nardone, "Part-time Workers: Who Are They?," *Monthly Labor Review* 109:2 (1986), p. 17.

5. Ibid., p. 18.

Chart 1. Index of full- and part-time employment and part-time employment as a proportion of total employment, 1968–85

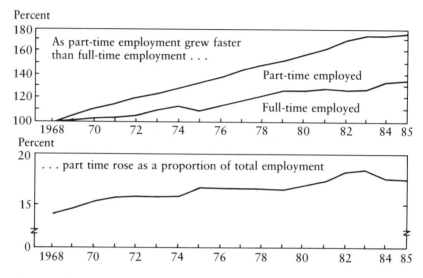

Source: Thomas J. Nardone, "Part-time Workers," *Monthly Labor Review,* February 1986, p. 16.

labor force and the high proportion of women among part-time employees. (See Tables 7 and 8.)

Many industries, as they turn increasingly to computerization of their accounting and marketing processes, are employing women to work at home on piece work rates where the companies will locate machines connected to company terminals. These machines deliver information and supervision as well as work products, while the women workers have the presumable advantage of being able to remain at home with their children—although isolated and working irregular, part-time hours.

In Sweden, where the highest part-time rate exists, almost the entire net growth in the labor force during the 1970s and 1980s was in the percentage of women workers, and that entirely in the number of part-timers. In Britain in the two decades between 1960 and 1980, the number of women in the paid labor force increased by 1.9 million. Almost 60 percent of that increase was in the service sector, especially in education, health, and local government, where 80 percent of the work is part-time.

The demand among women for part-time work has continued to grow in countries with high unemployment. Contrary to many predictions,

Table 7. Part-time work as a percentage of total employment in selected OECD countries and Austria

Country	1979	1986	% Growth
Austria	6.0	——	
Germany	11.2	12.3	1.1
Sweden	23.6	23.5	−0.1
United Kingdom	16.4	21.3	4.8
United States	16.4	17.4	1.0

Table 8. Women's share of part-time work in selected OECD countries and Austria

Country	%	Year
Austria	70.0	(1979)
Germany	89.8	(1984)
Sweden	86.6	(1986)
United Kingdom	88.5	(1986)
United States	66.5	(1986)

Source: Richard S. Belous, The Contingent Economy: The Growth of Temporary Part-time and Subcontracted Workforce, Washington, D.C.: National Planning Association, Report #289, 1989, pp. 51–52. For Austria, OeGB-Nachrichtendienst #2074, March 5, 1981, pp. 6–7.

part-timers have not been dismissed in vast numbers with mounting unemployment; indeed part-time work opportunities have grown; but even so, in most countries the supply of part-time jobs does not keep up with the demand, particularly from women.

In talking a few years ago with working mothers in nine countries, one of us asked them, "What kind of help do you need most?" Almost without exception, they asked first for more and better child-care facilities and then for opportunities to work part time.[6]

Who Works Part Time and How?

For the industrialized world generally, women make up the bulk of the part-time workers. (See Table 8.) The rigidity of an eight-hour day

6. Alice H. Cook, Working Mothers: Problems and Programs in Nine Countries, 1978.

is a forbidding demand upon many women. Among part-time workers are mothers of small children, both married and single, as well as mothers of older children still in school.[7] Some wives, even grandmothers, are fully occupied with the care of husbands. Part-timers are also single women caring for an infirm adult relative at home, girls or women in school or college, or mature women who have resumed or taken up new studies. Some women who want adult company seek companionship at work as a change from the isolation they suffer at home. Some women in transition between years of child care and housework to full-time work outside the home prefer to reenter the work world part time. Women making a transition in the other direction—from full-time work to less exacting schedules, as well as men or women whose ill-health or physical handicaps do not permit full-time work, may have to work part time. Women who appreciate some time of their own because they have been used to it, or women who have never had time of their own but now can afford it, are often happier with part-time than full-time work.

Men working part time are students, men trying a midlife change of occupations, or, increasingly, older men making a phased transition to full retirement. (Here Sweden is the model.) Some men and a few women are in what is often called "contingency work," or self-employment, part-time work in protest against the constraints of the traditional patterns of work organization in modern, industrialized society.[8]

If some workers want part-time work, others need it because family responsibilities, studies, or physical condition prevent full-time work. Still others have tried to get full-time work, but without success, and have taken part-time work as the next best; part-time employment is in fact partial unemployment for them.

There are many factors that decide whether a woman can take a paid job, and if part-time, at what hours. Unless she is single and childless, the limits to her work time are set by her access to facilities—public or

7. The fact that European schoolchildren are released soon after one o'clock means that children come home for their midday meal and are expected to have parental (usually maternal) supervision of homework for several hours in the afternoons. However, since summer school vacations are shorter than those in the United States, while summer vacations from work are almost everywhere four or more weeks, European parents have less difficulty with care of school-age children during vacations than U.S. parents.

8. De Neubourg details four reasons why people work part-time voluntarily: (1) they must combine family responsibilities with work; (2) paid work is not important enough to warrant working full time; (3) part-time work allows handicapped persons to find employment; and (4) a highly progressive income tax persuades some workers that the marginal utility of full-time work does not pay (de Neubourg, 1985, p. 559).

private, collective or individual, subsidized or not—for child care, transportation, shopping, laundry, cleaning, and even prepared meals. Other limits are set by her personal and family situation: the age of the youngest child and the number and spacing of other children, the presence at home of other dependents, and if she is married, the income and attitudes of her husband. For a woman who is a single parent, almost everything is harder, for she cannot make do on part-time earnings.

Too many discussions and statistical studies of part-time work stop with a yes or no distinction: Are you working part time or full time? Yet the number of hours that part-timers work, the times of the day or night, and the days of the week are equally important. The only feature common to part-time hours is that they are not full-time. Hours vary from a few per week to thirty or thirty-five a week; at the upper levels they merge into a full-time work schedule. Austria does not count hours of work under fourteen; Sweden and the United States designate any work of less than thirty-five hours a week, part-time.

Most part-timers have fixed schedules. Some have flextime on a schedule at least partly of their own choosing but within limits agreed upon or set by management. This arrangement means variable periods of starting and ending work, usually around a core time when everyone must work. Some workers are compelled to accept employers' unilateral changes of schedules without notice. All too few workers, however, have a written statement of what their schedule is, or a guarantee of its inflexibility. (See no. 3 of a proposed "Part-time Bill of Rights" at the end of this chapter.) In most arrangements, each part-timer is hired as an individual.

Recently, there has been a growth of interest in job-sharing and job-splitting. In job-sharing (or what the Swedes call "partner work") two people are jointly responsible for the whole of one full-time position. In job-splitting, each of the two has individual responsibility for her or his part of the full-time position. Their shares of the full-time position need not be equal, nor need the two salaries. A position may be shared or split in any one of many ways. One employee may take mornings and the other afternoons each day, with or without some overlap in hours on one or more days. Or the week may be split, each taking a few days, and perhaps spending one day together on the job. Employees may also work alternate weeks or even alternate half years.

Barclay's Bank, with headquarters in London, has a variety of plans for the 5,800 part-timers among its clerical staff of 53,000. Travel time to work in the head office departments is long for almost all employees, so the company does not split days but has two people filling one position by working alternate weeks. In this "twinning system," as Barclay's and other banks call it, two women may extend their twinning to include taking care of each others' children during time off from the bank. (A large Dutch grocery chain advertises for "paired mothers" to split jobs. They alternate days at work with days at home taking care of the small children of both families.) At the bank's branches, with many employees living nearby, especially in small towns, there is no job-splitting; part-timers put in three or four hours on each of the busiest two or three days per week.

A Norwegian experiment with job-sharing was designed to "bring the father back into the home" and permit the wife to enter the labor market under new conditions. A number of public and private employers took on pairs of parents with young children. Their schedules gave each parent half-time work more or less—no fewer than sixteen hours and no more than twenty-eight hours a week—and time which was to be spent at home with the children when the other parent was at work.

Job-sharing and job-splitting are found chiefly in female-dominated white-collar and administrative positions that do not require much, if any, supervision of other employees. In addition to distribution and banking, job-sharing arrangements exist in teaching, social work, libraries, clerical positions, and professional employment, including editing, publishing, and nursing.

In a number of countries, manufacturing firms have developed short daily shifts to take account of mothers' needs to be with their children. This willingness to accommodate was particularly true of firms during the economic boom preceding the "oil shock." Later investigations suggested that as the market became glutted with people seeking part-time work, employers became considerably less flexible in their offerings of shifts convenient to the applicant. Now, as a labor shortage emerges in the 1990s, many firms are again concerned with accommodating family needs. United Biscuits in Britain, for example, has short shifts: one from 11:45 A.M. to 3:15 P.M., another from 9:00 A.M. to 4:00 P.M. (in fact, work lets out at 3:45 P.M.), and a twilight shift from 5:15 P.M. to 9:15 P.M., when many fathers can be with their children and perhaps also assisting with household chores. Other firms have 6:00–10:00 P.M. twilight shifts. The children have one parent around all the time, but the man and woman get little time together.

Short shifts are not special to Britain. Among Swedish women part-timers, almost nine out of ten in the late 1970s were married to men working full time. "Most of the inconvenient hours of work—on part time, in evenings, at nights, and over holiday spells—fall to the mothers of two or more children," reported an officer of the metalworkers' union.[9] The quality of Swedish child-care arrangements is high; but the quantity is still deficient. Some mothers pay the price, in unsocial hours of work, as do many children, in long hours away from home. This price may be a blight on family life and on the possibilities of gender equality because women and not men bear the extra burdens that inadequate child-care arrangements entail.

Part-time arrangements during the regular work week is not the only way to consider the issues. Part time can be understood in terms of the year as well as the day or week. Since school systems still retain the schedules that they have inherited from a preindustrial age, when children helped in the fields, parents must now make what arrangements they can for the long holidays. Various firms in a number of countries offer women employment on a school-term basis. Mothers of school-age children are hired to work until school lets out for the summer vacation. In some cases, the employment relation terminates with the school year; other firms continue the employment relationship and the mother resumes work after the vacation. Only Sweden has legislated the vacations from work to coincide where possible with those from school, although Germany swings the dates of school vacations from province to province, year by year, so that parents can—and do—adjust vacations from work to coincide with those from school. (In both countries minimum vacations of four weeks a year are guaranteed to employed workers.)

The most innovative and radical proposal about working time and its distribution between part-time, full-time, and "no-time" work has come from a Swedish economist, Gösta Rehn, who in 1974 prepared a paper for OECD on "Life-long Allocation of Time." The paper is "a plea for establishing a deliberate policy to promote diversification and variability—in one word, flexibility—in the regulation and allocation of time for work, study, and leisure (including retirement), allowing for the greatest possible freedom of choice."[10]

What is proposed, in brief, is a lifetime reduction of working time by something like one-fifth from the present. These months might be used for studies, including training, an increase in vacations, and a shortening of working time by any of a wide range of alternatives. The plan would be financed by "a general income insurance" with "individual

9. Birger Viklund, "Working Hours in Sweden," *Current Sweden*, no. 189 (May 1978), p. 6.

10. Gösta Rehn, chair, Ad Hoc Group of Experts, "Lifelong Allocation of Time," 1974.

drawing rights for partly free utilisation, thus making it possible for the individual to use his/her rights in various respects interchangeably" throughout adult life. The plan deserves wide discussion for the possibilities it holds for men and women to divide working life between full-time, part-time, and leave periods that would permit adjustments to various stages of family and work demands. It could allow for periods of preparation and adjustment to new occupations or even new careers.

How Different Is Part Time from Full Time?

What in general distinguishes part-time from full-time work, beyond the shorter work week? There are different worlds of part time, ranging from responsible and interesting professional or administrative jobs to unskilled or semiskilled manual, clerical, or service jobs. Among the latter, part-time work is largely a female ghetto.

The pace of work in many part-time jobs is faster than that of full time. Management, in setting the pace or performance requirements for a three- or four-hour stint, does not allow for breaks during the short day or the fatigue that an eight-hour day would cause. Nor can part-timers slow down toward the end of their day as many do who work a full-time day.

Wages and salaries are likely to be somewhat lower than those of full-timers. There are so few men on the same sort of schedule in the same establishments with women part-timers that, under the restrictive language of the American and British equal pay laws, comparisons are seldom possible between the earnings of the two genders, and therefore the protection of an equal-pay law seldom applies.[11] Part-time employment reinforces gender segregation, and thus reinforces the wage gap between women's and men's earnings. Even more than women full-time employees, women part-timers are mostly in low-paid industries and services, and mostly in the poorer jobs within those industries.

The most significant differences in compensation occur not in straight piece or time rates but in forms of compensation for which part-timers may be ineligible under collective agreements or minimum wage or equal pay laws: notably in respect to merit and seniority payments and incentive bonuses. Where fringe benefits such as sick leave and maternity

---

11. The requirements for "equal pay for work of equal value" within the European Community have not yet been tested in respect to part-timers' compensation, so they remain undefined and unapplied.

leave are provided by law (in almost all industrial countries except the United States), at least some part-timers working a stated minimum of hours or earning stated minimum amounts are covered. If, as in the United States, coverage is left mainly to collective bargaining, these workers are likely to be left in the cold by their lack of organization, or even if organized, by their lack of power in the unions.[12]

Employers, who give much less in-service training to full-time female employees than to male, give almost none to part-timers. Generally they assume that if a person is looking for part-time work, she is not serious about her advancement in the firm.

The Union Effect

Part-timers are hard to organize. They have fewer contacts with their colleagues; a great many work in small enterprises that are particularly difficult to organize. Some work in isolation or semi-isolation, at home or on late shifts, or with no mobility during work hours. Most come and go without meal breaks or shorter breaks in which other employees can talk to each other. As paid work moves into the home this isolation increases and intensifies. Part-timers' attachment to the labor market is more tenuous than that of most full-timers. If, despite these obstacles, part-timers are union members, they are likely to be inactive. The combination of short work hours and extensive family obligations make it difficult to attend meetings with other members, even in daytime shifts, and it is difficult for those on other than daytime shifts even to find a shop steward with whom to file a grievance.

A vivid reminder of the problems of organizing women part-time employees came from the 1974 Swedish Equality Council's survey of part-time work. Union membership was higher among part-timers working over twenty hours a week than among those working "short part time." It was highest among those working on regular schedules, during normal working hours. Another indication of how problems of organizing affect the unionization of women part-time employees appeared in the higher rates of organization in the public sector (58 percent of women part-timers) than in the private sector (44 percent of same). More part-

---

12. In a U.S. survey by the Service Employees International Union concerning health care for low-paid workers, the union reported that, "while manufacturing companies generally provide insurance, employers in the service sector where workers are less likely to be unionized and often work parttime, are far less likely to provide insurance" (SEIU, "Access to Health Care: A System in Deep Trouble," c. 1987, p. 2).

timers are organized where there are large groups of employees under a single employer and where all the full-time workers themselves are organized.

The attitude of trade unions toward the effort to organize and represent part-timers depends to some degree on what remains to be done in organizing full-timers in union jurisdictions. If most workers are already organized, as in Sweden or Britain, unorganized women part-time workers represent more of a challenge than they do when even most full-timers remain unorganized. A much higher percentage of women part-timers is organized in the European countries that we studied than in the United States. The nation with the highest proportion of part-time work (Sweden), also had the highest percentage of part-timers who are union members. The reason may well relate not to the high percentage of part-timers so much as to the high rate of organization in that country.

Sections of European economies employing many part-timers are in the hands of public authorities and consumer cooperatives. Because of their affinities with the trade unions and labor or socialist political parties, these public authorities and cooperative employers are less likely than private employers to oppose unionization. Private and nonprofit institutions in the United States, such as hospitals, do not encounter similar pressures to recognize unions. In the United States a few unions such as those organizing retail clerks, where part-time work is a widespread condition of employment, seek to include part-timers proportionately in their benefit programs but meet with considerable opposition from employers because of costs.

In 1984 the Commercial, Banking, and Insurance Union of Germany (HBV) produced a model contract for part-time workers that included the following items: (1) specifying the beginning and ending hours of daily work; (2) describing the nature and extent of work; (3) detailing the amount and construction of salary, including all contractual and above-contractual payments; (4) specifying bonuses and other extra payments; (5) declaring that changes or extensions of these terms may be carried out only with permission of the works council, and any overtime or other extension of contract conditions must be paid at contractual rates; and stipulating that (6) part-time work must be limited to the five-day week; (7) part-timers have priority for increase in hours of work or for full-time openings; (8) daily work must not exceed four hours, or twenty hours per week; (9) part-timers must not be excluded from pension, bonus, or social fringe benefits; (10) part-timers must be paid by the same standards as full-timers; (11) part-timers have the same rights to all promotional, further training, and reeducation opportunities as other employees; and (12) if the part-timer receives less than 10 percent of the contribution limit for old age pensions, the employer must carry his/her contribution.[13]

Employer Demand

Some of the growth in employers' demand for part-timers in Europe during the 1960s and 1970s was simply the result of inability to find enough full-timers in a period of high employment. The continuing demand in less propitious times for part-time labor flows from a number of sources. In some cases, the part-timers meet the entire need; at other times they help bridge periods between full-timers' usual hours. Some of the demand arises at hours outside normal daytime schedules, in what Europeans call "the unsocial hours." Here the problems of part-time work meet those of shift work or any work outside standard daily schedules.

There are several reasons why employers need part-time workers.

(1) Some functions call for only a few hours of work each day, during daytime hours: the preparation and serving of school lunches, for example. Here the timing of the work suits many mothers of school children exactly. They need not leave home before their children do, and they are through in time for the children's return. Time and place of job often matter more to women part-timers than the amount of wages or job security.

(2) Some services and occupations must operate early and late, around the clock and on weekends, such as hospitals, public transport, postal service, telecommunications, journalism. They employ both part-time and full-time shift workers.

(3) Other services need only a few hours' labor a day (or night) but must operate later or earlier than standard hours: for example, the cleaning of buildings, which can begin only after the daytime staffs have vacated the premises.

(4) Consumers demand off-hours opening of shops and service establishments. In the past generation, there has been a vast increase in demand for consumer goods and services evening and weekends, and in some cases twenty-four hours a day: at stores, gasoline service stations, laundromats, dry cleaning establishments, semiprepared foods outlets, hotels, and restaurants. Many of these are the very products and ser-

---

13. OECD, "High Level Conference on the Employment of Women," *Women in the Labour Market: Analytical Report, Statistical Annex,* items 5 and 6, 1979, p. 29.

vices that women used to provide at home before they entered the labor force in such large numbers. Some of this demand for women part-time workers is thus the result of what other women need who work full time.

(5) Employers' try to minimize their requirements for labor. Employers add part-time help for daily or weekly peaks in various operations ranging from retail stores and restaurants to banks. Banks, for example, find two part-time employees more efficient for some routine clerical operations than a single full-time employee because of uninterrupted labor during the shorter period that each part-time employee works.

(6) Business firms want to amortize investments in costly new high-level technology more rapidly than the normal working day permits, because equipment such as computers quickly becomes obsolete. These are needs only in terms of the profitability of operations, not in terms of consumers or the nature of services, and they give rise to the problems of shift working as well as of part-time work.

(7) Employers desire flexibility in their work force. That means the ready ability to lay off and rehire, as business slackens or picks up, especially attractive for employers who are unwilling to take their chances on temporary or casual labor. They want reliable employees without the expense of being reliable employers. In fact, they can have this arrangement, except in periods of great labor shortage. Much labor force management is haphazard. Weakness in work organization and personnel planning is often disguised as flexibility, which means insecurity for workers.

Part-timers normally have more rights than temporary or casual employees but, since few in any of these categories are organized, most of them are ignorant of the rights they have under law or the rights they might gain under collective agreement.

What are the obstacles to employer demands for part-time work? One is the feeling of many people in management that employing part-timers is, as they told us, "just too much bother." Part of that bother comes from real or anticipated friction between full-time and part-time workers. Full-timers themselves may see the advent of part-timers as a serious threat to the wages and benefits of full-time work.[14] Where unions are strongly organized and in opposition to introducing part-time workers, union officers may add to pressures making management reluctant to use part-time workers.

---

14. Full-time unionized telephonists in Melbourne, Australia, commented to one of our team that part-time women telephonists "just want to get the money and escape the nervous strain."

The major stumbling block is the argument of cost. Employers claim that taking on two persons for four hours a day each is more expensive than taking on one person for eight hours, because of the expenses of recruitment and training, record-keeping and reporting, and employer-financed fringe benefits, sometimes including nursery facilities. Employers also cite the cost of turnover, generally higher among part-timers than full-timers. In addition, employer taxes for social security and workers' compensation based on the number of employees discourage the employment of part-timers. Taxes based on the payroll do not have that effect.

How much do employers know of relative costs of full-time and part-time employment? An extensive survey of part-time employment in the European Economic Community concluded that "there is little evidence that much systematic costing has been attempted." Employer claims of higher costs for part-timers "derive more from generalized inferences than from authenticated empirical evidence."[15] Moreover, "trade unions tend to be weakest in the services sector, where part-time employment predominates, and are not often able to acquire evidence with which to challenge such evaluations."[16]

Unionists and Feminists Are Uneasy with Part-time Work

The widespread ambivalence of male-dominated unions in trying to deal with problems of women workers in general is heightened in the case of part-time workers. Most German and Austrian unions are opposed to part-time work in principle. An Austrian study of the working conditions of white-collar workers noted that collective agreements in banks and savings institutions allow significantly worse conditions of pay for part-time than for full-time workers.[17] Swedish and British unions, by contrast, while criticizing part-time work, seek to improve its conditions.

There is natural concern among unionists that the inferior conditions of most part-time employment may pose threats to the standards of full-

15. Robinson, 1979, pp. 306–7.
16. Brigitte Stahn-Willig and Gerhard Baecker, "35 Stunden sind immer noch zu viel: Arbeitszeitprobleme in Lebenszusammenhang von Frauen," WSI Mitteilungen, January 1984, p. 21.
17. Helga Stubianek, "Die Entwicklung der Kollektivverhandlungen der Angestellten in Oesterreich: ihre Bedeutung fuer die Frauen," paper presented at the International Institute for Labour Studies Seminar, "Women and Industrial Relations," Vienna, September 12–15, 1979.

time employment. They argue that masses of unorganized part-timers weaken the unions' position in bargaining for full-timers. In the possibly greater output per hour of those who put in only a few hours a day at the workbench or in the factory-like office, the unions see the threat of a speedup for full-timers.[18] In the lower earnings of part-timers, the full-timers may see a threat to their own compensation. Unions also argue that the part-time work week weakens the movement for the long-run goal of a shorter standard work week. Some also argue that part-time work masks the extent of unemployment.

As for the part-timers themselves, their relative lack of organization is an implicit reproach to the unions. Unionists are divided as to their approach to these difficult colleagues. One view is that unions should make greater efforts to defend and improve the situation of part-timers, however difficult and costly the effort may have to be. A second view is that the unions' task is to emancipate part-timers to be either full-time workers or full-time homemakers, and they can best do this by opposing part-time work altogether.

There is, among unionists as among others, some understandable confusion about distinctions between part-time work on the one hand and temporary or casual labor on the other. Actually, taking on part-timers lessens the employers' recruitment of temporary labor or casual labor, categories which are even harder to organize and represent clearer threats to labor standards than do voluntary part-time employees.

In times of high unemployment, unionists have an understandable worry that the extension of part-time work will be not a supplement to full-time work but a poor substitute for it. They may try to limit the numbers or ratio of part-time jobs, and demand union consultation on the creation of part-time positions. Unionists prefer and even insist that workers work full time to be eligible for union protection and benefits.

Some feminist critics attack part-time work from another angle: that it permits the woman to continue to bear the brunt of the unequal labor in the home, with all its consequences for the relations of the genders both in the home and in the labor market. In 1976, Mai-Britt Carlsson, then chief women's officer of Sweden's TCO, in an address to the CCL Congress put it this way: "The fact that many women work part time

18. Karen Nussbaum of 9 to 5, National Association of Working Women, judges these conditions and the motivations for creating them very harshly: "Businesses' short-term strategies to increase productivity are forcing workers to accept lower standards of employment and reducing America's standard of living" ("Working at the Margins: Part-time and Temporary Workers in the United States," 9 to 5 Report, cited in BNA, special report, The Changing Workplace: New Directions in Staffing and Scheduling, 1986a, p. 4).

enables men to work full time, on terms regarded as acceptable on to-day's job market. It thereby contributes to preserving the traditional division of labor within the family, and to keeping alive a job market system that fails to take into consideration that people are obliged to spend time doing other things than working." [19] This criticism in excep-tional cases has won union support.[20] Like the dominant union posi-tion, many feminist criticisms are based on the belief that full-time paid work is the alternative that will lead to women's emancipation, and full-time work can do that only if men share the family work and the responsibilities of parenthood.

Feminists have good reason to continue challenging the prerogatives of male workers. Sweden is more egalitarian than most industrial soci-eties, yet a Swedish study showed that when both parents of small chil-dren worked full time, the man put in twenty minutes a day of work in the home, while the woman put in three hours a day. Swedish school-children asked to draw their fathers show them mostly staring at tele-vision screens or hiding behind their newspapers, but not at the kitchen sink or holding a broom.

Part Time, Full Time, No Time

Much criticism, whether unionist or feminist, assumes that women's choice is whether to work part time, full time, or no time. Actually their options are to work part time, full time, or not at all (outside the home). Some women come to part-time work from full-time work, others from full-time homemaking (which in Rehn's terms would be the "no time" option). Many an older woman who has worked full time would drop out of it entirely if she did not have the option of working part time; many a woman after having her first child cannot immediately reenter the labor market.

More specifically, many women turn to part-time jobs only after en-during long hours of full-time work plus home responsibilities. They

19. Mai-Britt Carlsson, address to the CCL, in *Proceedings, 1976*, p. 25.

20. For example, a resolution drafted by the Office and Professional Employees Inter-national Union (OPEIU) and submitted to the AFL-CIO executive council in February 1987 reads in part: "An argument to justify 'flexible working systems' is that women desire such flexible working hours because they have to reconcile family and professional responsibilities. In reality such practices merely reinforce the traditional distribution of roles in the family" (BNA, *Special Report*, 1986a. *The Changing Workplace*, p. 101). The *AFL-CIO News* reported that the 1987 AFL-CIO convention "endorsed a number of measures to improve family life," presumably including the OPEIU resolution (*AFL-CIO NEWS*, November 7, 1987, p. 3).

shorten their working days as the strain of full-time work becomes too great or as the family decides that it can do with less than two full-time incomes. Judgment as to when the strain on the woman is too great often depends upon when she and her partner think that they can do with less income.

Another time of choice occurs when the mother has her first child. In Sweden the growth of part-time work has given mothers an alternative to the departure from the labor market that used to characterize the "baby years." Swedish records of various cohorts of new mothers show the changes in labor force participation of those having their first child in 1975–77, as compared to those doing so in 1970–72. In the earlier period, 11 percent of such women changed from working full time to part time and 29 percent left the labor force. In the latter period, only three years later, 21 percent changed from full time to part time, and only 13 percent left the labor force.[21]

It is clear that in Sweden women are accepting the option of part-time work as an alternative to no time, and women elsewhere are as well. In Britain, in the years 1971–76, the number of women with dependent children who went into paid work increased by one-fifth. (This includes women with more than one child.) The proportion of women working full time remained steady after 1971. The increase in the proportion of women who worked was attributable solely to the numbers working part time.[22]

If women with children are to have any real choice between part-time and full-time work, there must be far more decent child-care facilities available at reasonable costs. The number of available facilities is insufficient almost everywhere for the preschool ages and almost nonexistent for after-hours care of younger school children. Transport, shopping, and other community services are needs almost as urgent as child care. These same needs for the single mother are even more urgent.

Do part-timers want more work? Women with household responsibilities working part time may look underemployed to some who speculate about what women should want. In 1974 a vast Swedish inquiry found that of those in part-time work, about one-third were doing "short part time," under twenty hours a week, and two-thirds "long part time," between twenty and thirty-four hours. Only 84,000 of 640,000 part-timers wanted more hours of work.

Fatigue is an insistent companion of the working woman, and an

21. Siv Gustafsson, "Women and Work in Sweden," *Working Life in Sweden*, no. 115 (1979b), p. 3.
22. *Population Trends*, no. 13 (1978).

enemy of equality. Tiring or boring work does not become less tiring or boring as the workday continues. Norwegian research in retailing found women part-timers to be healthier and less tired than full-timers; for example, they suffered less from lower back pain.

Part-time work can also be useful in maintaining job skills as well as health. The option of part-time skilled work may increase the willingness of some young women to take training, because it suggests that skills acquired before marriage can be kept up to date with part-time work while children are still small.

Some feminists argue that the ideology that underwrites part-time work contributes to sex inequality in the home, and can only be countered by getting rid of part-time work itself. Most trade unionists, although unwilling to deal with the problems part-time work presents, recognize that they cannot eliminate it. Union leaders, however, unlike their feminist critics, are in a position to prevent the abuses of part-time work. To do so, however, they must be responsive to the wishes both of women who want more and better regulated part-time jobs, and of full-time men and women employees who fear wage and work-place competition from exploited part-time workers—a balancing act for leadership that inevitably will lead to compromises.

Union Control of Part Time

"If only one word were to be used to describe the attitude of unions toward part-time work," the Canadians say, "that word would be 'ambivalent.'"[23] Yet these attitudes are changing and beginning to acknowledge part-time work as an accepted form of work, unless and until it in fact threatens full-time employment.[24] Unions in government and the service industries have been the first to recognize the need for a shift in policy.

Sweden is the nation making the largest use of part-time labor, and Sweden's LO has made the most comprehensive union demands in the interests of both part-time and full-time workers. This action follows a classic union tactic: if you can't stop a bad employer practice, at least reduce its damage by sharing in its administration or policy determination. The demands of LO have followed several lines: lower limits on the number of hours worked to qualify for social insurance coverage,

23. Commission of Inquiry into Part-time Work, *Part-time Work in Canada*, 1983, p. 93.
24. Isik U. Zeytinoglu, "Part-time Workers: Unionization and Collective Bargaining in Canada," IRRA Series, *Proceedings of the 39th Annual Meeting*, 1986, p. 448.

explain their rights to part-timers, limit unsocial and excessive hours, bargain locally for the creation of part-time positions, and guarantee a minimum number of hours of work.

In 1974, in its national agreement with the Swedish Employers' Confederation, LO was able to get a recommendation for a minimum of sixteen hours a week to qualify for social insurance, plus a recommendation that employers inform part-timers of their rights, and of the requirements for coverage under law and collective agreements.

Noting the continued increase of part-time work—"astronomical," it said in 1979, as the total of part-timers approached one million (almost one quarter of the labor force)—LO made demands regarding part-time work one of its three major new areas of negotiation for the next year's national bargaining. All working hours should be regulated, it said, and "the trade unions should gain control over part-time working."[25] Everyone should have the right to work at least twenty hours a week, but no one should have the right to work more than five days a week.

Some examples of how unions can take control of the use and conditions of part-time work are suggested by the alternatives developed in various European countries. In a metalworkers' local in Gothenburg in 1977, by local agreement the SKF plant could not on its own offer a woman a part-time position. If she herself asked for it, the company could give it to her, but only if the union approved. Even in the highly centralized bargaining context that existed then in Sweden, local unions still had control over the part-time issue.

An example of national concern for this issue is provided by the Belgian white-collar unions concerned about organizing part-time employment. As early as 1959, they won a national contract for part-time personnel from the association of chain stores. (Industry-wide national agreements have long been the general rule in Belgium.) Part-timers were to be in the same job classifications as full-timers. They were to have written contracts, specifying for one group a minimum of twenty-four hours a week and a maximum of 140 hours a month, a provision that made them eligible for social security benefits. A second group would have a minimum of only eight hours a week and a maximum of 110 hours a month. Since the lower range of hours did not automatically give social security coverage, employees in that range would be warned of the fact. Paid vacations and holiday entitlements were to apply to part-timers under the same conditions as full-timers. For a year's work, the paid vacation would be not less than twelve days. On ten public holidays, part-timers would get pro rata pay for the time off. In recruit-

25. *LO News*, January 1980.

ing for vacant full-time jobs, part-time workers would have priority. A final clause reassured the unions that the part-time system was in no case to constitute "a form of penalization of full-timers."

Occasionally part-timers have received pay above full-timers' rates or above the pro rata equivalent of full-timers' weekly or monthly salaries. During the period of labor shortages, Helsinki city hospitals offered nurses and auxiliaries higher rates in recognition of the fact that part-timers had some of the same fixed expenses, such as transportation, for part of a day as did those who came in for a full day's work. When the labor shortages came to an end, however, this recognition of part-timers' expenses also came to an end.

Some unions have tried to deal with the part-time issue through educational work. In Britain, NUPE launched an effort to bring women part-timers into paid released-time courses for new women shop stewards. The original proposal for the program was to offer full-day courses, but these were decidedly unpopular with the women. Their part-time work schedules—such as those of school-meal cooks and servers, and cleaning women—complemented their schedules of family responsibilities and children's routines. Men in such courses were full-timers, who received their full day's pay for attendance, but the women were asked to incur a day's expenses, with only their half-day's pay in reimbursement. They had to make special arrangements, often having to pay for child care during hours when they would normally have been at home. The solution to the problem was that NUPE's London division created a special course, with half-day sessions, open only to women.[26]

The Swedish commercial employees' union, Handels, had only about 60 percent of its potential constituency organized in the late 1970s. In consequence, organization of workers was high on the union's agenda. It conceived a plan to employ its own rank-and-file part-time members to reach the unorganized. Throughout the year it paid part-time members the equivalent of two weeks' wages to contact unorganized workers in small neighborhood shops.

In addition, Handels obtained contracts covering work beyond stores' normal daytime hours, obtaining premium pay for evenings, Saturdays, Sundays, and holidays. This clause was the trade-off for the union's acceptance of the lifting of legal restrictions it had earlier won on store hours during these periods; but since most of the work at the newly permitted hours is assigned to part-time employees, it is they who are the chief beneficiaries of this contract clause.[27]

26. Information obtained from interviews at NUPE headquarters, London, 1977.
27. Information obtained from interviews with Handels officials Malmö, 1976.

Rights under Law

"There is a superstition among too many part-timers that they have practically no rights under either social security or labor laws," a concerned local trade unionist told us. A number of European unions, however, have recognized a responsibility with regard to these rights in their collective agreements, part-timers' beliefs aside.

Three questions arise. What are the requirements for the eligibility of part-timers to benefits or protection under the laws of their respective countries? Where those requirements are too strict, how can they be liberalized to exclude as few part-timers as possible? How can part-timers be aided to learn more about the inevitably complex eligibility requirements for unemployment benefits, maternity benefits, or severance pay if they are laid off after years of employment?

In recent years trade union action has secured some significant broadening of coverage for part-timers. In Germany women's groups and the unions pushed for a liberalization of unemployment compensation requirements to take account of the realities of part-time work in working women's lives. In 1979 the trade union representatives on the self-governing BfA succeeded in changing the previous requirement that an unemployed part-timer had to accept a full-time job if offered one, or lose her unemployment benefits. Now an unemployed person who had been working part time, and who has sought a part-time job, may refuse an offer of a full-time job without losing her benefits, providing there are small children or family members at home needing her care. Moreover, part-timers are entitled to sickness insurance benefits if they work at least ten hours a week or forty-five hours a month.

In Britain, the action of trade union women's groups succeeded in broadening the original coverage of the Employment Protection Act of 1975 to assure part-timers a number of minimum basic rights. At the insistence of the TUC's women's advisory committee and general council, the labour government extended coverage to include part-timers working at least sixteen hours a week, as well as those working between eight and sixteen hours a week if they have worked for the same employer for five years. With this recognition of length of service, the part-timer, like the full-timer, qualifies for paid maternity leave and guaranteed reemployment, a minimum dismissal notice, a guaranteed wage payment if laid off or put on short-time, some remedy against unfair dismissal, and paid leave to arrange for training or to look for another job if laid off or dismissed.

Part-time employment may be the best way-station between full-time work and complete retirement. Recently a number of trade unionists and politicians have urged part-time work for workers nearing the retirement age as one way to create more employment. In Sweden men and women between sixty and sixty-five years old can reduce their work hours and receive compensation from old-age pension funds for up to 65 percent of the loss of earnings. To be eligible, they must reduce working time by at least five hours a week and continue to work at least seventeen hours a week.

This arrangement, of course, requires finding a suitable part-time job. At its 1976 convention, LO urged unions and employers to provide more part-time jobs and job-sharing to enable more men and women to benefit from this retirement plan. Within a year and a half of its introduction in 1976, 36,000 workers were receiving partial pensions, working part time and adapting to the eventuality of full retirement. (In the United States, a similar percentage would have meant over 900,000 prepensioners.)

Phased retirement may also be introduced in Britain by collective bargaining. A plan was negotiated by the Transport and General Workers Union with the South Wales firm of Aluminium Precision Extruders (part of a Norwegian hydroelectric company). Although T&G represented only the manual workforce, the company extended the contract provisions to the white-collar staff. With normal retirement for women at age sixty and men at age sixty-five, the company offered women of fifty-nine and men of sixty-four reduced work weeks in the last six months before retirement-age birthdays: one day a week off on full pay during the first two months, two days off during the second two months, and three days off during the last two months. That meant that preretirees in their last two months of employment, worked only Thursday and Friday each week, while drawing a full week's pay. Overtime during this period was banned.

The various forms of phased retirement in European countries may make a modest dent on the unemployment problem, but for individual employees, they ease the transition from full-time employment to full retirement. Perhaps most useful in the long run, they may serve to give legitimacy to part-time employment in general by including some men, and not just women, as part-timers.[28]

---

28. For proposals of this kind in the United States, see Hilda Kahne, *Reconceiving Part-time Work: New Perspectives for Older Workers and Women*, 1985.

A Bill of Job Rights

From the best collective agreements in Europe, progressive national legislation, and EEC initiatives there emerges what we call a "Bill of Job Rights for Part-time Workers." The necessary combination of collective bargaining and legislative action could wipe out the invidious distinctions, based upon the length of work weeks, between two groups of workers.

The need for change rests in what has come to be thought the immutable eight-hour day; but the eight-hour day is the result of reforms within this century. It was preceded by the ten-hour day, the twelve-hour day, and work from sunrise to sunset. It is not immutable, as European unions have decided in the face of the depressions of the 1970s and 1980s. German metalworkers went on strike for the thirty-five hour week and in 1990 won gradual reductions over the next five years to achieve it. Shortening of standard working hours gradually brings full-time and part-time workers closer and suggests in part what ought to be standard for the part-time worker—the security and standards enjoyed by the full-time worker. Until this happens, the part-time worker continues to be considered a marginal worker in the labor force.[29]

Bill of Job Rights for Part-time Workers

(1) Part-time work is legally recognized as a legitimate contribution to labor force participation, beginning with the definition of part-time work as a basis for full participation in labor market programs of training, benefits, entitlements, rights, and duties.

(2) Part-time workers must receive coverage under existing laws, through pro rata entitlements to financial benefits and allowances on vacations and other periods of leave.

(3) Employers must establish regular hours of work or agreed flextime. Employees may work hours beyond this schedule only on a voluntary basis and must receive premium pay for overtime and for work they perform during evenings, weekends, and holidays, whether this work is within their regular schedules or is performed as overtime. Wages and salaries must be set at least at the pro rata equivalent of pay for similar work by full-time employees.

29. See the full set of "Recommendations" in Commission of Inquiry into Part-time Work, 1983, pp. 29–32.

(4) Part-time employees are eligible for employer-sponsored leaves for care of newborn and adopted children.

(5) Minimum levels of eligibility for social insurance and support programs (child care, parental leaves, transportation allowances) are to be no less than half those for the standard work week, and no less for any employees with some specified years of continuous work experience.

(6) Discrimination against part-time employees in work assignments, safety, and health protection at the workplace is prohibited; and access to employer welfare facilities is guaranteed.

(7) Part-time workers will be provided opportunities on the same basis as full-time employees for in-service training, educational leave, and leave for training for union functions (shop steward, safety and health representative.)

(8) Part-time workers will be provided opportunities for promotion in accordance with qualifications and experience, and given priority, along with regular full-time employees, on bidding for vacant full-time positions, before there is hiring from outside. Full-time employees will be given priority in applying for new part-time positions.

(9) Part-time workers will be protected against arbitrary dismissal, have rights to severance pay, and have access to grievance machinery.

(10) Part-time workers will accumulate seniority in proportion to hours worked, and their seniority will determine the order of layoffs or dismissal for lack of work, and the order of recall. Priority layoffs of part-timers before others is forbidden.

(11) Newly inducted part-time employees will be informed by employers and union representatives of their rights under law and collective agreements, and of the hours to be worked and length of service required for coverage by labor laws and social security entitlements. The employment service and private placement agencies will give information requirements for coverage by law to those seeking part-time positions.

(12) Employers should as a rule offer part-timers at least the minimum number of hours to qualify for benefits under social insurance. Job seekers may nevertheless want shorter hours, but the choice should be theirs.

(13) Unemployed part-time workers should not be disqualified from unemployment compensation for refusal to accept full-time work.

(14) Legal requirements to phased retirement under both private and public pension rights will be set at age sixty-two for both men and women.

(15) Employers will encourage public discussion and proposals for the eventual introduction of programs granting lifetime mixtures of full- and part-time work, including years of leave.

The rights we have listed would create the conditions for the nondiscriminatory part-time work that the European Economic Community called for in 1982. Some of these rights already have been achieved by collective bargaining or law or a combination of the two in the countries that we studied, but they have not all been achieved in any one of them. Even more sweeping changes could be introduced with careful evaluation of the impact of present reforms and with serious attention to the spread of and safeguards on part-time work. The part-time alternative in work schedules presents an opportunity for a widespread, perhaps revolutionary, change in the relations between work and family, work and leisure. How might society be changed if basic assumptions about the rigidity of a day, a week, a lifetime of full-time work were to change? Such a question may be unanswerable now; but workers who see the possibilities of a different and less pressured organization of life may lead the way to answers in the future.

CHAPTER EIGHT

Health and Safety in the Workplace

In coming years we may see a shift in the emphasis and intensity of worker initiatives to promote health and safety in the workplace. . . . More and more we are learning that occupational exposures can impair both the health of the worker's future children and his or her ability to have those children. . . . Even if workers are willing to accept a degree of risk to their own health as a condition of employment, they may be far less willing to accept risks to their ability to bring healthy children into the world.

—Nicholas A. Ashford and Charles C. Caldart, "The Control of Reproductive Hazards in the Workplace: A Prescription for Prevention"

The dynamics of collective bargaining over health and safety measures have been significantly changed in recent years . . . with the passage of federal statutes providing for close regulation of health and safety matters.

—Charles W. Newcom, "Employee Health and Safety Rights under the LMRA and Federal Safety Laws"

Safety education must aim at being a powerful force for change.

—Kaj Eigstrand

Every industrial worker runs the same decisive risks whether he or she be strong as a bear or delicate as a flower. . . . The noise damages ears without exception, the air damages lungs without exception, the stress damages nerves without exception.

—Gøran Palm

In Willow Island, on the Ohio River in West Virginia, the right to life has hung in one case on the construction of a scaffolding and in another on the amount of lead in the pigment section of a chemical plant. Early in 1978, the scaffolding of a power plant's construction job collapsed, carrying fifty-one workmen to sudden death.

Just a few miles away and a few months later, a threat to life not yet in being was reported by seventeen women working in the thirty-year-old plant of the American Cyanimid Corporation, which produces over one hundred base chemicals. This is the women's story: all being of childbearing age, they were informed by the company that they would

Epigraphs: The first is from *Industrial Relations Law Journal* 5:4 (1983), p. 523; the second is from *Labor Law Journal* 32:6 (July 1981), p. 395; the third is from *Training and Education in Occupational Safety and Health in Sweden,* 1977, p. 21; the fourth is from *The Flight from Work,* 1977.

have to give up their jobs in sections of the plant using lead or various chemicals that might injure an unborn child through the mother. They would be transferred to lower-paying jobs in the janitorial department; some might lose their jobs altogether. There was one other possibility, however. If they were sterilized, they could keep their jobs. Directly or indirectly, company officials pressured them, some of the women said, to take that course, and they underwent sterilization at a local hospital. "I wish now that I'd been stronger," said one thirty-one-year-old, divorced mother of two children. "I didn't want to be sterile." Said another, "I did it because I was scared and I had to have the income." The company's spokesman said that it discourages sterilization: "If it was done, we did not sanction it."[1]

Anthony Mazzochi, at the time vice-president of the union to which the women belonged, the Oil, Chemical, and Atomic Workers (OCAW), saw the situation as a familiar one in OCAW's campaigns for health and safety: "Women are now being confronted with the dismal choice of relinquishing their right to have children, or their jobs. This is not the only company that is trying to force women out of the workplace, rather than clean it up."[2]

On October 12, 1979, the U.S. Occupational Safety and Health Administration (OSHA) cited American Cyanimid for willful violation of a clause of the 1970 Occupational Safety and Health Act that requires employers to provide work free from recognized hazards likely to cause death or serious physical harm. Eula Bingham, at the time head of OSHA, recalled that the reproductive health of both men and women workers was a part of OSHA's responsibilities: "No worker must be forced to

1. The federal appeals court finding on this point reads as follows: "In January and February of 1978, Glen Mercer, the Director of Industrial Relations, conducted a series of meetings for small groups of the Willow Island plant's female employees. At these meetings Mercer informed the women that hundreds of chemicals used at the plant are harmful to fetuses and that, consequently, the company had decided to exclude women of 'child-bearing capacity' from all departments of the plant where such chemicals were used. Mercer further declared that the company would deem any woman between the ages of 16 and 50 to be of childbearing capacity unless she presented proof that she had been surgically sterilized. A company doctor and nurse accompanied Mercer to these meetings and addressed the women. They explained to the women that such 'buttonhole surgery' was simple and that it could be obtained locally in several places. . . . The women were also told that the company's medical insurance would pay for the procedure, and that sick leave would be provided to those undergoing the surgery" (decision of District of Columbia Circuit in *OCAW v. American Cyanimid Company*, no. 81-1687, decided August 24, 1984).

2. OCAW leaflet, *Health and Safety in the Oil and Chemical Industry*, no date (1979?). See also "OSHA Inspecting American Cyanimid Plant following Complaint from OCAW," BNA, *Daily Labor Report*, no. 8 (January 11, 1979), pp. A-1–3.

sacrifice his or her right to conceive children in order to hold a job."[3] OSHA proposed only a $10,000 fine against American Cyanimid; the fine meant as much to the company as a nickel or a dime out of a worker's pocket.

An OSHA administrative judge dismissed the union's complaint on the grounds that the fetus protection policy is not a hazard within the meaning of the Act's general duty clause requiring employers to provide a workplace free from recognized hazards. "The employer neither controls nor creates the [economic and social factors that operate outside the workplace] as he controls work processes and materials." The Occupational Safety and Health Review Commission (OSHARC) rejected the union's appeal of the decision and sustained the company.[4] Then with the support of the American Civil Liberties Union (ACLU), the union turned once more to the courts. On August 28, 1984, the Eleventh Circuit Court of Appeals with Justice Bork and Justice Scalia (whose nominations to the Supreme Court a few years later caused debate) joined in sustaining the company's argument and the commission's decision. They concluded:

> The case might be different if American Cyanimid had offered the choice of sterilization in an attempt to pass on to its employees the cost of maintaining an ambient lead concentration higher than that permitted by law. But that is not the case. The company could not reduce lead concentration to a level that posed an acceptable risk to fetuses. The sterilization exception to the requirement of removal from the Inorganic Pigments Department was an attempt not to pass on costs of unlawful conduct but to permit the employees to mitigate costs to them imposed by unavoidable physiological facts.
>
> The women involved in this matter were put to a most unhappy choice. But no statute redresses all grievances and we must decide cases according to law. Reasoning from precedent, congressional intent, and the unforseeable consequences of a contrary holding, we conclude the American Cyanimid's "fetus protection policy" did not constitute a "hazard" within the meaning of the OSH Act.[5]

3. "OSHA Proposes Fines Totaling $269,710 on General Dynamics, American Cyanimid," BNA, *Daily Labor Report*, no. 199 (October 12, 1979), p. A-9.

4. "American Cyanimid Prevails in 'Fetus Protection Policy,' " ibid., no. 84 (May 1, 1981), p. A-6–7; text, E-1. For a full legal history of the case to this denial of *certiorari* by the Supreme Court, see "Case of Females Exposed to Lead," ibid., no. 197 (October 12, 1982), p. A-11.

5. "Court Blocks Challenge to American Cyanimid's 'Fetus Protection' Policy for Lead Exposures," ibid., no. 167 (August 24, 1984), p. A-1; text, "*Oil, Chemical and Atomic Workers Union v. American Cyanimid Company*, CA DC no. 81-1687, p. E-1–3.

The union thereupon turned to a plea under Title VII of the Civil Rights Act, and under threat of that action, American Cyanimid settled the case out of court. The terms of this settlement have not been made public, a condition often imposed by the guilty party in agreeing to a settlement.

Meanwhile, Willow Island had sparked the formation of the Coalition for Reproductive Rights of Workers. This coalition brought together representatives of trade unions, occupational health institutes, legal and civil rights groups, and women's organizations to defend both the health and the job rights of women and men threatened by toxic chemicals and other workplace hazards. "Fix the workplace and not the worker," demanded the Coalition of Labor Union Women.

Problems That Women Face

Women face five types of problems: the hazards that they share with men because they work in the same factories or offices or services; the hazards that are particularly those of women because of their segregation in a small number of so-called women's industries and women's occupations; the physical and especially the mental or psychosocial problems created by the double burden of paid work and unpaid family work; the risks involved in pregnant women's working in certain jobs; and the risks to women in jobs beyond their physical capacities.

Almost none of the risks is a risk to women alone. There are some men in most "women's industries" and some women in most "men's industries." Some men also suffer the combined strains of paid work environment and home responsibilities. There is no safety for women unless men workers are also protected, no safety for men unless women workers are also protected.

The Risks That Women and Men Share

At the beginning of this chapter we have quoted from a book that Gøran Palm wrote after a year's work on assembly operations at a large telephone equipment plant in Stockholm. As his account makes clear, the damage of unhealthy exposure at work is not gender specific.[6]

If something is known about the sources and the prevention of acci-

6. Gøran Palm, *Flight from Work*, 1979, p. 81. Palm worked for a year incognito at the L. M. Ericsson Company, the "Western Electric of Sweden."

dents and of disease, there is much that is unknown about the toxic substances that pollute the air of workplaces, about noise and other strains to the nervous system, and about the consequences of lack of autonomy, variety, and respect in working life. A flood of new materials have been produced, marketed, and introduced into the workplaces of the industrial countries. A list of new substances was prepared by the National Institute of Occupational Safety and Health (NIOSH) in 1973. It identified at that time over 12,000 toxic chemicals in American commercial and industrial life, and each year some 3,000 new chemicals are introduced into the American economy, with little study of their effects on human beings and few standards for their safe usage. The tragic consequences for working men and women exposed to vinyl chloride, benzene, lead, or asbestos (to name just a few) are only now becoming public knowledge.

Moreover, the consequences of any single toxic agent or any single stress factor are only part of the problem. Chemical, biological, physical, and stress hazards may combine in ways whose effects are more than the sum of their separate effects. This is called "synergism." For example, carbon monoxide and heat, amphetamines and overcrowding, or asbestos and smoking are known to produce synergistic effects. "The real world does not contain isolated hazards," Nicholas Ashford points out, "yet the combination effects are still only rarely studied."[7]

The measures that many employers find easiest and (in the short run) cheapest to adopt in order to reduce obvious threats to health and safety are protective devices for the worker to wear. The protective devices do not always fit, since faces are of different sizes, shapes, and hirsuite adornment. They are often so uncomfortable or lead to such losses of productivity that workers take them off. Most are made for men and not for women (at least in the trades in which women have not traditionally been employed). If they fit, they do not always work. Even if they seem to work, they may create problems as bad as those that they are designed to resolve: for example, ear plugs or protectors deprive operators of hearing and may disorient them in a prison of social isolation; they may cause infections and problems of the outer ear canal.

---

7. Nicholas Ashford, *Crisis in the Workplace: Occupational Disease and Injury*, 1976, p. 83. This book is a detailed survey by the then head of NIOSH. Although it is not written for a popular audience, it is entirely readable. *In These Times* in 1980 carried an article ("Valley of the Shadow of Death," 8:41) on Silicon Valley by Susan Martinez and Alan Ranio that stresses the "synergistic effect," i.e., the effect of a variety of chemicals that may be geometrically greater than the hazards of each individual substance.

The Risks of "Women's Occupations"

If some of the most dangerous occupations employ few women, there are a number of others that employ many women. In some of the typical women's industries and women's occupations, the risks to health are widespread. For example, the manufacture of men's clothing, employing about 320,000 women in the United States, looks from a distance like a rather benign industry. Yet its mechanical and chemical hazards have been documented in a NIOSH study (which had to be financed by a grant from the Amalgamated Clothing and Textile Workers Union of America [ACTWU]).[8]

Service operations employ many blue-collar women and expose workers to hazardous materials and conditions, including detergents and other chemicals for cleaning, heat, backstrain, and stress from irregular work schedules, from dealing with frustrated and unhappy clients, and from working unsocial hours. Such operations include the cleaning of buildings and work in laundries, dry cleaning establishments, beauty parlors, hotels, and restaurants. Nursing has many risks; social work with welfare clients, the aged, and prisoners can pile stress upon stress. Routine white-collar jobs, contrary to the general notion that they are safe and comfortable office work, expose millions of women to risks of accidents and occupational ailments. Technological advances have created new medical dangers, notably strains on eyes (from increased use of video display terminals [VDTs], for example), ears, and nervous systems.

Assembly-line methods, computer-based technology, and stepped-up production schedules have increased stress in many white-collar occupations. The size, layout, equipment, traffic patterns, pace of work, and relations between employees and supervisors in those inhuman landscapes that the Germans call "vast office spaces" all create problems that researchers are only beginning to study.[9] Even in the matter of accidents, many office workers are at considerable risk—from floor obstructions, top-heavy filing cabinets, poor lighting, rickety or unsuitable chairs, trailing telephone and light wires, and chemical substances. Offices are safe places only if they are made safe.

8. See Phyllis Lehman, "Women Workers: Are They Special?" in the U.S. Department of Labor's *Job Safety and Health*, April 1975. This useful publication was suppressed by short-sighted federal budget penny-pinching, just as the increase in occupational safety and health education in this country made such a magazine more useful than ever.
9. One of the foremost scholars in the field of social psychology is Bertil Gardell of the Swedish Social Science Research Council, who directs a working team on the social psychology of working life. For an introductory article on this approach, see "Psychosocial Aspects of the Working Environment," *Working Life in Sweden*, no. 1 (October 1979).

The Double Day

The double day is a fact of many working women's lives. They work at a paid job, then go home to another set of work responsibilities to maintain the household and family. Research shows that though a few men also work the double day (primarily those who are themselves single parents) and though a few more men spend more time on household responsibilities than their predecessors, the vast majority of domestic chores are done by women.

The problems may be largely physical—backstrain, to take a common example—and difficult to diagnose and treat if the woman continues to work the double day. Even more pronounced and recently gaining some of the attention that they merit, especially in the United States, are the psychosocial problems that result from physical combined with mental and emotional strain.

The human organism is so complex that it is often impossible (and usually wrong to try) to dissociate the factors that caused its malfunctioning. Ongoing research on the effects of the double day on work life and work capacity suggest that the stress of unrelieved responsibilities affects both work and home life. Yet most believe that the stress of work is a fact of life that one has to accept to hold a job. Indeed the cumulation of factors that produce job stress may be a major contributor to the tensions of the double day. Most modern physicians look beyond symptoms to the whole persons who live both at home and at work.[10]

Pregnancy

Pregnant workers and their unborn infants have been the object of much sentimental talk and some protective legislation, but they are also the growing subject of study. At the worksite, concerns about pregnant workers' well-being lead only to sporadic and often misguided action. There is little available knowledge of workplace risks to mother and fetus in the critical first three months of pregnancy. Only about two dozen workplace chemicals have been linked with miscarriages and birth defects—a statement about the level of ignorance, not safety. Few of the 20,000 chemicals common to work environments have been tested for

10. The British journal *Labour Research* has summarized the hazards of women's dual role of worker and mother as involving "low pay, shift work, payment by results, staff shortages and sexual and racial harassment . . . all factors identified as causing stress to women workers, in a National Union of Public Employees (NUPE) woman's course on stress at the workplace" (March 1988, pp. 18–20).

their effects on the expectant mother, the unborn child, or women and men in general. Yet almost any chemical the pregnant woman inhales, swallows, or absorbs through the skin may turn up in the fetus.

Ordinarily, women do not know during the first weeks after conception that they are pregnant, and those are weeks in which the embryo is at greatest risk. Among those who do know, many hesitate to inform supervisors or employers of their pregnancy out of well-founded fears of dismissal, or, if outright dismissal is forbidden by law, fear of harassment to make them quit.

Research on pregnancy and the workplace has shown that both women and men are at risk. For example, studies documenting the high miscarriage rate of the wives of men exposed to anesthetic gases when their spouses were not exposed show that anesthetic gases cause genetic damage to the sperm. A number of chemicals affect men's reproductive capacities, among them lead, benzene, cadmium, carbon disulfide, and the pesticide DBCP.

It was the danger to the male reproductive system that first called forth the international action necessary to fight occupational hazards. In 1977 the U.S. government discovered the danger associated with DBCP, a pesticide widely used to protect root crops. Fourteen of the thirty-seven men handling DBCP at a California chemical plant were found to be sterile or to have low sperm counts. The United States then set in motion, for the first time, the new International Occupational Safety and Health Hazard Alert developed by the ILO. From Geneva the ILO sent urgent messages to other countries to obtain the needed information on the use of the incriminated chemical and occupational exposure to it. As a result of this initiative, trade unions here and abroad continue to propose more international trade union action to detect, expose, and combat dangerous substances in the workplace.

Risks to Women in Jobs beyond Their Physical Capacities

On the average, the physical work capacity of women is lower than that of men of the same size and weight. With body weight the same, the maximal oxygen uptake of women is about 20 percent less than that of men, their hearts and lungs are smaller. They have about 24 percent of their body weight in fat, as compared to men's 18 percent; that fat is useful for long-distance swimming, but not for most jobs. They have shorter legs in relation to trunk than men, however, and that relationship is useful in lifting.

"It would be silly to try to place many women in the most strenuous jobs, where they could not perform as equals to many men," a Swedish physical anatomy expert, Dr. Irma Åstrand, told us. For some women, taking on such jobs would expose them to serious health risks, and not all these risks could be predicted by preemployment physical exams. Moreover, as she warned, "their failure at such jobs would reinforce stereotypes and make sensible change more difficult."

Employers, particularly in the heavy manufacturing and construction trades, have tended to exclude all women from jobs that many women are physically capable of doing. Though on average women may have smaller muscle capacities than men, there is also a great deal of overlap between the sexes. Determining objective measures of the physical demands of a job, and then determining objective measures of an individual's physical capabilities, is a step neither employers nor unions in these fields have wanted to undertake. In the United States with the introduction of EEOC guidelines on employment opportunity a beginning was made on the problem. But even if the guidelines were observed, at best they only prevented a qualified woman from being turned away. They could neither prevent women from taking jobs beyond their physical capacities nor require employers to adjust work and fit work clothing to women's needs. It is that issue that concerns us here.

Management and unions could do a good deal more than is usually done to make jobs physically easier. For example, most machines are built to men's sizes, most tools are designed for male hands, and most work clothing is designed for men's bodies.[11] A friend who is a woman miner did not receive shoes and gloves that fit her until the end of her career, and then only after she did the research in mail-order shopping to find manufacturers producing the sizes she needed.

Why Not More Action Sooner?

Why have women's health and safety at work been neglected until so recently? First, because most unions were doing very little to protect the health and safety of their members, male or female. There were a few notable exceptions, unions that established health services for members and their families, and a few that pressed employers for action on work hazards. Most tended to be absorbed in wage and job security issues. They bargained intensely for pay for the labor that their members furnished, but mostly disregarded the conditions under which they had to

11. One of our team visited an East German textile factory in the mid-1970s and was proudly shown looms made to women's sizes by a Czechoslovakian supplier. It was pointed out that the frequent reaching across looms that weavers accept as part of job content had been considerably eased with this somewhat smaller and shorter machine.

furnish that labor and the effects of those conditions on their health and lives. If they raised these issues at all, it was almost always on matters of injury, not disease: injury could be more readily seen by workers and by the employers (paying for workers' compensation). Health damage manifested itself more slowly and silently, and the costs were hard to calculate. Unions traditionally had settled for hazard and premium pay for work under hazardous conditions, rather than attacking the sources of hazard and discomfort. Safety stewards, where they existed, were among the least important union representatives, and of course there was only infrequent provision for their training. Joint union-management safety committees were rare, and those that existed were ill-equipped for their tasks. Union representatives were often discouraged by the inability or unwillingness of most management representatives on safety committees to reach decisions; the latter appeared to lack the power to decide issues. Recommendations of the committees became little more than suggestions to higher levels of management, and changes appeared slowly if ever. The National Labor Relations Board did not make safety and health mandatory subjects of collective bargaining until 1966. Moreover, before the 1970 passage of the Occupational Safety and Health Act, a U.S. employer who agreed to changes in the work environment in the interests of safety usually reduced the pay offer accordingly. Nor were incentives on the union side any more compelling. A candidate for union office might well conclude that he would win more votes by showing wage increases than writing safety clauses in the contracts he would negotiate.

The original state workers' compensation laws were passed early in the century; the labor movement did little else on safety and health in the political arena until the 1970s. As the Nader study group on disease and injury on the job reported in the Page-O'Brien study in 1973:

> The problems of occupational safety and health languished in the limbo of neglect for more than half a century. . . . Nobody paid heed to the inadequacy of existing state health and safety laws and their non-enforcement. Nor was there any attempt to arouse among the workers themselves an awareness of the full dimensions of the health and safety issue, nor a sense of responsibility for their own self-protection and survival. The labor movement was gradually building political muscle, but it did not press for the reduction of the frequency and severity of work accidents and diseases.[12]

12. Joseph A. Page and Mary-Win O'Brien, *Bitter Wages*, 1973, p. 59.

A second reason for the neglect of women's health concerns is that there has been a lack of information about the special problems of working women, and even less about the problems that they share with men. Male research workers in many studies simply have excluded the female members of the work force that they were studying—to "simplify the research design," as some researchers put it. In many attempts at research, the opposition of employers has stymied the researchers in their efforts to get at the medical and employment records of workers and to observe conditions in the workplace.

Some health research projects studying women alone have failed to examine the possible connection between their work experience and their medical experience. In the only major American survey of women who worked during pregnancy, the U.S. Public Health Service asked each woman about her husband's occupation, but not about her own occupation during her pregnancy. In her book *Women's Work, Women's Health,* Stellman has reproduced the Public Health Service questionnaire as if to satisfy her own, and her readers', incredulity in the face of the researchers' lack of scientific and human curiosity.[13] Study of work and women's health might well focus on clerical jobs, since three out of every four clerical workers in this country are women. Yet research on the health problems of clerical workers, men as well as women, is just beginning.

Of special concern for many women are psychosocial health problems. These arise from the structuring of work processes, the division of labor, systems of supervision, methods of wage payment (piece work, incentive pay), the hours of work and of relief, and the cumulative stress of work and personal lives.[14] Research on psychosocial health is controversial. It is often characterized as subjective, and it calls for study of human health as a matter of complex interrelationships. On the one hand, unions have been suspicious of psychosocial approaches that sought to find out how the worker could adjust to job stress, rather than how job stress could be minimized for her. Such research recalled the manipulative aims of management in its early enthusiasm for the "human

13. Stellman, 1977. The questionnaire appears on p. 142. An earlier book by Stellman and Daun dealt with hazards to both men and women. *Work Is Dangerous to Your Health: A Handbook of Health Hazards in the Workplace and What You Do about Them,* 1973. Women's Occupational Health Resource Center (WOHRC), an organization Dr. Stellman established, maintains a clearinghouse of materials on these subjects and publishes an occasional newsletter to which members may subscribe (WOHRC, 117 St. Johns Place, Brooklyn, N.Y. 11217).

14. See Gardell, 1977, p. 2, and Sheila Lewenhak, *Women and Trade Unions: An Outline History of Women in the British Trade Union Movement,* 1977, p. 283.

relations" approach, which was generally an approach hostile to, because a substitute for, unionism. To management, on the other hand, the study of the sources and remedies of excessive job stress has been suspect because it calls into question existing patterns of the organization of work and authority. Despite this historic controversy, white-collar unions in many countries have been analyzing, and by collective bargaining improving, the psychosocial conditions and possibilities of job satisfaction in their work environment and work processes.

A third factor in the neglect of women's occupational safety is that women in most countries were in a poor position to make effective demands for better health and safety, even had they had the information and the will to do so. Most forms of women's employment were until recently rather poorly organized, especially in the United States. Of those who were organized, a high percentage were in small enterprises or in industries of a marginal and technologically backward character, with many small, insecure firms. In their unions, women had little power and were almost entirely absent from important collective bargaining bodies, except in some local committees. Would they have done better than men on these matters at the collective bargaining table? Since they almost never had the chance, one cannot say; but could they have done less?

No doubt, women were not demanding enough, even under all these circumstances. Except where their unions were strong, however, or the women daring and knowledgeable about their rights beyond the ordinary man's daring and knowledge, the well-founded fears of victimization kept them from complaints about work hazards.

Fourth, in recent years a conscious or unconscious justification of women's risks by false reference to equality of the sexes has emerged. A surface acceptance, or a feigned acceptance, of equality has, among some, bred an indifference to the needs of working mothers, the psychosocial strains of the "double burden," and even the obvious needs of maternity.

A woman member of NUPE in northern England recalled returning home from work in a bus in which there was standing room only. "Alongside her stood a woman far advanced in pregnancy, while several healthy men occupied seats. The NUPE member asked one of them, 'Why don't you get up and give her your seat?' The man retorted, 'You want equality, don't you? This is equality!' To which she answered: 'She's bearing a child. What are you bearing?' "

More Union Interest

By the end of the 1960s, among workers and unions in the United States and in other industrial nations, serious concern slowly emerged over the rising toll of accidents and occupational disease. Workers and their unions began to demand study of the risks, to lobby for increased compensation for victims and survivors, more effective supervision of risk factors by government and employers, and more responsibility for labor representatives in safety and health administration. They placed greater stress on the manifold and complex causes of disease and debilitation that are slow in developing as compared to the more obvious risks of sudden fall, fire, or explosion. They began to pay more attention to the psychosocial problems of men's and women's health. In short, safety and health issues were being reordered as health and safety issues.[15]

This change in emphasis is reflected in the titles of three nations' relevant laws: the 1970 U.S. law is the Occupational Safety and Health Act; Britain's 1974 law is the Health and Safety at Work Act; and Sweden's 1977 law is the Working Environment Act. The word "environment" was meant to stress not only health as compared to safety, but the broad national policy that workplaces must be designed to suit human aptitudes, both physically and mentally, and that workers and their unions have the right to influence decisions on their work settings and work processes as a whole.

The increasing concern, and the changing goals of concern, with health and safety came from several sources. Scientists, public health authorities, doctors, and environmentalists (the latter seeing the factory as one of the worst polluters both inside and outside its walls) helped to make men, women, and their unions more sensitive to the awesome stream of new chemical products in their workplaces and to newly discovered risks of using supposedly well-known materials and processes. What was already known was alarming; what was not known yet was perhaps even more alarming. For example, industrial health experts have increased their estimates of the incidence of occupationally related cancer. In 1978, the National Cancer Institute, the National Institute of Environmental Health Sciences, and NIOSH estimated that occupationally related cancers would cause at least 20 percent of all cancer deaths in the decades

---

15. For brevity's sake, the terms "safety" and "health" are used alone even though one may mean both. "Safety steward" and "joint safety committee" are well-established terms, even when the more important and more difficult responsibilities of the positions are in the area of health rather than safety. The line of separation may be blurred; noise is a physical strain, but it may also be the cause of nervous disorders.

ahead. Later scientific estimates rose much higher, with increasing concern over exposures in nuclear arms plants, the dangers for nonsmokers in smoke-polluted environments, and recognition of hazards in new industrial chemicals and electromagnetic radiation. As more is known, estimates continue to rise, and the need for action in the workplace becomes clearer.[16]

New Opportunities for Women

At the beginning of the 1970s, European unions began to make major breakthroughs in winning recognition of the need for safety stewards and joint union-management safety committees, in an extension of their powers, and in their training for these functions. The breakthrough came first in Germany and Austria, with the extension in 1972 of the powers of works councils for the protection of safety and health.[17] Sweden and Britain, under new legislation and collective agreements, now require the election or appointment by the unions of thousands of safety stewards and of union members to joint safety committees. There are provisions for their training on paid released time.

Despite a tendency in many British shops to add the health and safety function to the shop steward's duties, a TUC conference concluded— without any binding force—that the disadvantages of appointing shop stewards as safety representatives outweigh the advantages. There are two primary disadvantages: first, the stewards are already very busy; and second, the elements of conflict with management in the stewards' bargaining and grievance functions could hamper the cooperation needed in safety and health work.

Increases in the numbers, the functions, and the training of worker representatives have meant more opportunities for women to acquire important leadership functions. In the case of safety functions, relatively few men have more applicable experience or training to offer than women. Women can now come forward as candidates, and on terms not as

16. For a study of the dangers of electromagnetic radiation, see Paul Brodeur, "Annals of Radiation," a three-part article in *The New Yorker*, 1989, June 12, pp. 51–86; June 19, pp. 47–73; and June 26, pp. 39–68. For greatly increased estimates of cancer and other diseases, see BNA, *Daily Labor Report*, "Medical Expert Says Occupational Disease Is More Prevalent than Officially Reported," no. 96 (May 19, 1989), p. A-6. The study undertakes an extrapolation from a New York State Report that showed three reported deaths from cancer against the researcher's estimate of over 1000.

17. We discuss in Chapter 3 the councils that are required by law in all but the smallest establishments and that function somewhat like shop steward councils in the United States or Britain.

unequal as usual, in union competition for office. In standing for work-place safety representatives, women may benefit from their stereotyped reputation for being more concerned than men with the human environment of their jobs. Some opinion surveys show that women rank working conditions and working relationships somewhat higher than men do, among the conditions they consider important in their jobs.

In the United States, women have established advocacy and research centers dealing with women's workplace exposures both to accident and disease.[18] Such centers have their roots in the efforts of women like the great American pioneer of public health and industrial medicine, Dr. Alice Hamilton, who earlier this century carried out investigations and introduced remedial programs under union, academic, hospital, settlement, and foundation sponsorship.[19]

Sweden: Bargaining, Law, and Local Union Action

The Swedish case exemplifies what unions can do through collective bargaining, government action, and training to address the problems of health and safety at work, when the problems are approached seriously, consistently, and democratically. In short, the Swedish unions have carried on the most ambitious collective bargaining, advocated the most ambitious laws, and developed the most extensive training programs on health and safety in the world.

The first national collective agreement on safety between labor and employer confederations was in 1942. It provided for the selection of safety stewards but gave them no real powers, and it was further vitiated by the traditional management emphasis on preventing workers' "unsafe acts." A 1949 law established a National Board of Occupational Safety and Health, which included representatives of trade unions and employer associations. There was little additional action, however, until dissatisfaction with working conditions became evident, and in 1967 LO concluded a broadly conceived national agreement with SAF. The Occupational Safety Act of 1974 was based upon the principles of that agreement, although its signatories continued to express their preference for solutions through collective bargaining.

The 1974 act gave union safety stewards the power to stop any pro-

18. See n. 13 for the work and publications of the WOHRC. A further source of information, particularly on research into Video Display Units (VDUs) and their effect on the women who operate them, is 9 to 5, Working Women, 1224 Huron Road, Cleveland, Ohio, 44115.

19. See Barbara Sicherman, *Alice Hamilton's Life in Letters*, 1984, as well as Alice Hamilton's autobiography, *Exploring the Dangerous Trades*, 1945.

cess that they considered an immediate danger to employees' lives or (a bolder innovation) to employees' health, pending a decision by the labor inspectorate. Employers had opposed the power to stop operations, but later recognized that the stewards were using it with good judgment. They then agreed to give any employee the right to suspend work that he or she considered unsafe in order to consult the safety steward.

LO and the cartel of private-sector white-collar unions, PTK, now also pressed forward along both the bargaining and the legislative routes. In 1976 the two federations signed a comprehensive agreement with SAF. Its principles were embodied in the Working Environment Act of 1977. The 1977 act was passed by a unanimous parliament, even though by then the socialists had lost their majority, and the socialist government that had initiated the legislation had been replaced by a so-called bourgeois government.

"Working conditions shall be adapted to the physical and psychological needs of the individual," says the law, in force since mid-1978. "The aim should be for work to be organized so that the employee himself or herself can influence his or her working situation," directly or through union representatives. In the planning and arrangement of work, "there must be due regard for the fact that individual persons differ in their aptitudes." The concept of work environment in the law includes such matters as job organization, working hours, wage payment methods, and, as LO stresses, "the entire psychological spectrum of working life." [20]

In 1985 the Swedish parliament enacted a law concerning occupational health and work adjustment. It establishes comprehensive occupational health services of a high standard suited to the needs that exist. The law allows the health stewards to investigate any case of ill health if there is suspicion that it may have something to do with work. It provides for monitoring for purposes of prevention and allows for participation of the chief health steward "right at the planning stage for new production, technology, or work organisation" in order to

20. In "Why Sweden Has Better Working Conditions than the U.S.," Don MacLeod, a technical consultant to the UAW who studied the workings of the law in Sweden, puts it this way: "The Swedish law refers to the concept of the 'Work Environment' rather than merely to 'occupational safety and health' as does OSHA. . . . Unlike OSHA, the Swedish law is clearly designed to give workers more say in their jobs—work should be arranged so that the worker can influence his or her work situation" (*Working Life in Sweden*, no. 28 [April 1984], p. 7). For a copy of the act, see Ministry of Labor, "The Working Environment in Sweden: New Legislation on the Working Environment: The Organisation and Administration of Occupational Health and Safety," 1977, pp. 25–36.

"take the employee's health and work adjustment into consideration."[21]

The Swedish law is a "framework law" in two essential respects: in
the setting of standards and in the implementation by collective bargaining. It gives the National Board of Occupational Safety and Health
wide powers to issue specific regulations. These are to embody the best
results of research and experience, not to set minimal requirements. The
unions' voice on the board deciding on research projects helps ensure
that they have a practical cutting edge. Rank-and-file workers take part
in cooperative research programs, along with employers, equipment
manufacturers, university and government experts, doctors, psycholo-
gists, and engineers. Said a leader of one research group, "We are forming a circle of communication between those who study and design industrial equipment, those who make it, those who buy it, and those
who use it every day." The language of standards is worked out by
committees of board officials and representatives of the labor unions
and employers' organizations. Moreover, the law creates a framework
within which local negotiations can take proper account of differences
from company to company in "needs, nature of the enterprise, organization and traditions," as outlined in the LO/PTK agreement with SAF.[22]

These parties understood that comparable local agreements would
follow the terms of both the Work Environment Act and the equally
path-breaking 1977 Act on the Joint Regulation of Working Life. The
latter expanded the scope of bargaining and the power of unions to
obtain information of almost all kinds from employers. That includes
the information necessary to monitor safety and health programs. (Unions
in the United States have just begun to obtain some of these powers.)

In cases of disputes about the scope of bargaining or about the demands of a union for information, the union's interpretation prevails
unless the employer can get a labor court to set it aside. All this was
included in order to support a strong union role in negotiation and in
action on health and safety (among other matters) and to help workers
and unions counter a great deficit of information. In particular, union
access to employer information supports the active and informed participation of local unions and especially of women, those who most need
access to factual data.

---

21. For details of trade unions' responsibility for implementation of the act and LO's
instructions to local trade union organizations for its implementation see LO's *Trade
Unions and Occupational Health Services*, 1986.

22. SAF-LO-PTK, *Working Environment Agreement*, 1977, p. 6.

Safety Stewards: Their Role, Power, and Function

Every workplace in Sweden employing five or more persons must have a safety steward. The steward can interrupt a machine, a working method, or a process that he or she considers an imminent threat to safety or health. The steward cannot be held liable for any loss from that stoppage of operations, even if it turns out that the reason was inadequate. The safety steward may also halt operations where the employer violates a ruling of the labor inspectorate. These provisions apply to white-collar as well as to manual workers.

By 1984, an army of 110,000 safety representatives had received training and were actively at work in Swedish firms. An additional 30,000 receive the forty-hour training each year.[23] Stewards who are committed to their mission can be "what no government inspector can be: someone on the spot continuously, to monitor employer performance on an ongoing basis," as Steven Kelman wrote when the law was new.[24]

The Joint Safety Committee

The joint safety committee, required in all establishments of over fifty employees, is "the central body for questions having to do with the working environment and company health services," says the SAF/LOP/TK agreement. "It is both a decision-making and an advisory body." To avoid the dithering ineffectiveness of a safety committee whose employer side (as so often in the United States) consists only of low-level personnel unable or unwilling to decide anything, at least one employer representative must come from the establishment's top management.

The union representatives have a majority of one on the committee. They are named, by election or appointment, by the local LO or PTK clubs at the ratio of their membership in the establishment. In case of a tie in union membership, the seat goes to the union that has the greater environmental hazards.

The safety committee does not have to wait until accident strikes or disease spreads to make or influence decisions. It can participate in the planning stages when management proposes the design of a new work-

23. MacLeod, 1984, p. 8.
24. Steven Kelman, "Occupational Safety and Health in Sweden: The Politics of Co-operation," *Working Life in Sweden*, no. 2 (December 1977), pp. 1–8. See also Kneeland Youngblood, "Safety Delegates and the Working Environment Act," *Current Sweden*, no. 204 (November 1978), pp. 1–10.

place, new or modified equipment, and new techniques or processes. The committee may deal with such matters not only in its own plant but with regard to any new plant its employer erects at another location, before there can yet be a safety committee there.

The safety committee negotiates the safety budget with management. Within the range of that budget, the committee's decisions are binding, and it may reach them by majority vote. On other matters, involving further company outlays, its decisions are binding only if unanimous. In cases of disagreement on such decisions, the union members may appeal to the labor inspectorate. While unions may consider the safety budget too small, at least union control means that it will be spent to solve serious work environment problems rather than merely to increase productivity.

The committee also has responsibility for the development of safety programs, the planning of safety training, and the distribution of safety information, as well as for monitoring employer compliance with regulations. In large enterprises of 1,000 to 2,000 employees, depending on the hazards of the operations, there must be a company health service. The committee and not the employer, according to the agreement, administers the company health service. It must approve the appointment of company doctors and safety engineers.

Union majorities on the committees controlling the company health service may eliminate one cause for concern that employees in the United States understandably show, that information revealed to company physicians, or turned up in company medical records may be used against them. As one American union team reported after visiting Sweden, "the fact that the doctor and nurse report to the safety committee seemed to allow them to worry more about the health of the workers than about company profits."[25] Swedish employees, and notably women, may feel freer than heretofore to bring up psychological or social problems with the workplace health staff.

Union stewards and safety committee members receive paid leave to attend to these duties. They are protected against interference with their work and against overt or covert retaliation by management by both law and a national collective agreement that covers almost everyone in private employment. They are further protected by the mutual recognition of unions and management of the need to share responsibility, cooperation, and power.

25. "If the Swedes Can Do It . . . ," *International Woodworker*, supplement, 1979?, p. 2.

Pooling Safety Work for Small Establishments

A high percentage of women work in small establishments (so do many men). Almost everywhere such establishments have even worse safety and health records than larger establishments. Most are incapable of developing proper safety programs, nor can they afford company medical services of their own. The cost of protective measures is likely to be high per employee, when compared with large establishments.

Many women and men in such companies feel helpless; others are close to a boss who works alongside his or her employees. In either case, workers, and especially unorganized workers, are unlikely to file complaints. No one has yet come up with a reason—except for the question-begging cliché (which is not a reason), "Life is unfair"—to explain why these employees should have to accept greater risks than the employees of larger establishments. Sweden has found a way by collective agreement and law to protect the employees of such establishments by pooling services on an area basis: joint company health centers for small and medium-sized firms. The medical adviser for LO has reported "positive experiences" with the joint centers. Regional safety stewards are working on a full-time basis among the establishments too small to have their own stewards. A program of loans on very advantageous terms (no repayment for two years; two years interest-free) makes sums up to about $25,000 available for small businesses to improve their working environments. The chief safety steward of the establishment has to approve any application for such a loan.

Employees working alone may face worse risks than those in small establishments. The law requires employers to give special attention to the risks of accident or ill health among those in solitary employment. Safety stewards may halt operations involving them on grounds of imminent danger.

The construction industry everywhere has its own hazards and its own problems of organization for safety. In Sweden and Germany there is a separate safety and health structure for the industry as a whole. Central and regional units are complemented by mobile units that serve the sites of construction. They may make the difference between safety and catastrophes such as those that continue to stain the pages of construction history in the United States.

Training Safety Stewards

Occupational health and safety training, as well as the distribution of a continuing stream of safety information, are the national responsibility of the Joint Industrial Safety Council created years ago by the two major labor confederations and the employer association. The costs of training are financed by employer contributions to the Swedish Working Environment Fund. Training takes place during paid work time; if it has to be done outside of work time, it is paid nevertheless, by agreement between the unions and employers.

When planning for the mass training of safety stewards in 1973, the LO representatives insisted that most training be carried out at local and plant levels and in the classic Swedish form of study circle discussions, rather than in lectures by company safety engineers. The employer representatives reluctantly agreed.[26] As a result, the unions have succeeded in centering much of the training on the stewards' own workplaces, with discussion of the problems closest to them. During the training the stewards make inspections, report trouble spots, and propose corrective measures. "To make these studies as realistic as possible, the aim is for stewards, foremen, and other staff categories all to attend the same study circles."[27] The residential schools are used by both labor federations and the larger national unions for the training of discussion leaders for these study circles and for the more advanced courses in steward training.

The basic course for stewards and foremen takes thirty to forty study hours. It includes six films that complement the course book. The courses are given in all but the very smallest workplaces. About 65 percent of all safety stewards and 45 percent of all foremen had taken the courses in the first five years of administration of the 1977 acts—a total of some 300,000 men and women. (A similar proportion of the American population would have put almost 8 million workers and foremen in basic safety courses. Actually in the United States, OSHA began making funds available for safety training to unions and teaching institutions such as university labor education centers about 1980.)

The Joint Industrial Safety Council's advanced courses cut across many industries, covering chemical health hazards, local safety work, lighting, noise, and the design of new workplaces. Hence the council provides funds to those branches of industry that wish, on the same joint union-

26. For study circles, see Chapter 4.
27. Birger Viklund, "Education for Industrial Democracy," *Current Sweden*, no. 132 (March 1977), p. 10.

management basis, to supplement the general courses with materials on their special work environments. Neither SAF nor LO sees this as in any way training these people to be safety experts. Rather the purpose is to make them appreciate the real and potential problems in their immediate environment. The ways in which health and safety hazards reveal themselves vary with the local settings, the firm's materials and products, its machines and the organization of its processes, and the customs and habits of people—supervisors and workers as well as workers among themselves—in their interactions within the shop. As LO's medical adviser explained it, the unions "have no desire to make the safety stewards into environmental or sampling experts. Their job is, together with employers, to act as qualified decision-makers. They need to possess general knowledge about the problems that exist, and general knowledge about details, so that they are able to make good use of the government officials and in-plant experts who are at their disposal."[28] As time goes on, a smaller proportion of the general training will be introductory and a larger proportion of it will be more advanced, specialized training geared to specific types of hazards and the problems of specific industries and occupations.

The collective agreements and legislation of the 1970s and 1980s have enabled the unions to mobilize a very large number of men and women as safety stewards and safety committee members, and to begin giving them the training necessary to detect hazards and press for their control or elimination. Training increases commitment. Commitment leads to more training, sharper monitoring of the work environment, and more preventive action. Yet thoughtful Swedes in labor circles, government, and research are far from complacent about the perils of industrial employment, or the pace of preventive measures and of education against those perils.

Television Courses

In Britain by 1978 the BBC and TUC had worked together on a series of seven films devoted to helping safety representatives and others to identify, understand, and control workplace hazards. Broadcast on two different days over two different channels, the twenty-five-minute programs had as their subjects the role of the safety and health representative, inspection and accident investigation, safe systems of work and

---

28. Eric Bolinder, "Worker Participation for Optimal Environment," *Arbetsmiljö*, no. 10B (1977), p. 28.

dealing with hazards, noise and vibration, dust, fumes and toxic materials, and a final program on "keeping up-to-date."[29]

The TUC has begun to address the historic indifference of many of its unions toward health and safety, by devoting a considerable part of its limited educational resources to these matters. The law provides for the election or appointment of safety stewards by the unions recognized within a workplace and protects their right to paid time for training, as well as for the performance of their duties as stewards. The Health and Safety Commission's code of practice on released time leaves such arrangements up to collective bargaining.

The TUC has insisted that the unions control the training. A number of employers offer further training on their own, and in some programs there is cooperation between unions and employers, although far less than in Sweden.

Video Display Terminals

Computer-based technology has offered severe challenges to a number of unions, white-collar and manual, both in industries where the new technology is shrinking employment and in those where it promises more employment. In the former the unions face serious problems in negotiating the terms of job security, career patterns, job classification, training, and retraining. In particular, they must confront the strains and risks in working steadily before VDTs or cathode ray tubes.

Hundreds of thousands of women sit in front of the "tube," or as the English say, the "box,"—in banks, insurance companies, hospital management offices, newspaper copyrooms, tourist and travel agencies, and postal, telephone, and other public service administrations. The use of VDTs is increasing with no end in sight, but the sight of many workers has been strained.

In an agreement with Ford, TASS and two other white-collar unions secured an understanding that there would be no dismissals as a result of introducing computers. In addition, the TUC's and the company's chief medical officers were to carry on discussions on the health implications of the use of VDTs. On the basis of research it had supported,

29. The BBC had a set of substantial background notes prepared for discussion leaders by specialists at the University of Aston at Birmingham, with notes for the final file written by the Birmingham Hazards Group, which is in touch with both shop stewards and safety stewards and can take up such delicate issues as disagreement between the two over the importance of risks (*Working for Safety: Background Notes*, 1978). The BBC also offered videotapes for union and employer use in training programs.

TASS advocated limiting each person's work on VDTs to a maximum of four hours a day and limiting anyone over forty-five to only occasional work on VDTs.

A British white-collar union that did much work on employment, job content and health aspects of the new computer-based technology was the Association of Professional, Executive, Clerical, and Computer Staffs. In APEX, the majority of members were women. It concentrated on the effects on its women members of using word processors. Its 1979 report, based on questionnaires sent to every local union and on examination of the available equipment, gave specific guidelines for the use of VDTs.[30]

Management and union agreed to prepare a safety-training syllabus for selected APEX members in each user department. Training was to include "an appreciation of the total system and its health and safety aspects." The agreement, moreover, took into account recommendations in the union's guidelines with regard to VDT glare, screen color, frequency of flicker, definition of characters, contrast control by the operator, and maintenance. Inadequate maintenance is a frequent source of operators' health difficulties, the APEX report noted.

The Austrian private-sector white-collar union, GPA, has been a leader in action-oriented research on worker health and computer use. It began its activities as early as 1959, with a bow to the pioneering work of the UAW in the United States, before computer technology hit Austria with full force. Then, in 1974, GPA held an international conference on "Human Choice and the Computer," which brought together computer experts, social scientists, and trade unionists. The conference set up a permanent international committee on "computers and society" within the International Federation of Commercial, Clerical, and Office Workers to process information as it was received. With the union's automation committee making intensive studies of management use of computers as a tool of supervision, GPA negotiators bargained for a ban on further introduction of computer surveillance of employees' individual performance. In the mid-1970s the union commissioned several studies to ascertain the consequences for members' health of using certain types of equipment. One study coupled scientific testing of objective difficulties (reduction of visual acuity and changes in color perception) with monitoring for psychosocial problems, such as headaches, and strain on the lens muscles in focusing. The GPA used its study to obtain agreements for rotation of operators to other work after each hour of VDT reading or for rest periods after two hours of such work.

30. APEX, Research Department, *Office Technology: The Trade Union Response*, 1979.

A German agreement between HBV and the Dresdner Bank differentiates between feeding information into the computer and reading from the screen. The agreement provides for ten minutes' break after each eighty minutes of feeding information, and ten minutes after each fifty minutes of reading information.

Unions in the United States as well as those abroad are sponsoring and encouraging major research on the questions. The leading ILO publication on questions of social and labor policy, *The Social and Labor Bulletin*, gives United States unions credit for being among the first to raise questions about the health hazards of VDTs.[31] The U.S. unions are credited with initiating the call "for greater collective bargaining" and pushing for "legislation at local, state and federal levels."[32]

Sweden called the first international scientific conference on work with video display units in 1986. It was attended by thirty-six trade union representatives from eight countries. Among American participants were representatives of the Ontario Public Service Employees, the Newspaper Guild, the Communications Workers of America, the National Association of Working Women, and the Service Employees International Union. In a statement issued at the conclusion of the meeting, the trade unionists said:

> We are far from establishing that VDUs cause birth abnormalities among users. But the increasingly strong possibility that this may be the case makes it essential to provide adequate protections immediately. The most important of these is the provision of adequate protection against Very Low Frequency (VLF) radiation. . . . The increased possibility of birth defects among VDU operators makes it imperative that both laboratory and epidemiological research be vigorously pursued and that operators be universally granted the right to transfer from VDU work when they become pregnant.[33]

In this country not only have unions and independent institutes undertaken studies, but some employers have been concerned as well about

31. *SLB*, "VDUs in the 1990s: Mounting Concern," no. 4 (1990), p. 379.

32. Among these union studies are: BNA, *Daily Labor Report*, "Office Workers' Union Tells Labor Subcommittee of Suspected Health Hazards from Workplace VDTs," no. 40 (February 29, 1984), pp. A-2–3; ibid., "Survey of VDT Users Reveals Link between Health Problems, Monitoring," no. 230 (November 29, 1985), pp. A-6–7; ibid., "VDT-Related Health Problems Called Serious National Threat," no. 11 (January 19, 1988), pp. A-4–5. This last report concludes, "Highly critical of computer monitoring, work quotas and speed ups, the report [done by 9 to 5, National Association of Working Women] recommends an end to these practices, maintaining that such work conditions result in a range of mental and physical stress-related illness."

33. Ibid., "Swedish Researchers Say Significant Questions Raised by Study of VDT Use and Pregnancy," no. 99 (May 22, 1986), p. A-3–4.

the possible ill effects of VDT usage on pregnant women. IBM, a major manufacturer of VDTs, conducted its own study of possible ill effects from computer use by pregnant women and all women in their reproductive years. The author of the study was an outside scientist. In an IBM house organ, he is reported as finding no relationship between birth defects and VDT emissions. He noted, however, that other studies did indicate the possibility of a relationship. Citing the high voltage and proximity of the transformer to the cover, he suggested shielding the covers of VDTs, a relatively inexpensive procedure. Thus although the expert found harmful exposures doubtful, he preferred to recommend erring on the side of caution and hence advised countermeasures against any possible damage to the user.

In Europe, the Council of Ministers, highest authorities in the EEC, have after long debate adopted a directive binding on the member states on standards for work on VDTs. It "sets out employers' obligations with regard to the safety of work stations. Employers are responsible for analyzing potential risks and ensuring that equipment complies with the standards set out in the annex to the Directive. They must also ensure that workers have enough pauses to rest their eyes and that they undergo regular eye tests."[34]

The issue of the degree to which VDTs are the source of health problems (and particularly of reproductive difficulties) is still open, although evidence seems to be mounting that some such association exists.[35] Whether dangers are the result of low-level radiation or of a variety of stresses, coupled with unfavorable working conditions (such as too much lighting, glare, improper seating, poor air conditions, and surrounding noise), is not yet clear. One probable result of the many studies and union activism is that at least new personal computers are better shielded than earlier models.

34. *SLB,* "Protection of Workers: Minimum Standards," no. 3 (1990), p. 308.

35. For several years in the United States, NIOSH has been at work on a study of the adverse effects on pregnancy from the use of VDTs. The Office of Management and Budget (OMB) has repeatedly held up the study on the grounds of its design; see BNA, *Daily Labor Report,* "OMB Decision Allows VDT Study but NIOSH Wary about Requirements," no. 112 (June 11, 1986), pp. A-12–13, and ibid., "Interviews with VDT Operators Complete; Reproductive Study Results Due Next Year," no. 169 (August 31, 1988), pp. A-1–2. Although this NIOSH study was promised for 1989, nothing appeared until 1991. The study that then appeared (ibid., 1991 #50, "NIOSH Study Finds No Link between VDT Use and Spontaneous Abortions," no. 50 [1991], p. A-1) is not the study presumably finished in 1989 and by no means the study NIOSH originally undertook. Its scope of investigation as originally planned and approved was considerably broader in terms of numbers of persons and types of machines that were to have been included. Critics of the study immediately entered their opinions: ibid., no. 71 (1991), p. A-1.

Measuring the Stress of Women's Jobs

The union that has been consistently active in studying many aspects of stress and its effect on women is the Austrian GPA. It cooperated with the Austrian Federal Institute for Health in a medical and socio-logical study of retail stores' check-out cashiers, almost all of whom are, as in the United States, women. The study examined the effects of dif-ferent patterns of moving goods past the point at which cashiers, usu-ally seated, ring them into the register. Most strenuous was the practice of the cashier's lifting goods from the customer's cart to the counter and then into another container (box, sack, or a second cart). Picking up, putting down, picking up again, the cashier might lift as much as five tons in the course of a peak day. The union ranked as best the continuous moving belt because it requires the customer to do most of the lifting. (In Germany, the HBV made its top priority the switch to moving belts in negotiating for store clerks.)

The GPA also identified the repeated complaints of union members about headaches, back problems, and circulatory disorders. Causes identified were drafts from nearby doors opening directly onto the street, work spaces too narrow for free bodily movement, poor lighting, noise and confusion around the cashier, and stress from the multiple demands of close attention to prices and accuracy while also having to do, in effect, customer relations work.

In another area, GPA undertook a large-scale technical study of the effects on physical and mental health of the noise, lighting, air condi-tioning, traffic patterns, and lack of privacy in "vast space" or "open plan" offices. The union turned to its members on works councils all over the country for proposals on remedial action. By law, the works councils have the right to examine and criticize management proposals for changes in plant and equipment, and to veto them if they fail to meet employees' needs for health and safety. The union took an active role in gradually training works councillors to use these rights. Its study gave it the basis for a checklist it could use in future evaluation of plans for the building, remodeling, or equipping of large-scale office space.

Union leaders reported that, thanks to the GPA publicity campaigns and bargaining based upon this research, the trend in Austria is away from the vast-space office. In Vienna we had difficulty in even finding such an office to visit, and the one that the union did find for us had recently installed room partitions to change traffic patterns and give workers more privacy.

Job evaluation is a way to rationalize wage structures within an establishment or a firm,[36] but it also can be used to locate the sources of the physical and mental strains of some women's jobs, and to analyze the possibilities of lessening those strains. Introducing the measurement of stress as an element of working conditions, effort, and responsibility—or however individual factors may be named—in a job evaluation scheme is not, however, unproblematic. One of the early and careful attempts to do this was in the study the DGB persuaded the German Federal Ministry of Labor to undertake in 1975.[37] The study was popularly known at the time as the "Ro-Ru Report" from the initial syllables in the names of its authors, Professor Rohmert, an industrial engineer, and Dr. Rutenfranz, an industrial medicine specialist. It asked what demands various jobs, notably those of assembly-line operations, made on employees (male and female), and whether the worker could stand up over time to the stress of these demands, notably in sensory and motor strain and nervous tension.

The differences between previous analyses and the Ro-Ru approach were many. The job evaluation scheme of the metal-industry collective agreement for Baden-Wuerttenberg had treated the "strain on sense and nerves" as one kind of strain. Thus a single figure had to carry the determination and evaluation of the intensity and the duration of "all activities of perception of the different senses, as well as vigilance, monotony, and time pressure."[38] The Ro-Ru study broke these strains down into fifty-one different items, giving a picture of multiple specific demands upon the worker at any one time and of multiple strains over time. It ascertained these strains by physiological measurements and laboratory tests, as well as by psychosocial observation and other information, in eleven major sectors of employment, ranging from metalworking and clothing manufacture to civil service occupations.

Many of the job evaluation schemes preceding Ro-Ru and the wage structure based on them had assigned low values to the strains in many women's jobs as compared to the values given to the heavy muscular effort demanded of many men's jobs. Ro-Ru showed that such so-called light work entailed heavier total strain, from ever-repeated small muscle

36. See the discussion of job evaluation in Chapter 5. In it, we show how job evaluation has been used by unions to make progress toward equal pay for work of comparable value.

37. The Ro-Ru Report is discussed at some length in Chapter 5. The West German Parliament in Bonn issued an English summary: see Josef Rutenfranz and Walter Rohmert, *The Ergonomic Assessment of Burden and Stress in Various Industrial Workplaces*, 1977.

38. F. J. Chapple, Electrical, Electronic, Telecommunication, and Plumbing Union (EETPU), *Equal Pay and Job Evaluation*, 1975, p. 2.

effort of unvarying machine-paced tasks, than did the occasional heavy lifting in men's jobs. The earlier evaluations, concluded the Ro-Ru study, were not based on scientific findings but on traditional male-dominated evaluation of the relative worth of tasks performed by men and women.[39]

Job evaluation should be not only a means to get equal pay for work of comparable worth but also "the first step in focusing attention on the nature of work performed by women," as a large British workers' union said. That "will lead to serious efforts to restructure work in such a way that the industrial life of our female members is enriched."[40]

A Women's Health Manual for Works Councillors

Male (and even female) safety stewards or works councillors have sometimes failed to see the special health problems of female work-mates. Training courses have been too general or too infrequent to take up many of their problems. So the women's division of the German Textile and Clothing Workers Union mobilized the union's experts to prepare a women's health manual to inform and sensitize works councillors in its industries.

Work and Stay Healthy, as the manual was entitled, offered a mini-refresher course and outlined an action program to improve health-related working conditions for women. In highly readable form with many drawings, printed on loose-leaf sheets for easy updating, it set out a number of major problems and minimum acceptable standards for meeting them. For women who work sitting, it showed the back and leg support needed, ideal chair heights, and a number of other items in a checklist. For those who work standing, it pointed out the dangers of varicose veins, reduced oxygen flow to the brain, and the consequent need for movement and alternation between upright and sitting postures. The steward was urged to find out which of the standing jobs could be changed to permit sitting, and whether folding chairs might permit workers to sit occasionally without leaving their workposts. The manual gave similar information on work tables, desks, lighting, noise

39. Unfortunately the Ro-Ru Report lies yellowing in a ministry file. Soon after it was accepted by the DGB and the metalworkers, the employers' association rejected it. The government changed soon thereafter from Social Democratic to conservative Christian Democratic, and the new labor minister took the report and its recommendations off the ministry agenda.

40. Industrial Relations Services, *Health and Safety Information Bulletin,* no. 9 (September 1976), pp. 1, 5.

levels, air circulation and air conditioning, working hours and work breaks, and the proper location and equipping of lockers, toilets, washrooms, sickrooms, and restrooms.

Relevant sections of the German federal laws and regulations were included and quoted in full for easy reference. Because enforcement may vary from place to place, the union's women's division included actual accounts from attempts made by its staff around the country. These demonstrated differences in the cooperation works councillors might expect from factory inspectors in various areas as unions press employers for compliance.

A step-by-step plan of action for the works councillors began with placing the improvement of women's working conditions on the works council agenda. The council would then create a committee to work with departmental representatives to investigate and report on needed corrections in shop floor and office conditions. It would then decide on whether to call in the factory inspectorate. The step-by-step plan also offered an appropriate form for presenting demands to management. It called for identifying specific conditions requiring further investigation or immediate correction to achieve compliance with the law and good practice.

Like grievances about other working conditions, those about health and safety are related to the immediate circumstances of the workplace—its lighting, work organization, demands, and burdens. The key to remedy, insofar as it can be found and implemented by members of the workforce, depends on workers' sensitivity to hazards and their acquaintance with procedures for dealing with them. These procedures include the statement of workers' rights in law and collective agreement, some knowledge of what workers in comparable plants have been able to accomplish, and a clear picture of how complaints can be handled both within the plant and under the law.

German trade union women in Hesse—the heavily industrialized area around Frankfurt—alerted the regional women's committee to unsafe practices and health hazards in many area plants. The committee turned to the state authorities, and succeeded in persuading them to carry out a sweeping investigation that turned up over 9,000 serious violations of the laws, and a much larger number of less serious violations, in some 2,000 enterprises who together employed 94,000 women. The worst conditions were in the smaller enterprises, many of which were not large enough to have works councils.

Members of the women's committee went on television to publicize the results of the investigation. They demanded more adequate routine inspections, better follow-up of compliance by violators, and tougher sanctions for those still refusing to comply. They roused other labor groups and women's organizations to lobby for their program. They persuaded the Ministry of Labor in Hesse to issue a brochure to help workers identify violations of the law and to register complaints; at the same time they continued their educational campaign where it had begun, at the grass roots.

When Is an Occupational Disease "Occupational"?

Officials in government or enterprise are far too slow in recognizing work-connected origins of ailments. If employers experienced comparable lags in the delivery of supplies or payment of bills, they would surely resort to extreme and immediate measures.

The Austrian trade union federation (OeGB) and the semigovernmental Chamber of Labor have a standing joint committee charged with bringing the very incomplete list of diseases officially recognized as work-connected up to date. The committee, for example, has studied a number of diseases and disabilities from which women suffer as a result of long-term physical exposure, one-sided muscular exertion, and continued nervous strain (all analyzed in the Ro-Ru report in neighboring Germany), including varicose veins, tendonitis, and certain nerve diseases.

Recognition of such ailments as work-connected would make their victims eligible not only for workers' compensation but also for job transfer or vocational rehabilitation. To meet such a standard women and their unions will need the leverage that only scientific and legal authorities can supply if workers are to get employers to take some of the preventive measures that industrial medicine already suggests are useful, particularly when the symptomatology indicates the condition is the result of a combination of exposures at work with conditions at home. When the Swedes in 1985 revised their 1977 law on industrial injuries, they included among the diseases and injuries for which workers' compensation will be paid, psychosomatic disorders, stomach ulcers, myocardial infarctions, and damage to mental health. In all cases, if the employer is to succeed in denying responsibility for the condition, he or she must bear the burden of proof by showing that complainants' injuries or sickness are not a result of the job.

No Dismissal for Ill Health without Consulting the Employee

Several British tribunal decisions have required an employer to consult with an employee before a dismissal decision involving his or her fitness to work, when he or she has suffered from illness held not to be work-connected. For example, one Employment Appeals Tribunal has ruled that an employer cannot rely solely on a doctor's opinion but must consult the employee before reaching a decision on dismissal. Another EAT ruled:

> Discussions and consultation will often bring to light facts and circumstances of which the employers were unaware, and which will throw new light on the problems. The employee may wish to seek medical advice on his own account, which, brought to the notice of the employers' medical advisers, will cause them to change their opinion. There are many possibilities. Only one thing is certain, and that is if the employee is not consulted . . . an injustice may be done.

Union representatives usually can advise members on such matters. Sometimes, when a medical condition prevents an employee from doing her old job, they may suggest another job in which she can be productively employed with the same employer—perhaps with retraining.

In Sweden, such a case would require consultation with the employee and with the union, and if necessary retraining for another job (without cost to the employee). Adjustment committees exist in plants and offices, composed of representatives of unions, management, and the local employment service, to help older workers, handicapped or ailing workers, youth, and women to obtain and hold jobs that they can perform despite diminished capacity for their old lines of work or inexperience in new lines of work.

Preventive Medicine

Unions have been slow to help workers detect health problems by encouraging or providing them with the right to routine medical examination, such as annual eye examinations for VDT users or ear examinations for workers exposed to continuous loud noise. A few unions have established medical clinics where their members can go for such examinations on their own volition, and some of these encourage workers to go annually. Among these are the garment workers' unions in the United States. In England, a 1977 local agreement at a Thorn Electrical

Industries plant in Enfield gave its 2,000 employees paid time off for breast and cervical cancer screening at a local health clinic. The speedy and effective negotiation with Thorn was largely the work, we were told, of a woman senior steward at the Enfield plant.

In many European countries national health systems provide preventive as well as emergency and therapeutic services to every citizen. The Thorn agreement was based on such a provision. In this country, where such facilities exist even nominally only for the poor and the aged, a few unions have followed the seamen and—for a time—the miners, as well as the early and continuing example of the International Ladies' Garment Workers and the Amalgamated Clothing and Textile Workers Unions in setting up a system of health centers for members, paid for by employer contributions based on the number of employees. Alternatively, other unions have included community services committees in their structure. Committee members are able to advise fellow workers where and when medical examinations are available through one of the voluntary health agencies in the community or at local hospitals.

The Right Not to Be Born Disabled

"Five weeks ago British employers became responsible for a new hidden workforce," wrote a leading London industrial relations journal when the Congenital Disabilities (Civil Liability) Act came into force in 1976. The law was a product of the public horror at the disabling of children by their pregnant mothers' use of the drug thalidomide. The law made an employer responsible for damages to a child born disabled as a result of any breach of duty in the conditions of either parent's employment, whether the employer's fault was one of negligence or violation of a statute. The duty owed an employee was in effect extended to an employee's unborn children. The right to make such a claim was limited to a child surviving at least forty-eight hours after birth.

It was precisely this kind of claim that American Cyanimid sought to avoid in the case recounted at the beginning of this chapter. Among the thousands of claims made by Indian workers at Bhopal against Union Carbide, the American chemical company responsible for the explosion there (and later for a leakage of chemicals in its West Virginia plant), were claims of reproductive damage. Union Carbide avoided years of litigative expense by making a mass settlement with the Indian government and the lawyers for claimants.

In the United States, the extent of the employer's responsibility for workers' reproductive health raised the question of federal preemption of state legislation on health and safety. Conflicts arose particularly as newborn federal agencies—such as the Nuclear Regulatory Commission (NRC)—claimed to override state laws and regulations. The problem was settled before the Supreme Court in 1984 in the case of *Silkwood v. Kerr-McGee Corporation*. Silkwood's survivors sought a Supreme Court reversal of the Tenth Circuit's decision that the Atomic Energy Act and the NRC's regulation of radiation hazards "preempts the . . . authority vested in the states to provide health and safety protections for their citizens." The Silkwood heirs, who had received a multiple substantial award in the district court, were supported in their appeal to the circuit court by amicus briefs from several states, led by the State of Wisconsin. The U.S. Justice Department, however, sided with Kerr-McGee in arguing that the corporation was liable for considerably lesser damages under federal terms. The final decision lay with the Supreme Court, which by a vote of five to four held that "federal regulation of safety in the nuclear power industry at least does not preempt a jury's award of punitive damages under state tort law.[41] Thus, it marginally maintained the principle of federal superiority to the states while allowing a petitioner to fare better under state than federal dicta.

With the continuing introduction of new chemicals into industry, toxicologists must determine which chemicals and interactions of chemicals have antenatal properties.[42] Until this knowledge-base is complete, unions offer two sources of assistance to their members: to insist upon preventive measures wherever there is presumptive evidence of damage to the bodies of workers and their unborn children; and to assist members whose children are at risk by helping them take damage cases to the courts.

In Britain, the Association of Scientific, Technical, and Managerial Staffs began negotiating in the late 1970s to address one cause of tragedy and eventual claims. With 77,000 women among its membership of

41. BNA, *Daily Labor Report*, "Supreme Court Permits Punitive Damages for Lab Worker Contaminated by Plutonium," no. 7 (January 12, 1984), p. A-12.

42. In a BNA Special Report of a recently issued study, *Pregnancy and Employment: The Complete Handbook on Discrimination, Maternity Leave, and Health and Safety*, 1987, the following summary appears: "One government source estimated that 15 million to 20 million jobs in the United States expose workers to chemicals that may cause reproductive injury. . . . NIOSH estimates that nine million workers are exposed to radio frequency/microwave radiation, which can cause infertility and embryonic death in animals; more than half a million workers are exposed to glycolethers, known to cause defects in animals. And about 200,000 hospital and industrial workers handle ethylene oxide and anesthetic gases, both associated with miscarriages in humans" (p. 57). See also BNA, *Daily Labor Report*, "Workplace Health Issues for Pregnant Workers Pressing Employers for More Attention, Report Says," no. 137 (October 26, 1987), p. A-12, and *SLB*, "Protection of Workers: Minimum Standards," no. 3 (1990), p. 308.

770,000, ASTMS included the following clause in contracts, beginning with several publishing firms: "If an infection arises in the workplace which, according to informed medical opinion, would be injurious to the health of unborn children, the [pregnant] employee will be allowed absence without loss of pay." Among the infections that the union foresaw were both well-known and lesser-known dangers to pregnant women.

The duties of British union health and safety representatives in general include examining workplace activities and, through the union or its national confederation's medical services, getting medical opinion on substances used in work processes in order to identify those that might damage an unborn child through its mother or father. Union medical services are more and more becoming alert to the dangers to male as well as female reproductive systems. They are endeavoring now to have those substances specifically named in codes of safe operations for members of both sexes as well as in codes of safe employee conduct. When conditions are unsafe for pregnant workers, the immediate remedy they seek is leave with pay or transfer to safer jobs, with retention of pay rates, seniority, and fringe benefits. The ultimate remedy, namely the production of safer compounds, lies beyond union power to insist upon.

German law requires the employer to change a pregnant employee's place and type of work—with no loss of pay—if her doctor believes that her regular job is dangerous or potentially dangerous to her or the fetus. In Austria, after the first five months of pregnancy, a woman by law need not do any piece work, or any work similar to it, if there is danger to her of fatigue. The EEC Commission on June 28, 1990, completed a series of six directives to the member states on "Health and Safety Rights of Workers." The sixth directive defines carcinogens and "specifies employers' obligations in assessing risks, in setting up protective systems and equipment to avoid workers' exposures to such risks, and in reducing or eliminating the use of carcinogenic agents."[43] This action by the highest authority in the EC explicitly places responsibility for improvement upon employers in the twelve member states. In doing so, however, it strongly implies the right of unions where they find laxity or neglect to bring grievances to employers or to the labor courts in the manner provided by national law for handling union members' complaints.

In this country, several unions, as well as a number of institutes con-

43. For comparison of health conditions in European countries prior to the effective date of implementation of the EC directive, see "Health and Safety Rights of Workers in 17 Countries," *European Industrial Relations* Review, no. 83 (April 1989), pp. 4–12.

cerned with industrial disease, and a few employers have undertaken studies of the possible ill effects of VDT usage on pregnant women.[44] The NIOSH study, announced and drafted as definitive, met with difficulties in the federal Office of Management and Budget, as well as within NIOSH itself. Although it was announced for publication in 1989, it did not appear until 1991, and then considerably changed and limited from its original design.[45] The numbers of persons and industries studied were limited to the telephone industry in two occupations, and the range of machines that might be involved now covered only two.[46] The authors said the study was not designed to assess whether subclinical fetal loss might be affected by VDT use. (Subclinical or early fetal loss pertains to the earliest stages of pregnancy, before a woman suspects she is pregnant.) Nor did the study address the association between spontaneous abortion and physical or psychological stress, "two factors that may accompany the use of VDTs."[47] Critics of the study immediately called attention to these and other shortcomings.[48]

Conclusion

The issues raised in this chapter are among the most recent and the most baffling for unions to attempt to control. The effects of the use of many materials and electromagnetic rays are still the subject of controversy and investigation. Both advocates and critics of the findings that have been produced recognize that the outcomes will be largely determined by political bodies, and both find themselves used by lawmakers, prosecutors, and complainants. The costs of decisions, no matter which way they go, are great, whether for employers or workers. But it is not only the present generation that may be affected. Whether the issues arise from exposure to machines or to chemicals, one of the questions has to do with the next generation of both men and women whose

44. BNA, *Daily Labor Report,* "Office Workers Union Tells Labor Subcommittee of Suspected Health Hazards from Workplace VDTs," no. 40 (February 29, 1984), pp. A-2–3; "Survey of VDT Users Reveals Link between VDT Users, Monitoring," no. 230 (November 29, 1985), pp. A-6–7; "Pacific Northwest Bell Forms Committee on VDT-related Programs," no. 27 (1986), p. A-2.
45. Theresa M. Schnorr et al., *Video Display Terminals and the Rise of Spontaneous Abortion,* NIOSH Publications on Video Terminals (revised), 1991.
46. Ibid., p. 728.
47. BNA, *Daily Labor Report,* "NIOSH Study Finds No Link between VDT Use and Spontaneous Abortions," no. 50 (1991), p. A-1.
48. Ibid., "Supporters of Tougher Standards Criticize NIOSH Miscarriage Study," no. 72 (April 12, 1991), p. A-1.

parents worked in these exposed zones. Because lawmakers have for generations seen the woman worker as the producer of children, the first reaction is—as Willow Island so clearly demonstrated—to remove women from the danger zone. But when research turned to these effects on the male reproductive system, the definition of both equality and safety was broadened to include men. A major question now is that of assessing the employer's responsibility for both male and female workers. In the meantime scientists and regulatory agencies remain unsure of how they may best proceed to solve these problems with the information they have at hand.

One aspect of the situation is certain, however. The union's role cannot be to perform the scientific investigations, nor to produce the best solutions. It can promote training of its members who staff safety committees to recognize dangers, to advocate caution in situations where scientists offer contradictory findings, and to serve as advocates for their members who believe they have been subjected to hazardous exposures.

The Miners Union with their campaign against "brown lung" may have been the first union to call attention to the fact that disease as well as unsafe environments endangers the lives of their members. OCAW, in the early days of its organization in the 1940s, similarly realized it had to deal with chemical hazards. The UAW has followed these forerunners, as it has undertaken to prosecute several fetal protection cases; and the SEIU, as it turned to organizing thousands of government office workers, has been the leader in California in advancing legislation regulating the use of VDTs.[49] In taking on an advocacy role, the unions not only are defending endangered women workers, but they are challenging the long-standing acceptability of chemical and magnetic exposures for males, particularly the notion that "hazard pay" is adequate compensation for men to accept these dangers.

Knowledgeable administrators of government programs and attorneys in the field, such as Nicholas Ashford and Charles Caldart, believe that only independent institutions can both demonstrate the objectivity and acquire the funds necessary to meet the investigative and administrative tasks involved in identifying hazards and defining solutions to control their use.[50] They place heavy responsibility on the several state

---

49. San Francisco is reported to be the first city adopting local legislation to mandate VDT safety standards. Although its ordinance was being challenged by two employers, it went into effect on January 26, 1992. BNA, *Daily Labor Report*, no. 17 (January 27, 1992), pp. A-13–14.

50. Nicholas A. Ashford and Charles C. Caldart, "The Control of Reproductive Hazards in the Workplace: A Prescription for Prevention," *Industrial Relations Law Journal* 5:4 (1983), pp. 523–63. The authors outline a series of regulatory laws, in addition to

and federal agencies concerned with workplace environment and its hazards, as well as upon the "self-help mechanisms" that they suggest to individuals choosing to go to the courts for help. Recent thinking in the dispute resolution community of mediators and arbitrators selects this area as one in which voluntary dispute resolution can play an active role. Since such procedures are common to the experience of unions and employers, it is possible that these methods may appeal to both sides as a means of lowering the intensity of disputes over health and safety issues, and at the same time providing settlements much more expeditiously than the courts can do. The bottleneck, however, is with the research institutions. The very fact of the introduction of perhaps as many as 30,000 new chemical combinations in the course of a year into the production process is an overwhelming one for scientific institutions to face and for administrative staffs in state and federal government to respond to. The pressures of interest groups and their representatives within as well as outside government politicize the issues. It is in this area that even an Ashford becomes uncertain of the future.

---

which they enumerate legal grounds for "self-help mechanisms." They conclude that among "the various regulatory and legal mechanisms one should not lose sight of the political context," and add, "It is the extent to which these avenues can be used as political, as well as legal, tools that will ultimately determine whether they can safeguard the reproductive health of workers and their offspring" (p. 563).

Amelioration of the Work
and Family Conflicts

Efforts to improve the conditions affecting women's work in Western Europe and the United States are by implication also struggles for equality in the workplace. Such struggles have caused conflicts within unions as well as between unions and employers. The contest is clearly drawn and well understood; yet the changes necessary to help workers fulfill responsibilities both at home and at work are difficult to bring about, at best occurring slowly and by inadequate degrees.

The grounds of the contest lie in job segregation. The practices that spring from that source are all well documented. They begin with the assignment of women to relatively few occupations designated as "women's work," a measure that still effectively bars women from nontraditional occupations. To combat this effect, the struggle for change sets goals of unlimited access to training; decent working conditions, including freedom from sexual harassment; access to adequate health and safety measures; and equal pay for work of equal value. But achievement of these goals is handicapped by long social tradition that builds resistance to statutory approaches and inhibits changes through collective bargaining.

Indeed, many of women's concerns are not widely perceived as labor market issues: women's "second shift" in the home; their responsibility for children's nurturance and education whether they are marriage partners or single parents; their vulnerability as they become "displaced homemakers" who, as a consequence of widowhood or divorce, must seek entry or long-delayed reentry into the labor market, unprepared for the current requirements of waged work; women's presumed lower career aspirations that are in fact due to social and cultural beliefs about women's skills and abilities, and due as well to a long history of education for girls in the household rather than the technical arts. Vivid confirmation of the consequences of these circumstances grows with the increasing evidence that most of the poor are women and their children—a circumstance embodied in the recently coined phrase "the feminization of poverty."

In contrast, working women are united in their view of these problems as major labor market issues. Male workers sometimes join women in support of both their personal and their labor market goals, but usually only when they see the issue as one in which they too have a direct stake. Examples would be the struggle against a two-tiered system of wages and benefits or for health and safety measures that benefit women and men alike.[1]

Women's Special Problems: Causes and Effects

The special problems women face are highlighted when a few manage to enter male-dominated occupations and trades in search of the relatively high wages and good benefits available there. When these women appear men protect their turf against intrusion with various forms of harassment: men neglect to teach safety information to women; men give women hard and dangerous jobs without adequate preparation; men haze women as they do apprentices, even damage their machines, forget to give them new instructions for new batches of work; and they sexually harass and isolate women on the job to keep them estranged and defensive.

Cockburn offers a sensitive analysis of just how and why men feel sufficiently threatened to engage in such hostile, even life-threatening, practices.[2] In her view, they see their concepts of both job and skill as threatened by women joining them. Men understand skill as something learned, different from women's so-called innate ability to do work that requires neither fostering nor perfecting; skill is demanded by the job and accumulated through long experience. According to Cockburn, a political definition of skill emerges from the historically determined means of its acquisition through long practice and tutelage from other men. Skill acquired by men for men's work is honorific; the skills associated with women's work are adapted to limber fingers, not to strong backs and large muscles. Job and skill are closely allied to what men do. Women who undertake to do men's jobs, diminish, even pollute, these qualities.

1. The development of a two-tiered system to limit competition is a "devil's pact" struck between senior employees and their employers to limit the opportunities of new, incoming workers by stipulating that they receive a lower scale of wages, do simpler tasks, and receive less training, while the old guard continue at the old or even an improved rate of wages. The net effect, even if temporarily protecting some, is to degrade the work and limit job opportunity for all—thus the "devil's pact." See Cynthia Cockburn, *Brothers: Male Dominance and Technological Change*, 1983. She notes that a divisive strategy of a two-tier labor pool allows for a pool of unorganized, unprotected labor available to scab, constituting a lower-class stratum in the working class (p. 23).

2. Ibid., p. 113.

Moreover, they challenge the accepted characteristics of appropriate gender roles and identities. One can almost say that "skill" is a masculine noun. Men thus have vested interests in separating themselves from women at work and in maintaining the fiction that men and women cannot manage the same job and skill levels, even when these distinctions are highly arbitrary and differ from workplace to workplace.[3]

However basic these issues are, they arise only rarely, for most women still work in gender-segregated jobs. The fact of segregation is often explained as the consequence of an extension of women's work in the home or, more recently, as peculiarly suited to their aptitude for small muscle activity and their preference for monotonous and repetitive work that allows them even at work, if need be, to center their lives on home and children. Indeed, it is precisely because women's work in factory, office, and service trades meets these conditions that the struggle for labor market equality has nowhere succeeded.

Underlying these facts is the long-standing social definition of home as an appropriate place for women. "The domestic code," as Alice Kessler-Harris has traced it historically,[4] still dominates much of the thinking about the home in relation to the workplace. The nineteenth-century vision of woman—on a pedestal as the representation of motherhood, innately concerned for ethical values, the embodiment of self-sacrifice, and willingly submissive and subordinate to the head of family—continues to distort the realities of women's lives. As a consequence, working women are confined to a narrow range of occupations; they are excluded from the majority of jobs and therefore from many unions or, alternatively, admitted to unions as members of a secondary and isolated class; they are supervised at work by males; and they are paid low wages.

In a few instances, women's unions have been organized. In these cases members developed a remarkable degree of self-consciousness, through the growing sense that women's problems had a common thread both of cause and effect, running across national boundaries and diverse occupations.

The fact of continuing job segregation testifies to the durability of many outworn concepts. Women in the work force continue to be seen as temporary. Their prime tasks still are perceived as centering on reproduction, despite the fact that the birthrate in the industrialized countries has sunk below the level of reproduction of the population, family

3. On this point, see also Ronnie J. Steinberg, "The Social Construction of Skill: Gender, Power, and Comparable Worth," *Work and Occupations*, special issue, "Skill," 17:4 (November 1990), pp. 449–82.

4. Alice Kessler-Harris, *Women Have Always Worked*, 1981.

size is shrinking, and the time women take away from work after the births of their children is shorter even than the legal allowances for maternity leave.[5] Yet responsibility for home tasks and childrearing remains, as it has for centuries, almost entirely in women's hands. As a consequence many working mothers turn out of necessity for a number of years to part-time work, with the result that it has come to be associated with women.[6] Like women's work generally it is devalued and poorly paid, while unions for these very reasons resist its spread and neglect the women employed in it. This does not mean, however, that unions have focused instead on women as full-time workers. Union traditions see women who work full-time as anomalies—as justified in working only if they are single or widowed, or otherwise working out of dire need.

Undeniably, economic and social forces have contributed to a gradually changing context for women's labor—among them, inflation throughout the industrialized world that requires two incomes to meet family needs, the views propagated by the women's movement, and the growing number of women heads of family resulting from the rising rates of divorce. Increasingly, women everywhere in the Western world are working for wages and salaries with shorter interruptions in their working lives as they limit the size of their families to one or two children. Indeed, many have decided to give priority to career over children and have none. Yet, so powerful is the effect of systemic socialization about gender roles that cultural and interpersonal expectations of women have been remarkably slow to change. Few men have been willing to share the burdens of homemaking and childrearing, and so women continue to carry these, working two shifts as best they can. Arlie Hochschild estimates their efforts come to an extra month of work per year.[7]

Women who seek opportunity in the union hierarchy in effect take on a third shift; and those who do so usually are single, widowed, or with grown children. Under these circumstances they are at a serious

5. Here it is again noted that the United States among the industrialized countries has no legal allowance for maternity leave and that where individual firms provide time for leave, almost none pays for this leave. At best, companies provide some assurance about reemployment. Almost no unions have opposed this trend. A countermovement may be taking place in Sweden, despite its high percentage of working women. Marianne Sandstrom of the Swedish *Arbetslivcentrum,* in discussing "Parenthood and Working Life" at an informal meeting in Stockholm on June 27, 1990, noted that "Sweden has now the highest fertility rate of the industrialized countries at 2.1 children per woman of childbearing age."

6. See Chris de Neubourg, "Part-time Work: An International Quantitative Comparison," *International Labour Review* 124:5 (1985), pp. 559–76.

7. Arlie Hochschild with Anne Machung, *The Second Shift: Working Parents and the Revolution at Home,* 1989, p. 26.

disadvantage, since they start the climb up the union ladder comparatively late in life. While a few have reached the top, they have done so, like their counterparts in the corporations, under unusual circumstances and often at sacrifice of family life.

Women Mediate the Work-Family Conflict

Women are under enormous pressure to mediate between work and family—to carry the contradictions of this duality on their own shoulders. The social forces for change that have swept women into the labor market have pushed women to change faster than men. As Hochschild points out, women today are more different from their mothers than men are from their fathers.[8] The influx of women into paid work and the increased power in the home that a wage brings has raised women's sense of entitlement not only on the job but also in the home. Self-interestedly, men resist carrying burdens their fathers never carried, and they overrate the concession "to help out" around the house, seeing what they do as a great improvement over their fathers' behavior.

Yet, despite growing differences between men and women in aspirations and expectations, it is clear that widespread, open conflict has not broken out in the home.[9] Male resistance is often accepted by women, in part because they too have been socialized to accept women's subordinate role, but in part out of a realistic weighing of alternatives. They see the close link between their low earning power and the negative costs of divorce,[10] in terms of the emotional as well as economic deprivations of single motherhood.[11] Independence bought by pressing men to do more sharing than they will accept is too hard won. Whatever give-and-take occurs between husbands and wives takes place against this background. Hochschild believes that women in working couples feel pressed to accept whatever help men choose to offer as a "gift."[12] A woman may well feel grateful that her husband agrees to her working, even when she gets no assistance from him in the tasks of the home.

In the process of transition—however little its roots are understood

8. Ibid., p. 56.

9. Although the ever-rising divorce rate may be a contrary indicator, we are not aware of studies that explain the causes of divorce in terms closely related to wifely revolt on this score.

10. See Lenore J. Weitzman, *The Divorce Revolution: the Unexpected Social and Economic Consequences for Women and Children in America*, 1985.

11. Terry Arendell, *Mothers and Divorce: Legal, Economic, and Social Dilemmas*, 1986.

12. Hochschild with Machung, 1989, p. 18.

and however ad hoc adjustments are worked out—the structure and behavior of the family are necessarily undergoing change as well. Women's workday is not infinitely expandable and so mothers must contrive a variety of ways of fitting in everything. They cut down on housework, redefine their role as homemakers, and, according to Hochschild, they cut down on child care. If they have enough money, they hire surrogates. Working-class women have different strategies. Because child care is costly they try to parcel it out to family members. Although child care is more available in some countries than in others, nowhere is it totally available, affordable, or satisfactory. Nonetheless, its broad acceptance as a major aid to dual-earner families means that some of the historic texture of family life, family socialization of children, and family support systems is in process of change.[13] Even the structure and makeup of the family are undergoing change so radical that neither lawmakers nor social agencies can assume that their support systems and regulations meet the current needs of the contemporary family.

The Role of Unions

Unions have tended to overlook the changing dynamics of family life. This failure arises in part because the structure of the family and its internal contracts and arrangements do not submit to collective bargaining approaches or processes, limited as they are to labor market issues. Yet many of the problems with which unions attempt to deal— including the central problem of equal employment opportunity—stem from persisting inequalities within the family. It is evident that the labor union, as a significant social institution and an essential labor market body, must be cognizant of the handicaps with which women enter the realm of work, recognizing that these are handicaps working men do not share. Unions must learn to add them to the equality equation.

✓ However dimly unions have understood the root causes of women's problems at work, we found in Europe a number of union programs that—often serendipitously—met women's needs. The more radical ones were in Scandinavia, but social policy in European countries is longer established and more generous than is the case in the United States, including national health insurance, paid maternity leave, parental leave, housing assistance, child allowances, and child care. While the trade unions have supported many of these moves, they have left drafting and

13. Myra H. Strober, "Two-Earner Families," in *Feminism, Children, and the New Families*, ed. Sanford M. Dornbusch and Myra H. Strober, 1990.

implementation to the national, provincial, or city governments, while keeping watchful eye and guiding hand on the outcome through their affiliated or closely associated labor party.

Examples of direct trade union action to correct inequities at work through collective bargaining of course exist. The most striking ones are the attempts to reevaluate the work of women in Germany and England, and the Swedish attempt to narrow the gap between low- and high-paid workers, an approach that was more successful in bringing women's pay close to men's than programs in any other country.[14]

A major conclusion from our work, then, is that the revolution to bring equality for women into the workplace will never succeed until the problems of equality within the home are addressed. Since intervention in the home is not perceived to be the function of a labor market institution, an approach that unions could undertake is to aid in reorganizing the workplace to accommodate it to the needs of family. Because we were looking for operating programs, we have not dealt with this aspect of the problem, although research in several of these countries is now underway. Indeed concern with the causes and outcomes of part-time work is now a major topic of investigation almost everywhere.[15] Many individual unions for whom this is a special issue have begun to regulate part-time conditions and payments in their contracts.

Union Programs as Models

Everywhere, we found, women face harassment at work, particularly when they are introduced into male-dominated professions. Trainers of women for work in these fields have prepared them in some instances for facing these problems. One specific tactic was not to introduce women singly into companies or occupations, nor to isolate them in one or two departments or shifts in a plant, but to spread them throughout the occupations. Training for nontraditional work includes making evident

14. However, this advance may no longer continue. A 1990 visit to Sweden's *Arbetslivcentrum* confirms press information that unions there have now largely given up the "solidary wage policy."

15. For Austria, see "Part-time Employment: A Woman's World," *OeGB Nachrichtendienst*, no. 2074 (1981). For Germany, see Ingrid Kurz-Scherf, "Tarifvertraeglichen Bestimmungen zur Teilzeitarbeit in ausgewaehlten Tarifbereichen," *WSI Mitteilungen*, 1984; and Hedwig Rudolf, "Modern Working Times, Recent Developments in Germany—More Stress and Less Rewards for Women," *Equal Opportunities International*, no. 2 (1984), pp. 10–14. For Great Britain, see B. Ballard, "Women Part-time Workers: Evidence from the 1980 Women and Work Survey," Department of Employment *Gazette*, 92:9 (1984); "Changing Patterns of Part-time Work in the United Kingdom," *European Industrial Relations Review*, November/December 1988, pp. 10–14; and "Moving Towards Part-time Equality," *European Industrial Relations Review*, November/December 1988, p. 6.

that schools and families have socialized men and women for separate roles and separate statuses. It includes providing a realistic picture of persisting discrimination, teaching women to identify and confront it and then giving them support during the early months of their employment. Equally important are program evaluations such as the ones CEDEFOP has financed and published. This organization has accepted and promoted the conclusion reached in a number of German and Swedish training experiments, that women—especially those who have not previously or recently worked—learn better and faster when training programs are designed especially for women. It has also recognized that both vocational and personal counseling, because of women's early socialization in family and school, can play an important part in a training program's success. The inclusion of child care as part of the program also has been shown to be an essential component of programs to support women's advancement in the workplace.

A movement that has made more progress in Europe than in the United States is that for paid educational leave. In some countries such leave is in part provided by law, thus assuring that persons elected to works councils can undertake training for these posts. In contrast, training and retraining for advancement in the firm are commonly the products of negotiation.

Health and Safety

An area in which European unions have made great strides is in the improvement of health and safety regulations for workers. Unions in Sweden have been the most successful, but German and Austrian unions have adequate inspection services and standard-setting institutes studying work hazards. European unions have achieved rights of co-determination in matters of health and safety, exemplified in the health and safety stewards on the floor of factories (and occasionally of offices), and in the creation of joint labor-management committees with power to halt dangerous work and to recommend improvements in machines, procedures, and materials. In Sweden, health and safety stewards have the right to stop work that they consider dangerous.

An attempt in the early 1970s by German unions to reform systems of job evaluation would have looked systematically at women's jobs in terms of stress and strain. The study's report was not implemented, however, because the employers' association decided not to accept either the principle or the proposal worked out by experts. This report remains instructive to American advocates of revised job evaluation tech-

niques concerned with issues of comparable worth, and of job evaluation generally.

Unions in both Germany and Sweden have been active in bargaining
for relief from the demands VDTs put upon thousands of women operators. They have negotiated frequent rest periods during the day, as
well as the opportunity for pregnant women to be relieved of work on
computers altogether. This concern not only with the effects of eye-
strain but also with the possible reproductive damage that can be traced
to the computer's electromagnetic field is in sharp contrast to the long-
delayed and considerably modified study of this subject by NIOSH.

Shorter Hours

Many of the improvements in working conditions achieved by European unions reflect an understanding of the special conditions under
which women work and of the pressure of unrelieved family duties. The
concern with shortening working time and indeed the duration of working life is one of the central themes of European unions. The powerful
metalworkers' union of Germany has recently negotiated the last steps
toward the achievement of a thirty-five hour week, to be attained by
the mid-1990s.[16]

To be sure, much of this concern for achieving shorter working hours
has little to do with benefiting families. Rather it is in consideration of
the threat of general unemployment presented through mechanization,
computerization, and even robotization of work both in factory production and in the white-collar occupations, Yet, men and women differ
in how they prefer to reshape the hours of work. Women want shorter
days, while men prefer either shorter work weeks or shorter work years.
Hence, many of the agreements actually reached through this effort have
disregarded women's concerns. Only Sweden allows both parents of
preschool children to work a shortened six-hour day.

Training

An indirect and positive result of the introduction of high technology
is the additional pressure it puts on training programs to improve skills
both of workers who remain in these occupations and of unemployed
workers retraining for new tasks. Since women's unemployment in all
countries except Britain is at a higher rate than men's, measures for

16. *IMF Bulletin*, Summer 1990, p. 1.

training and retraining the unemployed are designed in particular for women, financed by the EC social fund and carried out through CED-EFOP (more recently through the EC's European Network of Training Programs for Women, IRIS).

Indeed, the integrated labor and product market to be established by 1992, and destined to include not only the present EC member states but eventually most of the rest of Europe and possibly Turkey, will provide considerably more mobility for those seeking work. In anticipation of 1992, CEDEFOP is now deeply engaged in developing occupational job descriptions for both training and employment that will obtain uniformly throughout the EC.

Women in Union Leadership

Within the unions, in all of the countries in our study, are efforts to bring women into leadership positions—in Germany, there are the Frauenfoerderplaene; in Britain and Sweden, "positive action programs." Some are more systematic and compelling than others, but their purpose is to place women in elected and appointed positions of leadership in the unions themselves, at least until their numbers in these positions closely approach the proportion of women in the unions' memberships.

While special programs for women have deep historical roots in Germany and Austria, dating back to the very origins of the unions, they were a by-product of the fact that women were isolated within the labor market; there were relatively few working women, and the unions assumed that they were a lesser class without the protection of the law. The provision of women's sections within the unions in effect emphasized their special and inferior place within the labor market. With the reorganization of these unions after the Second World War, many of the same motives operated to continue this historic practice.

Today's women's division, as an institution, has taken on a new function. It is now the voice of women seeking equality both in the labor market and in the family. In Germany, in particular, it has allied itself with the organized women's lobby, the German Council of Women. Its voice is heard in the national parliament as well as in the trade union congress.

Such coalitions with other women's organizations have been particularly successful in Germany and England. The growing interest of continental countries in setting up equality centers in towns and cities has encouraged union women as well as unorganized workers to find advice, counseling, and legal assistance when equal opportunity legislation appears to have been neglected or violated.

An important consequence of many of the efforts to form alliances and create a common front in the battle against patriarchy is evident precisely in these coalitions across class lines. The expressions of concern and of demands arising from such efforts have made the subject of discrimination and its relief a part of the public conversation concerned with policies that benefit working women.

Sweden had a women's department, but the trade union executive board abolished it in the 1970s in the name of equality. It was replaced with a committee on the family to which men as well as women were appointed. We found that Swedish women are now seeking their own organization and using it to elect women officials and bring women's issues before local, regional, and national trade union meetings. Moreover, in 1990 interviews, we learned of new experiments in all-women's educational programs.

Britain's history differed decidedly from these other countries. In the early 1920s when the Women's Trade Union League amalgamated with the Trades Union Congress it negotiated for a number of seats for women on the TUC executive board, a move other countries accepted only fifty years later. Britain's annual conference of "unions catering to women" serves as the major gathering for a discussion of women's issues and decisions about which issues to bring to the TUC itself.

Among these examples of women's union organizations, the German one had the most impressive structure, replicated, as it is, in each of the national unions, in each district office, and in many of the local unions and shops. Its systematic provision for meetings and educational programs, for staff appointments and consultations, and for national congresses that were scheduled to precede the trade union conventions in order to formulate and present women's issues for union debate, spoke to the mobilization of maximum power and influence. It is out of these divisions that the Frauenfoerderplaene come and more than half of the unions have now adopted such plans. The major shortcoming in this program is its lack of an independent budget.

Throughout our study trade union women recognized their lack of assertiveness and training for organizational tasks. To a considerable degree the education departments of the unions have met some of their needs. The regular presentation of special courses for women at the DGB schools, the coopting of women's division staff members to teach in the union programs, the recognition in a decentralization program that it is more difficult for women to attend a resident school than is the case with men (and therefore that more classes have to be held in local or regional schools)—all of these adjustments to meet women's needs represent positive changes.

One important purpose of the "promotion plans"—the Foerderplaene—is to bring women into the collective bargaining process because if they are involved it is more likely that their interests will be represented at the bargaining table. Though it is unclear how much difference women bargainers will make (since there are so few), it is clear that in unions where women make up at least a substantial minority of members, women's issues receive prominence when women participate in the bargaining. Such issues include regularization of part-time work, introduction of flextime, improvement of maternity leave with job security on return to work, assistance with or even provision of child care, a compensation system based on bias-free evaluation of the value of women's work, the inclusion of women on joint health and safety committees, and union monitoring of equal opportunity for women in hiring, on-the-job training, and promotion.[17]

Work and Family

The trade union as it functions in Europe and the United States has the power and means to propel change in the relationships of work and family in the modern, postindustrialized world. Unions, clearly, have tried to grapple with problems stemming from women's special responsibilities for the family and their effect on women's working conditions. A basic difference between the United States and Europe is that the European countries have national social programs that provide maternity and child health care, widespread child-care facilities, child allowances, parental leave, and housing assistance to large families. In addition, Sweden has focused its public policy on the welfare of the child and thus to some degree has subordinated labor market policy to family policy. Most of the officials with whom we spoke saw two primary reasons for the high percentage of working women: the Swedish tax policy that taxes individual rather than spousal incomes, and the equitable treatment of part-time work. Moreover, they credit the increase in the average number of years women work to the state's central concern with child and maternity health and welfare.

Everywhere unions are able to negotiate with employers for benefits

17. See Action Program of the ETUC, as well as the Women's Action Program, 1988–93, of the EC for a complete list of issues affecting working women.

above the level provided by statute. This is the outcome particularly in those unions in which women are collective participants in union affairs through a women's section of the unions.

In their work within union structures, women bring their problems and needs as both workers and family members to the attention of shop stewards, works councillors, local officers, bargaining committees, and teachers in educational and training programs. The unions' responses in terms of special programs, together with accommodations in the scheduling and structure of these programs, are the bona fides that can assure women that their problems are recognized, and that they are being looked upon as full members of these organizations. Paradoxically, then, unions must fully recognize and make accommodations to women's double shift, even as they try to eliminate it. We have found no country and no set of trade unions attacking the basic source of injustice. Progressive thinking consists in making adjustments not only to the double shift but also to programs whose goal is its elimination. Whether we like it or not, a gender revolution is in progress. For the women who are part of it, either as activists or as passive participants, it is a very difficult revolution. It calls inevitably for a drastic reorganization of work and the workplace to take account of familial needs and obligations. Organized groups of women within unions are propelling the movement forward as the logical instrument to achieve the recognition of women as equal members of the union, the workplace, and society.

Abbreviations

ABF	Workers Education Association (Sweden)
ACAS	Advisory Council and Arbitration Service (U.K.)
ACTWU	Amalgamated Clothing and Textile Workers (U.S.)
AFA	Airline Flight Attendants (U.S.)
AFL	American Federation of Labor (U.S. until 1957)
AFL-CIO	American Federation of Labor–Congress of Industrial Organizations (U.S.)
AFSCME	American Federation of State, County, and Municipal Employees
ALA	American Library Association
AMS	The Swedish Labor Market Board *(Arbeitsmarkstyrelseu)*
ANA	American Nurses' Association
APEX	Association of Professional, Executive, Clerical, and Computer Staffs (U.K.)
ASTMS	Association of Scientific, Technical, and Management Staffs (U.K.)
AT&T	American Telephone and Telegraph Company
AUEW	Amalgamated Union of Engineering Workers (U.K.)
BBC	British Broadcasting Corporation
BDA	Federation of German Employers *(Bund der deutschen Arbeitgeber)*
BfA	The German Labor Market Board *(Bundesanstalt fuer Arbeit)*
BIBB	The National Institute for Vocational Training *(Bundesinstitut fuer Berufsbildung* (Germany)
BNA	Bureau of National Affairs (U.S.)
BVG	Basic Workplace Labor Relations Law *(Betriebsverfassungsgesetz)* (Germany)
CAC	Central Arbitration Commission (U.K.)
CBI	Confederation of British Industry
CCL	Canadian Congress of Labor
CDU	Christian-Democratic Union (Germany)
CEC	Commission of the European Community
CEDEFOP	Commission for Vocational Training in the European Community
CHCJ	Community High Court of Justice (EC)
CIO	Committee (later, Congress) of Industrial Organizations (U.S.)
CLUW	Coalition of Labor Union Women (U.S.)
CREW	Center for Research on European Women (Brussels)
CUTW	Connecticut Union of Telephone Workers (U.S.)
CWA	Communications Workers of America

DAG   Independent White-collar Union *(Deutsche Angestellten Gewerk-schaft)* (Germany)
DBW   The Vocational Education Institution of the German Federation of Labor *(Deutsches Bildungswerk)*
DGB   German Federation of Labor *(Deutscher Gewerkschaftsbund)*
DGB Protokoll   Congress Proceedings of the DGB (Germany)
EAT   Employment Appeals Tribunal (U.K.)
EC   *See* EEC
EEC   European Economic Community, composed of twelve European nations (also EC) (Brussels)
EEOA   Equal Employment Opportunity Act (U.S.)
EEOC   Equal Employment Opportunity Commission (U.S.)
EETPU   Electrical, Electronic, Telecommunication, and Plumbing Union (U.K.)
EGB   European Trade Union Federation *(Europaeischer Gewerkschaftsbund)* (Brussels). *See* ETUC
EIT   Engineering Industry Training Board (U.K.)
EOC   Equal Opportunities Commission (U.K.)
EPA   Equal Pay Act (U.S.)
ETUC   European Trade Union Confederation (Brussels)
ETUI   European Trade Union Institute (Brussels)
FIET   International Federation of Commercial, Clerical, and Technical Employees *(Federation Internationale d'Employés Technicale)* (Geneva)
GMB   General Municipal, Boilermakers and Allied Trades Union (U.K.)
GMWU   General and Municipal Workers Union (U.K.)
GNP   Gross National Product
GPA   Trade Union of Private Sector White-collar Workers *(Gewerkschaft der Privatangestellten)* (Austria)
GTB   Union of Textile and Clothing Workers *(Gewerkschaft Textil und Bekleidung)* (Germany)
GTBL   Trade Union of Textile, Clothing, and Leather Workers *(Gewerkschaft der Textil, Bekleidung, und Lederarbeiter)* (Austria)
Handels   Swedish Union of Commercial Employees
HBV   Commercial, Banking, and Insurance Union *(Handel, Banken, und Versicherung)* (Germany)
HMSO   His/Her Majesty's Stationery Office (the British government's publications office)
IBEW   International Brotherhood of Electrical Workers (U.S.)
ICFTU   International Confederation of Free Trade Unions (Brussels)
IDS   Incomes Data Services (U.K.)
IGM   Industrial Union of Metalworkers *(Industrie Gewerkschaft Metall)* (Germany)
ILGWU   International Ladies Garment Workers Union (U.S.)
ILO   International Labour Organisation (or, for its administration, International Labour Office) (Geneva)

IMBE	Industrial Union of Metal, Mining, and Energy Workers (Austria)
IMF	International Metalworkers' Federation (Geneva)
IRIS	European Network of Training Schemes for Women
IRRA	Industrial Relations Research Association (U.S.)
IT	Industrial Tribunal (U.K.)
ITB	Industrial Training Board (U.K.)
ITF News	*International Transport Federation News* (Geneva). *See* ITWF
ITS	International Trade Secretariats (variously located)
ITWF	International Transport Workers Federation (Geneva)
IWY	International Women's Year
Kommunal	Swedish Union of Local Government Employees
LO	Swedish Confederation of Labor *(Sverige Landesorganisation)*
Metall	The short name for the IGM in Germany, Austria, and Sweden
MSC	Manpower Services Commission (U.K.)
MSF	Manufacturing, Science, and Finance Workers Union (U.K.) (includes TASS and APEX)
NALGO	National Association of Local Government Officers (U.K.)
NAS	National Academy of Science (U.S.)
NCCL	National Council on Civil Liberties (U.K.)
NEA	National Education Association (U.S.)
NGG	Food and Restaurant Workers Union *(Nahrung, Gaststaetten, und Genuss)* (Germany)
NGO	Non-governmental International Women's Organisations (in conference at the same time as the U.N. International Women's Conferences during the Women's Decade, 1975–85)
NIOSH	National Institute of Occupational Safety and Health (U.S.)
NLRA	National Labor Relations Act (U.S.)
NLRB	National Labor Relations Board (U.S.)
NRC	Nuclear Regulatory Commission (U.S.)
NUM	National Union of Miners (U.K.)
NUPE	National Union of Public Employees (U.K.)
NWLB	National War Labor Board (U.S.)
OCAW	Oil, Chemical, and Atomic Workers Union (U.S.)
OECD	Organisation for Economic Cooperation and Development (composed of 28 nations) (Paris)
OeGB	Austrian Trade Union Confederation *(Oesterreichischer Gewerkschaftsbund)*
OeTV	Public Workers Union *(Oeffentliche Dienste, Transport, und Verkehr)* (Germany)
OMB	Office of Management and Budget (U.S.)
OME	Office of Management Education (U.K.)
OPEIU	Office and Professional Employees International Union (U.S.)
OSHA	Occupational Safety and Health Administration (U.S.)
OSHARC	Occupational Safety and Health Review Commission (U.S.)
PTK	Cartel of white-collar workers' unions in the private sector for pur-

	poses of collective bargaining with the Swedish Employers' Association
RWDSU	Retail, Wholesale, and Department Store Union (U.S.)
SACO/SR	Swedish Association of Academic, Professional, and Managerial Officers
SAF	Swedish Employers' Federation *(Svenska Arbetsgivarefoereningen)*
SDP	Social Democratic Party (Sweden)
SEIU	Service Employees International Union (U.S.)
SIF	White-collar Workers' Union in the private sector (Sweden)
SLB	*Social and Labour Bulletin* (ILO)
SOFI	Sociological Research Institute *(Soziologisches Forschungsinstitut* (University of Goettingen, Germany)
SPD	Social Democratic Party of Germany *(Sozial-Demokratische Partei Deutschlands)*
TASS	Technical, Administrative, and Supervisory Staffs (section of the AUEW, U.K., until 1985). *See* MSF
TCO	Swedish Central Organization of Salaried Employees *(Tjaenstemans Centralorganisationen)*
Textil	Textile and Clothing Workers Union (Sweden)
TGWU	Transport and General Workers Union (also T&G) (U.K.)
TOPS	Training Opportunities Scheme (U.K.)
TUC	Trades Union Congress (U.K.)
UAW	United Automobile Workers (U.S.)
UCLEA	University and College Labor Education Association (U.S.)
USCRC	United States Civil Rights Commission
USDOL	United States Department of Labor
VDT	Video Display Terminal
VDU	Video Display Unit
VLF	Very Low Frequency
WB	Women's Bureau, Department of Labor (U.S.)
WEA	Workers' Educational Association (U.K.)
WLB	War Labor Board (World War II) (U.S.)
WOHRC	Women's Occupational Health Resource Center (U.S.)
WOW	Wider Opportunities for Women
WSI	Trade Union Research Center (*Wirtschafts- und Sozialwissenschafts* Institut) (Germany)
WTUL	Women's Trade Union League (U.S. and U.K.)
YOP	Youth Opportunities Program (U.K.)

References

Aaron, Benjamin. 1985. "The NLRB, Labor Courts, and Industrial Tribunals: A Selective Comparison." *Industrial and Labor Relations Review* 39:1, pp. 35–45.

ACAS. 1978. *Code of Practice on Time Off for Trade Union Duties and Activities*. London.

Acker, Joan. 1989. *Doing Comparable Worth: Gender, Class, and Pay Equity*. Philadelphia: Temple University Press.

——, and Donald R. van Houten. 1974. "Differential Recruitment and Control: The Sex Structure of Organizations." *Administrative Science Quarterly* 39:1, pp. 35–45.

AFL-CIO News. 1987. "The AFL-CIO Convention." November 7, p. 3.

Aichholzer, George, Peter Kowalski, Lutz Burkhardt, and Gerd Schienstock. 1986. *Vocational Training in Austria*. Berlin: CEDEFOP.

AMS. 1985. *Labour Market Training*. Solna: Swedish Labour Market Board.

APEX, Research Department. 1978. *Topics: Unemployment*. London: APEX.

——. 1979. *Office Technology: The Trade Union Response*. London: APEX.

Arendell, Terry. 1986. *Mothers and Divorce: Legal, Economic, and Social Dilemmas*. Berkeley: University of California Press.

Ashford, Nicholas A. 1987. *Crisis in the Workplace: Occupational Disease and Injury*. Cambridge: MIT Press.

——, and Charles C. Caldart. 1983. "The Control of Reproductive Hazards in the Workplace: A Prescription for Prevention." *Industrial Relations Law Journal* 5:4, pp. 523–63.

Atkin Committee. *See* War Cabinet Committee.

Bain, George Sayers. 1983. *Industrial Relations in Great Britain*. Oxford: Basil Blackwell.

Baker, Helen. 1942. *Women in War Industries*. Princeton: Princeton University Press.

Ballard, B. 1984. "Women Part-time Workers: Evidence from the 1980 Women and Work Survey." *Department of Employment Gazette* 92:9, pp. 409–16.

Balser, Diane. 1987. *Sisterhood and Solidarity: Feminism and Labor in Modern Times*. Boston: Southend Press.

Barkin, Solomon, ed. 1975. *Worker Militancy and Its Consequences, 1965–1975: New Directions in Western Industrial Relations*. New York: Praeger.

BBC. 1978. *Working for Safety: Background Notes*. London: Villiers House.

Beccali, Bianca. 1984. "From Equality to Difference: Women and Trade Unions in Italy." *Feminist Review*, no. 16 (April), pp. 47–49.

Bellante, Donald, and Sunne Brandmeyer. 1989. "The Impact of the Employment and Earnings of Women." Pennsylvania State University Conference,
Department of Labor Studies, "Women and Unions." March.

Beller, Andrea H. 1984. "Occupational Segregation and the Earnings Gap."
Paper presented at the U.S. Civil Rights Commission Consultation, Washington, D.C., June 6–7.

Belous, Richard S. 1989. *The Contingent Economy: The Growth of Temporary,
Part-time, and Sub-contracted Workforce.* Washington, D.C.: National Planning Association.

Benya, Anton. 1969. *Wochenpresse.* October 6.

———. 1981. *Oesterreichische Nachrichtendienst,* no. 2074 (March 5).

Bergmann, Barbara. 1974. "Occupational Segregation, Wages, and Profits When
Employers Discriminate by Race and Sex." *Eastern Economic Journal* 1:2–3
(April/July), pp. 103–10.

Black, Naomi. 1989. *Social Feminism.* Ithaca: Cornell University Press.

Blaxall, Martha, and Barbara Reagan, eds. 1976. *Women and the Workplace:
The Implications of Occupational Segregation.* Chicago: University of Chicago Press.

BNA. 1944. *In re Bendix Aviation Corporation, Bendix Products Division, and
the United Automobile Workers.* Case 2941-D, September 20, 1943. In *War
Labor Reports: Wage and Salary Stabilization,* vol. 11. Washington, D.C.:
BNA.

BNA, *Daily Labor Report.* 1981. "American Cyanimid Prevails in 'Fetus Protection Policy.'" No. 84 (May 1), pp. A-6–7.

———. 1982. "Case of Females Exposed to Lead." No. 197, p. A-11.

———. 1983. "Supreme Court to Hear Arguments in Karen Silkwood Case." No.
5 (January 10), pp. A-3–4.

———. 1984a. "Supreme Court Permits Punitive Damages for Lab Worker Contaminated by Plutonium." No. 7 (January 12), p. A-12.

———. 1984b. "Office Workers' Union Tells Labor Subcommittee of Suspected
Health Hazards from Workplace VDTs." No. 40 (February 29), p. A-2–3.

———. 1984c. "Court Blocks Challenge to American Cyanimid 'Fetus Protection
Policy' for Lead Exposures." No. 167 (August 24), p. A-1. Text, "American
Cyanimid Co.," CADC 81-1687, p. E-1–3.

———. 1985a. "Employers Advised to Preempt VDT Regulations through Voluntary Action." No. 87 (May 6), pp. A-2–5.

———. 1985b. "IBT Reacts Strongly to VDT Story." No. 87 (May 6), p. A-5.

———. 1985c. "Survey of VDT Users Reveals Link between VDT Users, Monitoring." No. 230 (November 29), pp. A-6–7.

———. 1986a. "Pacific Northwest Bell Forms Committee on VDT-Related Programs." No. 27, p. A-2.

———. 1986b. "Swedish Researchers Say Significant Questions Raised by Study
of VDT Use and Pregnancy." No. 99 (May 22), pp. A-3–4.

———. 1986c. "OMB Decision Allows VDT Study, but NIOSH Wary About
Requirement." No. 112 (June 11), pp. A-12–13.

——. 1987. "Workplace, Health Issues for Pregnant Workers Pressing Employers for More Attention, Report Says." No. 137 (October 26), p. A-12.

——. 1988a. "VDT-Related Health Problems Called Serious National Threat." No. 11 (January 19), pp. A-2–3.

——. 1988b. "Interviews with VDT Operators Complete: Reproduction Study Results Due Next Year." No. 169 (August 31), pp. A-1–2.

——. 1989. "Medical Expert Says Occupational Disease Is More Prevalent than Officially Reported." No. 96 (May 19), p. A-6.

——. 1991a. "NIOSH Study Finds No Link between VDT Use and Spontaneous Abortions." No. 50, p. A-1.

——. 1991b. "Supporters of Tougher Standards Criticize NIOSH Miscarriage Study." No. 72 (April 12), p. A-1.

BNA, *Special Report*. 1986a. *The Changing Workplace: New Directions in Staffing and Scheduling*. Washington, D.C.: BNA.

——. 1986b. *Work and Family: A Changing Dynamic*. Washington, D.C.: BNA.

——. 1987. *Pregnancy and Employment: The Complete Handbook on Discrimination, Maternity Leave, and Health and Safety*. Washington, D.C.: BNA.

Bolinder, Eric. 1977. "Worker Participation for Optimal Environment." *Arbetsmiljö*, no. 10B.

Brandstaller, Traudl. 1982(?). *Frauen in Oesterreich: Bilanz und Ausblick*. Vienna: Frauenservicestelle fuer allgemeine Frauenfragen, Bundeskanzleramt.

Braverman, Harry. 1974. *Labor and Monopoly Capital: The Degradation of Work in the Twentieth Century*. New York: Monthly Labor Review Press.

Bridenthal, Renate, Atina Grossman, and Marion Kaplan. 1984. *When Biology Became Destiny: Women in Weimar and Nazi Germany*. New York: Monthly Review Press.

Brodeur, Paul. 1989. "Annals of Radiation." *New Yorker*. Part I: "Hazards of Electro-Magnetic Fields," June 12, pp. 51–88; Part II: "Something Is Happening," June 19, pp. 47–73; Part III: "Video Display Terminals," June 26, pp. 39–68.

Brody, Doris Cohen. 1975. "American Labor Education Service, 1927–1962: An Organization in Workers' Education." Ph.D. diss., Cornell University.

Broedel, Reiner, Erna Schmitz, and Erwin Fauss. 1982. *A Comparative Study of Denmark, the Netherlands, Ireland, the United Kingdom, and the Federal Republic of Germany*. Berlin: CEDEFOP.

Business Week. 1985. "Don't Duck Comparable Worth." January 28, pp. 140–41.

Castles, Stephen, and Godula Kosack. 1973. *Immigrant Workers and Class Struggle in Western Europe*. New York: Institute of Race Relations, Oxford University Press.

CCL. 1976. *Proceedings 1976*. Ottawa: CCL.

CEC. 1976. *Vocational Guidance and Training for Women Workers*. Brussels: EEC.

——. 1981. *A New Community Action Programme on the Promotion of Equal*

Opportunity for Women, 1982–1985. Brussels: EEC Commission, 1-917 758, December.

CEDEFOP. 1983. "Innovative Training and Employment for Women." Seminar Report, Manchester. Luxembourg: CEDEFOP.

Centre for Educational Research and Innovation. 1976. *Development in Educational Leaves of Absence.* Paris: OECD.

Chapple, F. J. 1975. *Equal Pay and Job Evaluation.* London: EETPU.

Chickering, Roger. 1980. Review of Dörte Winkler, *Frauen im Dritten Reich. Business History Review* 54:136 (Spring).

Christensen, Kathleen. 1987. *A New Era of Home-based Work: Directions and Policies.* New York: Henry Holt.

Christl, Josef, and Michael Wagner. 1982. "Die Stellung der Frau in der oester- reichischen Lohn- und Gehaltspyramide." *Wirtschaft und Gesellschaft* 8:1 (January), pp. 77–96.

Cicourel, Aaron V., and John T. Kitsuse. 1963. *The Educational Decision Makers.* Indianapolis: Bobbs-Merrill.

Clark, G. 1982. *Working Patterns: Part-time Work, Job Sharing, and Self-Employment.* London: Manpower Services Commission, HMSO.

Clegg, Hugh A. 1972. *The System of Industrial Relations in Great Britain.* Oxford: Basil Blackwell.

Clot, Isabelle Savoy. 1984. "What Equality for Women: The Swiss Experiment." *Labour and Society* 9:1 (January/March), pp. 87–104.

Cockburn, Cynthia. 1983. *Brothers: Male Dominance and Technological Change.* London: Pluto Press.

Cole, G. D. H. 1952. *A Short History of the British Working-Class Movement, 1789–1947.* London: George Allen Unwin.

Commission of Inquiry into Part-time Work. 1983. *Part-time Work in Canada.* Ottawa: Publication Distribution Center.

Commons, John R., ed. 1905. *Trade Unionism and Labor Problems.* Boston: Ginn and Co.

Cook, Alice H. 1962. "Dual Government in Unions." *Industrial and Labor Relations Review,* April, pp. 323–49.

———. 1978. *Working Mothers: Problems and Programs in Nine Countries.* Rev. ed. Ithaca: Industrial and Labor Relations Press, Cornell University.

———. 1983. *Comparable Worth: The Problem and States' Approaches to Wage Equity.* Honolulu: Industrial Relations Center, University of Hawaii, Manoa.

———. 1985. *Comparable Worth: A Case Book of Experience in States and Localities.* Honolulu: Industrial Relations Center, University of Hawaii, Manoa.

———. 1987. *Comparable Worth Supplement.* Honolulu: Industrial Relations Center, University of Hawaii, Manoa.

———. 1990. "Implementation of Comparable Worth in the United States." Paper presented at IRRA spring meeting, Buffalo, N.Y., May 1–3.

———, Val R. Lorwin, and Arlene Kaplan Daniels, eds. 1984. *Women and Trade Unions in Eleven Industrialized Countries.* Philadelphia: Temple University Press.

Corcoran, Jennifer. 1981. "U.K. Sex Discrimination and the European Court." *Equal Opportunities International* 1:1, pp. 18–22.

Cousins, Frank. 1969. *TUC Report*. London: TUC.

Coussins, Jean. 1976. *The Equality Report*. London: National Council of Civil Liberties, Rights for Women Unit.

Daniels, Arlene Kaplan. 1988. *Invisible Careers: Women Civic Leaders and the Voluntary World*. Chicago: University of Chicago Press.

de Neubourg, Chris. 1985. "Part-time Work: An International Quantitative Comparison." *International Labour Review* 124:5, pp. 559–76.

Deutscher Bundestag. 1983. *Unterrichtung durch die Bundesregierung ueber Erfahrungen mit der Gleichbehandlung von Maennern und Frauen am Arbeitsplatz betreffendem Teil des arbeitsrechtlichen EG-Anpassungsgesetzes*. Bonn: Drucksache 10.14. March 31.

DeVault, Marjorie. 1991. *Feeding the Family: The Social Organization of Caring as Gendered Work*. Chicago: University of Chicago Press.

DGB. 1983. *Kongress Protokoll*. Duesseldorf: DGB.

Dornbusch, Sanford M., and Myra H. Strober, eds. 1990. *Feminism, Children, and the New Families*. New York: Guilford Press.

Edwards, Richard, Paolo Geronna, and Franz Toedtling, eds. 1986. *Unions in Crisis and Beyond: Perspectives from Six Countries*. Dover, Mass.: Auburn.

Eiger, Norman. 1981. "Labor Education and Democracy in the Workplace." *Working Life in Sweden*, no. 22 (April), pp. 1–12.

Eigstrand, Kaj. 1977. *Training Education in Occupational Health and Safety in Sweden*. Stockholm: National Board of Occupational Safety and Health.

Elliott, Ruth. 1984. "How Far Have We Come? Women's Organisations in the Unions of the United Kingdom." *Feminist Review*, no. 16, pp. 53–55.

Ellis, Valerie. 1982. *The Role of the Trade Unions in the Promotion of Equal Opportunities*. London: EOC/SSRC Joint Panel on Equal Opportunities.

England, Paula. 1984. "Explanation of Job Segregation and the Sex Gap in Pay." Paper presented at the U.S. Civil Rights Commission Consultation, Washington, D.C., June 6–7.

EOC. 1980a. *Annual Report*. Manchester: HMSO.

——. 1980b. *Women and Trade Unions*. Manchester: HMSO.

Equal Opportunity Review. 1988a. "Equal Value: A Union Update." No. 22 (November/December), pp. 9–15; 34–37.

——. 1988b. "Negotiating for Equality." No. 22 (November/December), pp. 31–34.

——. 1988c. "Unions: Still a Long Way to Go." No. 22 (November/December), p. 4.

ETUC/ETUI. 1983. *Women's Representation in Trade Unions*. Brussels: ETUC/ ETUI.

——. 1987. *Women in Trade Unions in Western Europe*. Brussels: ETUC/ ETUI.

——. 1989. *Positive Action for Women in Western Europe*. Brussels: ETUC/ ETUI.

European Industrial Relations Review. 1987. "Changing Conditions of Part-Time Work in the United Kingdom." November/December, pp. 6–12.

——. 1989. "Health and Safety Rights of Workers in Seven Countries." No. 183 (April), pp. 14–21.

Evans, Sarah, and Barbara Nelson. 1989. *Wage Justice: Comparable Worth and the Paradox of Technical Reform*. Chicago: University of Chicago Press.

FIET. 1975. *Program for Women Salaried Employees*. Geneva: FIET.

Fisher, Marguerite. 1948. "Equal Pay for Equal Work Legislation." *Industrial and Labor Relations Review* 2:1 (October), pp. 50–57.

Frauen. 1989. "Kollektivvertraege Ueberpruefen: Die Gleichbehandlunskommission Bekommt eine Vorsitzende." December, p. 4.

——. 1990. "Frauenarbeit neu Bewerten." February, p. 3.

Frauen und Arbeit. 1980. "Nach 18 Jahren Lohnstreit hoeher Gruppierung." August/September, p. 20.

——. 1982. "Forderungen des DGB zur Durchsetzung der Gleichen Rechte und Chancen der Frauen-Lohndiskriminierung: Lohngleichheit fuer Maenner und Frauen." No. 10 (October), pp. 7–8.

——. 1983. "Frauenarbeit zur Durchsetzung der gleichen Rechte und Chancen der Frauen." [Arbeitsmaterial fuer die Gewerkschaften.] July, pp. 2–10.

——. 1984. "FIET Weltkongress." January, p. 16.

Freeman, Richard B., and James L. Medoff. 1984. *What Do Unions Do?* New York: Basic Books.

Fryer, Bob, Andy Fairclough, and Tom Manson. 1974. *Organisation and Change in the National Union of Public Employees*. Coventry: University of Warwick.

Galbraith, John K. 1973. *Economics and the Social Purpose*. Boston: Houghton Mifflin.

Gardell, Bertil. 1977. "Psychosocial Aspects of the Working Environment." *Working Life in Sweden*, no. 1 (August), pp. 1–6.

Gaudart, Dorothea. 1977. "Gleiche Berufschancen fuer Frau und Mann." *Enquete der Gewerkschaft der Privatangestellten*. Vienna: GPA.

——, and Rose Marie Greve. 1978. "Analysis of the Discussions—International Symposium on 'Women and Labour.'" International Institute for Labour Studies, Vienna, September 12–15.

GMWU. n.d. *Bargaining for Equality*. London: G&MWU.

Goldschmidt-Clermont, Luisella. 1983. *Unpaid Work in the Household: A Review of Economic Evaluation Methods*. Geneva: ILO.

GPA. 1978. *Men and Women: Equal Partners in Society*. Vienna: GPA.

——. 1979. *Our School Books: Reflection of Our Society*. Vienna: GPA.

Great Britain Royal Commission on Labour. 1893. *The Employment of Women: A Report to Parliament on the Conditions of Work in Various Industries in England, Wales, Scotland, and Ireland*. London: HMSO. (See also Orne et al.)

Gustafsson, Siv. 1979a. "Male-Female Lifetime Earnings Differentials and Labor Force History." Paper presented at the seminar "Studies in Labor Market Behavior: Sweden and the United States," Stockholm, July 10–11, Arbetslivcentrum, Working Paper Series.

———. 1979b. "Women and Work in Sweden." *Working Life in Sweden*, no. 115 (December), pp. 1–4.

———. 1986. "Trende in der Entwicklung zur Gleichberechtigung." Paper presented at the seminar "Equality between Women and Men in Sweden and Switzerland," Stockholm, March 18, Arbetslivcentrum, Working Paper Series.

Hamilton, Alice. 1945. *Exploring the Dangerous Trades*. New York: Little, Brown.

Harlan, Sharon R., and Ronnie J. Steinberg, eds. 1989. *Job Training for Women: The Promise and Limits of Public Policy*. Philadelphia: Temple University Press.

Harrison, J. F. C. 1965. *Society and Politics in England, 1780–1960*. New York: Harper and Row.

Hartmann, Heidi I., ed. 1987. *Computer Chips and Paper Clips*. Washington, D.C.: National Academy Press.

Hawley, Amos H., ed. 1979. *Societal Growth*. New York: Free Press.

Hegelheimer, Barbara. 1977. *Berufsqualification und Berufschancen von Frauen in der Bundesrepublik Deutschland*. Berlin: Max Planck Institut fuer Bildungsforschung.

———. 1982. *Equal Opportunity and Vocational Training: In-Firm Training and Career Prospects for Women in the Federal Republic of Germany*. Berlin: CEDEFOP.

Hertz, Rosanna. 1986. *More Equal Than Others: Women and Men in Dual-Career Marriages*. Berkeley: University of California Press.

Hewlett, Sylvia Ann. 1985. *A Lesser Life: The Myth of Women's Liberation in America*. New York: Morrow.

Hochschild, Arlie M. 1983. *The Managed Heart: Commercialization of Human Feeling*. Berkeley: University of California Press.

———, with Anne Machung. 1989. *The Second Shift: Working Parents and the Revolution at Home*. New York: Viking Press.

Hooks, Janet M. 1944. *British Policies and Methods in Employing Women in Wartime*. Bulletin 200. Washington, D.C.: Department of Labor, Women's Bureau, GPO.

Hunt, Judith. 1975. *Organising Women Workers*. London: WEA.

———, and Shelley Adams. 1980. *Women, Work, and Trade Union Organisation*. London: WEA.

ICFTU. 1978a. *Integration of Women into Trade Union Organisations*. Brussels: ICFTU.

———. 1978b. *Women's Charter of Working Rights*. Brussels: ICFTU.

IDS. 1984. *Employment Law Handbook: Sex Discrimination and Equal Pay*. London: Gresham Press.

IGM. 1986. *Frauenfoerderplan*. Frankfurt: IGM.

———. 1988. *Working Hours: Dreams, Wishes, and Demands of Women*. Frankfurt: IGM Women's Division.

ILO. 1950. "Equal Remuneration for Men and Women Workers for Work of Equal Value." 33d Session, International Labour Conference, Geneva.

———. 1974a. *Paid Educational Leave: Proposed Texts*. Geneva: ILO.

———. 1974b. *Report IV (2)*. 59th Session, International Labour Conference.

———. 1985a. "Convention 156." *Official Bulletin* 63, series A, no. 2.

———. 1985b. *Equal Opportunities and Equal Treatment for Men and Women in Employment*. 71st Session, Report no. VII. Geneva: ILO.

———. 1987. "Women Workers: Protection or Equality." *Conditions of Employment*. Geneva: ILO.

Industrial Relations Service. 1976. *Health and Safety Information Bulletin*. No. 9 (September).

International Labour Review. 1941. "The Employment of Women in Germany under the National-Socialist Regime." 44:6, pp. 617–59.

———. 1942. "The Employment of Women in Germany." 45:3 (March).

International Woodworker. 1979 (?). "If the Swedes Can Do It. . . ." Supplement, 44:10.

ITF News. 1988. "Women's Conference." P. 5.

Jacoby, Robin Miller. 1977. "The British and American Women's Trade Union Leagues, 1890–1925." Ph.D. diss., Harvard University.

Jangenas, Bo. 1985. *The Swedish Approach to Labour Market Policy*. Stockholm: Swedish Institute.

Kahne, Hilda. 1985. *Reconceiving Part-time Work: New Perspectives for Older Workers and Women*. Totowa, N.J.: Rowman and Allanheld.

Kamerman, Sheila B. 1980. "Child Care and Family Benefits: Policies of Six Industrialized Countries." *Monthly Labor Review* 103:11, pp. 23–28.

———. 1983. "Child Care Services: A National Picture." *Monthly Labor Review* 106:12, pp. 35–39.

———, and Alfred J. Kahn, eds. 1978. *Family Policy: Governments and Families in Fourteen Countries*. New York: Columbia University Press.

Kassalow, Everett. 1963. *National Labor Movements in the Postwar World*. Evanston, Ill.: Northwestern University Press.

Kelman, Steven. 1977. "Occupational Safety and Health in Sweden: The Politics of Cooperation." *Working Life in Sweden*, no. 2 (December), pp. 1–8.

Kessler-Harris, Alice. 1981. *Women Have Always Worked*. Old Westbury, N.Y.: Feminist Press.

———. 1982. *Out to Work: A History of Wage-Earning Women in the United States*. New York: Oxford University Press.

Kornbluh, Joyce, and Mary Fredrickson. 1984. *Sisterhood and Solidarity: Workers Education for Women, 1914–1984*. Philadelphia: Temple University Press.

Koziara, Karen S., Michael H. Moscow, and Lucretia Dewey Tanner, eds. 1987. *Working Women: Past, Present, and Future*. Washington, D.C.: BNA.

Kurz-Scherf, Ingrid. 1984. "Tarifvertraegliche Bestimmungen zur Teilzeitarbeit in ausgewaehlten Tarifbereichen." *WSI Mitteilungen* 34:3, pp. 138–53.

——. 1986. "Von der Emanzipation des Bruennenmaedchens in Heilbaedern: Frauendiskriminierung, Frauenfoerderung durch Tarifvertrag und Tarifpolitik." *WSI Mitteilungen* 39:8, pp. 537–48.

Labour Research. 1988a. "Stress at the Workplace." March, pp. 18–20.

——. 1988b. "Working for Equality within the Unions." May, p. 9.

Landau, Eva C. 1985. *The Rights of Working Women in the European Community*. Brussels: Commission of the European Communities, European Perspective Series.

Lawrence, Elizabeth. 1989. "Shop Stewards in Local Government, Gender, and Union Activities." Paper presented at the Pennsylvania State University conference "Women and Unions." March.

Lehman, Phyllis. 1975. "Women Workers: Are They Special?" *Job Safety and Health* 3:4 (April), pp. 5–13.

Lewenhak, Sheila. 1977. *Women and Trade Unions: An Outline History of Women in the British Trade Union Movement*. New York: St. Martin's.

Lewis, Suzan, and Cary L. Cooper. 1989. *Career Couples: Contemporary Lifestyles and How to Manage Them*. London: Unwin Paperbacks.

Lipset, Seymour, Martin Trow, and James Coleman. 1956. *Trade Union Democracy*. Glencoe, Ill.: Free Press.

Lloyd, Cynthia, ed. 1975. *Sex Discrimination and the Division of Labor*. New York: Columbia University Press.

LO. 1970. *The Trade Unions and Family Policy*. Stockholm: LO.

——. 1976a. *Education—Preparing for Work and Democracy: Report to the 1976 Congress of the Swedish Trade Union Federation, Summary*. Stockholm: LO.

——. 1976b. *The Trade Union Movement and Family Policy*. Stockholm: LO.

——. 1979. *Trade Union Education in Sweden*. Stockholm: Prisma.

——. 1980. *This Is How We Work for Equality between Men and Women in Working Life and in Trade Unions*. Stockholm: LO.

——. 1985. *LO's Role in the Framing and Implementation of School and Educational Policy Reforms in Sweden*. Stockholm: Prisma.

——. 1986. *Trade Unions and Occupational Health Services*. Stockholm: LO.

Lopata, Helene Z. 1971. *Occupation Housewife*. New York: Oxford University Press.

Lorwin, Val R. 1975. "The Black and the Red: Christian and Socialist Labor Organization in Western Europe." Paper presented at 14th International Congress of Historical Sciences, San Francisco. Pp. 22–29.

Losseff-Tillmans, Gisela. 1978. *Frauenemanzipation und die Gewerkschaften, 1800–1975*. Wuppertal: Hammer.

MacLeod, Don. 1984. "Why Sweden Has Better Working Conditions Than the U.S." *Working Life in Sweden*, no. 28 (April), pp. 1–10.

Mansbridge, Albert. 1920. *An Adventure in Working-Class Education*. New York: Longmans Green.

Martinez, Sue, and Alan Ranio. 1980. "Valley of the Shadow of Death." *In These Times* 8:41.

Matthews, Tony. 1978. *Trade Union Studies: A Partnership in Adult Education between the BBC, the TUC, and the WEA.* London: BBC.

Meidner, Rudolf, and Berndt Öhman. 1972. *Fifteen Years of Wage Policy.* Stockholm: LO.

Milkman, Ruth, ed. 1985. *Women, Work, and Protest: A Century of U.S. Women's Labor History.* Boston: Routledge and Kegan Paul.

Ministry of Labor, Sweden. 1977. *The Working Environment in Sweden: New Legislation on the Working Environment; The Organisation and Administration of Occupational Health and Safety.* Stockholm: Ministry of Labor.

Moberly, Robert B. 1987. "Temporary Part-time and Other Atypical Employment Relations in the U.S." *Labor Law Journal* 318:11, pp. 689–96.

Moccio, Francine. 1989. "Experiencing Gender Integration in the Building Trades." Paper presented at the Pennsylvania State University Department of Labor Studies Conference "Women and Unions," March.

Muench, Joachim. 1986. *Vocational Training in the Federal Republic of Germany.* Berlin: CEDEFOP.

Myrdal, Alva. 1971. *Towards Equality: A Report to the Swedish Social-Democratic Party.* Stockholm: Prisma.

NALGO. 1975. *Equal Rights Working Party Report.* London: NALGO.

Nardone, Thomas J. 1986. "Part-time Workers: Who Are They?" *Monthly Labor Review* 109:2, pp. 13–17.

Nash, Al. 1981. *Ruskin College: A Challenge to Adult Education.* Ithaca: Industrial and Labor Relations Press, Cornell University.

National Advisory Committee on Emancipation. 1977. *Report.* The Hague.

Needleman, Ruth, and Lucretia Dewey Tanner. 1986. "Women and Unions: Current Issues," *Labor Studies Journal* 10 (Winter 1986).

Negt, Oscar, Christine Morgenroth, and Edzard Niemeyer. 1990. "Organizationsphantasie, Vernetzung, Projekte—neue Elemente der Einheitsgewerkschaft." *Gewerkschaftliche Monatshefte,* July, pp. 446–55.

Nelson, Anne. 1989. "Women as National Union Leaders." Paper presented at the Pennsylvania State University Department of Labor Studies Conference "Women and Unions." March.

———, and Barbara Wertheimer. 1975. *Trade Union Women: A Study of Their Participation in New York City Locals.* New York: Praeger.

Newcom, Charles W. 1981. "Employee Health and Safety Rights under the LMRA and Federal Safety Laws." *Labor Law Journal* 32:7, pp. 395–423.

Nielsen, Georgia. 1982. *From Skygirl to Flight Attendant.* Ithaca: Industrial and Labor Relations Press, Cornell University.

Nielsen, Ruth. 1983. *Equality Legislation in a Comparative Perspective: Toward State Feminism.* Copenhagen: Women's Research Center in Social Science.

9 to 5, National Association of Working Women. 1985. *Hidden Victims: Clerical Workers, Automation, and the Changing Economy.* Cleveland: 9 to 5.

Oakley, Anne. 1976. *Women's Work: The Housewife, Past and Present*. New York: Vintage Books, Random House.

OCAW. 1979(?). *Health and Safety in the Oil and Chemical Industry*. Denver: OCAW.

OECD. 1979. "High Level Conference on the Employment of Women." *Women in the Labour Market: Analytical Report, Statistical Annex*. Items 5 and 6. Paris: OECD.

——. 1986. *Girls and Women in Education: A Cross-national Study of Sex Inequalities in Upbringing and in Schools and Colleges*. Paris: OECD.

OeGB Nachrichtendienst. 1981. "Part-time Employment and Women's Work." No. 2074.

Oels, Monika, and Suzanne Seeland, eds. 1985. *Equality of Training Opportunity and Vocational Training Five Years On . . . Vocational Training Measures for Women in the European Community*. Berlin: CEDEFOP.

Oesterreichische Studiengruppe Automation und industrielle Arbeit. 1978. *Differenzierende Bestimmungen fuer Maenner- und Frauenarbeit in den oesterreichischen Kollektivvertraegen*. Vienna: GPA.

OME. 1972. *Equal Pay: First Report on the Implementation of the Equal Pay Act of 1970*. London: HMSO.

Orne, Eliza, Clara E. Collett, May E. Abram, and Margaret H. Irwin (Lady Commissioners, Great Britain Royal Commission on Labour). 1893. *The Employment of Women: Reports on the Conditions of Work in Various Industries in England, Wales, Scotland, and Ireland*. London: HMSO.

Page, Joseph A., and Mary-win O'Brien. 1973. *Bitter Wages*. New York: Grossman.

Palm, Gøran. 1977. *Flight from Work*. Cambridge: Cambridge University Press.

Pfarr, Heide M., and Klaus Bertelsmann. 1985. *Gleichbehandlungsgesetz: zum Verbot der unmittelbaren und der mittelbaren Diskriminierung von Frauen im Erwerbsleben*. Wiesbaden: Hessendienst der Staatskanzlei in Zusammenarbeit mit der Zentralstelle fuer Frauenfragen beim hessischen Ministerpraesidenten. Kassel: Herkules Druck.

Piva, Paolo, and Chiara Ingrao. 1984. "Women's Subjectivity to Union Power and the Problem of Work." *Feminist Review*, no. 16 (April), pp. 50–54.

Qvist, Gunnar. 1974. *Statistik och Politik: Landesorganisationen och Kvinnorna pa Arbetsmarknaden*. Stockholm: Prisma.

Ratner, Ronnie S. [Ronnie J. Steinberg], ed. 1980. *Equal Employment Policy for Women: Strategies for Implementation in the United States, Canada, and Western Europe*. Philadelphia: Temple University Press.

Rehn, Gøsta. 1974. *Lifelong Allocation of Time*. Paris: OECD, Directorate for Social Affairs, Manpower, and Education, Social Affairs and Industrial Relations Division. Processed.

Reimer, Rita Ann. 1986. "Work and Family Life in Sweden." *Social Change in Sweden*, no. 34 (April).

Remick, Helen. 1979. *Strategies for Creating Sound, Bias-free Job Evaluation and the EEOC: The Emerging Issue.* New York: New York Industrial Relations Counsellors.

——, ed. 1984. *Comparable Worth and Wage Determination: Technical Possibilities and Political Realities.* Philadelphia: Temple University Press.

Report for International Women's Year. 1975. Stockholm: Swedish Institute.

Reskin, Barbara, ed. 1984. *Sex Segregation in the Workplace: Trends, Explanations, Remedies.* Washington, D.C.: National Research Council, National Academy Press.

Richbell, Suzanne. 1976. "De Facto Discrimination and How to Kick the Habit." *Personnel Management* (London) 8:11 (November), pp. 30–33.

Rights of Women in Europe. 1983. *Women's Rights and the EEC: A Guide for Women in the United Kingdom.* London: Rights of Women in Europe.

Robinson, Olive. 1979. "Part-time Employment in the European Community." *International Labour Review* 118:3, pp. 299–314.

Rohmert, Walter, and Josef Rutenfranz. 1975. *Arbeitswissenschaftliche Beurteilung und Beanspruchung an unterschiedlichen industriellen Arbeitsplaetzen.* Bonn: Bundesminister fuer Arbeit und Sozialordnung.

Rudolf, Hedwig. 1984. "Modern Working Times: Recent Developments in Germany—More Stress and Less Rewards for Women." *Equal Opportunities International,* no. 2.

Ruggie, Mary. 1984. *The State and Working Women: A Comparative Study of Britain and Sweden.* Princeton: Princeton University Press.

Ruhnke, Irmgard. 1973. "Zur Ideologie gewerkschaftlicher Frauenarbeit." Diplomarbeit. Berlin: Freie Universitaet.

Rutenfranz, Josef, and Walter Rohmert. 1977. *The Ergonomic Assessment of Burden and Stress in Various Industrial Workplaces.* Annex 1 to Printed Matter, 8.547. Bonn: Bundestag.

Sabel, Charles. 1979. "Rationalization and Unemployment in Germany: Their Impact on a Fragile Truce." IRRA *Proceedings,* 32d annual meeting, pp. 316–24.

SAF-LO-PTK. 1977. *Working Environment Agreement.* Stockholm: Joint Industrial Safety Council.

Sandberg, Elisabet. 1975. *Equality Is the Goal: A Swedish Report for International Women's Year.* Stockholm: Swedish Institute.

Schmidt, Folke, ed. 1978. *Discrimination in Employment.* Stockholm: Almqvist Wiksell.

Schnorr, Theresa M., et al. 1991. *Video Display Terminals and the Risk of Spontaneous Abortion.* NIOSH, Publications on Video Display Terminals. Cincinnati: U.S. Department of Health and Human Services, Public Health Service. pp. 727–33.

Scott, Hilda. 1982. *Sweden's "Right to Be Human": Sex Role Equality—the Goal and the Reality.* Armonk, N.Y.: M. E. Sharpe.

SEIU. 1987. *Access to Health Care: A System in Deep Trouble.* Washington, D.C.: SEIU.

Shields, Mark. 1981. "Labor Fights Back." *Washington Post National Weekly*, September 18.

Sicherman, Barbara. 1984. *Alice Hamilton's Life in Letters*. Cambridge: Harvard University Press.

Simon, Carl, and Ann White. 1982. *Beating the System: The Underground Economy*. Boston: Auburn House.

SLB. 1990. "Protection of Workers: Minimum Standards." No. 3, p. 308.

———. 1990. "VDUs in the 1990s: Mounting Concern." No. 4, pp. 378–79.

Smith, Robert J., and Ella Lury Wiskell. 1982. *The Women of Suye Mura*. Chicago: University of Chicago Press.

Smolkin, Shelley. 1979. "When a Homemaker Loses Her Job." *Working Woman*, July, p. 18.

Soldon, Norbert C. 1978. *Women in British Trade Unions, 1874–1976*. Totowa, N.J.: Rowan and Littlefield.

———, ed. 1985. *The World of Women's Trade Unionism: Comparative Historical Essays*. Westport, Conn.: Greenwood Press.

Stahn-Willig, Brigitte, and Gerhard Baecker. 1984. "35 Stunden sind immer noch zu viel: Arbeitszeitprobleme in Lebenszusammenhang von Frauen." *WSI Mitteilungen*. 37:1 (January), pp. 14–23.

Steinberg, Ronnie J., 1982. *Wages and Hours: Labor and Reform in Twentieth-Century America*. New Brunswick, N.J.: Rutgers University Press.

———. 1990. "The Social Construction of Skill: Gender, Power, and Comparable Worth." Special issue, "Skill," *Work and Occupations* 17:4 (November), pp. 449–82.

Stellman, Jeanne. 1977. *Women's Work, Women's Health*. New York: Pantheon.

———, and Susan P. Daun. 1973. *Work Is Dangerous to Your Health: A Handbook of Health Hazards in the Workplace and What You Do about Them*. New York: Vintage Books.

Stone, Katherine. 1973. *Handbook for Oil, Chemical, and Atomic Workers Women*. Denver: OCAW.

Stubianek, Helga. 1979. "Die Entwicklung der Kollektivverhandlungen der Angestellten in Oesterreich: ihre Bedeutungen fuer die Frauen." International Institute for Labour Studies seminars. Paper presented at the "Women and Industrial Relations" symposium, Vienna, September 12–15.

Szalai, Alexander, ed. 1972. *Use of Time: A Multinational Study*. Paris: Mouton.

TASS. 1985(?). *Equal Rights*. London: TASS.

TCO. 1978. *TCO's View of Family Policy and Equal Opportunities*. Stockholm: TCO.

Toelle, Helga. 1980. "Do We Need an Anti-Discrimination Law?" Friedrich Naumann Foundation Conference, Bonn, August.

Tomandl, Theodor, and Karl Fuerboeck. 1987. *Social Partnership: The Austrian System of Industrial Relations and Social Insurance*. Ithaca: Industrial and Labor Relations Press, Cornell University.

Treiman, Donald J. 1979. *Job Evaluation, an Analysis Review: Interim Report to the EEOC.* Washington, D.C.: National Academy of Science.

———, and Heidi I. Hartmann. 1981. *Women, Work, and Wages: Equal Pay for Jobs of Equal Value.* Washington, D.C.: National Academy of Science.

TUC. 1969. *Trades Union Congress Report.* London: TUC.

———. 1978. *Trades Union Congress Report.* London: TUC.

———, Department of Employment. 1980. *Youth Employment and Vocational Training: The Material and Social Standing of Young People during Transition from School to Work in the United Kingdom—United Kingdom Contribution to a Comparative Study in the Member States of the European Communities.* Berlin: CEDEFOP.

———, *Women Workers' Bulletin.* 1984. No. 4.

U.S. Commission on Civil Rights. 1985. *Comparable Worth: An Analysis and Recommendations—A Report.* Washington, D.C.: GPO.

U.S. Department of Labor, Women's Bureau. 1942a. *Your Questions as to Women in War Industries.* Bulletin 194. Washington, D.C.: GPO.

———. 1942b. *Equal Pay for Women in War Industries.* Bulletin 196. Washington, D.C.: GPO.

van Hemeldonck, Marijke. 1978. *Europese Beweging.* April.

Veblen, Thorstein. 1899. *The Theory of the Leisure Class: An Economic Institution.* New York: Macmillan.

Viklund, Birger. 1977. "Education for Industrial Democracy." *Current Sweden,* no. 152 (March), p. 4.

———. 1978. "Working Hours in Sweden." *Working Life in Sweden,* no. 7 (September).

Von Moltke, Konrad, and Norbert Schneevoight. 1977. *Educational Leaves for Employees.* San Francisco: Jossey-Bass.

War Cabinet Committee (The Atkin Committee). 1919. *Women in Industry.* London: HMSO.

Warne, Colston, ed. 1945. *Yearbook of American Labor: War Labor Policies,* vol. 1. New York: Philosophical Library.

———, ed. 1949. *Labor in Postwar America: Yearbook of American Labor.* Brooklyn: Remsen Press.

Wassen-van Schaveren, Paula. 1977. *Planning the Emancipation of Women.* The Hague: Dutch National Advisory Committee on Emancipation.

Webb, Beatrice. 1919. "Minority Report." *War Cabinet Committee Report,* pp. 278–84. London: HMSO.

Webb, Sidney. 1902. *Problems of Modern Industry.* London: Longmans Green.

Weitzel, Renate. 1983. *Berufliche Bildung nach dem Arbeitsfoerderungsgesetz: Rechtliche und institutionelle Bedingungen der Teilnahme von Frauen im Vergleich zu Maennern.* Berlin: Wissenschaftszentrum.

Weitzman, Lenore J. 1985. *The Divorce Revolution: The Unexpected Social and Economic Consequences for Women and Children in America.* New York: Free Press.

Wertheimer, Barbara M. 1975. *Focus on Women Unionists.* New York: School of Industrial and Labor Relations (Metropolitan District), Cornell University.

——. 1977. *We Were There: The Story of Working Women in America.* New York: Pantheon.

——, ed. 1981. *Labor Education for Women Workers: An International Comparison.* Philadelphia: Temple University Press.

Wilensky, Harold. 1968. "Women's Work: Economic Growth, Ideology, Structure." *Industrial Relations* 7:3, pp. 235–48.

Willborn, Steven. 1989. *A Secretary and a Cook: Challenging Women's Wages in the Courts of the United States and Great Britain.* Ithaca: Industrial and Labor Relations Press, Cornell University.

Willis, Paul. 1981. *Learning to Labor: How Working-class Kids Get Working-class Jobs.* New York: Columbia University Press.

Willms, Angelika. 1983. *Auf dem Weg zur berufliche Gleichstellung der Maennern und Frauen: Entwicklungspezifischen Segregation des Arbeitsmarktes und ihre Determinanten, 1925–1980.* Arbeitspapier no. 36, Universitaet Mannheim.

Windmuller, John P., ed. 1987. *Collective Bargaining in Industrialized Market Economies: A Reappraisal.* Geneva: ILO.

Winkler, Dörte. 1977. *Frauen im Dritten Reich.* Hamburg: Hoffman and Campe.

Wistrand, Birgitta. 1982. *Swedish Women on the Move.* Stockholm: Swedish Institute.

Witt, Matt. 1987. "Labor Tries a New Tactic." *Washington Post National Weekly,* May 28, p. 32.

WLB. 1944. *Report, Wage and Salary Stabilization,* vol 11. Washington, D.C.: BNA.

Wolf, Irene, and Walter Wolf. 1991. *How Much Less: Earning Disparities between Women and Men in Austria.* Vienna: Ministry of Social Affairs.

Working Life in Sweden. 1985. "Swedish Collective Bargaining in Transition." No. 30 (November), pp. 1–8.

Yohalem, Alice. 1980. *Women Returning to Work.* Montclair, N.J.: Allenheld Osmun.

Youngblood, Kneeland. 1978. "Safety Delegates and the Working Environment Issues." *Current Sweden,* no. 204 (November), pp. 1–10.

Zeytinoglu, Isik U. 1986. "Part-time Workers: Unionization and Collective Bargaining in Canada." *IRRA Proceedings,* 39th annual meeting, New Orleans, December 28–30.

Index

abortion: and IGM, 96; and ILO, 27; local union support for, 67; and NALGO Report, 64; and progressive agenda, 21
Academy of Labor, 109
Acker, Joan, 42
ACTWU. *See* Amalgamated Clothing and Textile Workers Union
AFA. *See* Airline Flight Attendants
Affiliated Schools for Workers. *See* American Labor Educatioin Service
affirmative action: and EEOA, 106; Executive Order (U.S.), 28; in German unions, 57–58, 102; in labor market, 22; in local union (U.S.), 43; in training programs, 190; in union education, 113–14; for union employees, 104; in wage equity, 190
AFL-CIO. *See* American Federation of Labor–Congress of Industrial Organizations
AFSCME. *See* American Federation of State, County, and Municipal Employees
Airline Flight Attendants, 100, 104
alternative schedules, ANA, 104. *See also* hours; part-time work
Amalgamated Clothing and Textile Workers Union (U.S.), 248–49
Amalgamated Union of Engineering Workers (U.K.), 69, 156
American Cyanamid Corporation, 218–28, 249
American Federation of Labor–Congress of Industrial Organizations, 85
American Federation of State, County, and Municipal Employees, 74
American Labor Education Service, 119–20
American Nurses Association, 65, 85, 104
American Telephone and Telegraph Company, 74
AMS. *See* Arbetsmarknadstyrelsen
ANA. *See* American Nurses Association
anti-unionism: and Conservative government (U.K.), 82; as U.S. phenomenon, 14

APEX. *See* Association of Professional, Executive, Clerical, and Computer Staffs
apprenticeship, 169, 172, 178
Arbetsmarknadstyrelsen (Swedish Labor Market Board): accepts child-centered society, 188; aims for full employment, 187; local structure of, 187; and pay equity, 150; supports continuing education and retraining, 187–88; and vocational training for women, 173
arbitration: awards, 20; private (U.S.), 80; voluntary dispute resolution in health and safety cases, 253
Ashford, Nicholas A., 217, 221, 253
Association of Professional, Executive, Clerical, and Computer Staffs (U.K.): action on VDTs, 240; education on equality, 130–31; encourages VOP, 186; and pay equity, 155
Association of Scientific, Technical, and Management Staffs (U.K.), 251
ASTMS. *See* Association of Scientific, Technical, and Management Staffs
Astrand, Irma, 225
AT&T. *See* American Telephone and Telegraph Company
AUEW. *See* Amalgamated Union of Engineering Workers
Austria: action on VDTs, 240; barriers for working women, 180; centralized bargaining, 104; collective bargaining, 83–84; decentralized education, 116; educational leave, 121–22; equal opportunity, 148–49; Equal Treatment Commission, 161; extension of agreements, 81; GPA programs, 130, 149, 180, 240–43; health and safety, 243; hot lines, 60, 114; ILO, 27; individual pay equity complaints, 154; part-time work, 195, 205; postwar union reorganization, 10–12; pregnancy protection, 148; status of women, 30; union demands, 92; vocational training, 179–81; wage regulation, 93; wages in wartime, 180; women's conference, 64; women's

Austria (cont.)
courses, 127; women's division, 50, 68–69; works councils, 86–87

Baker, Helen, 143
Barclay's Bank, 197
Barkin, Solomon, 84
Belous, Richard S., 195
Benya, Anton, 79
Bingham, Eula, 218
blue-collar workers: 2, 12. See also class
Bork, Robert, Justice, 219
breadwinner, 19, 36; and collective bargaining, 136
Brody, Doris Cohen, 120
Burgmuller, Alfred, 180–81

CAC (U.K.). See Central Arbitration Commission
Caldart, Charles C., 217, 253
Campbell, Bea, 17, 21
career choice, 169; "career ladders," 177; parental decisions, 178
Carlsson, Mai-Britt, 206
CEDEFOP, 176; and job segregation, 177; and women's training, 261–62. See also vocational training
Central Arbitration Commission (U.K.), 152
centralization: in Austrian bargaining, 83; benefit to women, 85–86, 104, 105; in Swedish bargaining, 105; of union power, 46–47
Chamber of Labor (Austria), 84, 148; and joint committee on occupational diseases, 247; and wages, 162
Charlton, Val, 17, 21
chemical workers, 129–30. See also Oil, Chemical, and Atomic Workers
child allowances: Germany, 24, 31; Nordic countries, 33
child care: central to labor-management policy, 34; during education programs, 113–15; five support goals, 33; in Hessen, 67; laissez-faire policy, 34; necessary to women's full-time work, 208; in Nordic countries, 33; not labor market issue, 255; by older women, 116–17; state responsibility for, 74, 102–4; and Swedish unions, 70; during World War II, 24
child labor, 20, 136, 137
child welfare: basic to labor market policy (Sweden), 24, 105; and equality goal, 41; linked to national health insurance, 74

Christl, Josef, 149
Clark, I.G., 191
class: and Communist Manifesto, 22; in education, 108–9; middle-class values, 20; in vocational training, 170
closed shop, 82
Clot, Isabelle Savoy, 191
CLUW. See Coalition of Labor Union Women
Coalition of Labor Union Women (U.S.), 50–51, 65, 76; and health and safety, 220; and women's education, 127
coalitions: German Council of Women, 40, 63, 131, 264; U.K. experience, 264. See also Women's Trade Union League
Cockburn, Cynthia, 256
co-determination: Austria, 92, 181; Germany, 92, 181; and health and safety, 262; origin, 25
collective bargaining: airlines (U.S.), 100; in U.K., 81–82, 108–9; comparison of U.K. and Sweden, 34, 164; "custom and practice," 82; discrimination in collective agreements, 94–96; on equal pay, 14, 162; family equality, 260; local negotiations within framework, 233; major union function, 46, 79–106; monitoring results of, 38; multiunion (U.K.), 85; "peak bargaining," 84, 149; procedures and results, 79–82; small establishments, 236. See also part-time work; pay equity
—women in bargaining: on bargaining committees, 7, 25–26, 79–106; education for, 107, 266; effect of extension of agreements, 81; on women's issues, 85, 102–3
Communications Workers of America; 74, 241
Community High Court of Justice, 38, 39, 90; Belgium, 147; citations of Germany, 151; decisions on equal pay, 146; EOC, 147–53
conciliation, 88, 248
conservatives: effect on equal pay (Britain), 153; and trade unions (Austria), 160; in U.K. government, 82; in U.S. government, 103–4; and working women, 21, 40
Cook, Alice H., 195
Corcoran, Jennifer, 90
courts: class action, 167; on pay equity (U.S.), 163–67; on protective legislation, 23–24. See also labor courts
Cousins, Frank, 135, 168

CWA. *See* Communications Workers of America

DAG. *See* Deutsche Angestellten Gewerkschaft decentralization: effect on barriers to women in unions, 116; in trade union education, 116
Deutsche Angestellten Gewerkschaft (German White-Collar Workers Union), 67, 83; and child care, 115; and vocational training, 183
Deutscher Frauenrat (German Council of Women), 65, 131. *See also* coalitions
Deutscher Gewerkschaftsbund (German Federation of Labor), 96; pay equity study, 150–51, 158–59; 244–45; structure, 67, 83, 96; vocational training, 183; women's division, 66; works council elections, 100–101. *See also* Ro-Ru study
DGB. *See* Deutscher Gewerkschaftsbund
discrimination: in Austria, 97–98, 148, 161; barriers producing, 49; in contracts, 149; at end of war (U.S.), 144; by fellow workers and shop stewards, 90; in German unions, 94; and grapevines, 60; and hierarchy, 35; and law (Sweden), 158; monitoring of, 52; against part-timers, 213; seniority results in, 95; sex, 95; training in antidiscrimination, 261–62; in unions, 90, 97; in vocational training, 189–90; and women's equality centers, 265; in women's wages, 135–61
Displaced Homemakers, 175–76, 256
divorce, 258, 259
"domestic code": concept, 19–20; effect on social policy, 22–23, 74, 257
domestic work, 177
double burden: constraints on women's activities, 56, 59; examples, 21, 23; extra month of work, 258; family responsibilities, 189; health hazards in double day, 92, 223, 228; part-time work a response to, 207; personal, not labor market issue, 255; support systems to relieve, 35; and unions, 267
dual-earner family, in Sweden, 31
dual labor market, 35

early retirement, 95
EAT. *See* Employment Appeals Tribunal
educational system: academic, 169; adult, continuing education, 176; barriers to equality, 112–13; "bridge schools"

(Germany), 176; coeducation, 170; European compared to U.S., 262; gender bias in, 176; gender-labeled careers, 170; place for vocational education, 169; technical colleges (U.K.), 176; Sweden's vocational education, 188
EEC or EC. *See* European Economic Community
EEOC. *See* Equal Employment Opportunity Commission
Eigstrand, Kaj, 217
emancipation, 7–8
employers: attitudes of European compared to U.S., 93; burden of proof in litigation, 247; and carcinogens at workplace (Europe), 251; German association rejects wage study, 151; health and safety agreements (Sweden), 231–38; motivations, 95; organization of, in U.K., 85, 152; organization of, in Sweden, 84, 149; responsible for unequal pay, 161; sponsors of child care (U.S.), 102; subsidies for hiring unemployed (Sweden), 187
employment, 5–6, 7; Employment Protection Act (U.K.) and part-timers, 212; Employment Service (Austria), 180–81; part-time work, 191–207; Swedish policy and practice, 187–88
Employment Appeals Tribunal (U.K.), 90, 247
EOC. *See* Equal Opportunities Commission
Equal Employment Opportunity Commission (U.S.), 147–48, 164
equality:
—in family, 14, 40–41, 105; definition of, 32; and division of labor, 27; in Germany, 31; and ILO, 27; union support of joint responsibility for, 260
—gender, 9, 28, 105, 135, 137, 178; bias in schools, 189; and GPA (Austria), 97; international norm, 37; in Sweden, 37–38; and TUC (U.K.), 97; in U.S., 74
—labor market: and affirmative action, 22; attention to, 32–33; as dependent on equality in family, 261; and dual labor market, 35–37; EC program, 39; and education, 29; equal opportunities in, 3; and fatigue, 209; in Germany and Austria, 36; goals of, 255; and laws, 20; outworn concepts, 40, 113; and sex harassment, 255; in Sweden, 36, 182; and training programs, 189; in U.S., 36–37, 188;

equality (*cont.*)
war's end brings regression, 144, 162, 165
—and legal redress: burden of proof (EEC), 39; in Europe, 134; individual, 40; in U.S., 155
—ombudsman: Austria, 161; Sweden, 40
—within trade unions, 37, 68–69, 71–72, 130, 155–60, 181; agreements written in masculine (Germany), 94; goals and reality, 7–9; as monitor of equality law, 266; officers more concerned than rank-and-file, 85; policy, 86; women's activity, 14; and women's divisions, 96, 265; women's place in, 3–4; women's support of, 82
—in workplace: 6, 79; in EC, 38; education of men on, 129–30; equal opportunity coverage, 3; Sweden, 162; union monitoring of, 266
Equal Opportunities Commission (U.K.), 152–54
equal opportunity: coverage, 3; Swedish law, 162; worldwide demand for, 177–78
equal pay for equal work, 178; and administration of EEOC (U.S.), 147; advocates of, 137–38; constitutional requirements (Germany), 138; in early unions, 138; throughout EC, 31, 161; history of, 4, 135; legislation for (U.S.), 145, 147; piece rates, 137; standard rate, 135, 137, 138; studies, 138–39, 140, 143; union interest in, 144; during world wars, 139–44
equal pay for work of equal value, 103, 145–61; and collective bargaining, 103; definition of equal value, 145; EC policy on, 38, 146–47; and FIET, 96; and Ford workers, 97–98; and ILO, 145–46; implementation of, 146; slow growth of, 48; TASS, education on, 127; U.S. Women's Bureau model law, 147
equal pension rights, 161; in EC, 31
equal treatment: Commission (Austria) administers Equal Opportunity Act, 148, 160, 161, 162; German development, 182; job segregation and, 177–78; policy goal, 20
ETUC, ETUI. *See* European Trade Union Confederation and European Trade Union Institute
European Economic Community: CEDE-FOP, 176–77; commissioners, ix; directives, 242, 251; and equal pay, 146–47;

and health and safety, 251; and law in U.K., 39; monitoring equality, 38; and part-time work, 216; social fund, 146–47; Treaty of Rome, 146; Women's Action Programmes, 38–39
European Trade Union Confederation and European Trade Union Institute, 96, 99
Executive Order 11246 (U.S.), 28

factory inspection, in Hessen, 67
family: and church doctrine, 22; definition of, 10, 21; law, 14, 17–18, 22, 33, 105; men in, 21, 257, 259; unions and, 260; wage, 19–20, 145
—and work, 19, 92; consequence, women in low-status jobs, 76; governments' policies, 17–41; inequalities in labor market, 61; NALGO Report, 64; need women's voices and participation, 74; two elements give rise to conflict, 5–7, 255; unequal sharing in family, 51, 66; women's attempts to resolve conflict, 215, 259; women's strategies, 266–67
family policy, 24, 28; Austria, 30; "domestic code" and women, 25, 66; Germany, 30, 182; as labor market regulation, 25; as maternity protection, 25; as natalism, 24, 25; U.S., 32
Federation Internationale d'Employés Technicale (International Federation of Commercial, Clerical, and Technical Employees), 96, 240
feminization of poverty, 255, 259
FIET. *See* Federation Internationale d'Employés Technicale
Fisher, Marguerite, 144
foreign workers, 28, 96, 124
Fraser, Douglas, 42
Frauen und Arbeit, 89, 101
Fredrickson, Mary, 120
Freeman, Richard B., 43

Galbraith, John K., 191
G&MWU. *See* General and Municipal Workers Union
Gaudart, Dorothea, 180
General and Municipal Workers Union (U.K.), 60, 61, 100; and pay equity, 155, 157
Germany:
—education system, 169–70; "bridge schools," 176; career counseling, 171; continuing education, 176; educational leave, 121–23; union education, 59, 106–31; vocational educa-

tion in, 182–84; women's courses,
127–31
—family in, 29–31
—labor market: apprentice system, 172,
187; Basic Law, 150; cable spinners,
91; collective bargaining, 83–84; Employment Promotion Act, 182; extension of agreements, 83–84; ruling on
part-time unemployed, 212
—international agencies, influence of, 27
—political parties, 47
—trade unions: equality within, 150; and
health and safety law, 251; local cartels, 46; membership, 56; opposition
to part-timers, 205; policy, 25; program, 67, 92; women leaders, 61;
women's divisions, 50, 64, 246
—women's wages: in wartime, 141–42;
and labor courts, 154; and Ro-Ru
study, 150–51, 244–45
Gewerkschaft der Privat Angestellten
(Trade Union of Private Sector White
Collar Workers, Austria): collective
agreements, 97; and discrimination,
149; education and research, 130; publications, 138; study of effect of stress
on women, 243; study of "large space"
work environment, 243; and VDT
study and program, 240–41; women's
status in, 180
Gewerkschaft Textil und Bekleidung
(Trade Union of Textile and Clothing
Workers,), Germany 245–46
Gewerkschaft Textil, Bekleidung, und
Lederarbeiter (Trade Union of Textile,
Clothing, and Leather Workers, Austria), 116, 128
Goldman, Emma, 50
GPA. See Gewerkschaft der Privat Angestellten
Great Britain, 10–11, 24, 29, 31, 60, 73;
affirmative action, 18; bargaining structure, 81–82, 99; centralization of union
structures in, 46; Congenital Disabilities
Act, 249; educational leave, 141–42;
employer responsibility for damage to
unborn child, 249; EOC, 147; grievance
handling, 97; health and safety stewards, 238–39; influence of international
agencies, 27; labor courts, 90; national
union discipline, 91; on-the-job training, 173; part-time work, 205, 212; pay
equity, 151–55; phased retirement,
213; political parties, 48, 153; union
education, 100, 106–10; vocational
training system, 184; wages in wartime,

140, 142–43; women leaders, 61;
women's' divisions, 50, 64–68
grievance handling: cable spinners, 91;
under collective agreements, 80; on discrimination, 267; duty of fair representation (U.S.), 93–94; European compared to U.S. system, 90–91; forced
quits, 97; health and safety, 246;
honey-makers, 91; labor courts, 86–88;
on labor grades, 91; part-timers' eligibility, 215; works councils, 88
Grospiron, A. F., 1
GTB. See Gewerkschaft Textil und Bekleidung
GTBL. See Gewerkschaft Textil, Bekleidung, und Lederarbeiter

Hamilton, Alice, 231
Hammond, M. B., 139
Handel, Banken, und Versicherung (Commercial, Banking, and Insurance Union,
Germany), 202, 241
Handels (Sweden), 115, 211
Harlan, Sharon, 188
HBV. See Handel, Banken, und Versicherung
health and safety, 5, 27, 217–54; cancer
screening (U.K.), 248–49; chemical
workers' exposures, 217; electromagnetic exposures, 230; employers' preventive measures, 247–48; factory inspectors, 246; German chemical
workers' union education, 129–30;
hearing damage, 217–21; industrial
health experts, 229; joint safety committees, 230; lung damage, 217; male
reproductive hazards, 224; nerve damage, 217; nuclear factories, 230; occupational disease, 229–30, 247–48;
pregnant workers' rights, 251; psychosocial problems controversy, 227–28;
remedies, 247; right to live, 217; risks
in offices and service trades, 222; risks
to children, 217; risks women and men
share, 220–21; safety education, 217–
30; safety measures, clothing, 221;
safety stewards, 120–21, 229–32, 237,
251; strain in overwork, 224–25; "synergism," 221; unions' concern, 225–26,
229; violations of law (Germany), 246;
women's role in, 266; women's special
concerns, 220, 227; workers' compensation, 226, 247. See also VDT
Hegelheimer, Barbara, 174, 178, 183–84
Hochschild, Arlie, 28, 259

homework, 20, 137, 194; home-based
  work, 14; isolation of, 201
hours, 27; and FIET, 96; and German
  unions, 92; "lifetime allocation of
  work," 199; shift work, 199; shorter,
  92, 199, 263; in Sweden, 92, 105; "unsocial hours," 199
housework, 18, 19

IBEW. *See* International Brotherhood of
  Electrical Workers
IBM. *See* International Business Machines
ICFTU. *See* International Confederation of
  Free Trade Unions
IGM. *See* Industrie Gewerkschaft Metall
ILGWU. *See* International Ladies Garment
  Workers Union
ILO. *See* International Labour Organisa-
  tion
industrial democracy, 25
industrial revolution, 19–20
Industrial Training Board (U.K.), 185
Industrial Tribunal (U.K.), 90
Industrie Gewerkschaft Metall (Industrial
  Union of Metalworkers, Germany), 57–
  58, 107; approves Ro-Ru study, 151;
  education, 129–30; strike for shorter
  hours, 214; women members, 56, 96;
  women's courses, 126–27; women's
  promotion programs, 58
infirm and elderly care, 32
information hotlines, 60
Ingrao, Chiara, 17, 21
intergovernmental agencies, 26
International Brotherhood of Electrical
  Workers (U.S.), 74
International Business Machines, 242
International Confederation of Free Trade
  Unions, 57–58, 60
International Labour Organisation: Convention on educational leave, 122–23,
  192; Convention 100 on equal pay for
  work of equal value, 145–46, 163; definition of part-time work, 192; labor
  representation, 62; and male reproduc-
  tive hazards, 224; standard-setting in
  protective legislation, 26; union educa-
  tion, 107
International Ladies Garment Workers
  Union (U.S.), 248–49
International Trade Secretariats, 63, 96
ITB. *See* Industrial Training Board
IT. *See* Industrial Tribunal
ITS. *See* International Trade Secretariats

job evaluation, 4; Bendix case, 141; EOC
  (U.K.) implementation of pay equity,
  152–53; German chemical workers,
  130; GMWU, 100; NALGO flat pay increases, 157–58; planned but unused by
  LO (Sweden), 163; Ro-Ru study, 244–
  45; TCO, 163
job security, 87, 96
job segregation, 73, 76, 136–37, 257; in
  Austria, 162, 180; effect on union elections, 53; effect on union life, 51; effect
  on vocational training, 181, 189; in the
  household, 27; initiated in U.S. after
  study, 166–68; and marginal work, 18;
  root of family/work conflict, 255; in
  service trades, 177; in Sweden, 164
Jones, Jack, 90, 91

Kahn, Alfred J., 24, 29
Kamerman, Sheila B., 24, 29
Kanter, Rosbeth Moss, 34
Kessler-Harris, Alice, 19–20, 257
Kommunal (Sweden), 125
konzitierte Aktion (Austria), 83
Kornbluh, Joyce, 120
Kurz-Scherf, Ingrid, 79

labor contracts, "rights" and "interests,"
  80
labor courts, 80, 86–87, 88; Community
  High Court of Justice, 90; enforcement
  of pay equity, 159; in Germany, 91; in
  U.K., 90
labor-management relations, 26; collective
  bargaining, 79–106; Europe compared
  with U.S., 93; and social justice, 79;
  subject of training, 109; U.S. legislation
  on, 94
labor market: male domain in, 28; part-
  timers' weak connection with, 201;
  structure and state intervention, 35;
  Swedish women in, 87; U.K. and Sweden compared, 34; U.S. vocational
  training policy, 188; women in, 81, 87
labor parties: education of leaders, 109;
  U.K., 152; unions and, 91
late entry, 169. *See also* reentry
Lawrence, Anne T., 171
laws and legislation, 7; on collective bargaining (U.K.), 110; German Basic Law,
  150–51; U.K. pay equity, 151–52; on
  union powers and behavior, 80; U.S. labor relations, 94
layoff: dismissal notice, 212; notice of

(Sweden), 187; and works councils (Germany), 84
living wage, in wartime, 140
LO. *See* Sverige Landesorganisationen
Lorwin, Val R., 47

male dominance:
—in family, 136; in Germany, 31; and homemaking, 258–59
—on labor market, 21, 28, 165; male norms govern, 178; males' advancement (Austria), 180; men feel threatened, 256; vocational training, 173
—in unions, 2, 51, 68–69, 71, 75, 82, 257; attitude toward part-time workers, 205, 257; hostility to women at local level, 104; in pay equity, 135, 160; in union education, 112–13, 130
—in works councils, 88, 160
Manpower Services Commission (U.K.), 185–86
Mansbridge, Albert, 118
Manufacturing, Science, and Finance Workers Union (U.K.), 155
marriage, 21; partnership in, 18, 30, 52, 207; in Sweden, 31, 33, 207
marriage law: in Austria, 30; in Germany, 30–31, 66, 68
Marx, Eleanor, 50
maternity leave, 24, 74, 94, 257; in Austria, 30; in Germany, 31–32; for part-timers, 212; in U.S., 32
Mazzocchi, Anthony, 218
Medoff, James L., 43
Metall (Austria, Germany, Sweden): and affirmative action, 57–58; and education, 129, 161; women members of, 56, 96; women's courses, 126–27
minorities, among workers, 2, 3, 113
motherhood, 23, 30, 257; cost of single status, 259; women workers and reproduction, 253. *See also* maternity leave
MSC. *See* Manpower Services Commission
MSF. *See* Manufacturing, Science, and Finance Workers Union
Muench, Joachim, 168
Muste, A. J., 44

Nahrung, Gaststaetten, und Genuss (Food and Restaurant Workers Union, Germany), 91
NALGO. *See* National Association of Local Government Officers

Nardone, Thomas J., 193
Nash, Al, 109
National Association of Local Government Officers (U.K.): equality program, 157; Equal Rights Working Party, 51–52; family responsibility and equal rights, 51
National Council on Civil Liberties (U.K.), 63, 156
National Education Association (U.S.), 65, 85
national health insurance, 74, 94; emergency and therapeutic services, 249; link to industrial medicine, 249; and maternity and child care programs in Europe, 32
National Institute of Occupational Safety and Health (U.S.): designation of toxic chemicals, 221; study of clothing industry, 222; study of VDTs and pregnancy, 252
National Labor Relations Act and National Labor Relations Board (U.S.), 85, 226
National Union of Miners (U.K.), 155
National Union of Public Employees (U.K.), 53, 61; education for part-timers, 211; equality and pregnancy, 228
Nazis and unions, 11, 83, 141
NCCL. *See* National Council on Civil Liberties
NEA. *See* National Education Association
Nelson, Anne, 127
Newcom, Charles W., 217
Newspaper Guild (U.S.), 241
NGG. *See* Nahrung, Gaststaetten, und Genuss
Nicolay-Leitner, Ingrid, 152, 161
9 to 5, National Association of Working Women (U.S.), 241
NIOSH. *See* National Institute of Occupational Safety and Health
NLRA and NLRB. *See* National Labor Relations Act and National Labor Relations Board
nontraditional occupations: and CEDE-FOP (Germany), 183; in European Community, 39; in Germany, 92; and MSC (U.K.), 185; preparation for entering, 169; training for, 261–62; vocational counseling through LO (Sweden), 172
NUM. *See* National Union of Miners
NUPE. *See* National Union of Public Employees

O'Brien, Mary-Win, 226
OCAW. *See* Oil, Chemical, and Atomic Workers
Occupational Safety and Health Administration (U.S.), 218–19
OECD. *See* Organisation for Economic Cooperation and Development
Oeffentliche Dienste, Transport, und Verkehr (Public Workers Union, Germany), 61, 99
OeGB. *See* Oesterreichischer Gewerkschaftsbund
Oels, Monika, 171, 174–75
Oesterreichischer Gewerkschaftsbund (Austrian Trade Union Confederation), 61, 83, 96; and equal opportunity law, 148; influence on vocational training, 181; joint committee on occupational disease, 247; women's division, 148–49, 162
OeTV. *See* Oeffentliche Dienste, Transport, und Verkehr
Oil, Chemical, and Atomic Workers (U.S.), 253
Organisation for Economic Cooperation and Development, 27, 170
OSHA. *See* Occupational Safety and Health Administration

Page, Joseph A., 226
Palm, Goran, 126, 217, 220
parental leave, 102; in Sweden, 105
part-time work, 5, 27, 191–216; Belgian unions' plan for regularizing, 240; Bill of Rights for, 214; black and white workers in, 193; characteristics of, 191, 200–201; and childbirth, 208; cost of, 205; definitions of, 192; demand for, 193–94, 205, 208; employer's needs for, 202. 257; Equality Council Survey, 201; family/work demands, 198–99; forms of, 195; friction with full-time workers, 214; in Germany, 31, 195; HBV model contract for, 202; homework, 194; ineligible for full-time benefits, 201–5; job-sharing or job-splitting, 197; LO position, 209; reasons for seeking, 195; response to double burden, 207, 261; schedules of workers, 197; in service trades, 194; in Sweden, 92, 105, 187–88, 191–216; Sweden, U.K., and U.S. compared, 195; Swedish and U.K. unions seek improvements, 205–6; training opportunities, 174; unions opposed to, 205–7; women pre-

dominate in, 195; women's careers damaged by, 206–7
pay equity, 135–61; Austrian studies of, 160–62; and collective agreements, 166; cost of, 165; in Germany, in Ro-Ru study, 261; positive effect, 166; trade union efforts, 155, 266; in U.S., 155, 165, 266
pension rights, for displaced homemakers, 176; in EC, 27, 38; Sweden, 105; U.K. practice, 251
People's High Schools (Sweden), 124
Piva, Paolo, 17, 21
political parties, 13, 47–48, 67; "Greens," 92; Labour, 98, 152; SDP (Sweden), 163
"positive action," 29; EC, 39; Western Europe, 99
pregnancy, 24; and ASTMS bargaining, 251; European and U.S. policies contrasted, 24; German law on, 251; and U.K. health and safety representatives' duties, 251
private sector, 39
Private Sector White-collar Workers (Sweden), 70, 163; individual salary system, 164
progressives, 21–22
promotion: in trade unions, 3; on the job, 24, 76; in part-time work, 215
protective legislation, 12; definition of, 23–24; and ILO, 26; and pregnancy, 221, 223; support systems, 3; training officers on, 109
public sector: in EC, 139; equal rights in, 22; executive boards of unions, 102; training older women, 174; welfare state, 182; and women's equality, 174

Quataert, Jean, 135
Qvist, Gunnar, 141

Ramm, Theo, 38
reentry: and apprenticeship, 172; in Austria, 180; preparation for, 175; of U.K. women, 185–86
Rehn, Gosta, 199, 207
released time: educational leave (Sweden), 121–23; for training, 55; in U.K., 110; for works councils, 88, 100, 108
religious affiliation: German and Austrian unions, 83–84; influence of canon law, 22; and traditional values, 11
remand, 125
"reserve army," 18; U.K. women as members of, 187

reserved seats, on executive boards, 3, 61–62, 71, 104
Retail, Wholesale, and Department Store Union (U.S.), 100
retirement, 212. *See also* pension rights
Richbell, Suzanne, 173
Rohmert, Walter, 244
Ro-Ru study, 150–51, 244–47, 262
Ruggie, Mary, 22, 35–36, 164
Ruskin College, 109, 120
Rutenfranz, Josef, 244
RWDSU. *See* Retail, Wholesale, and Department Store Union

SAF. *See* Svenska Arbetsgivarefoereningen
Scalia, Anthony, Justice, 219
Schmidt, Folke, 23–24
Schneevoigt, Norbert, 120, 176
Seeland, Suzanne, 171, 184–85
SEIU. *See* Service Employees International Union
seniority, 95; for part-timers, 215
Service Employees International Union (U.S.), 74; and VDTs, 24, 253
service trades, 137, 177; women in, 174
severance pay, for part-timers, 212, 215
sex harassment, 173, 256
shift work, 95
shop stewards, 85; and national union discipline, 90–91; and part-timers, 201; in U.K., 82, 99
SIF (TCO). *See* Private Sector White-collar Workers
Silkwood case, 250
single parents, 27, 52; in EC, 39; and part-time work, 208
social policy, 2, 8; and collective bargaining, 79; in Europe, 266; for part-timers, 197, 199, 207, 212–16; in public and private agencies, 22; in Sweden, 267; unions build on public policy, 106; in U.S., 260; women's issues in public sphere, 30, 261
social security: and labor laws on part-time in Europe, 212; law as subject of training, 109; in U.K., 31
Society of Graphical and Allied Trades (U.K.), 99
solidary wage (Sweden), 4, 14, 86, 92, 105, 149; effect of, 154, 261; policy, 162
Steinberg, Ronnie, 188
Stellman, Jeanne, 7, 227
Stone, Katherine, 1
strain and stress: education programs (Sweden), 123; GPA studies, 243; rec-
ognition of, 92; Ro-Ru study, 150, 151, 244–45
strikes: of Ford workers (U.K.), 97–98; of IGM (Germany), 214; Swedish general strike, 84; in U.K., 82; as ultimate bargaining tool, 94
study circles (Sweden), 70, 124; LO "remand," 125; Metall, 116–17; teaching methods in, 117; with television, 119
Summers, Tish, 79
Svenska Arbetsgivarefoereningen (Swedish Employers Association), 84, 149
Sverige Landesorganisationen (Swedish Confederation of Labor), 69–70, 84, 86, 96; and education, 115–16, 117, 124; financing union education, 125; and health and safety, 231–36; jobs for pre-retirement workers, 213; and part-time work, 209; solidary wage, 149–50; wage policy, 162; women's division abolished, 265
Sweden:
—collective bargaining, 84, 92; centralization in, 46; women's gains in, 105
—education: adult, 176; leave for, 121–23; People's High Schools, 124; union, 110; vocational, 123, 187–88
—family policy, 31; child welfare, 34
—health and safety, 231–38; law, 232–34; and VDTs, 241; working environment, 222
—labor market policy, 4–5; avoiding unemployment, 187; foreign workers, 28; gender equality, 24–25; phased retirement, 213
—political parties, 48
—tax policy, 31, 105, 266
—trade unions, 37, 45, 69–70, 84, 86, 96; and education, 125; and phased retirement, 213; on part-timers' conditions, 205–6, 209; role in health and safety issues, 231–36; wage policy, 149–50, 162; and women, 69, 105, 265

T&G. *See* Transport and General Workers Union
TASS. *See* Technical, Administrative, and Supervisory Staffs
taxation: in Nordic countries, 33; in Sweden 31, 105; in U.K., 31
Taylor, Frederick, 6
TCO. *See* Tjaenstemans Centralorganisationen
Technical, Administrative, and Supervisory Staffs (U.K.); 59–73, 100; bargain-

Technical (*cont.*)
ing on VDTs, 239–40; education, 116, 127; support of pay equity, 156. *See also* Manufacturing, Science, and Finance Workers Union
technology: introduction of new, 92, 95, 96; retraining for, 174; U.S. government support for training in, 189
Title VII, Civil Rights Act (U.S.), 28, 164
Tjaenstemans Centralorganisationen (Swedish Central Organization of Salaried Employees), 69–70, 84, 96, 99; education program, 124; "remand" to study circles, 125; wages, 149–50, 163–64
Toelle, Helga, 135
Trades Union Congress (U.K.), 61, 64, 81; and benefits for part-timers, 212; critique of British vocational education, 185; Dagenham auto workers, 97–98; education, 110, 118, 238–39; educational leave, 121–22; equal pay, 150, 152, 157; equal rights committee, 157; health and safety issues, 239; safety stewards, 230; and VDTs, 239–40; vocational training policy, 186; women's meeting, 265
traditional values: Austria, 180; domestic code, 19, 23; male breadwinner, 19, 136; as reflection of religious values, 11; and union education, 107; and women's work life, 160
Transport and General Workers Union (U.K.), 82, 90, 155
tripartite representation, 26; Austrian vocational training, 179; labor courts, 88; pay equity, in U.K., 152
TUC. *See* Trades Union Congress
two-tiered system, 256

UAW. *See* United Automobile Workers Union
UCLEA. *See* University and College Labor Education Association
UMW. *See* United Mine Workers of America
unemployment, 14; compensation for part-timers, 212; and demand for part-timers, 194; effect of phased retirement on, 213; in Germany, 31, 92
Union Carbide, 249
unions
—affiliations of, 53–54, 59, 62–63, 65; in TUC, 81
—careers in, 52, 58–60; women in leadership, 264–65

—Community Service Committees (U.S.), 249
—conventions of, 57, 96; in Austria, 149
—critics of, 125–26
—demands of: on ecology, 92; on education, 131; on "forced quits" (U.K.), 97; for regulating part-time work, 209–10; for women's issues, 103, 131
—education in, 4, 43, 58–59, 76, 107–31; affirmative action, 113–14; barriers to, 110–13; child care and, 113–15; correspondence courses, 113, 117; decentralization of, 116; European systems compared with U.S., 100, 108–9; family programs (LO), 115; financing of, 112, 125; German system, 108–9; "informal," 107; leadership training, 111, 115–17, 124, 265; model structure (U.K.), 111; outreach, 124; for part-timers, 211, 215; purpose of, 107, 126–31, 265; for safety stewards, 237–38, 253; subject matter, 109; Swedish system, 70, 115, 117; teaching methods, 117–20; television in, 117–20, 237–38; university programs, 281; in U.S., 119–20; women and, 96, 107
—elections in, 43, 53, 57–58, 70, 99; in U.S., 100; of women health and safety stewards, 230
—functions of, 42–46; administrative benefits, 80, 103; advocates for health and safety, 230, 253; education, 107–31; enforcement of pay equity, 160; health and safety stewards, 230; laws defining scope of, 80; representation of members, 80
—internal politics of: caucuses, 44–45; religious affiliation, 67; "voice," 43–76
—leadership of, 66; women leaders, 264–66. *See also* unions: education in
—local meetings of, 52–53; families present, 53; in Hessen, 67; in Sweden, 70; "town meeting," 44; workplace meetings, 53
—membership of, 66, 71, 73, 81, 103; DGB, 56; Europe compared to U.S., 100
—policies of: industrial democracy, 25; unions legitimized, 25; women and, 22–23. *See also* arbitration; co-determination; conciliation; hours; strikes
—power and decision-making in, 45, 46, 47, 60, 71, 75, 80, 102–3; Europe

compared with U.S., 93–94; and
leaders, 102; scientific studies of,
253; source of, in collective bargaining, 80
—staffs of, 43, 45, 52, 58
—structure of: for bargaining, 80, 85;
confederations, 2, 12, 45, 56–57, 84;
departments, 67, 71–72; education,
108–31; IGM (Germany), 96; independent of state and management,
12; industrial unions, 81–83; key to
union success, 86; ladies' auxiliaries,
49; local unions, 45–46, 52, 82, 84;
and part-time work (Sweden), 210;
and politics, 12, 42–76; and purpose,
71; regions' and districts' (Germany),
83; special place for women in, 71–
72, 76; women's gains in, 104
—task forces of, 63–64
—"voice" of, 70, 76; rank-and-file, 97;
representation of members, 79–80; of
women's divisions, 264
—and women: and centralization, 105;
and early policy, 3, 22–23, 264–65;
and new technology, 96; and pay differentials, 161; reserved seats for, 61;
special organizations for, 51; and
wage gap, 86; "woman question,"
49; women's conferences, 64; wom-
en's handicaps, 43; women's leadership, 3, 264–65
—women's divisions of, 3, 46, 50, 51,
56–58, 60–61, 65, 71–72; in Austria, 68–69; in Germany, 131, 246
—youth in, 45
United Automobile Workers Union (U.S.):
and VDTs, 240, 253; women's division,
65, 102
United Biscuits, 198
United Mine Workers Union (U.S.), 253
United Nations, and gender equality, 37
United States:
—adaptation of European programs, 73;
U.K. influence on union structure,
81
—health and safety: chemical exposures,
250; national health program debated, 74; NIOSH and toxic substances, 219; overlapping federal enforcement agencies, 250; reproductive
health law, 249–50; Silkwood case,
250; studies of VDTs and pregnacy,
252; trade unions' concerns with
VDTs, 229, 241–42
—law and litigation: American Cyanamid,
217–29; class actions, 155; NLRB re-

quirements, 226; protective legislation, 23–25
—part-time work, 192, 194
—political parties, 47
—trade unions: CLUW, 50; collective bargaining, 85; independent of state,
11–12; NLRB requirements, 226;
union presidents, 100; women's divisions, 65–68; women's educational
programs, 127–28
—wages: equal pay and Title VII, 147–
48; equal pay for work of equal
value, 147–64; Supreme Court decisions on, 23–24
University and College Labor Education
Association (U.S.), 120, 128
university labor education, 76

vacations, 94, 210
van Hemeldonck, Marijke, 42
van Houten, Donald R., 42
VDTs. See video display terminals
Veblen, Thorstein, 168
video display terminals, 239–42; and eye-
strain, 248; NIOSH study of, 252, 263;
and reproductive hazards, 252; and rest
period, 239–40
Viklund, Birger, 116
vocational counseling, 169, 171–72; in
Austria, 180; gender bias in, 189; gender differences in, 171; isolation of
schools from working life, 171; need
for better counseling, 178; needs of
counselors, 171; for nontraditional vocations, 187; in school, 171; support
staff, 189
vocational training, 4–5, 14, 18, 95, 104,
168–90; in Austria, 181–83; CEDE-
FOP, 176; drop-outs, 178; Europe compared with U.S., 94; and gender, 170,
174–89; German system of, 31, 92,
181–83; and guidance, 169; in-service
and on-the-job, 173–74; IRIS, 264; for
nontraditional work, 209; and part-time
work, 209; rarely available, 174; reentry training, 175, 179; refresher courses,
175; requirements, 171, 178; retraining,
173–74; support staff, 178, 179; in
Sweden, 187; trade union influence,
181, 190; for unemployed women, 264;
in U.S.: 188–89; women's motivations,
178; women's programs neglected, 189;
women's special needs, 174, 176–78,
183; youth's special needs (Germany),
184

vocations, freedom of choice in, 169
von Moltke, Konrad, 120, 176

"wage kitty" (Sweden), 163
wages: Austrian wage gap, 160; CHCJ
  dicta, 153; definition of, 153; differentials, 161–63; early studies (U.K.),
  138–39; in Germany, 92, 94–95, 96,
  130, 138; integrated with national economic policy, 163; low wages justified,
  135–38; pay equity, 166; pay gap, 86,
  134, 136, 137; and Ro-Ru study, 151;
  in Sweden, 149–50, 161, 163; trade
  union policy and practice, 22–23, 67,
  86, 95, 135–67; and women, 22–23,
  66, 86
Wassen-van Schaveren, Paula, 7
Webb, Beatrice, 140
Wedderborn, Dorothy, 49
Weimar Republic (Germany), 86
Wertheimer, Barbara M., 107, 120
white-collar workers, 83; Austria, 97; Belgium, 210; U.K., 100, 239–46
Wilensky, Harold W., 17, 21, 171
Witt, Matt, 93
women and labor market, 18, 62, 66,
  136; in EC, 39
women officers, 58, 60, 61, 71, 85; insufficient representation of women, 128;
  promotion programs in Germany, 264;
  single, widowed, or with grown children, 258–59; works councils, 88
Women's Action Programme (EC), 38–39
Women's Bureau (U.S.), 147
women's culture, 75, 76
women's domestic role, 20, 22, 257
women's issues, 60, 63, 70, 88, 94–98,
  102–3; education on, 128; family matters, 131; and government, 102; not

seen as labor market issues, 255; wom-
  en's unions, 104–5; Year of Working
  Woman (Germany), 66–68. See also sex
  harassment; wages
women's professions, 136
"women's proper place," 18, 71, 75, 76,
  136, 137, 257
Women's Trade Union League (U.K. and
  U.S.), 50, 75, 120, 265
women's unions, 50, 257; AFA and ANA,
  104
women's work, 20, 25, 102, 135, 255,
  257; chemical workers (Germany),
  129–30; "light work," 136; struggles
  for equality, 255
work, definition of, 9. See also women's
  work
workers' compensation: employers' burden of proof, 247; for industrial disease, 245–47; for psychosomatic disorders (Sweden), 247; for safety, 226
workers' rights, 22; in law and collective
  bargaining, 246; no dismissal for ill-
  health, 248; not to be born disabled,
  249–52; in Sweden, 248
work reorganization, 267
Works Councils: 55, 85, 86–87; elections,
  87, 88; Health Manual for Women
  White-collar Workers, 245–46; law
  (Germany), 99–100; powers over health
  and safety, 230; powers to enforce pay
  equity, 160; training of councilors,
  100–101; women in, 100–101

Year of the Working Woman (Germany),
  66–67, 150

zero-sum, 104
Zetkin, Klara, 50

Library of Congress Cataloging-in-Publication Data

Cook, Alice Hanson.
  The most difficult revolution : Women and trade unions / Alice H. Cook with Val R.
Lorwin and Arlene Kaplan Daniels.
     p.   cm.
  Includes bibliographical references and index.
    ISBN 0-8014-1916-6 (alk. paper).—ISBN 0-8014-8065-5 (pbk. : alk. paper)
    1. Women in trade-unions—Europe. I. Lorwin, Val R. (Val Rogin), 1907–
1982. II. Daniels, Arlene Kaplan. 1930–   . III. Title.
HD6079.2.E85C66   1992
331.4'78'094—dc20   92-52747